THE WORLDLY AND HEAVENLY
WISDOM OF 4QINSTRUCTION

BY

MATTHEW J. GOFF

BRILL
LEIDEN · BOSTON
2003

This book is printed on acid-free paper.

Library of Congress Cataloging-in-Publication Data

Goff, Matthew J.
    The worldly and heavenly wisdom of 4QInstruction / by Matthew J. Goff.
        p. cm. — (Studies on the texts of the desert of Judah, ISSN 0169-9962 ; v. 50)
    Rev. ed. of author's thesis (Ph. D.).
    Includes bibliographical references and index.
    ISBN 90-04-13591-X (alk. paper)
        1. 4QInstruction. 2. Wisdom—Religious aspects—Judaism. 3. Judaism—Doctrines. I.
    Title. II. Series.

    BM488.A15G64 2003
    296.1'55—dc22   2003057066

ISSN   0169-9962
ISBN   90 04 13591 X

PRINTED IN THE NETHERLANDS

THE WORLDLY AND HEAVENLY WISDOM
OF 4QINSTRUCTION

STUDIES ON THE TEXTS
OF THE DESERT OF JUDAH

EDITED BY

F. GARCÍA MARTÍNEZ

ASSOCIATE EDITOR

P.W. FLINT

VOLUME L

FOR DIANE

CONTENTS

ACKNOWLEDGMENTS

This study is a revised version of my dissertation, which I wrote under the direction of John J. Collins. I am grateful for his assistance with this book, both at the dissertation stage and in the revision process. He helped enormously with both tasks and gave feedback to multiple drafts. The final result would have been much poorer if not for his contribution. I would also like to thank Michael Fishbane and Tikva Frymer-Kensky, the other members of my dissertation committee, for their assistance.

Work began on this study in its dissertation form in Fall 2000. The bulk of the writing was completed in New Haven, Connecticut. I revised the work for publication in Savannah, Georgia, where I moved to start working at Georgia Southern University as an Assistant Professor of Religious Studies.

There are many who have helped with this project. Several friends and colleagues read and provided feedback on drafts of chapters. They include Samuel Adams, Shannon Burkes, Yonder Gillihan, Daniel Harrington, Dale Martin, Matthew Neujahr, and Eibert Tigchelaar. Their efforts improved the overall quality of the project. I thank them for their contributions. Daryl Jefferies and Sarah Tanzer provided me with copies of their dissertations. I am also grateful to Torleif Elgvin, Catherine Murphy, Loren Stuckenbruck, and Eibert Tigchelaar for making forthcoming publications available to me (some of which have since appeared in print). Tigchelaar deserves additional thanks for his patience as I asked him numerous questions about Hebrew fonts. I also appreciate the help of Eric Prince, a recent graduate of Georgia Southern, who proofread the entire manuscript with care and attention. Lanell Vanlandingham, of the Department of Literature and Philosophy, showed impressive restraint as I drained the office toner supplies during the revision process. My chair, Bruce Krajewski, and the rest of the department, was also supportive while I balanced my first year of teaching with work on the manuscript.

Special thanks go to John Strugnell. During the 2001 New England regional meeting of the Society of Biblical Literature, I met with him to discuss 4QInstruction. We also spoke about a draft of Chapter 1 at his home. He was under no obligation yet offered me guidance and feedback. From both him and John Collins I learned that a good scholar is committed to student development.

The transcription of the Hebrew of 4QInstruction follows the standard format of the DJD series.

Aspects of Chapters 2 and 4 were presented at two SBL meetings—in April 2002 at Brandeis University for the New England regional meeting, and in November 2002 at the annual meeting in Toronto. Ideas from this study have also appeared in *Dead Sea Discoveries* 10 (2003) and in a review article in *Journal of Biblical Literature* 122 (2003) on three recent books in the STDJ series.

I thank Florentino García Martínez for including my work in the STDJ series and for his enthusiastic support. I have enjoyed working with him. I am also grateful for the assistance of Brill's editorial staff, especially Mattie Kuiper and Pim Rietbroeck.

Savannah, Georgia
June 30, 2003

ABBREVIATIONS

Abbreviations generally follow the guidelines given in Patrick Alexander et al., *The SBL Handbook of Style* (Peabody: Hendrickson, 1999). This study also uses the following abbreviations, which are not listed in *The SBL Handbook*:

AOAT   Alter Orient und Altes Testament
ANTZ   Arbeiten zur neutestamentlichen Theologie und Zeitgeschichte
SBM   Stuttgarter biblische Monographien
SSU   Studia Semitica Upsaliensia
YJS   Yale Judaica Series

CHAPTER ONE

COMMON WISDOM?: THE WORLDLY AND HEAVENLY
WISDOM OF 4QINSTRUCTION

1. INTRODUCTION

4QInstruction, which has also been titled "Sapiential Work A" and
"Musar Le-Mevin," is the longest wisdom text of the Dead Sea Scrolls
corpus.[1] At least six copies[2] of 4QInstruction were found at Qumran
(1Q26, 4Q415-18, 423), all of which are in Herodian script.[3] This

---

[1] "Sapiential Work A" was the working title of the document before it was formally
published in volume 34 of the Discoveries of the Judean Desert series (henceforth "*DJD
34*"). "Musar Le-Mevin" (Instruction for a Maven) is the title given to the composition by
the editors of *DJD 34*. See John Strugnell and Daniel J. Harrington, *Qumran Cave
4.XXIV: Sapiential Texts, Part 2. 4QInstruction (Mûsār Lĕ Mēvîn): 4Q415ff. With a re-
edition of 1Q26* (DJD 34; Oxford: Clarendon, 1999), 3. Torleif Elgvin is the editor of
4Q423. Since 1Q26 is a manuscript of the composition, it has also been referred to as
"1/4QInstruction," "1Q/4QInstruction," or simply "Instruction." In this study the designation "4QInstruction" will be used.

[2] It is possible that there are more than six. Elgvin has argued that there are two copies
of 4QInstruction preserved among the approximately 300 fragments that comprise 4Q418.
E.J.C. Tigchelaar has discerned three. In *DJD 34* only a small portion of 4Q418 fragments are presented as attesting manuscripts aside from the main 4Q418 copy. The matter
is "purely of codicological interest" and does not affect the interpretation of 4QInstruction
(*DJD 34*, 227). See Torleif Elgvin, "The Reconstruction of Sapiential Work A," *Revue de
Qumran* 16 (1995): 559-80; E.J.C. Tigchelaar, "Towards a Reconstruction of the Beginning of 4QInstruction (4Q416 Fragment 1 and Parallels)," in *The Wisdom Texts from
Qumran and the Development of Sapiential Thought* (ed. C. Hempel, A. Lange, and H.
Lichtenberger; BETL 159; Leuven: Leuven University Press/Peeters, 2002), 99-126;
idem, *To Increase Learning for the Understanding Ones: Reading and Reconstructing
the Fragmentary Early Jewish Sapiential Text 4QInstruction* (STDJ 44; Leiden: Brill,
2001), 15-17.

[3] This would, according to Cross's dating of Qumran scripts, date the manuscripts to
the late first century BCE. Most copies are in early Herodian (30-1 BCE). Strugnell has
dated 4Q416 to be older than the other Herodian manuscripts by about twenty-five years.
See *DJD 34*, 76. 4Q423 and 1Q26 are considered to be in middle Herodian, a script that
is dated to 1-30 CE. Several commentators have noted that the late date of the manuscripts underscores the significance of the text for the community at Qumran. See *DJD
34*, 2; John J. Collins, *Jewish Wisdom in the Hellenistic Age* (OTL; Louisville: Westminster John Knox, 1997), 117; Torleif Elgvin, "An Analysis of 4QInstruction" (diss.; Hebrew University of Jerusalem, 1997), 10. See also Frank Moore Cross, "The Development

amount rivals the number of manuscripts of key texts such as the Damascus Document (8) and the War Scroll (7) and suggests that the wisdom
text was important for the sectarian community.[4] In 1999, after over
forty years of editorial work, 4QInstruction was formally published in
DJD 34 by John Strugnell and Daniel Harrington.[5]

---

of the Jewish Scripts," in *The Bible and the Ancient Near East* (ed. G.E. Wright; New
York: Doubleday, 1961), 133-202.

   In terms of the manuscripts that comprise 4QInstruction, note that there has been
speculation that 4Q419 is part of the composition. The basis of this claim is that there is
material common to 4Q419 8 ii 7 and 4Q416 2 ii 2-3. The relevant part of the latter text
reads: "if] he closes his hand, [then the spirit of all] flesh [will be gathered]" (cf. Deut
15:7). Earlier Elgvin considered 4Q419 a 4QInstruction text but later changed his mind.
See his "Admonition Texts from Cave 4," in *Methods of Investigation of the Dead Sea
Scrolls and the Khirbet Qumran Site: Present Realities and Future Prospects* (ed. M.O.
Wise et al.; Annals of the New York Academy of Sciences 722; New York: New York
Academy of Sciences, 1994), 180.   Daniel Harrington contends that 4Q419 and
4QInstruction are two separate works.   See his *Wisdom Texts from Qumran* (London:
Routledge, 1996), 73.   4Q419 stresses themes such as the Law of Moses, the Aaronic
priesthood, and cultic purity.   These topics are not prominent in 4QInstruction.   (See
section 2 of Chapter 6.)   There is no compelling reason to identify 4Q419 as a text of
4QInstruction. In the official edition of 4Q419, it is not considered part of 4QInstruction.
See Stephen J. Pfann et al., *Qumran Cave 4.XXVI: Cryptic Texts and Miscellanea, Part I*
(DJD 36; Oxford: Clarendon, 2000), 320-32.   Strugnell and Harrington suggest that
4Q419 quotes 4QInstruction. See *DJD 34*, 95.   See also Armin Lange, *Weisheit und
Prädestination: Weisheitliche Urordnung und Prädestination in den Textfunden von
Qumran* (STDJ 18; Leiden: Brill, 1995), 45.

   [4] D. Dimant, "The Qumran Manuscripts: Contents and Significance," in *Time to Prepare a Way in the Wilderness* (ed. D. Dimant and L.H. Schiffman; STDJ 16; Leiden:
Brill, 1995), 36-37.

   [5] The first 4QInstruction text to be published was 1Q26. It appeared in *DJD 1*. See D.
Barthélemy and J.T. Milik, *Qumran Cave 1* (DJD 1; Oxford: Clarendon, 1955), 101-02.
See also Daniel J. Harrington, "The Raz Nihyeh in a Qumran Wisdom Text (1Q26,
4Q415-418, 423)," *Revue de Qumran* 17 (1996), 549.   Milik identified 1Q26 as "un
apocryphe" that is evocative of the testament and instruction genres.   Strugnell reported in
1956 that four Cave 4 manuscripts had been identified that were similar to 1Q26. See his
"Le travail d'édition des fragments de Qumrân: Communication de J. Strugnell," *Revue
Biblique* 63 (1956): 64-66.   He also mentioned that four or five other sapiential works
were found among the Cave 4 material. Over the next few years major fragments such as
4Q416 2, 4Q417 1 and 2, and 4Q418 81 were purchased. This helped the editors realize
that these and other fragments formed part of a large sapiential composition. By 1959 the
fragments of Sapiential Work A had been numbered, transcribed, and entered into the
concordance used by the editorial team (*DJD 34*, xiv). Strugnell's work on 4QInstruction
accelerated in 1992 when he began his collaboration with Daniel J. Harrington (ibid., xv).
Emmanuel Tov helped establish their editorial partnership.   See Hershel Shanks, "Chief
Scroll Editor Opens Up: An Interview with Emanuel Tov," *Biblical Archaeology Review*
28 (May/June 2002), 33.   Also note that Tigchelaar, *To Increase Learning*, 5-13, provides
an excellent history of the editing of 4QInstruction.

   The first full publication of 4QInstruction texts occurred in 1992, in the second fascicle
of Ben Zion Wacholder and Martin Abegg, *A Preliminary Edition of the Unpublished
Dead Sea Scrolls: The Hebrew and Aramaic Texts from Cave Four* (Washington, D.C.:

In this chapter I will begin with some comments on the state of the text of 4QInstruction and relevant scholarly literature. I will then provide an overview of 4QInstruction's wisdom.

2. THE TEXT OF 4QINSTRUCTION

4QInstruction is a long composition that survives in tattered remnants. It is comprised of over 425 fragments.[6] It has been suggested that the original text of one 4QInstruction manuscript, 4Q418, was as long as the Hodayot or the Temple Scroll.[7] The largest extant fragment contains the partially damaged four columns of 4Q416 2.[8] The existence of an additional 4QInstruction fragment has come to light.[9] The reconstruction of

---

Biblical Archaeology Society, 1992). For 4QInstruction manuscripts, see ibid., 44-154, 166-73. See also Tigchelaar, *To Increase Learning*, 13-15. Parts of 4QInstruction were also published in 1992 in the much-maligned book, Robert Eisenman and Michael Wise, *The Dead Sea Scrolls Uncovered* (New York: Barnes and Noble, 1992). See ibid., 241-55. They translated only a few 4QInstruction texts and do not include major fragments such as 4Q415, 4Q423, and 1Q26. See John Strugnell and Daniel J. Harrington, "Qumran Cave 4 Texts: A New Publication," *Journal of Biblical Literature* 112 (1993): 491-99.

Another pre-*DJD 34* translation of 4QInstruction appeared in Michael Wise, Martin Abegg, Jr., and Edward Cook, *The Dead Sea Scrolls: A New Translation* (San Francisco: HarperSan Francisco, 1996), 378-90. They entitle the text "The Secret of the Way Things Are," which is their translation of the *raz nihyeh*. At the time 4QInstruction was poorly understood, and this is reflected in this edition. For example, the editors understand 4Q412 1 as the beginning of the composition, a text now considered a separate document. See also Geza Vermes, *The Complete Dead Sea Scrolls in English* (New York: Penguin, 1997), 402-12.

[6] Eibert J.C. Tigchelaar, "The Addressees of 4QInstruction," in *Sapiential, Liturgical and Poetical Texts from Qumran: Proceedings of the Third Meeting of the International Organization for Qumran Studies, Oslo 1998* (ed. D. Falk et al.; STDJ 35; Leiden: Brill, 2000), 62.

[7] *DJD 34*, 2. Elgvin has speculated that 4QInstruction was originally one and a half times larger than the Damascus Document. See his "'To Master His Own Vessel': 1 Thess 4:4 in Light of New Qumran Evidence," *New Testament Studies* 43 (1997), 605.

[8] According to Strugnell, 4Q416 2 was damaged when it was brought to the Rockefeller Museum by Kando, the infamous manuscript dealer. It was exposed to perspiration when Kando wrapped it around his chest to hide it during a police search. This caused its skin to shrink and darkened some of the surface of the leather. See *DJD 34*, 73. According to Lena Liebman, a conservator at the Rockefeller Museum, this damage was caused when 4Q416 was treated in the 50's or 60's with castor oil. See Elgvin, "An Analysis of 4QInstruction," 13, note 7. There is no reason to doubt Strugnell's account of the damage. As pointed out to me by Tigchelaar (personal communication), it is possible that the fragment could have been blemished by perspiration and later treated with castor oil.

[9] See Émile Puech and Annette Steudel, "Un nouveau fragment du manuscrit 4QInstruction (XQ7 = 4Q417 ou 4Q418)," *Revue de Qumran* 19 (2000): 623-27. The text in question was published in *DJD 36* as XQ7, "XQUnidentified Text." Its editor was Armin Lange. A Finnish pastor bought the fragment from the Bedouin in 1960 in Jerusa-

individual texts is aided by the presence of multiple 4QInstruction manuscripts among the Dead Sea Scrolls.[10] This text has 'synoptic' material,
and interpretation is often aided by variants.[11]

4QInstruction's poor state of preservation hinders assessment of its
overall structure. Stegemann has argued that it is possible to estimate the
number of columns that came between a given text and the inward end of
a scroll based on changes in distance between wear patterns.[12] Elgvin
adopts Stegemann's methods to reconstruct 4QInstruction. For example,
he estimates that there were four columns between 4Q417 2 ii and 4Q417
1 i, with 4Q417 2 coming earlier in the composition.[13] From this one can
deduce that 4Q416 2 also comes before 4Q417 1, since 4Q416 2 and

---

lem. When he died it became the property of the State of Israel. XQ7 was not assembled
with the rest of the 4QInstruction fragments because the Israel Antiquities Authority never
informed John Strugnell of its existence (personal communication). Puech and Steudel
identify XQ7 as a 4QInstruction text because its orthography, paleography, and other
manuscript characteristics match those of 4Q417 and 4Q418. The approximately nine
fully visible words of XQ7 generally occur in wisdom texts, with most of them found in
4QInstruction. Not enough survives of XQ7 to speculate on the main themes it originally
addressed. The disclosure of the fragment does not have a significant impact on the interpretation of 4QInstruction. See also Tigchelaar, *To Increase Learning*, 125.

[10] Some of the most important overlaps are 4Q415 11 → 4Q418 167; 4Q416 1 →
4Q418 1-2; 4Q416 2 i-ii → 4Q417 2 i-ii; 4Q416 2 iv → 4Q418 10; 4Q417 1 i → 4Q418
43; 4Q418 69 ii → 4Q417 5; 4Q418 81 → 4Q423 8; 4Q423 3 → 1Q26 2; 4Q423 4 →
1Q26 1. For a fuller list of 4QInstruction's overlaps, see Tigchelaar, *To Increase Learning*, 148-50.

[11] Ibid., 151-53.

[12] Hartmut Stegemann, "Methods for the Reconstruction of Scrolls from Scattered
Fragments," in *Archaeology and History in the Dead Sea Scrolls* (ed. L.H. Schiffman;
Sheffield: Sheffield Academic Press, 1990), 189-220. The basic principle of this method
is that the distance between wear patterns will decrease as one moves from the outward
end of a wrapped scroll to its inward end. The change in distance between wear patterns
is roughly constant, depending on how tightly or loosely the scroll was wrapped. If one
only has a small fragment but is able to measure the distance between wear patterns, it is
possible to estimate the change in distance between wear patterns in the original scroll. It
is therefore possible to estimate the distance between a given text and the inward end of
the scroll. See also Annette Steudel, "Probleme und Methoden der Rekonstruktion von
Schriftrollen," in *Qumran—die Schriftrollen vom Toten Meer: Vorträge des St. Galler
Qumran-Symposiums vom 2./3. Juli 1999* (ed. M. Fieger et al.; Freiburg/Göttingen:
Universitätsverlag/Vandenhoeck & Ruprecht, 2001), 97-109.

[13] Elgvin measures the turn of the scroll for 4Q417 2 to be 13 cm, and 9.9 cm for
4Q417 1. 4Q417 1 "thus derives from a more internal part of the scroll than" 4Q417 2.
Therefore 4Q417 2 is closer to the outward end of the scroll than 4Q417 1. If true, 4Q417
2 was closer to the beginning of the composition than 4Q417 1. If one assumes a constant
decrease in circumference of 4 mm per turn, this would place approximately 58 cm between the two fragments, a distance that would leave enough room for 4 columns of 13 cm
in length. A 4 mm turn is materially possible, but it is not the only estimate one can use.
See his "The Reconstruction of Sapiential Work A," 569. One should keep in mind that in
pre-*DJD 34* scholarship on 4QInstruction, 4Q417 1 was numbered as 4Q417 2, and vice
versa.

4Q417 2 are variants of the same text. Such knowledge might have helped one reconstruct the text of 4QInstruction if more of it had survived. But as it stands one can say little about its overall structure. An attempt to reconstruct 4Q418 has been made but it is of limited value.[14] The editors of *DJD 34* offer no reconstruction of their own of the text as a whole. Tigchelaar likewise concludes "we do not have sufficient materials and evidence to place the *Instruction* fragments in subsequent columns of a manuscript or of the composition."[15] Reconstructing 4QInstruction is a moot point insofar as interpretation of the composition is concerned since its available content does not appear to be arranged in any discernible fashion. This is often the case with wisdom compositions.[16]

One notable exception regarding placement of 4QInstruction material is 4Q416 1. Most scholars consider it the beginning of the work because the fragment has an unusually wide right margin (3.3 cm).[17] This could not be fully explained if it were placed in the middle of the composition. The final judgment is prominent in 4Q416 1. If it is at the beginning, the text provides the eschatological perspective with which the rest of the composition should be understood.[18] *1 Enoch* opens with a judgment scene that performs a similar function. Elgvin previously argued against viewing 4Q416 1 in this way but has rescinded his criticism.[19]

---

[14] A. Steudel and B. Lucassen have completed a reconstruction of 4Q418. It is currently not published and is summarized in *DJD 34*, 19-20.

[15] *To Increase Learning*, 161. Tigchelaar does contend, however, that a "relative reconstruction" is possible. By this he means that certain texts can be identified, primarily through analysis of the overlaps of 4QInstruction texts, as occurring near others in the original composition. For example, based on his reconstruction of 4Q418a (ibid., 126-39), its overlaps with 4Q416 and 4Q417 suggest these texts originally were from the first portion of 4QInstruction. See ibid., 159. Overlaps with 4Q418a also indicate that 4Q418 167 was on a sheet following the one that began with 4Q418 9. See ibid., 163.

[16] James L. Crenshaw, *Old Testament Wisdom: An Introduction* (Atlanta: John Knox Press, 1981), 73; Alexander Di Lella and Patrick W. Skehan, *The Wisdom of Ben Sira* (AB 39; New York: Doubleday, 1987), 4.

[17] Harrington, *Wisdom Texts*, 41; John Kampen, "The Diverse Aspects of Wisdom at Qumran," in *The Dead Sea Scrolls after Fifty Years: A Comprehensive Assessment* (2 vols.; ed. P.W. Flint and J.C. VanderKam; Leiden: Brill, 1998), 1.227; Tigchelaar, *To Increase Learning*, 161.

[18] Collins, *Jewish Wisdom*, 126; André Caquot, "Les textes de sagesse de Qoumrân (Aperçu préliminaire)," *Revue d'histoire et de philosophie religieuses* 76 (1996), 7.

[19] Personal correspondence. Elgvin's reading of 4Q416 1 left its wide right margin unexplained. He claimed that material from 4Q416 1 2-4 is found in 4Q418 73 at the bottom of a column and in 4Q418 201 at the top of a column, suggesting that there was material before 4Q416 1. See his "The Reconstruction of Sapiential Work A," 566. Elgvin's understanding of 4Q418 73, which has no visible bottom margin, presumed his own reconstruction of 4Q416 1. Since 4Q418 201 clearly preserves a top margin, 4Q418 73 was thought to preserve a bottom margin, although none is clearly visible, since it was

3. SCHOLARLY ASSESSMENTS OF 4QINSTRUCTION

4QInstruction is considered a wisdom text because in terms of form and content it is similar to the traditional wisdom of Proverbs.[20] Like Proverbs, this Qumran text contains admonitions and is concerned with the practical affairs and ethical conduct of its addressee.[21] The text gives instruction on topics such as marriage (4Q416 2 ii 21) and the timely payment of debts (4Q417 2 i 21-23). 4QInstruction often echoes advice found in biblical wisdom. For example, both Proverbs and 4QInstruction warn against going surety, the practice of pledging an item of value, including one's life, as collateral in order to obtain credit.[22] Both texts urge one to practice filial piety, as does the fifth commandment (Prov 23:22; 4Q416 2 iii 15-16). There is also continuity between the educational mission of 4QInstruction and that of Proverbs, as laid out in its prologue (Prov 1:1-7; 4Q418 81 17).

The editors of *DJD 34* understand 4QInstruction as a Second Temple wisdom text in terms of its correspondences with Proverbs.[23] Strugnell

---

understood to precede fragment 201. His views have been criticized in *DJD 34*, 83-84, and Tigchelaar, "Towards a Reconstruction," 106-07. See also idem, *To Increase Learning*, 155.

[20] Also demonstrating 4QInstruction's affinities with the sapiential tradition, the composition has been compared to Ahiqar. See H. Niehr, "Die Weisheit des Achikar und der *musar lammebin* im Vergleich," in *The Wisdom Texts from Qumran*, 173-86.

[21] "Admonition" (Mahnwort) is defined by Michael Fox as "a warning against improper behavior, usually given in vetitive (negative imperative) form." See his *Proverbs 1-9* (AB 18a; New York: Doubleday, 2000), 14. Philip Nel argues that the admonition is typically connected to a motivation clause that is necessary for understanding the coherence of the admonition form. See his *The Structure and Ethos of the Wisdom Admonitions in Proverbs* (BZAW 158; Berlin/New York: Walter de Gruyter, 1982), 74, 125. See further his "Authority in the Wisdom Admonitions," *Zeitschrift für die alttestamentliche Wissenschaft* 93 (1981): 418-26.

[22] 4Q418 88 3, "Take care for yourself lest you go surety"; Prov 17:18, "It is senseless to give a pledge, to become surety for a neighbor" (cf. 22:16).

[23] Strugnell's assessments of 4QInstruction are also available in "The Sapiential Work 4Q415ff. and the Pre-Qumranic Works from Qumran: Lexical Considerations," in *The Provo International Conference on the Dead Sea Scrolls* (ed. D.W. Parry and E. Ulrich; STDJ 30; Leiden: Brill, 1999), 595-608; idem, "More on Wives and Marriage in the Dead Sea Scrolls (4Q416 2 ii 21 [Cf. 1 Thess 4:4] and 4QMMT, B)," *Revue de Qumran* 17 (1996): 537-47. For additional work by Harrington on 4QInstruction, see *Wisdom Texts*, 40-59; idem, "The Qumran Sapiential Texts in the Context of Biblical and Second Temple Literature," in *The Dead Sea Scrolls Fifty Years After Their Discovery: Proceedings of the Jerusalem Congress, July 20-25, 1997* (ed. L.H. Schiffman, E. Tov, and J.C. Vander-Kam; Jerusalem: Israel Exploration Society/Shrine of the Book, Israel Museum, 2000), 256-62; idem, "Ten Reasons Why the Qumran Wisdom Texts are Important," *Dead Sea*

and Harrington observe that the text exhibits, like the Book of Proverbs, no interest in national traditions. The word "Torah," for example, is not attested in 4QInstruction, nor is "Israel."[24] Other wisdom texts, such as Ben Sira and the Wisdom of Solomon, display a pronounced interest in national traditions. Strugnell and Harrington conclude that 4QInstruction is a "'missing link' in the history of the common (i.e. non-sectarian) Jewish wisdom traditions, datable between Proverbs and Sirach."[25] A dating of the third or early second century BCE is proposed so that 4QInstruction may be seen as exemplifying a stage of Jewish wisdom that is not yet combined with national traditions.[26] From this dating it naturally follows that 4QInstruction could not be a product of the Qumran community, although the large number of manuscripts suggests that it was a popular text for its members.[27] The editors of *DJD 34* suggest that the original purpose of 4QInstruction was to train sages for employment in royal centers of administration in the Persian, Ptolemaic or Seleucid periods.[28] They also contend that these administrative sages were priests.[29]

Strugnell and Harrington's assessments of 4QInstruction account for its numerous points of contact with Proverbs and Ben Sira. All three texts share wisdom commonplaces. But is the wisdom of 4QInstruction "common"? Many important elements of 4QInstruction resonate with the apocalyptic tradition and have no analogue in biblical wisdom. They include the following:

Discoveries 4 (1997): 245-55; idem, "Wisdom at Qumran," in *The Community of the Renewed Covenant: The Notre Dame Symposium on the Dead Sea Scrolls* (ed. E. Ulrich and J. VanderKam; Notre Dame: University of Notre Dame Press, 1994), 137-53. See also section 3.5 of this chapter.

[24] *DJD 34*, 25, 27. Note, however, that "Israel" has been tentatively reconstructed in 4Q417 24 1: [ראל]שׂי עמו, "his people Is[rael]." See ibid., 207.

[25] Ibid., 31.

[26] Stegemann also dates the Qumran wisdom literature to be older than the second and first centuries BCE. He emphasizes that this corpus continues the ancient Near Eastern wisdom tradition. For this reason he argues "None of the contents of these new finds requires a date of authorship later than the fourth or third century B.C." See his *The Library of Qumran: On the Essenes, Qumran, John the Baptist, and Jesus* (Leiden/Grand Rapids: Brill/Eerdmans, 1998), 100.

[27] *DJD 34*, 30. In his preliminary reports of 4QInstruction Strugnell considered it to be a sectarian composition. See "Le travail d'édition," 64.

[28] *DJD 34*, 21. See also Torleif Elgvin, "Priestly Sages? The Milieus of Origin in 4QMysteries and 4QInstruction," in *Sapiential Perspectives: Wisdom Literature in Light of the Dead Sea Scrolls. Proceedings of the Sixth International Symposium of the Orion Center, 20-22 May 2001* (ed. G. Sterling and J.J. Collins; Leiden: Brill, forthcoming).

[29] See section 2 of Chapter 6.

- reliance on revelation through the frequently used phrase "the mystery that is to be" (רז נהיה)[30]
- appeal to a heavenly book (the vision of Hagu)
- a focus on eschatological judgment
- the elect status of the addressee, who is in the lot of the angels (4Q418 81 4-5)
- the promise of eternal life made to the addressee

Strugnell and Harrington demonstrate an awareness of these features of the text in their comments on individual passages. They understand 4QInstruction as a whole, however, in terms of a wisdom trajectory based on Proverbs and Ben Sira that cannot explain its apocalyptic worldview. Assessing the content of 4QInstruction requires accounting for both its practical advice and revealed wisdom.

Aside from the editors of *DJD 34*, there have been to date three major efforts to interpret 4QInstruction—by Armin Lange, Torleif Elgvin, and Eibert Tigchelaar. In what follows their work and that of other relevant scholars will be assessed, and then I will outline this study's approach to 4QInstruction.

3.1 Armin Lange

4QInstruction asserts that God endowed the cosmos with a sense of order at the moment of creation.[31] The association of Lady Wisdom with creation in Proverbs 1-9 emphasizes the rational structure of the natural world. Lange understands the sapiential tradition primarily as an effort to describe this ordering principle: "Schon in der Weisheit selbst ist die Vorstellung von einer präexistenten weisheitlichen Urordnung in den Kontext prädestinationischen Denkens rückt."[32] This influences his understanding of the רז נהיה. It for him "bezeichnet somit ein Phänomen, das ethische, historische, nomistische, eschatologische und urzeitliche Komponenten in sich vereinigt. Es handelt sich um eine Welt-bsw.

---

[30] The term "revelation" has been defined as "any divine disclosure of knowledge communicated by visionary or prophetic means" and "the manifestation of heavenly realities in a historical context." See Markus Bockmuehl, *Revelation and Mystery in Ancient Judaism and Pauline Christianity* (Grand Rapids: Eerdmans, 1990), 2. The theme of revelation is discussed in Chapter 2.

[31] See section 4.2 of Chapter 2.

[32] *Weisheit und Prädestination*, 40. His views on 4QInstruction are also available in "Wisdom and Predestination in the Dead Sea Scrolls," *Dead Sea Discoveries* 2 (1995): 340-54; idem, "Die Weisheitstexte aus Qumran: Eine Einleitung," in *The Wisdom Texts from Qumran*, 17-26.

Schöpfungsordnung."[33] The רז נהיה in 4QInstruction elevates the traditional sapiential assertion of the world's rational structure to the status of revealed knowledge.

Basing an assertion of order upon revelation is, for Lange, a reaction to the "crisis of wisdom" that is exemplified by Job and Qoheleth. These books have been understood as a critical response to the conventional claim that righteousness will be rewarded and wickedness punished, a view that undergirds the ethical advice of Proverbs.[34] In this formulation, Job and Qoheleth demonstrated the bankruptcy of traditional wisdom and encouraged the development of new forms of sapiential thought.[35] For Lange 4QInstruction is an example of the new kinds of wisdom speculation produced by this crisis.

Lange understands the vision of Hagu as similar to the mystery that is to be. It is another way that revelation is used to raise beyond human critique the sapiential assertion that a rational order is embedded in the world. He explains the vision's association with the book of remembrance (4Q417 1 i 15-16) as an attempt to give support to the legitimacy of this rational principle because its validity was considered weak and open to question. Lange argues that when "diese fraglich gewordene und verborgene Ordnung zu einem auf den himmlischen Tafeln schriftlich fixierten 'Bauplan' des Seins wurde, wurde ihre Wahrheit und Wirklichkeit bestärkt, gleichsam mitfixiert."[36]

---

[33] Lange, *Weisheit und Prädestination*, 60.

[34] For a traditional formulation of the crisis, see K. Galling, *Die Krise der Aufklärung in Israel* (Mainzer Universitätsreden 19; Mainz: Verlag der Johannes Gutenberg-Buchhandlung, 1952). That Job and Qoheleth represent a sapiential crisis has been questioned. J. Crenshaw has pointed out the antiquity of skepticism in Israel, as evident in texts such as Isaiah 5:19 and Zephaniah 1:12; this suggests that such views should not be associated exclusively with Job and Qoheleth. See his *Old Testament Wisdom*, 196. G. von Rad has asked "is it at all feasible that two individual works will have brought about a rethinking of later Israel's understanding of the world?" See his *Wisdom in Israel* (London/Valley Forge: SCM Press Ltd./Trinity Press International, 1972), 237. R. Murphy remarks that, while Qoheleth challenges traditional wisdom, he is still a "sage" (חכם; 12:8) and should not be understood as attacking the wisdom tradition but rather considered "in the light of this tradition with which he 'quarrels.'" See his *The Tree of Life: An Exploration of Biblical Wisdom Literature* (3rd ed.; Grand Rapids: Eerdmans, 2002 [orig. pub., 1990]), 55.

[35] Anticipating Lange's view, J. Coert Rylaarsdam writes "The real contribution of Job and Ecclesiastes was to help to smash the too limited, earth-bound arena of traditional Jewish eschatology, which the great prophetic movement had utterly failed to do. By their rigid analysis and merciless criticism of life in the light of the orthodox doctrine of rewards, the pessimistic writers paved the way for a new eschatology." See his *Revelation in Jewish Wisdom Literature* (Chicago: University of Chicago Press, 1946), 89.

[36] *Weisheit und Prädestination*, 92.

Lange understands 4QInstruction as the eschatologizing of biblical wisdom.[37] For him 4QInstruction confirms *in toto* von Rad's understanding of apocalypticism as an eschatological outgrowth from the sapiential tradition.[38] He views the final judgment in 4QInstruction (e.g., 4Q416 1 13) as an eschatological elaboration of the traditional Tat-Ergehen-Zusammenhang, the connection between deed and consequence that is assumed by traditional wisdom.[39] This is also how Lange understands the role of judgment in the Book of Mysteries (1Q27, 4Q299-301) and the Treatise on the Two Spirits of 1QS. 4QInstruction also shares terminology with these two texts, such as אל דעות (1QS 3:15; 4Q299 35 1; 4Q417 1 i 8) and רז נהיה (e.g., 1Q27 1 i 4). These similarities are used to posit a common milieu. All three texts are representative of the "post-crisis" phase of the wisdom tradition. He does not consider them compositions written by the Dead Sea sect, but acknowledges that they were used by this group.[40]

---

[37] Before Lange, John G. Gammie discussed an "eschatologization of wisdom" that he associated with a rising sense of national self-identity in the sapiential tradition. See his "From Prudentialism to Apocalypticism: The Houses of the Sages amid the Varying Forms of Wisdom," in *The Sage in Israel and the Ancient Near East* (ed. J.G. Gammie and L.G. Perdue; Winona Lake: Eisenbrauns, 1990), 479-97. 4QInstruction does not support this characterization since it shows minimal interest in national affairs.

[38] *Weisheit und Prädestination*, 301-06. See also von Rad, *Wisdom in Israel*, 263-83. He argues that apocalypticism represents an eschatological development of sapiential thought, as found in material such as Qoheleth 3. In that text it is asserted that there is a right time for all things, and this perspective, according to von Rad, is given an eschatological orientation in apocalypticism. Puech has credited von Rad with seeing that "la sagesse est comme mère de l'apocalyptique." See his "Apports des textes apocalyptiques et sapientiels de Qumrân à l'eschatologie du judaïsme ancien," in *Wisdom and Apocalypticism in the Dead Sea Scrolls and in the Biblical Tradition* (ed. F. García Martínez; BETL 168; Leuven: Peeters-Leuven University Press, forthcoming).

Gustav Hölscher also argued that wisdom is the source of apocalypticism. See his "Die Entstehung des Buches Daniel," *Theologische Studien und Kritiken* 92 (1919): 113-38. See further S.L. Cook, *Prophecy and Apocalypticism* (Minneapolis: Fortress, 1995), 11; E. Elizabeth Johnson, *The Function of Apocalyptic and Wisdom Traditions in Romans 9-11* (SBLDS 109; Atlanta: Scholars Press, 1989), 55-56.

[39] *Weisheit und Prädestination*, 188-90. The Tat-Ergehen-Zusammenhang explains why the righteous will be rewarded and the wicked destroyed by their own devices (e.g., Prov 26:27), as opposed to direct intervention by God (Vergeltung), the norm in prophetic literature. This topic is discussed in section 2 of Chapter 2.

[40] Lange understands sapiential sections of the sectarian texts as the incorporation of older material. For example, he notes that CD 2:2-13, which is a sapiential pericope, is sandwiched between two passages that, in different ways, present the history of the community (1:1-2:2 and 2:14-4:12). He argues that his concept of a sapiential Urordnung "wird in der Damaskusscrift funktionalisiert" and given a role in the sect's understanding of itself (*Weisheit und Prädestination*, 270). The presence of the Treatise in the Community Rule is viewed similarly.

In *Weisheit und Prädestination*, Lange's conclusions are based on close studies of a few pericopes, without examination of 4QInstruction as a whole. His analysis focuses on 4Q417 1 i. This major fragment has apocalyptic elements, such as appeal to a heavenly book, but has little practical wisdom. This prevents a proper assessment of 4QInstruction's combination of practical and apocalyptic elements.

More recently, Lange has argued that both 4QInstruction and Mysteries have important cultic concerns and attach great importance to the Torah.[41] He claims that these two texts should be situated in the Jerusalem Temple. He also argues that the second epilogue of Qoheleth (12:12-14) stems from this same setting:

> In den nichtessenischen Weisheitstexten aus Qumran (4QInstruction and Mysteries) dokumentiert sich vielmehr auch eine von Koh kritisierte weisheitliche Schule, die ich im folgenden als Tempelweisheit bezeichnen möchte.[42]

Qoheleth's second epilogue, 4QInstruction, and Mysteries are understood as having similar positions regarding the Torah and the cult. On that basis, Lange posits that they all stem from the Jerusalem Temple. The circles that produced this material are dated to the period of the Maccabean crisis since this is a period of unrest and disagreement centered around the Temple.[43] However, even if one were to grant that the Torah and the cult are major themes for the epilogue of Qoheleth (and

---

[41] Armin Lange, "In Diskussion mit dem Tempel: zur Auseinandersetzung zwischen Kohelet und weisheitlichen Kreisen am Jerusalemer Tempel," in *Qohelet in the Context of Wisdom* (ed. A. Schoors; BETL 136; Leuven: Leuven University Press/Peeters, 1998), 113-60. A version of this article is available in English as "Eschatological Wisdom in the Book of Qohelet and the Dead Sea Scrolls," in *The Dead Sea Scrolls Fifty Years After Their Discovery*, 817-24. See also his "Die Endgestalt des protomasoretischen Psalters und die Toraweisheit," in *Der Psalter in Judentum und Christentum* (ed. E. Zenger; Herders Biblische Studien 18; Freiburg: Herder, 1998), 101-36. Lange has also examined the phrase הפיל גורל in 4Q418 81 5. See his "The Determination of Fate by the Oracle of the Lot in the Dead Sea Scrolls, the Hebrew Bible and Ancient Mesopotamian Literature," in *Sapiential, Liturgical and Poetical Texts from Qumran*, 39-48. He examines sapiential terminology in his "Kognitives *lqh* in Sap A, im Tenak und Sir," *Zeitschrift für Althebraistik* 9 (1996): 190-95.

[42] "In Diskussion mit dem Tempel," 145. He argues that these three texts are all critical of Qoheleth's skeptical attitude towards the cult, a view he sees in texts such as "God is in heaven, and you upon earth" (5:1). See ibid., 156. This claim is supported by the contention that Mysteries is citing Qoheleth. For example, Lange argues that the expression יותר ל- of 1Q27 1 ii 3 is dependent on the use of this construction in Qoheleth 6:8, 11; and 7:11. He also contends that the word שגג ("inadvertent sin") in 1Q27 6 2 is the result of engagement with Qoheleth 5:5, which also uses this term. See ibid., 125. The terminology of the Book of Mysteries that for Lange reflects a "Kohelet-Rezeption" is too common to posit direct engagement with Qoheleth.

[43] Ibid., 157.

this is easier to claim with regard to the Torah—see 12:13—than the cult), it does not follow that it should be located at the Temple. 4QInstruction has cultic concerns (e.g., 4Q418 103 ii) and uses the Torah (cf. 4Q416 2 iii 19), but they are not major preoccupations in the work and do not require a Temple setting. If 4QInstruction had such a provenance one would expect a more nationalistic stamp. It has no Zion theology and does not predict the eschatological restoration of the Temple in the manner of 11QTemple 29:8-10. The Temple is by no means an important theme of 4QInstruction. These assessments also apply to Mysteries. Lange's common Sitz-im-Leben for Qoheleth 12:12-14, 4QInstruction, and the Book of Mysteries should be seen in light of his understanding of 4QInstruction and Mysteries as a response to the "crisis of wisdom."

4QInstruction, Mysteries, and the Treatise do not directly engage the skepticism of Qoheleth or the complaints of Job. This suggests that they are not responding to a "crisis of wisdom." 4QInstruction can nevertheless be seen, as Lange suggests, as eschatologizing biblical wisdom since it combines practical wisdom with an apocalyptic worldview. Lange himself, in my opinion, does not fully treat this combination because his understanding of biblical wisdom tends to focus exclusively on its affirmation of the rational principle of order that God gave the cosmos. There is no substantial engagement with the practical wisdom of either Proverbs or 4QInstruction.

Lange's use of von Rad is also problematic. Von Rad's thesis has sparked fruitful reflection on the relationship between wisdom and apocalypticism. After von Rad's work, H.-P. Müller posited the origins of apocalypticism to be the "mantic wisdom" of dream interpretation and omens.[44] Michael Stone examined the "lists of revealed things" found in apocalyptic literature and argued that they stemmed originally from the sapiential tradition.[45] But, as is well known, von Rad's thesis cannot

---

[44] H.-P. Müller, "Mantische Weisheit und Apokalyptik," *Congress Volume: Uppsala 1971* (VTSup 22; Leiden: Brill, 1972), 268-93. See also Andreas Bedenbender, "Jewish Apocalypticism: A Child of Mantic Wisdom?" *Henoch* 24 (2002): 189-96 (*The Origins of Enochic Judaism: Proceedings of the First Enoch Seminar. University of Michigan, Sesto Fiorentino, Italy, June 19-23, 2001* [ed. G. Boccaccini]).

[45] M.E. Stone, "Lists of Revealed Things in the Apocalyptic Literature," in *Magnalia Dei: The Mighty Acts of God* (ed. F.M. Cross et al.; Garden City: Doubleday, 1976), 414-51. See also John G. Gammie, "Spatial and Ethical Dualism in Jewish Wisdom and Apocalyptic Literature," *Journal of Biblical Literature* 93 (1974): 356-85; Benedikt Otzen, "Old Testament Wisdom Literature and Dualistic Thinking in Late Judaism," in *Congress Volume: Edinburgh 1974* (VTSup 28; Leiden: Brill, 1975), 146-57; Robert Coughenour, "The Wisdom Stance of Enoch's Redactor," *Journal for the Study of Judaism* 13 (1982): 47-55; Martin Hengel, *Judaism and Hellenism* (2 vols.; Philadelphia: Fortress, 1973), 1.209-10; James C. VanderKam, "The Prophetic-Sapiential Origins of

stand as originally presented.[46] Both wisdom and apocalypticism can be understood as deterministic and revealed knowledge in apocalyptic literature is often presented as wisdom (e.g., *1 En.* 93:10). Nevertheless the two traditions are quite different. Proverbs has no interest in history, whereas a concern with history is a hallmark of apocalyptic literature. The wisdom tradition generally presupposes a stable atmosphere in which one can prosper through hard work and common sense, but in apocalypticism the prevailing mood is often of upheaval and crisis.[47] Furthermore, the epistemology of the two traditions is entirely different. While apocalypses generally appeal to supernatural revelation, in traditional wisdom knowledge is typically derived from experience and the observation of the natural world.

3.2 Torleif Elgvin

Elgvin has produced a comprehensive study of 4QInstruction.[48] Many of the arguments of this work have already been published.[49] He identifies material in the composition that has affinities with biblical wisdom. 4QInstruction, he observes, contains admonitions, as does Proverbs and

---

Apocalyptic Thought," in *From Revelation to Canon: Studies in Hebrew Bible and Second Temple Literature* (JSJSup 62; Leiden: Brill, 2000), 241-54; J.Z. Smith, "Wisdom and Apocalyptic," in *Map Is Not Territory* (Chicago: University of Chicago Press, 1978), 67-87; Andreas Bedenbender, *Der Gott der Welt Tritt auf den Sinai: Entstehung, Entwicklung und Funktionsweise der Frühjüdischen Apokalyptik* (ANTZ 8; Berlin: Institut Kirche und Judentum, 2000), 62-87, 264-65.

[46] John J. Collins, "Wisdom, Apocalypticism and Generic Compatibility," in *Seers, Sibyls and Sages in Hellenistic Roman Judaism* (JSJSup 54; Leiden: Brill, 1997), 385-404. See also Shannon Burkes, *God, Self, and Death: The Shape of Religious Transformation in the Second Temple Period* (JSJSup 79; Leiden: Brill, 2003), 253-62.

[47] For an idiosyncratic view of Proverbs as "literature for crisis," see Ellen F. Davis, *Proverbs, Ecclesiastes, and the Song of Songs* (Louisville: Westminster John Knox, 2000), 13-18.

[48] "An Analysis of 4QInstruction." This work is forthcoming as *Wisdom and Apocalyptic in 4QInstruction* (STDJ 38; Leiden: Brill).

[49] See, for example, Torleif Elgvin, "Early Essene Eschatology: Judgment and Salvation according to Sapiential Work A," in *Current Research and Technological Development on the Dead Sea Scrolls: Conference on the Texts from the Judean Desert, Jerusalem, 30 April 1995* (ed. D.W. Parry and S.D. Ricks; STDJ 20; Leiden: Brill, 1996), 126-65; idem, "Wisdom and Apocalypticism in the Early Second Century BCE—The Evidence of 4QInstruction," in *The Dead Sea Scrolls Fifty Years After Their Discovery*, 226-47; idem, "Wisdom, Revelation, and Eschatology in an Early Essene Writing," in *Society of Biblical Literature Seminar Papers 1995* (SBLSP 34; Atlanta: Scholars Press, 1995), 440-63; idem, "The Mystery to Come: Early Essene Theology of Revelation," in *Qumran between the Old and New Testaments* (ed. F.H. Cryer and T.L. Thompson; JSOTSup 290; Sheffield: Sheffield Academic Press, 1998), 113-50; idem, "Wisdom With and Without Apocalyptic," in *Sapiential, Liturgical and Poetical Texts from Qumran*, 15-38.

Ben Sira. Elgvin characterizes the admonitions as relating to "specific fields of life" such as family, ethics, farming, and financial affairs.⁵⁰ He also documents aspects of 4QInstruction that have affinities with apocalyptic literature, such as revelation, eschatological judgment, and the periodization of history. The apocalyptic material of the composition is for him found for the most part in its "discourses," whereas the connections to biblical wisdom are primarily in its admonitions.⁵¹

Elgvin classifies the practical and apocalyptic portions of 4QInstruction into different strata. For him "the composition represents a conflation of two literary layers."⁵² He understands the admonitions as comprising an originally autonomous work that consisted of practical advice in the tradition of Proverbs 10-31. This "secular" work was later incorporated into apocalyptic, eschatological discourses by early Essene circles.⁵³ The author of the second stratum is not associated directly with the Qumran Essenes because 4QInstruction has none of the key markers of this group, such as sectarian use of the word יחד, the Teacher of Righteousness, or any of the institutional hierarchy described in the Community Rule and the Damascus Document.⁵⁴ Elgvin dates the admonitions to the early second century BCE, and thus close to Ben Sira, while granting that they could have derived from the third century. In his dissertation Elgvin argued that the discourses were written between 160 and 130 BCE, but he has since shifted to a pre-Maccabean dating.⁵⁵

In Elgvin's view, the *yaḥad* community was formed when the people responsible for 4QInstruction, who were non-priestly lay teachers,

---

⁵⁰ Elgvin, "Wisdom and Apocalypticism," 227.

⁵¹ The term "discourse" is a broad form-critical category that characterizes teachings not expressed in a single proverb. It is an elaborate, extended meditation on a topic. This form has also been called "didactic narrative" or the "wisdom poem." See Murphy, *The Tree of Life*, 10; Crenshaw, *Old Testament Wisdom*, 38-39.

⁵² Elgvin, "Wisdom and Apocalypticism," 226. Lange has supported this view. On the basis of the eschatological judgment in 4Q416 1 and the practical wisdom of 4Q417 2 i, he claims that "der *MLM* (Musar Le-Mevin) eine Redaktion erfahren hat." See his "In Diskussion mit dem Tempel," 127.

⁵³ "Wisdom and Apocalypticism," 246. Elgvin originally argued that 4QInstruction is a product of the Qumran community but revised this position. See his "Admonition Texts," 193.

⁵⁴ יחד does, however, appear in 4QInstruction but it contains no explicit sectarian use of this word. See Eibert J.C. Tigchelaar, "הבא ביחד in *4QInstruction* (*4Q418* 64 + 199 + 66 par *4Q417* 1 i 17-19) and the Height of the Columns of *4Q418*," *Revue de Qumran* 18 (1998): 589-93.

⁵⁵ Elgvin, "An Analysis of 4QInstruction," 185. See also his "Priestly Sages?" The pre-Maccabean position is suggested by the fact that 4QInstruction displays no sense of political upheaval or familiarity with the Maccabean crisis. These factors, however, do not *a priori* exclude a later date. My assessments regarding the date of 4QInstruction are summarized in section 3 of Chapter 6.

merged with priestly groups.[56] In his dissertation Elgvin argues that this pre-Essene community of teachers found self-identity in the figure of Noah: "God's revelation to Noah is a model for understanding end-time secrets."[57] The author of 4QInstruction saw Noah as "a model for the life of the elect."[58] Noah is not, however, presented as a major figure in 4QInstruction, and this assessment has not been endorsed.

Elgvin's conclusion that 4QInstruction is a composite work is problematic.[59] When dealing with such a fragmentary text it is difficult enough to discern the text in its present state, let alone posit different strata. Attributing the sapiential material to an early layer and the apocalyptic portions to a later one depends on a rigid notion of generic purity. The problem is analogous to the approach of Jesus Seminar scholars to Q, the sayings source of Matthew and Luke.[60] The perspective is that wisdom and apocalypticism are mutually exclusive traditions, with the former early and the latter late. In the case of 4QInstruction, this view hinders an appreciation of its combination of practical wisdom with an apocalyptic worldview.

Elgvin has also examined the relationship between 4QInstruction and *1 Enoch*.[61] He explains the affinities between the two texts by positing that the wisdom text reflects direct literary dependence on *1 Enoch*. Both compositions include an appeal to revelation in the form of a heavenly book (e.g., *1 En.* 90:20; 93:1-2; 4Q417 1 i 15). 4QInstruction, like the *Epistle of Enoch* and the *Apocalypse of Weeks*, is addressed to an elect

---

[56] "Wisdom and Apocalypticism," 247.

[57] Elgvin, "An Analysis of 4QInstruction," 66. This view reflects his reconstruction of 4Q416 1 with 4Q418 73 and 201. The first line of 4Q418 201 reads: נהיה הודיע אל נח[. Elgvin takes נח to be the biblical Noah and appends this fragment to the second visible line of 4Q416 1, following the material he adds to this line from 4Q418 73. Thus while 4Q416 1 2 according to the transcription in *DJD 34* is ולתכן חפצו֯, the line according to Elgvin reads (4Q418 201 material in solid underline; 4Q418 73 material in dotted underline): ולתכן חפצו [על כל עולה ואשר?}ל{נהיה הודיע אל נח קץ בפן?]. He translates this as: "and establish His will over all evil. He made known to Noah what was (?) to come, period upon period." See his "An Analysis of 4QInstruction," 238-39. Rejecting this reconstruction, Strugnell and Harrington, *DJD 34*, 422, hold that "there is no overlapping of this text with the parallel manuscripts." Moreover, they do not read נח as Noah, but as נח]לת, "inheritance." See also Tigchelaar, "Towards a Reconstruction," 107.

[58] "An Analysis of 4QInstruction," 71. See also his "Early Essene Eschatology," 136, 148.

[59] Kasper Bro Larsen, "Visdom og apokalyptik i Musar leMevin (1Q/4QInstruction) [Wisdom and Apocalyptic in Musar leMevin (1Q/4QInstruction)]," *Dansk Teologisk Tidsskrift* 65 (2002): 1-14. See also section 3.5 of this chapter.

[60] See John S. Kloppenborg, *The Formation of Q* (Harrisburg: Trinity Press International, 1999 [orig. pub., 1987]), xi. See also Collins, "Wisdom, Apocalypticism and Generic Compatibility," in *Seers, Sibyls and Sages*, 401-04.

[61] See section 2.3 of Chapter 5.

group with a privileged role in the eschatological scenario.[62] Both texts
posit the destruction of the wicked at the eschatological judgment and the
ultimate salvation of the righteous. 4QInstruction and the *Epistle of
Enoch* both understand their audiences as poor (e.g., 4Q416 2 iii 8; *1 En.*
94:1-9). On the basis of these similarities, Elgvin argues that "Enochic
traditions are the primary sources of inspiration for the eschatological
discourses" of 4QInstruction.[63] Elgvin speculates that the vision of Hagu
could refer to the *Apocalypse of Weeks*, the *Animal Apocalypse*, or
both.[64] He also identifies 4QInstruction's mystery that is to be as the
"sevenfold wisdom" given to the elect in the *Apocalypse of Weeks* (*1 En.*
93:10).[65]

While Elgvin draws attention to important similarities between
4QInstruction and *1 Enoch*, positing a literary relationship between them
is not warranted.[66] There is no explicit evidence of literary dependence.
Moreover, there are substantial differences between the two texts. The
Epistle of Enoch never refers to its audience as "poor," but rather to the
"righteous" who are abused by the wealthy (e.g., *1 En.* 96:1-8).
4QInstruction, by contrast, frequently reminds the addressee that he is
poor.[67] Additionally, there is no anger directed towards the rich in
4QInstruction, whereas disdain for the wealthy is a major preoccupation
of the *Epistle of Enoch*. The two texts also have different modes of revelation. *1 Enoch* never mentions the mystery that is to be, and
4QInstruction has no otherworldly journeys or visions interpreted by an
angel. Although Elgvin speculates that the vision of Hagu represents an
Enochic work, it is not evident that the vision should be understood as an
actual document. It is associated with a book in heaven (4Q417 1 i 15-
16) and is never treated as a physical text.[68] His association of
4QInstruction's mystery that is to be with the "sevenfold wisdom" of the
Apocalypse of Weeks highlights the fact that both texts portray the elect
as recipients of divine knowledge. These texts do not, however, necessarily have the same elect group, or the same revelation, in mind.

---

[62] Elgvin, "Wisdom With and Without Apocalyptic," 29.

[63] Elgvin, "An Analysis of 4QInstruction," 169. See also G.W.E. Nickelsburg, "The
Epistle of Enoch and the Qumran Literature," *Journal of Jewish Studies* 33 (1982): 333-
48.

[64] Elgvin, "An Analysis of 4QInstruction," 170.

[65] Ibid., 63.

[66] See Loren T. Stuckenbruck, "4QInstruction and the Possible Influence of Early Enochic Traditions: An Evaluation," in *The Wisdom Texts from Qumran*, 245-61; Michael
Knibb, "The Book of Enoch in the Light of the Qumran Wisdom Literature," in *Wisdom
and Apocalypticism in the Dead Sea Scrolls and in the Biblical Tradition*.

[67] See section 3.3 of Chapter 4.

[68] See section 2.3 of Chapter 3.

Enochic literature was popular in the late Second Temple period. This is suggested by the Aramaic Enoch manuscripts found at Qumran and the description of Enoch in *Jubilees* 4. It is reasonable to suppose that the author of 4QInstruction, as Elgvin suggests, was familiar with Enochic material. If so, he borrowed ideas from it, not actual phrases.

3.3 Eibert J.C. Tigchelaar

Eibert J.C. Tigchelaar has studied both physical[69] and interpretative aspects of 4QInstruction.[70] His book, *To Increase Learning for the Understanding Ones* (cf. 4Q418 221 3), is a valuable supplement to *DJD 34*. In this work he thoroughly examines all available sources for the text of 4QInstruction—the PAM photographs, the *Preliminary Concordance* of the Dead Sea Scrolls produced in the 1950's, and the fragments themselves. Tigchelaar offers transcriptions of 4QInstruction fragments, and is clear when his readings differ from those of *DJD 34*. While the differences between the editions of texts in *To Increase Learning* and *DJD 34* are often minor, it is useful to compare the two versions.[71]

At times Tigchelaar proposes versions of 4QInstruction texts that differ significantly from those of *DJD 34*. Generally these "new" texts are the product of novel joins and overlaps. For example, Tigchelaar tentatively suggests that 4Q418 238 should be placed at the top of 4Q416 1, which is generally considered the beginning of the composition.[72] In this case the first visible word of 4QInstruction would be משכיל. If Tigchelaar's reconstruction is granted, the beginning of 4QInstruction highlights the educational intent of the composition to an extent previously unknown.[73] Tigchelaar underscores this theme by positing that the first column of 4Q418, which is another version of the beginning of the composition, ended with 4Q418 221 and 222.[74]

---

[69] See his "הבא ביחד in *4QInstruction*"; idem, "Towards a Reconstruction."

[70] See, for example, his "The Addressees of 4QInstruction," 62-75; idem, "Eden and Paradise: The Garden Motif in Some Early Jewish Texts," in *Paradise Interpreted: Representations of Biblical Paradise in Judaism and Christianity* (ed. G.P. Luttikhuizen; Leiden: Brill, 1999), 37-57.

[71] Tigchelaar writes regarding his book that "Many comments are marginal, but in other cases my alternative readings may further the study of the text." See *To Increase Learning*, 27.

[72] Ibid., 183.

[73] This reading relates to the possibility that 4QInstruction is a product of the Qumran sect. The War Scroll, for example, begins with the phrase למשכיל, and this is often thought to be the case for the Community Rule (see also 1QSb 1:1; 4Q403 1 i 30; 4Q511 2 i 1).

[74] *To Increase Learning*, 189. 4Q418 221 2-3 reads: "... to make all the simple ones understand ... [and to in]crease learning for the understanding ones."

Tigchelaar's composite texts are plausible and merit consideration, but in general should not be considered definitive. He is clear when they are offered as hypothetical possibilities.[75] Because of the fragmentary state of the text of 4QInstruction, total confidence in a given reconstruction is rarely possible.

Regarding interpretive issues, Tigchelaar is perhaps best known for his contention that 4QInstruction's addressee "could be anyone in society" rather than a student in a specific school setting.[76] This view is at odds with the position of the editors of *DJD 34* that the text was designed to educate a specific audience of scribal priests. For Tigchelaar the diversity of the addressees, who are comprised of farmers, people engaged in business, and craftsmen, "suggests a more general audience than only a special class of students."[77] Therefore 4QInstruction, in his view, was not written by the Dead Sea sect.

The possibility that the word משכיל may appear at the beginning of the 4QInstruction has led Tigchelaar to re-consider his claim that the composition is not the product of a pedagogical setting.[78] While granting that 4QInstruction may envision a משכיל devoted to increasing the learning of the "understanding ones," Tigchelaar still argues, on the grounds that the text has a diversity of addressees, that it is written for "a more general audience than only a special class of students."[79] It is certainly true that 4QInstruction is devoted to a range of different addressees. It does not necessarily follow that the text was addressed to a "more general audience." The addressees of 4QInstruction, despite their occupational differences, have elect status. The mystery that is to be is revealed to them and they are taught that they are in the lot of the angels (4Q418 81 4-5). Even if the word משכיל does not appear at the beginning of 4QInstruction, the text seems designed to provide instruction for a specific group.

---

[75] *To Increase Learning*, 183.

[76] "The Addressees of 4QInstruction," 75.

[77] Ibid., 68.

[78] *To Increase Learning*, 245. Tigchelaar had previously disputed that the figure of the teacher should be seen in the composition. See "The Addressees of 4QInstruction," 68. Whether the word משכיל appears at the beginning of the work or not, it seems clear that the authorial voice of 4QInstruction is that of a teacher. The composition is addressed to a student, the *mebin* who is asked repeatedly to learn and study. Since there is a student it is safe to presume a teacher, although such an office is rarely mentioned in the text (e.g., 4Q418 81 17), and never in relation to its author.

[79] *To Increase Learning*, 248.

3.4. Other Contributions to the Study of 4QInstruction

Several other scholars have contributed to the study of 4QInstruction. Esther Chazon has compared the treatment of Adam in 4QWords of the Luminaries (4Q504-06), 4QParaphrase of Genesis and Exodus (4Q422), 4QInstruction, and Ben Sira 17.[80] These texts in various ways combine the tradition of humanity's dominion over creation (Gen 1:27) with Adam's stewardship over the garden of Eden (2:15). After comparing them, she concludes that there may be a literary relationship between 4Q422 and 4Q504-06.

Jörg Frey has compared the term "flesh" (בשר) in 4QInstruction with the use of the word σάρξ in the letters of Paul.[81] Both Paul and 4QInstruction understand "flesh" as negative and base; both also contrast "flesh" with "spirit." For this reason Frey suggests that Paul may have read a text like 4QInstruction as part of his Pharisaic education.[82] The possibility that Paul drew upon Palestinian wisdom traditions attested in 4QInstruction merits more consideration.[83]

Charlotte Hempel has examined 4QInstruction and other Qumran wisdom texts such as the Book of Mysteries and 4QWays of Righteousness (4Q420-21) vis-à-vis the rulebooks of the Qumran community.[84] Hempel asks if the Qumran wisdom texts should be considered products of the Dead Sea sect. She grants that sectarian elements and influence from the sapiential tradition might exist in the Qumran wisdom corpus "alongside one another."[85] She observes that the rulebooks have phrases that are also found in the wisdom texts, such as the mystery that is to be (1QS 11:3-4), and the term משכיל (e.g., 4Q417 1 i 25; 1QS 9:12-26). 4QInstruction includes a "vision of Hagu" whereas undisputedly sectarian texts mention a "Book of Hagu."[86] While not claiming outright that

---

[80] Esther Chazon, "The Creation and Fall of Adam in the Dead Sea Scrolls," in *The Book of Genesis in Jewish and Oriental Christian Interpretation: A Collection of Essays* (ed. J. Frishman and L. van Rompay; Leuven: Peeters, 1997), 13-24.

[81] Jörg Frey, "The Notion of 'Flesh' in 4QInstruction and the Background of Pauline Usage," in *Sapiential, Liturgical and Poetical Texts from Qumran*, 197-226. In the same volume, see Heinz-Wolfgang Kuhn, "The Wisdom Passage in 1 Corinthians 2:6-16 between Qumran and Proto-Gnosticism," 240-53. See also Jörg Frey, "Die paulinische Antithese von 'Fleisch' und 'Geist' und die palästinisch-jüdische Weisheitstradition," *Zeitschrift für die neutestamentliche Wissenschaft* 90 (1999): 45-77; idem, "Flesh and Spirit in the Palestinian Jewish Sapiential Tradition and in the Qumran Texts: An Inquiry into the Background of Pauline Usage," in *The Wisdom Texts from Qumran*, 367-404.

[82] Frey, "The Notion of 'Flesh' in 4QInstruction," 225.

[83] See the excursus of Chapter 3.

[84] Charlotte Hempel, "The Qumran Sapiential Texts and the Rule Books," in *The Wisdom Texts from Qumran*, 277-95.

[85] Ibid., 279.

[86] See section 1 of Chapter 3.

the wisdom texts are products of the Qumran community, she highlights "the presence of a number of overlapping terms and ideas between the material that describes organizational matters in the Rules and the sapiential texts."[87]

In the same volume in which Hempel's article appears, George Brooke analyzes the use of scripture in 4QInstruction and other wisdom texts from Qumran.[88] He offers a "preliminary taxonomy of some of the uses of scripture" in this material.[89] Some wisdom texts presume the instructional value of scripture. For example, the teaching on marriage in 4Q416 2 iii 20-iv 5 is based on an interpretation of Genesis 2-3.[90] Brooke also contends that in the Qumran wisdom texts "scriptural wisdom traditions are made eschatological."[91] 4QInstruction can be understood in this way since it combines wisdom reminiscent of Proverbs with an apocalyptic worldview.[92]

Daryl Jefferies has published a study of the admonitions of 4QInstruction.[93] He offers a critical edition and form critical exposition of selected 4QInstruction texts. The citation format of 4QInstruction that

---

[87] Hempel, "The Qumran Sapiential Texts," 295.

[88] George J. Brooke, "Biblical Interpretation in the Wisdom Texts from Qumran," in *The Wisdom Texts from Qumran*, 201-20.

[89] Ibid., 202.

[90] Ibid., 213.

[91] Ibid., 220.

[92] There are several articles in *The Wisdom Texts from Qumran* that contribute to the study of 4QInstruction, aside from essays in this collection mentioned elsewhere in this chapter. For example, John Strugnell, in his "The Smaller Hebrew Wisdom Texts Found at Qumran: Variations, Resemblances, and Lines of Development," 31-60, compares attestations of words in wisdom texts such as 4Q184 and 302 with the vocabulary of 4QInstruction and biblical wisdom texts. He relies on the handwritten concordance of the Dead Sea Scrolls produced in the 1950's. A. Schoors, "The Language of the Qumran Sapiential Works," 61-95, is a philological study of the vocabulary of 4QInstruction and other wisdom texts from Qumran. Christfried Böttrich, in "Früjüdische Weisheitstraditionen im slavischen Henochbuch und in Qumran," 297-321, argues that *2 Enoch* is an important source for understanding sapiential thought in Hellenistic-Roman Judaism. She notes several similarities between *2 Enoch* and 4QInstruction. Both, for example, stress the theme of creation. See ibid., 318. James H. Charlesworth, "The Odes of Solomon and the Jewish Wisdom Texts," 323-49, argues that the *Odes of Solomon*, like 4QInstruction, combines practical wisdom with an apocalyptic worldview. For example, the *Odes* include both paraenesis (20:6) and mystery language (8:10-11). See ibid., 347. J. Dochhorn claims that 4QInstruction and the *Apocalypse of Moses* attest similar exegetical traditions regarding Genesis 3:17-19. See his "'Sie wird dir nicht ihre Kraft geben'—Adam, Kain und der Ackerbau in 4Q423 2₃ und Apc Mos 24," 351-64.

[93] Daryl Jefferies, *Wisdom at Qumran: A Form-Critical Analysis of the Admonitions in 4QInstruction* (Gorgias Dissertations, Near Eastern Studies 3; Piscataway: Gorgias Press, 2002). This is the published version of his 2001 dissertation from the University of Wisconsin-Madison.

this book employs makes it difficult to use.[94] On the basis of common terminology he argues that 4QInstruction should be considered a product of the Qumran community.[95] Jefferies disagrees with the editors of *DJD 34* that 4QInstruction is a "missing link" between Proverbs and Ben Sira, arguing instead that "4QInstruction is better situated in the development of Jewish wisdom between Sirach and later more Hellenized forms of Jewish wisdom such as Pseudo-Phocylides."[96] For this reason he dates 4QInstruction to 150-100 BCE.[97] The basis for this view is that 4QInstruction uses "the Hellenistic monostich" whereas Ben Sira favors the couplet. Since Pseudo-Phocylides is fully integrated into the wider Hellenistic world, 4QInstruction is seen in an intermediate position between the two in terms of Hellenistic influence.[98] Even if one were to grant that the monostich is Hellenistic, Hellenism should not be taken as an important criterion for assessing the Sitz-im-Leben of 4QInstruction. The composition never explicitly shows familiarity with or interest in the contemporary international world. Gentiles, for example, never appear in a prominent way in the text.

Some recent books on the Dead Sea Scrolls, while not devoted to 4QInstruction exclusively, include significant discussion of the composition. Two examples are Catherine M. Murphy's *Wealth in the Dead Sea Scrolls* and Crispin H.T. Fletcher Louis's *All the Glory of Adam*.[99] Murphy's book provides a "thick description" of the disposition of wealth in the Qumran community.[100] Murphy offers the first extensive examination

---

[94] Jefferies classifies the admonitions he studies into six categories—for example, "Dealing with Others," "Requiring the Proper Lifestyle," and "Money Matters." Each section is numbered. 4QInstruction texts are placed into each section accordingly. For example, in section 6, entitled "Achieving and Maintaining your Inheritance," 4Q417 2 i 1-5 is text "A," lines 6-13 text "B," etc. Throughout the dissertation Jefferies prefers his own citation format rather than the system in common use—that is, using not "4Q417 2 i 1-5" but "6.A." See *Wisdom at Qumran*, 265. For example, in ibid., 79-90, he outlines the 4QInstruction texts he analyzes without using the standard citation format.

[95] Ibid., 59.

[96] Ibid., 320.

[97] Ibid., 77.

[98] His understanding of the monostich is similar to that of Miriam Lichtheim. See her *Late Egyptian Wisdom Literature in the International Context: A Study of Demotic Instructions* (OBO 52; Göttingen: Vandenhoeck & Ruprecht, 1983). For more on Pseudo-Phocylides, see Pieter van der Horst, *The Sentences of Pseudo-Phocylides* (Leiden: Brill, 1978); John J. Collins, *Between Athens and Jerusalem* (2nd ed.; Grand Rapids/Livonia: Eerdmans/Dove, 2000 [orig. pub., 1983]), 168-74.

[99] Catherine M. Murphy, *Wealth in the Dead Sea Scrolls and the Qumran Community* (STDJ 40; Leiden: Brill, 2002); Crispin H.T. Fletcher-Louis, *All the Glory of Adam: Liturgical Anthropology in the Dead Sea Scrolls* (STDJ 42; Leiden: Brill, 2002).

[100] *Wealth in the Dead Sea Scrolls*, 24.

of the presentation of poverty in 4QInstruction and its financial advice.[101]
She contends that 4QInstruction places its financial advice against a
theological backdrop that highlights the dominion of God.[102] Murphy
also emphasizes that the addressee's elect status and his eschatological
rewards are described with economic terms such as פעלה ("reward") and
נחלה ("inheritance").[103] Eschatological rewards are designed to resolve
economic injustices in the present.

Murphy emphasizes that 4QInstruction gives a range of financial advice. For example, she understands 4Q417 2 i 1-6 as providing instruction on proper comportment when in the presence of nobles.[104] By contrast, 4Q417 2 i 17-21 presumes that the addressee lacks food.[105] The
author also observes that 4QInstruction's ethical ideals are associated
with financial instruction. For example, 4Q416 2 ii 18-iii 8 teaches that
the addressee should avoid wasteful excesses of food and drink and resist
the temptation to squander a loan that has been deposited him with
him.[106] Both teachings stress moderation and caution.

Fletcher-Louis, in *All the Glory of Adam*, argues that Second Temple
literature attests an "angelomorphic anthropology." He contends that at
the time some Jews were thought to have "lived an angelic life and possessed an angelic identity or status."[107] That is, they possess a heavenly
form of human existence. According to Fletcher-Louis, 4QInstruction,
like other Second Temple texts, presents humanity in angelomorphic
terms. This is clear, he claims, in 4Q417 1 i 14-18, which speaks of a
"spiritual people" that was created "according to the likeness of the holy
ones."[108]

Fletcher Louis devotes particular attention to 4Q418 81.[109] He contends that this text is addressed to Aaronic priests. This is based on the
fact that it tells one to glorify God. Line 3 alludes to Numbers 18:20, a
priestly text. According to line 4, the addressee has been established
לקדוש קודשים. Portraying Aaron as an angelomorphic priest, Fletcher-
Louis takes this phrase to mean "Aaron is 'holy of holies.'"[110] Aaron,
however, is not a major figure in 4QInstruction, making it unlikely that

---

[101] Ibid., 163-209. See also Benjamin G. Wright III, "The Categories of Rich and Poor in the Qumran Sapiential Literature," in *Sapiential Perspectives*.
[102] *Wealth in the Dead Sea Scrolls*, 166.
[103] Ibid., 167. This topic is addressed in Chapter 4.
[104] Ibid., 175.
[105] Ibid., 179.
[106] Ibid., 189.
[107] *All the Glory of Adam*, 4.
[108] Ibid., 113-18.
[109] See section 2.4.3 of Chapter 3.
[110] *All the Glory of Adam*, 179.

the language of holiness in 4Q418 81 alludes to him. Since the composition has limited interest in cultic affairs, it is more likely that it describes the addressee's elect status in priestly terms, not that he is a priest.[111]

---

[111] There have been other scholarly contributions to 4QInstruction. Before the publication of *DJD 34*, André Caquot provided a preliminary general survey and translation of several manuscripts of the Qumran wisdom literature, including some of the key texts of 4QInstruction. See his "Les textes de sagesse de Qoumrân," 5-30. Patrick Tiller, in his study of the phrase "eternal planting" in Second Temple literature, argues that the expression should not be taken as proof that 4QInstruction is a product of the Qumran community. See his "The 'Eternal Planting' in the Dead Sea Scrolls," *Dead Sea Discoveries* 4 (1997): 312-35. Geza Vermes has claimed that 4QInstruction should be considered a composition of the Dead Sea sect on the basis of its affinities with writings such as the Community Rule and the Hodayot. See his *The Complete Dead Sea Scrolls*, 402. Giovanni Ibba examines similarities between 4QInstruction and the Book of Mysteries. See his "Il 'Libro dei Misteri' (1Q27, f.1): testo escatologico," *Henoch* 21 (1999): 73-84. Matthew Morgenstern argues that the phrase בית מולדים has an astrological sense. See his "The Meaning of בית מולדים in the Qumran Wisdom Texts," *Journal of Jewish Studies* 51 (2000), 141-44. James Scott examines the use of the Korah tradition in 4Q423 5. He argues that 4QInstruction has a sectarian provenance. The mention of Korah in 4Q423 is considered a reference to "schismatics within the congregation" who denounced the Teacher of Righteousness early in the history of the community. See his "Korah and Qumran," in *The Bible at Qumran: Text, Shape, and Interpretation* (ed. P.W. Flint; Grand Rapids: Eerdmans, 2001), 182-202. Following Elgvin, Jay E. Smith has argued that the word כלי in 4Q416 2 ii 21 refers to the phallus, against the position of Strugnell that it should be interpreted as "wife." See Jay E. Smith, "Another Look at 4Q416 2 ii.21, a Critical Parallel to First Thessalonians 4:4," *Catholic Biblical Quarterly* 63 (2001): 499-504. See also *DJD 34*, 109. Cana Werman uses 4QInstruction to help explain the enigmatic "Book of Hagu" that is mentioned in writings of the Dead Sea sect. In her opinion, 4QInstruction calls on its addressee to "meditate both on his own life and on the course of history." The Book of Hagu similarly contained instruction based on "meditations on creation and history." See her "What is the Book of Hagu?" in *Sapiential Perspectives*. Werman also briefly examines 4QInstruction in a study of the role of engraved tablets in *Jubilees*. See her "'The חורה and the תעורה' Engraved on the Tablets," *Dead Sea Discoveries* 9 (2002): 75-103. Stefan Beyerle, in his wide-ranging study of apocalyptic theology, discusses 4QInstruction's utilization of Genesis 1-3. See his "Und dann werden die Zeichen der Wahrheit erscheinen ..." (Habilitationsschrift; Rheinischen Friedrich-Wilhelms-Universität, 2001), 523-33. (This work will be published in Brill's JSJSup series.) In the present study, the use of Genesis 1-3 in 4QInstruction is discussed in Chapter 3. Loren T. Stuckenbruck suggests that 4Q418 81 construes the elect community to which it is addressed as participating to some extent with the angels. See his "'Angels' and 'God': Exploring the Limits of Early Jewish Monotheism," in *Exploring Early Jewish and Christian Monotheism* (ed. L.T. Stuckenbruck and W. Sproston North; New York/London: Continuum, forthcoming). This topic is addressed in section 2.4.3 of Chapter 3. Lawrence H. Schiffman studies legal aspects of 4QInstruction in his "Halakhic Elements in the Sapiential Texts," in the *Sapiential Perspectives* volume mentioned above. He also briefly treats the text in *Reclaiming the Dead Sea Scrolls* (ABRL; New York: Doubleday, 1995), 203-06. See further Tigchelaar, *To Increase Learning*, 18-19.

3.5 Studies of Wisdom and Apocalypticism in 4QInstruction

Recently there has been a great deal of interest in 4QInstruction's combination of traditional wisdom and apocalypticism. Elgvin's claim that the composition's sapiential and apocalyptic portions represent separate redactional strata was examined above. Lange has reached a similar view, whereas Larsen has called Elgvin's redactional scheme into question.[112] Larsen explores how 4QInstruction merges practical wisdom and supernatural revelation. He contends that the *raz nihyeh* of 4QInstruction represents a "radical rejection of experiential knowledge." Even though the composition does not completely deny experiential wisdom (i.e., 4Q423 5 5-6), Larsen is certainly correct when he claims that the ethical and practical advice of the composition has been "transferred into an apocalyptic frame of reference." He considers 4QInstruction "en ideologisk hybrid," a wisdom text with an apocalyptic worldview.[113]

Larsen draws on the work of John Collins. He has examined 4QInstruction's combination of traditional wisdom themes, such as filial piety and marriage, with apocalyptic themes, such as judgment and revelation.[114] Collins concludes "the new evidence from Qumran shows that wisdom, even Hebrew wisdom, cannot be identified with a single worldview."[115] He prefers to define wisdom simply as "instructional material." 4QInstruction demonstrates that sapiential forms can accommodate types of thought which are quite alien to the traditional wisdom of Proverbs. The "coherence of wisdom literature" is to be found in its function as pedagogical material rather than identification with a particular worldview.[116] He believes that 4QInstruction has affinities with the writings of the Dead Sea sect but that the text should not necessarily be identified as a product of that group.[117]

Collins has also studied 4QInstruction's eschatology. The composition's depiction of the final judgment and history is similar to that of

---

[112] Lange, "In Diskussion mit dem Tempel," 127; Larsen, "Visdom og apokalyptik," 14.

[113] Ibid., 4.

[114] See John J. Collins, "Wisdom Reconsidered, in Light of the Scrolls," *Dead Sea Discoveries* 4 (1997): 265-81; idem, *Jewish Wisdom*, 117-125.

[115] "Wisdom Reconsidered," 281.

[116] This is in contrast to the view of J.L. Crenshaw who, in his classic introduction to wisdom literature, argues that wisdom should be understood as "a marriage of form and content." He contends that one finds in wisdom literature distinctive views of the world consistently bound with the same literary forms. See Crenshaw, *Old Testament Wisdom*, 19; Collins, "Wisdom Reconsidered," 266. Note also von Rad, *Wisdom in Israel*, 25.

[117] John J. Collins, "The Eschatologizing of Wisdom in the Dead Sea Scrolls," in *Sapiential Perspectives*. This issue is examined in section 2 of Chapter 6.

apocalyptic texts. He has compared how 4QInstruction and the Wisdom of Solomon reflect influence from the apocalyptic tradition.[118] There are obvious differences between the two texts. While the Wisdom of Solomon is heavily influenced by Hellenistic philosophy, 4QInstruction shows no familiarity with this tradition. Nevertheless they are both Jewish wisdom texts that use the term "mystery" to denote knowledge regarding the created order, and both associate this understanding with righteousness.[119]

Daniel Harrington has also examined 4QInstruction vis-à-vis wisdom and apocalypticism. In a comparison of 4QInstruction and *4 Ezra*, he argues that the former contains "wisdom in an apocalyptic context" whereas the latter "reveals apocalyptic wisdom."[120] This distinction is meant to emphasize that, while having apocalyptic elements such as revelation, 4QInstruction in terms of genre is a sapiential text, whereas *4 Ezra* is an apocalypse.

Harrington has also compared 4QInstruction with Ben Sira.[121] There are topics that both texts address in similar ways. For example, both compositions recommend filial piety and are wary of borrowing.[122] 4QInstruction's combination of practical wisdom and apocalypticism, he argues, is a trait that distinguishes it from Ben Sira.[123] This is a helpful distinction. Ben Sira dismisses the contemplation of esoteric wisdom, urging people instead to rely on the Torah: "Reflect upon what you have been commanded, for what is hidden is not your concern. Do not meddle in matters that are beyond you, for more than you can understand has been shown you" (3:22-23; cf. 34:5). While 4QInstruction professes to disclose revealed mysteries, Ben Sira dismisses appeals to revelation beyond that of Sinai.

---

[118] John J. Collins, "The Mysteries of God: The Category 'Mystery' in Apocalyptic and Sapiential Writings," in *Wisdom and Apocalypticism in the Dead Sea Scrolls and in the Biblical Tradition*. See also Shannon Burkes, "Wisdom and Apocalypticism in the Wisdom of Solomon," *Harvard Theological Review* 95 (2002): 21-44.

[119] The ethical function of the mystery that is to be has also been stressed by Émile Puech. See his "Apports des textes apocalyptiques et sapientiels." This topic is examined in Chapter 2. He has also argued that the eschatology of 4QInstruction is similar to that of the main texts of the Qumran community. This issue is addressed in section 2.1 of Chapter 5.

[120] Daniel J. Harrington, "Wisdom and Apocalyptic in 4QInstruction and 4 Ezra," in *Wisdom and Apocalypticism in the Dead Sea Scrolls and in the Biblical Tradition*.

[121] Daniel J. Harrington, "Two Early Jewish Approaches to Wisdom: Sirach and Qumran Sapiential Work A," *Journal for the Study of the Pseudepigrapha* 16 (1997): 25-38. A slightly revised version of this article is available in *The Wisdom Texts from Qumran*, 263-75.

[122] These issues are examined in Chapter 4.

[123] Harrington, "Two Early Jewish Approaches to Wisdom," 37.

By contrast, James Aitken argues that the theology of Ben Sira accords well with 4QInstruction.[124]   He contends, for example, that Ben Sira's dismissal of esoteric speculation in 3:21-24 should not be taken as his definitive position on the issue because he portrays God as a revealer of secrets: "I (Wisdom) will set him again upon the straight path and reveal to him my secrets (גליתי לו מסתרי)" (4:18; cf. 39:6-8; 42:19).[125] Ben Sira's approval of revealed knowledge, he observes, is also evident in his description of Isaiah: "By his dauntless spirit he saw the future … He revealed what was to occur to the end of time, and the hidden things before they happened" (48:24-25).[126]   Aitken concludes: "In comparing Ben Sira and *Sapiential Work A* it can be seen that the Wisdom text is explicit where Ben Sira is implicit."[127]

By trying to downplay the differences between Ben Sira and 4QInstruction, Aitken overstates their similarities. Ben Sira clearly uses language of concealment and revelation. His claims that Lady Wisdom possesses secrets and that God disclosed special knowledge to Isaiah indicate a departure from traditional wisdom. The Book of Proverbs could not be a source for such views. Yet they do not warrant the assertion that the mindset of Ben Sira is compatible with an apocalyptic worldview, even if one qualifies this outlook as "implicit" as opposed to a more "explicit" apocalyptic perspective. Ben Sira associates God with the revelation of secrets in a way that is quite different from 4QInstruction. The Qumran wisdom text provides revelation to an elect group. Ben Sira understands God's secrets as available to any clever, eager student of wisdom. The "secrets" can be found by any diligent student of Torah: "If you desire wisdom, keep the commandments, and the Lord will lavish her upon you" (1:26). Wisdom's secrets are rare and valuable but are not restricted to an elect community. While Ben Sira's description of the revelation of knowledge to Isaiah is in tension with his dismissal of esoteric wisdom in 3:21-24, it is not implied that one who acquires wisdom can obtain the knowledge given to Isaiah. While praising a revered figure of biblical lore, Ben Sira makes an exceptional claim of revelation that is not presented as a goal of instruction.

---

[124] James Aitken, "Apocalyptic, Revelation and Early Jewish Wisdom Literature," in *New Heaven and New Earth: Prophecy and the Millennium. Essays in honour of Anthony Gelston* (ed. P.J. Harland and C.T.R. Hayward; VTSup 77; Leiden: Brill, 1999), 181-93.

[125] Ibid., 189. This translation is from Di Lella and Skehan, *The Wisdom of Ben Sira*, 168. See also Núria Calduch-Benages, "God, Creator of All (Sir 43:27-33)," in *Ben Sira's God: Proceedings of the International Ben Sira Conference, Durham, Ushaw College 2001* (ed. R. Egger-Wenzel; BZAW 321; Berlin/New York: de Gruyter, 2002), 93-95.

[126] Aitken, "Apocalyptic, Revelation and Early Jewish Wisdom Literature," 190.

[127] Ibid., 193.

García Martínez has also examined the role of revealed wisdom in 4QInstruction.[128] The title of his paper, "Wisdom at Qumran: Worldly or Heavenly?" is a word play on the title of the present study. In 4QInstruction the basis of the acquisition of wisdom is the mystery that is to be. For that reason he argues that the wisdom of 4QInstruction "is not worldly *and* heavenly wisdom, it is revealed wisdom, and thus thoroughly heavenly."[129]

García Martínez, like scholars such as Collins, Larsen, and Harrington, observes that the mystery that is to be has a central role in 4QInstruction. Generally exhortations to obtain wisdom occur in the context of the mystery that is to be rather than observation of the natural world. In that sense it is possible to characterize the wisdom of 4QInstruction as heavenly. But the mystery that is to be involves more than disclosing heavenly knowledge. The bestowal of this revelation is intended to shape one's behavior. For example, 4Q416 2 iii 15-19 combines the mystery that is to be with a call to practice filial piety. This does not mean that the mystery that is to be reveals that parents should be honored. The mystery that is to be shows the addressee the extent of God's dominion over the created order. Knowing this larger truth demands conduct that befits this knowledge. It calls for a way of life that is characterized by humility and reverence. In this sense the mystery that is to be fosters 'worldly' wisdom—knowledge that is eudemonistic and practical. 4QInstruction offers the addressee both heavenly and worldly wisdom.

Published in 1999, 4QInstruction is still in the early stages of research. The theme of poverty in the text has not been fully examined. Its depiction of the eschatological rewards that await the righteous also warrants more investigation. 4QInstruction's interpretation of Genesis 1-3 merits further study, and raises the corollary issue of the status of the Torah in the composition. These topics are important for understanding 4QInstruction's practical advice and its apocalyptic worldview.

4. THE CORE ISSUE

The central concern of this study is how 4QInstruction should be understood in relation to wisdom and apocalypticism. 4QInstruction is a peda-

---

[128] Florentino García Martínez, "Wisdom at Qumran: Worldly or Heavenly?" in *Wisdom and Apocalypticism in the Dead Sea Scrolls and in the Biblical Tradition*.

[129] Italics his. See "Wisdom at Qumran." Also note Alexander Rofé, "Revealed Wisdom: From the Bible to Qumran," in *Sapiential Perspectives*.

gogical composition devoted to the ethical development of its intended audience. It accomplishes this by giving instruction in the tradition of biblical wisdom on practical topics such as debts and family. It also does this by disclosing divine mysteries that provide knowledge on topics such as the extent of God's dominion over the created order and the imminence of his judgment. These teachings reflect its apocalyptic worldview. The author of 4QInstruction wanted the addressee to live in light of the revelation given to him. The knowledge that had been disclosed was intended to encourage him to live ethically and piously. 4QInstruction's apocalyptic worldview provides the broader theological context in which its concern for the addressee's ordinary life is to be understood.

Chapter 2 treats the theme of revelation in 4QInstruction. The epistemology of both traditional wisdom and apocalypticism is examined so that the role of revelation in 4QInstruction may be better understood vis-à-vis these traditions. I argue that the epistemology of 4QInstruction is compatible with that of Daniel and *1 Enoch*, since all three texts purport to disclose knowledge that would not otherwise be available in the human realm. Through revelation the addressee acquires knowledge about the deterministic divine framework that orchestrates the flow of events. This revelation influences instruction on topics, such as history, creation, and eschatology. The addressee's daily life is also shaped by this knowledge.

Chapter 3 analyzes the vision of Hagu pericope (4Q417 1 i 13-18). This section examines the enigmatic details of this passage, such as the "spiritual people" who are given this vision and the "fleshly spirit" who is not. It also discusses the use of the word אנוש in this pericope. This term can be read as referring to humankind, Enosh, or Adam. This passage comprises a teaching upon which the addressee is to ponder and reflect. The intent of this teaching, I argue, is for the addressee to identify with the "spiritual people." He is to be like the "spiritual people" and avoid living like the "fleshly spirit." In this chapter I contend that the text's interpretation of Genesis 1-3 is important for understanding these two contrasting types of humankind. 4QInstruction's use of Genesis 1-3 is also placed in its late Second Temple context.

Chapter 4 examines 4QInstruction's concern for the addressee's practical affairs, as exemplified by its interest in his poverty and by the financial advice it gives him. 4QInstruction, it will be argued, appropriates traditional sapiential views on poverty and modifies them to accommodate the elect status of the addressee. Although few scholars have examined the theme of poverty in 4QInstruction, in this chapter I suggest that poverty is an important context for the text's ethical advice and the presentation of the addressee's elect status.

Chapter 5 analyzes 4QInstruction's eschatological horizon. It examines 4QInstruction's description of the final judgment in relation to the theophanic tradition. The composition presents judgment as occurring at the final stage of history. The chapter also discusses the contrasting eschatological fates proclaimed for the righteous and the wicked. In it I contend that eternal life with the angels is promised to the addressee. He has affinity with the angels and is told to be like them. The "eternal joy" that is promised to him is a full realization after death of his relationship with the angels during his life.

The final chapter will summarize my assessments regarding the wisdom of 4QInstruction and its Sitz-im-Leben, giving particular attention to how the text should be understood vis-à-vis *1 Enoch* and the Qumran sectarian community.

CHAPTER TWO

"UNDERSTAND YOUR MYSTERIES":
THE THEME OF REVELATION IN 4QINSTRUCTION

1. INTRODUCTION

4QInstruction is exceptional among sapiential texts because of its prominent appeals to revelation. Two phrases of the composition, רז נהיה and
חזון ההגוי, refer to the revelation of heavenly knowledge. This chapter
focuses on רז נהיה; the "vision of Hagu" will be treated in Chapter 3.
While 4Q417 1 i is the only text of 4QInstruction that mentions the vision of Hagu, רז נהיה occurs over twenty times in the composition.[1] רז
נהיה is central for the overall theme of revelation in 4QInstruction,
whereas the vision of Hagu is part of a single teaching about the "spiritual people" and the "fleshly spirit."

The phrase רז נהיה is difficult to interpret. First, the word רז should
be considered. It is a term of Persian provenance that can be translated
as "secret" or "mystery." Pahlavi *raz*, Middle Persian *r'z*, and Modern
Persian *raz*, for example, all mean "secret, mystery." The word is employed in Persian texts such as *Denkard* (*Madau*). The relevant portion
reads: "*pad nimez i az waxš ewarzed o razig gyag ku padiš amarg daštar
<i> tan ta frašgird pad dadar kam*" (598.20).[2] Its translation reads: "By
order of the spirit, his immortal preserver moves his body to a secret
place (where it is kept) until the (eschatological) Renovation, according
to the Creator's will." *Denkard* 6.214 also attests this use of the word

---

[1] See, for example, 4Q415 6 4; 4Q416 2 i 5 (par 4Q417 2 i 10-11); 4Q416 2 iii 9, 14,
18, 21 (par 4Q418 9 8, 15; 4Q418 10 1, 3); 4Q417 1 i 3, 6, 8, 18, 21 (par 4Q418 43 2, 4,
6, 14, 16); 4Q417 1 ii 3; 4Q418 77 2, 4; 4Q418 123 ii 4; 4Q418 172 1; 4Q418 184 2; and
4Q423 4 1, 4 (par 1Q26 1 1, 4). The phrase has also been plausibly reconstructed in
4Q415 24 1; 4Q416 17 3; 4Q418 179 3; 4Q418 190 2-3; 4Q418 201 1; 4Q418c 8; 4Q423
3 2; 4Q423 5 2; and 4Q423 7 7. In many of these instances the mystery that is to be is
preceded by the preposition ב. The phrase רז נהיה is prefixed by a *mêm* in 4Q416 2 iii 21.
It is used without a preposition in 4Q416 2 iii 14.

[2] This citation was pointed out to me by Bruce Lincoln, University of Chicago. Also
the phrase "*raz-kirrog*" means "the craftsman of the mystery."

raz: "*arzanig bawišn pad harw raz [i pay] gar i yazd ud yazdan 'dyn'y ...*
'dynyx i yazdan ud raz i paygar i xweš az kas-ez nihan nest ... ud raz i xir
i xweš aweš nimayend." The translation of this text reads:

> One ought to be worthy with regard to every mystery of the battle of the
> gods and with regard to the gods' secrecy (?) ... The secrecy (?) of the gods
> and the mystery of their battle are not hidden from any one ... and they (the
> gods) show him the mystery of their things.[3]

This Avestan material underscores that the word רז can refer to secret
knowledge of an eschatological magnitude.[4]

רז is used in Second Temple sources to refer to supernatural revelation. The word occurs in the Book of Daniel, primarily as a term for the
revelation of the interpretation of Nebuchadnezzar's dream. In this story
רז also signifies the revelation of eschatological knowledge. Daniel
praises a God "who reveals mysteries (גלא רזין), and he has disclosed to
King Nebuchadnezzar what will happen at the end of days" (2:28). According to the Aramaic manuscripts of *1 Enoch*, this composition also
uses the word רז in relation to the disclosure of eschatological knowledge. In chapter 106, Enoch reveals knowledge about the final judgment, and claims that the Lord gave him this knowledge: "I know the
mysteries (רזי) of the holy ones, for that Lord showed (them) to me"
(4QEn^c 5 ii 26-27; cf. 106:19).

The use of the term רז in 4QInstruction has similarities to its usage in
Daniel and *1 Enoch*. The word refers to eschatological revelation
(4Q417 2 i 10-12). This knowledge is grounded in a larger framework.
The "mystery" of the רז נהיה refers to God's dominion and mastery of

---

[3] Aturpati-i Emetan, *The Wisdom of the Sasanian Sages (Denkard VI)* (trans. S.
Shaked; Boulder: Westview Press, 1979), 82-84. Another related Persian *raz-* word is
rašatenhe, a verb that denotes destruction of an eschatological magnitude. See Christian
Bartholomae, *Altiranisches Wörterbuch* (Strassburg: Verlag von Karl J. Trübner, 1904),
1527.

[4] The word רז, however, can refer to secrets that are not eschatological. For example,
an inscription from an Ein Gedi synagogue formed by a craft guild warned members not
"to disclose the secret (רזה גלי) of the city to Gentiles." See Moshe Weinfeld, *The Organizational Pattern and the Penal Code of the Qumran Sect* (NTOA 2; Fribourg/Göttingen:
Éditions Universitaires/Vandenhoeck & Ruprecht, 1986), 25, 58-64. Note that this inscription was probably written several centuries after the close of the Second Temple
period. For the secular use of רז, cf. Sir 8:18 and 12:11. See also Armin Lange, "In
Diskussion mit dem Tempel: zur Auseinandersetzung zwischen Kohelet und wei-
sheitlichen Kreisen am Jerusalemer Tempel," in *Qohelet in the Context of Wisdom* (ed. A.
Schoors; BETL 136; Leuven: Leuven University Press/Peeters, 1998), 130; *DJD 34*, 29;
B. Rigaux, "Révélation des Mystères et Perfection à Qumran et dans le Nouveau Testa-
ment," *New Testament Studies* 4 (1958), 241; A. Schoors, "The Language of the Qumran
Sapiential Works," in *The Wisdom Texts from Qumran and the Development of Sapiential
Thought* (ed. C. Hempel, A. Lange, and H. Lichtenberger; BETL 159; Leuven: Leuven
University Press/Peeters, 2002), 91.

the created order. God created the world by means of this mystery (4Q417 1 i 8-9).[5] Through this mystery the addressee perceives that a deterministic framework governs the flow of events.[6] Therefore, by understanding this mystery he can perceive how the created order functions: "And you, understanding son, gaze into the רז נהיה and know [the path]s (נתיבו[ת])[7] of all life. The way that one conducts himself he appoints over [his] deed[s] (התהלכו יפקוד על מעשׂ[יו])" (4Q417 1 i 18-19).[8] Contemplation of God's comprehensive plan results in learning many different aspects of the natural order. For example, through the study of the mystery that is to be the addressee can learn the knowledge of good and

---

[5] See section 4.2 of this chapter.

[6] See section 4.3 of this chapter.

[7] Only the final *tāw* of this word remains. Strugnell and Harrington, *DJD 34*, 166, suggest that it is too hazardous to reconstruct and make several suggestions, such as נחלת, גורלות, and נתיבות, all of which are "contextually plausible supplements." In their transcription of 4Q417 1 i they leave ת[ ] unreconstructed. But in their translation of the fragment they supply "the paths of" in this lacuna, indicating that they understand the Hebrew as נתיבות. This reconstruction is also offered by Torleif Elgvin, "An Analysis of 4QInstruction" (diss.; Hebrew University of Jerusalem, 1997), 256. Tigchelaar opts not to reconstruct ת[ ]. See his *To Increase Learning for the Understanding Ones: Reading and Reconstructing the Fragmentary Early Jewish Sapiential Text 4QInstruction* (STDJ 44; Leiden: Brill, 2001), 52. Lange opts for נחלת. See his *Weisheit und Prädestination: Weisheitliche Urordnung und Prädestination in den Textfunden von Qumran* (STDJ 18; Leiden: Brill, 1995), 51. The poor state of preservation of this word makes assessments of its original form tentative. I support the view that the word should be reconstructed as נתיבות. Although not conclusive on material grounds, semantically it works well.

[8] There is some disagreement regarding the reconstruction of the phrase transcribed here as יפקוד על מעשׂ[יו]. None of the various options yield translations that are substantially different semantically. Elgvin, "An Analysis of 4QInstruction," 256, reads בפקודת מעשׂ[י ל[א, which produces the translation, "and its walking according to what is appointed for the creatur[es of G]od." There are not enough letter traces to reproduce a *bêt*. The reconstruction ל[א is possible but not required. Jefferies adopts the ל[א מעשׂ[י transcription of Elgvin and reads *hê* instead of *bêt*. See his *Wisdom at Qumran: A Form-Critical Analysis of the Admonitions in 4QInstruction* (Gorgias Dissertations, Near Eastern Studies 3; Piscataway: Gorgias Press, 2002), 266. Strugnell and Harrington, *DJD 34*, 151, also read *hê* instead of *bêt* and transcribe מעשׂ[י without the word אל. This is translated "And the manner of walking that is appointed for [his] deed[s]." They argue that *hê* is to be favored for the פקד verb because two vertical descenders are visible. See ibid., 154. This is also the transcription favored by Tigchelaar, *To Increase Learning*, 52. However two such descenders are not discernable upon examination of PAM 41.942. Based on the photograph, *yôd* is to be favored over *hê*. Reading *hê* instead would not produce any major semantic difference, although הפקוד could be rendered as a passive, as in *DJD 34*, 155. In either case it is clear that the manner of walking is appointed by God.

As for מעשׂ[י, I follow *DJD 34* and supplement it with a *wāw* and *yôd*. "His deeds" works better than Elgvin's "creatures of God" in terms of the phrase's parallelism with "paths of life." God has predetermined one's deeds and the knowledge of the mystery that is to be gives the addressee insight into the framework orchestrating life. Although the transcription of 4Q417 1 i 18-19 is not fully recoverable, its meaning clearly included an assertion that the ways of humankind are established by God.

evil (4Q417 1 i 6-8). The extent of God's dominion over the cosmos is presented as a revealed truth that allows the addressee to acquire wisdom.[9] This theology has a tremendous influence upon 4QInstruction's understanding of creation, history, and eschatology. In what follows I discuss 4QInstruction's presentation of these topics.

In this chapter, I argue that the Niphal portion of the רז נהיה emphasizes that divine mastery extends throughout the entire chronological scope of the created order.[10] 4Q417 1 i 3-4 and 4Q418 123 ii 3-4, for example, connect the mystery that is to be with the past, present, and future. This mystery gives the addressee the ability to understand the full chronological extent of God's deterministic framework.

Scholars have offered many different ways to translate רז נהיה. De Vaux, in an early analysis of the Cave 1 text of the Book of Mysteries (1Q27), argued that the phrase should be translated as "le mystère passé."[11] This opinion was based on biblical examples where the Niphal of the verb היה refers to a completed action (e.g., Prov 13:19; Judg 20:3). Soon thereafter I. Rabinowitz observed that the context of 1Q27 demands that the phrase be translated as "a mystery to be," since 1Q27 1 i 3-7 refers to the eschatological judgment.[12] Milik's edition of Mysteries in *DJD 1* translates the phrase as "le mystère future." Barthélemy uses this translation in the preliminary edition of 1Q26.[13] Scholars have since generally favored a translation of the phrase that emphasizes a future sense, while some have offered translations that do not stress the temporal dimension of the phrase.[14]

---

[9] While 4QInstruction presents God's mastery as a revealed mystery, throughout the Hebrew Bible it is presented as a self-evident fact. Jon Levenson, for example, has written "We can capture the essence of the idea of creation in the Hebrew Bible with the word 'mastery.'" See his *Creation and the Persistence of Evil: The Jewish Drama of Divine Omnipotence* (Princeton: Princeton University Press, 1988), 3.

[10] This topic is examined in section 4.1 of this chapter.

[11] Roland de Vaux, "La Grotte des manuscrits hébreux," *Revue Biblique* 66 (1949), 605.

[12] See his "The Authorship, Audience and Date of the De Vaux Fragment of an Unknown Work," *Journal of Biblical Literature* 71 (1952), 22.

[13] *DJD 1*, 102, 104.

[14] This is evident in the translation "le mystère future de l'avenir" of A. Caquot. See his "Les textes de sagesse de Qoumrân (Aperçu préliminaire)," *Revue d'histoire et de philosophie religieuses* 76 (1996), 9. Related is Helmer Ringgren's "the coming mystery." See his *The Faith of Qumran: Theology of the Dead Sea Scrolls* (Philadelphia: Fortress, 1963), 21. D. Harrington prefers "the mystery that is to be/come." See his *Wisdom Texts from Qumran* (London: Routledge, 1996), 49. J.J. Collins uses the similar translation "the mystery that is to be" in his "Wisdom Reconsidered, in Light of the Scrolls," *Dead Sea Discoveries* 4 (1997), 272. L.H. Schiffman attempts to find some middle ground between de Vaux and Rabinowitz: "the mystery of that which was coming into being." See his "4QMysteries[a]: A Preliminary Edition and Translation," in *Solving*

34   CHAPTER TWO

The temporal meaning of the word makes translating this phrase inherently problematic. I doubt whether any translation can fully convey its temporal sense. Any translation of נהיה must specify a single tense—past, present, or future. The word itself, however, is trying to convey the fact that the רז נהיה extends throughout all of history. I opt for the translation "the mystery that is to be" that is used by Collins and very similar to the one chosen by Harrington (see above note). While no translation is fully adequate, this rendering of the phrase is better than other choices that have been suggested. It does not imply an exclusive future sense to the extent suggested by the rendering "the mystery to come" or "le mystère future." The translation "mystery that is to be" establishes that the phrase has a temporal meaning, even though it does not fully convey it, whereas the translations offered by scholars such as García Martínez, Lange, and Ibba do not stress the expression's temporal sense. While the option "mystery that is to be" can be criticized, it appears to be the best translation available.

The interpretation of the mystery that is to be in 4QInstruction is aided by the occurrence of the phrase in the Book of Mysteries and the Com-

---

Riddles and Untying Knots: Biblical, Epigraphic, and Semitic Studies in Honor of Jonas C. Greenfield (ed. Z. Zevit et al.; Winona Lake: Eisenbrauns, 1995), 210. In the official edition of Mysteries he translates the phrase as "the mystery that was coming into being." See Torleif Elgvin et al., *Qumran Cave 4.XV: Sapiential Texts, Part 1* (DJD 20; Oxford: Clarendon, 1997), 36. Elgvin opts for "the mystery to come" while disputing that רז נהיה has an "exclusive future meaning." See his "An Analysis of 4QInstruction," 78. The "mystery to come" is also the translation preferred by the editors of *DJD 34* and Catherine Murphy. See her *Wealth in the Dead Sea Scrolls and the Qumran Community* (STDJ 40; Leiden: Brill, 2002), 207. Charlotte Hempel translates the phrase as "the mystery to be." See her "The Qumran Sapiential Texts and the Rule Books," in *The Wisdom Texts from Qumran*, 284. See also Jefferies, *Wisdom at Qumran*, 65; Otto A. Piper, "The 'Book of Mysteries' (Qumran 1 27): A Study in Eschatology," *Journal of Religion* 38 (1958), 96; John J. Collins, *Jewish Wisdom in the Hellenistic Age* (OTL; Louisville: Westminster John Knox, 1997), 121-25; Markus Bockmuehl, *Revelation and Mystery in Ancient Judaism and Pauline Christianity* (Grand Rapids: Eerdmans, 1990), 42-56; Daniel J. Harrington, "The Raz Nihyeh in a Qumran Wisdom Text (1Q26, 4Q415-418, 423)," *Revue de Qumran* 17 (1996): 549-53; Kasper Bro Larsen, "Visdom og apokalyptik i Musar le-Mevin (1Q/4QInstruction) [Wisdom and Apocalyptic in Musar leMevin (1Q/4QInstruction)]," *Dansk Teologisk Tidsskrift* 65 (2002), 8-13; Schoors, "The Language of the Qumran Sapiential Works," 86-87.

Examples of translations that do not stress the temporal meaning of the phrase include F. García Martínez's "the Mystery of Existence," which is also preferred by R. Eisenman and M.O. Wise, A. Lange's "Geheimnis des Werdens," and G. Ibba's "mistero dell'esistenza." See Florentino García Martínez and Eibert J.C. Tigchelaar, *The Dead Sea Scrolls Study Edition* (2 vols.; Leiden: Brill, 1997-98), 1.67; Robert Eisenman and Michael Wise, *The Dead Sea Scrolls Uncovered* (New York: Barnes and Noble, 1992), 241; Lange, *Weisheit und Prädestination*, 97; Giovanni Ibba, "Il 'Libro dei Misteri' (1Q27, f.1): testo escatologico," *Henoch* 21 (1999), 77.

munity Rule.[15]   In these texts it refers to the divine control of reality. This is additional evidence that the phrase refers to God's deterministic dominion in 4QInstruction.   In the Book of Mysteries the expression signifies the total temporal jurisdiction of God's providence.   1Q27 1 i 3-4 (par 4Q300 3 3-4) reads:

> But they did not know the mystery that is to be, and the former things (קדמוניות) they did not consider.   Nor did they know what is to come upon them. And they did not save their lives from the mystery that is to be.[16]

The Book of Mysteries uses the mystery that is be to refer to the divine control of history with emphasis on the final judgment.   In 1QS 11:3-4 the speaker claims that he has received revelation: "For from the source of his knowledge he has disclosed his light, and my eyes have observed his wonders, and the light of my heart the mystery that is to be (רז נהיה)."[17]   The mystery that is to be is part of the content of the revelation. It is in parallelism with God's "wonders" (נפלאותיו).   The speaker also claims that he knows the "truth of God" (11:4). In this text the mystery that is to be is presented as knowledge about God's might and his eternal nature.

4QInstruction underscores the theme of God's dominion with the phrase רזי פלא ("wondrous mysteries").   4Q417 1 i 2 is a fragmentary text that tells the addressee: "[And] upon the wondrous myster[ies of the God of the Awesome Ones you shall ponder] (וֹ]בֹרזֹ פלאֹ]י אל הנוראים) [תֹשכיל)" (cf. 4Q418 43 1).   The phrase רזי פלא also occurs in 4Q417 1 i 13: "Then you will know the glory of [his] m[ight, together wi]th his wondrous mysteries (כבוד עֹ]וֹזו עֹ]ם רזי פלאו), and the mighty acts of his deeds (גבורות מעשיו)" (cf. 4Q417 20 2; 4Q418 219 2).[18]   In this line רז is

---

[15] Elgvin has reconstructed the phrase רז נהיה in 4Q413 (4QComposition concerning Divine Providence) 1-2 4-5. See his "The Mystery to Come: Early Essene Theology of Revelation," in *Qumran between the Old and New Testaments* (ed. F.H. Cryer and T.L. Thompson; JSOTSup 290; Sheffield: Sheffield Academic Press, 1998), 132.   After the visible כאשר גלה אל[of 4Q413 4, Elgvin supplies the phrase אוזן מבינים ברז נהיה (cf. 4Q418 123 ii 4).   This produces the line "as God opened the ears of those who understand to [sic] the mystery to come."   This reconstruction is not used in the official edition of 4Q413. Its editor, Elisha Qimron, points out that the word אל is in Paleo-Hebrew, suggesting that it should be translated as "God" rather than as a preposition. See *DJD 20*, 169.

[16] For this translation, see *DJD 20*, 38. 1Q27 1 i 3 is similar to 4Q417 1 i 3, which connects the mystery that is to be to מעשי קדם. Also note 4Q418 148 ii 6. It exhorts one to "set (your heart?) to understanding the former things (בינה לקדמוניות שים ל[ב])."

[17] See Hempel, "The Qumran Sapiential Texts and the Rule Books," 284; Alfred Mertens, *Das Buch Daniel im Lichte der Texte vom Toten Meer* (SBM 12; Stuttgart: Echter KBW Verlag, 1971), 124-30.

[18] The reconstruction of the word עֹ]וֹז is difficult due to erosion of the fragment's ink. The traces of an *'ayin* are visible. Elgvin, "An Analysis of 4QInstruction," 257, reads עֹ]וֹ֯ז. He has also transcribed the word as עֹ]ולם. See his "The Mystery to Come," 140. This

parallel to גבורה.[19] The word רז is used to convey the power and dominion of God.

The phrase רזי פלא refers to the transmission of revealed knowledge
elsewhere in late Second Temple literature.[20] In 1QS 11:4-5 the speaker
declares that the truth of God is his support and that the light in his heart
is "from the mysteries of his wonder" (מרזי פלאו). God's mysteries are
revealed to leaders of the sect so that they may pass on knowledge of his
splendor to the rest of the community. In 1QS 9:18-19 the Maskil is
stipulated to teach the community the "mysteries of wonder and truth"
(רזי פלא ואמת) so that group members may "walk perfectly ... in all that
has been revealed to them." This is also the case in the Hodayot. In
1QH 9:21 and 15:26 the speaker claims to have had "wonderful mysteries" revealed to him. In 10:13 the speaker praises his appointed role as a
teacher of revealed knowledge: "You have set me like a banner for the
elect of justice, like a knowledgeable mediator of wondrous mysteries
(רזי פלא)" (cf. 5:8). God is also praised for teaching the elect his "wondrous mysteries" in 1QH 19:10 (cf. CD 3:18).[21]

---

reading is also adopted by Jefferies, *Wisdom at Qumran*, 265. Strugnell and Harrington,
DJD 34, 160, argue that the space after the *'ayin* is too large for עד and too small for עולם.
For this reason they opt for עוז. The reading in *DJD 34* is favored here. It is also adopted
by Tigchelaar, *To Increase Learning*, 52. The gap between the initial *'ayin* of the word in
question and the *mēm* of the word מ[is 7 mm. Given that letters in 4Q417 are 2.0-2.5
mm in length, this allows for three letter spaces. See *DJD 34*, 143. The עוז] supplement
with its thin letters fits this space well, whereas the space is too small for the reading עּ[ולם
because of the large size of final *mēms* in this fragment. Moreover the possibility of
reading עּ[ולם is weakened by the fact that the phrases that accompany it both end in a
masculine suffix, "mysteries of his wonder" and "the mighty acts of his deeds." This
suggests that the word used to reconstruct עּ[should also end in a suffix. The reconstruction "His might" is also attractive because עּ[is in conjunction with the phrase "mysteries
of his wonder."

[19] Cf. 4Q299 5 2, "[migh]ty mysteries of light" (גב[ו]רות רזי אור]); CD 13:8, "mighty acts
of his wonder" (גבורות פלאו); Sir 42:21, "mighty acts of his wisdom" (גבורת חכמתו). The
Talmud (*b. Meg.* 3a) describes Targum Jonathan as containing mysteries that Jonathan
acquired from Haggai, Zechariah, and Malachi. The mysteries were so powerful that
when they were revealed the land of Israel "quaked over an area of four hundred
parasangs by four hundred *parasangs*, and a Bath Kol came forth and exclaimed, 'Who is
that that has revealed my secrets to mankind (מי הוא זה שגילה סתריי לבני אדם)?' Jonathan b.
Uzziel thereupon rose and said, 'It is I who have revealed thy secrets to mankind.'" Note,
however, that this passage does not use רז but סתר. See Ringgren, *The Faith of Qumran*, 9.
Elgvin, "An Analysis of 4QInstruction," 80, points out that רז is used in Targums Neofiti
and Jonathan on Genesis 49:1 to refer to secret knowledge that God prevents Jacob from
disclosing to his sons.

[20] Tigchelaar, *To Increase Learning*, 204-05; Elgvin, "The Mystery to Come," 132.

[21] The phrase רזי פלא may also be in the Book of Mysteries in 1Q27 1 i 7. According to
García Martínez and Tigchelaar, this line attests the expression רזי פלא. See their *Dead
Sea Scrolls Study Edition*, 1.66. Schiffman, however, reconstructs the phrase as "myster-
ies of Belial." He nevertheless asserts that פלא is present. See *DJD 20*, 37. He argues

In both the Community Rule and the Hodayot God's "wondrous mysteries" are revealed to the speaker to legitimate a deterministic perspective. In 1QS the Maskil who is given the רזי פלא is to walk "in compliance with the regulation of every period and in compliance with the worth of each man: he should fulfill the will of God in compliance with all revelation for every period" (9:12-13; cf. 3:15). The "wondrous mysteries" of 1QH 9:21 are associated with the statement that "in the wisdom of your knowledge you have determined their course before they came to exist" (ll. 19-20).[22] The phrase "wondrous mysteries" helps establish that a divine plan has been revealed to the elect.[23]

Scholarship has observed that the mystery that is to be refers to an overarching divine plan. Writing about the Book of Mysteries, Schiffman comments that the רז נהיה "refers to the mysteries of creation, that is, the natural order of things that depends on God's wisdom, and to the mysteries of the divine role in the processes of history."[24] Collins similarly writes that the mystery that is to be "seems to encompass the entire divine plan, from creation to eschatological judgment."[25] According to Harrington, the phrase refers to a written composition:

---

that the word פלא had to have been a mistake because context suggests that a negative word should follow רז. There does not, however, appear to be enough space to read "Belial," but his assessment that a negative word follows רז is sound. De Vaux's 1949 reconstruction leaves out the word in dispute: "et tous ceux qui détiennent les mystères de ... ne seront plus." See his "La Grotte des manuscrits hébreux," 605-06. The word after רז is not visible in the PAM photo of the fragment. One cannot state conclusively that the text contains the phrase רזי פלא.

[22] M. Delcor, *Les Hymnes de Qumran (Hodayot)* (Paris: Letouzey et Ané, 1962), 85-86; Svend Holm-Nielsen, *Hodayot: Psalms from Qumran* (Aarhus: Universitetsforlaget, 1960), 22. See also the War Scroll: "For great is the p[lan of] your [glo]ry, and your marvelous mysteries (רזי נפלאותיכה) in [your] height[s]" (14:14; cf. 4Q491 8-10 i 12). The phrase נפלאותי[רֹ]ז[י] occurs in a fragmentary passage of the Songs of the Sabbath Sacrifice (4Q401 14 ii 2; cf. 4Q403 1 ii 27; 4Q181 1 i 4-5). See Esther Eshel et al., *Qumran Cave 4.VI: Poetical and Liturgical Texts, Part 1* (DJD 11; Oxford: Clarendon, 1998), 208. Note that Ephesians uses the term mystery to refer to a divine plan orchestrating reality: "he has made known to us the mystery (μυστήριον) of his will, according to his good pleasure that he set forth in Christ, as a plan for the fullness of time, to gather up all things in him, things in heaven and things on earth" (1:9-10; cf. 3:9). See further Bockmuehl, *Revelation and Mystery*, 199-200.

[23] Also note that 1QS 11:19 associates "your holy plans" (מחשבת קורשכה) with the phrase "to gaze into the abyss of your mysteries" (להביט בעומק רזיכה).

[24] Lawrence Schiffman, "4QMysteries^b: A Preliminary Edition," *Revue de Qumran* 16 (1993), 204. See also Bockmuehl, *Revelation and Mystery*, 54; Tigchelaar, *To Increase Learning*, 205; Schoors, "The Language of the Qumran Sapiential Works," 87.

[25] Collins, *Jewish Wisdom*, 122.

It (רז נהיה) seems to be a body of teaching that concerns behavior and eschatology. It is probably an extrabiblical compendium, not the Torah ... it
may have been the 'Book of Meditation' (see 1QSa 1:6-8).[26]

He also suggests that the phrase may refer to the Book of Mysteries.[27]
Harrington observes that the רז נהיה is associated with behavior and
eschatology. But the teachings associated with this mystery are never
construed as citations from a separate document. Wacholder and Abegg
understand both the mystery that is to be and the vision of Hagu as "sectarian title(s)" of literature of the Qumran community, including
4QInstruction, that had an authoritative status comparable to that of the
Torah.[28] This interpretation has not been endorsed because is not clear
how 4QInstruction could be citing itself.[29]

The mystery that is to be has already been revealed to 4QInstruction's
addressee. For example, 4Q418 123 ii 4 reads: "His period which God
revealed to the ear of the understanding ones through the mystery that is
to be" (cf. 4Q416 2 iii 18). He is told to "gaze" (נבט) upon,[30] "examine"
(דרש), "meditate" (הגה) upon, and "grasp" (לקח) it.[31] It is reasonable to
ask how the addressee contemplated the mystery that is to be. This cannot be recovered fully but some speculation is possible. Whereas in
biblical wisdom one is often told to "hear" (שמע) instruction, in
4QInstruction the frequency of נבט with regard to the mystery that is to
be underscores a more visual understanding.[32] In rabbinic Hebrew נבט
can refer to having a vision.[33] This suggests that gazing upon the mystery that is to be might have been a type of visionary experience. When
the mystery that is to be is referred to as a past event, there is a compo-

---

[26] Harrington, *Wisdom Texts*, 49.

[27] Harrington, "The Raz Nihyeh in a Qumran Wisdom Text," 553.

[28] Ben Zion Wacholder and Martin G. Abegg, *A Preliminary Edition of the Unpublished Dead Sea Scrolls: The Hebrew and Aramaic Texts from Cave Four* (2 vols.; Washington, D.C.: Biblical Archaeology Society, 1992), 2.xiii. They speculate that "Present
indications are that the Vision of the Haguy and the Mystery of Being refer to the same
compositions that are included in this fascicle."

[29] See *DJD 34*, 3.

[30] 4Q416 2 i 5 (par 4Q417 2 i 10); 4Q417 1 i 3, 18 (par 4Q418 43 2, 14). See also
4Q418 123 ii 5. Note that the words נבט and רז are used together in 1QS 11:19.

[31] See 4Q416 2 iii 9 (par 4Q418 43 4 (par 4Q417 1 i 6), and 4Q418 77 4.
See Elgvin, "The Mystery to Come," 133.

[32] Eibert J.C. Tigchelaar, "The Addressees of 4QInstruction," in *Sapiential, Liturgical
and Poetical Texts from Qumran: Proceedings of the Third Meeting of the International
Organization for Qumran Studies, Oslo 1998* (ed. D. Falk et al.; STDJ 35; Leiden: Brill,
2000), 68; *DJD 20*, 164. Note, however, 4Q418 177 4: ... וקח בינה האזינה, "take instruction and heed ..." (cf. 4Q412 1 5-6).

[33] See, for example, *b. Sanh.* 101b: "He (Nebat) had a vision (word play with "Nebat")
but he did not see (ראה, that is, understand it properly)."

nent of hearing; it is revealed to the "ear" of the addressee.[34] Contemplation of the mystery that is to be probably involved reflection upon teachings that had already been given.

In order to emphasize the connection between the mystery that is to be and the knowledge it provides, 4QInstruction describes its teachings as "mysteries" (רזים): "O wise son, understand your mysteries (התבונן ברזיכה)" (4Q417 1 i 25; cf. Sir 47:12). 4Q416 2 ii 8-9 uses the term "mysteries" in a way that is parallel to "statutes": "And do not let go of your statutes (חוקיכה; cf. Prov 4:13). [Care]fully observe your mysteries (ברזיכה השמר // [מא[דה)."[35] The word "statutes" may refer to teachings that the addressee is to follow, and perhaps the Torah.[36] In 4Q418 177 7a the addressee is admonished to "know his mysteries (רזוו)."[37] Even though the mystery that is to be is not explicitly mentioned in every teaching of 4QInstruction, the phrase signifies knowledge about how the natural order functions. The text's teachings encourage the addressee to better understand and succeed in the world. In this sense the mystery that is to be pertains to all of the composition's instruction, including its practical advice. Its teachings are "mysteries" that are grounded in the larger mystery that is to be. The composition merges a pedagogical and eudemonistic ethos with appeals to revelation.

4QInstruction combines practical wisdom with an apocalyptic worldview. This raises the question of how the composition should be understood in relation to the sapiential and apocalyptic traditions. Lange and Elgvin reach opposite conclusions on this point. Lange argues that 4QInstruction uses the mystery that is to be to reestablish the legitimacy of the traditional sapiential assertion that God made the world with wisdom, a view that had been weakened by the "crisis of wisdom."[38] For him, therefore, the mystery that is to be stresses continuity between 4QInstruction and older wisdom. Both 4QInstruction and Proverbs assert that the world has an inherent sense of order. The Qumran wisdom text makes this claim through the mystery that is to be and Proverbs through Lady Wisdom, whose presence at creation establishes that the world was made with wisdom.

Elgvin, by contrast, considers the רז נהיה to be

---

[34] See 4Q416 2 iii 18; 4Q418 123 ii 4; 4Q418 184 2; 4Q423 4 4 (par 1Q26 1 4); 4Q423 5 1; and 4Q423 7 6.

[35] Regarding the transcription of the word [מא[דה, I follow Tigchelaar, *To Increase Learning*, 46-47. Strugnell and Harrington reconstruct [לנפש]כה. See *DJD 34*, 90. Tigchelaar points out that the lacuna is not wide enough for this many letters.

[36] See section 4.4 of this chapter.

[37] Tigchelaar, *To Increase Learning*, 111, transcribes this word as רזיו.

[38] *Weisheit und Prädestination*, 60. See Chapter 1 for a summary of his views.

a comprehensive word for God's mysterious plan for creation and history, his plan for man and for redemption of the elect ... *raz nihyeh* represents an apocalyptic reinterpretation of the concept of divine Wisdom, that stresses the esoteric nature of God's revelation.[39]

Whereas Lange emphasizes 4QInstruction's continuity with older wisdom, Elgvin sees in the mystery that is to be a break between 4QInstruction and traditional wisdom. As reviewed in Chapter 1, Elgvin posits two compositional strata in 4QInstruction, an early layer of practical wisdom and a later one characterized by apocalyptic theology. For Elgvin, the mystery that is to be epitomizes the second stratum. According to this view, the mystery that is to be demonstrates how an apocalyptic mindset takes over and reorients the traditional sapiential understanding of creation. Important for this perspective is that in 4Q417 1 i 8-9 God created the world ברז נהיה, not בחכמה.[40]

How the mystery that is to be should be understood vis-à-vis wisdom and apocalypticism is in dispute. 4QInstruction should be considered a wisdom text because it draws on traditional wisdom in terms of form and content. Yet its appeals to revelation distinguish it from older wisdom.[41] Biblical wisdom promotes the acquisition of knowledge through perception of the natural order. The addressee of 4QInstruction, however,

---

[39] Torleif Elgvin, "An Analysis of 4QInstruction," 80-81; idem, "Wisdom and Apocalypticism in the Early Second Century BCE—The Evidence of 4QInstruction," in *The Dead Sea Scrolls Fifty Years After Their Discovery: Proceedings of the Jerusalem Congress, July 20-25, 1997* (ed. L.H. Schiffman, E. Tov, and J.C. VanderKam; Jerusalem: Israel Exploration Society/Shrine of the Book, Israel Museum, 2000), 235.

[40] See section 4.2 of this chapter.

[41] Knowledge derived from the created order, however, has been understood as a form of revelation by scholars such as G. von Rad, J. Crenshaw, and R. Murphy. See L.G. Perdue, "Revelation and the Problem of the Hidden God in Second Temple Wisdom Literature," in *Shall Not the Judge of All the Earth Do What is Right?: Studies on the Nature of God in Tribute to James L. Crenshaw* (ed. D. Penchansky and P.L. Redditt; Winona Lake: Eisenbrauns, 2000), 201-22. Practical wisdom provides insight into how the natural world functions. The knowledge that is disclosed to the wise in Proverbs includes an awareness of the general operating principles by which reality operates. It reveals the nature of God in that from the ordered nature of reality an intelligent creator can be deduced. For example, Prov 16:4 reads "The Lord has made everything for its purpose, even the wicked for the day of trouble." See also 20:12; 21:30-31. Proverbs can be said to offer a 'Newtonian' form of revelation. Isaac Newton viewed his rationality as a sacred tool he could use to perceive the mind of God. See Michael J. Buckley, *At the Origins of Modern Atheism* (New Haven/London: Yale University Press, 1987), 138. If one grants that Proverbs has a form of revelation, it is entirely different from that of 4QInstruction. For other scholars who subscribe to the view that traditional wisdom includes a type of revelation, see Philip Nel, *The Structure and Ethos of the Wisdom Admonitions in Proverbs* (BZAW 158; Berlin/New York: Walter de Gruyter, 1982), 115; Bernhard W. Anderson, *Contours of Old Testament Theology* (Minneapolis: Fortress, 1999), 274; Lennart Boström, *The God of the Sages: The Portrayal of God in the Book of Proverbs* (Stockholm: Almqvist & Wiksell, 1990), 43.

learns about the world through the contemplation of revealed knowledge. In terms of pre-Christian Jewish literature, the epistemology of 4QInstruction has its closest parallels in the apocalypses.[42] A central feature of apocalyptic literature is the disclosure of heavenly knowledge that would not otherwise be available in the human realm.[43] 4QInstruction's reliance on revelation is an aspect of its apocalyptic worldview. The composition's assertion that rewards and punishments will be meted out after death is also apocalyptic. Some will inherit "glory" and others "ini[qu]ity" (4Q417 2 i 10-12). 4QInstruction, like many apocalyptic texts, asserts that history is ordained to have a specific end. 4Q416 4 1, for example, teaches that there is a final "period of wrath" in which judgment is to occur.[44]

Israel's sapiential tradition was both conservative and flexible. Great value was placed on wisdom that was handed down from generation to generation. Yet the wisdom tradition was able to merge with other ideas and newer developments. As Ben Sira's reception of traditional wisdom incorporates covenantal theology, 4QInstruction combines practical wisdom with an apocalyptic worldview. 4QInstruction attests a transformation of wisdom. The composition has many of the same concerns of traditional wisdom yet connects them to the mystery that is to be. This has no precedent in biblical wisdom. It is not required to attribute 4QInstruction's wisdom to a crisis in the sapiential tradition or to assume that its author considered traditional wisdom in need of revision. 4QInstruction's apocalyptic worldview is more simply understood as a

---

[42] There are other Jewish traditions in which רז and other mystery terms are important, such as rabbinic magical texts and *hekhalot* mysticism. These traditions achieved prominence after the Second Temple period and are beyond the purview of this study. It is possible that the use of רז in these literatures has some degree of continuity with the use of mystery terminology in Second Temple material. For more information, see Mordecai Margalioth, *Sepher Ha-Razim* (Jerusalem: Yediot Achronot, 1966); Gershom Scholem, *Origins of the Kabbalah* (Princeton: Princeton University Press/Jewish Publication Society, 1987 [orig. pub., 1962]), 106-23; Michael A. Morgan, *Sepher Ha-Razim: The Book of Mysteries* (Chico: Scholars Press, 1983); Jens-Heinrich Niggemeyer, *Beschwörungsformeln aus dem "Buch der Geheimnisse" (Sefär ha-razim): Zur Topologie der magischen Rede* (Hildesheim/New York: Georg Olms Verlag, 1975); Steve Savedow, *Sepher Rezial Hemelach: The Book of the Angel Rezial* (York Beach: Samuel Weiser, 2000); Emil Schürer, *The History of the Jewish People in the Age of Jesus Christ* (rev. ed.; ed. G. Vermes, F. Millar, and M. Black; 3 vols.; Edinburgh: T. & T. Clark, 1973-87), 3.342-79. For the use of the word רז in rabbinic literature, see also H.W. Basser, "The Rabbinic Attempt to Democratize Salvation and Revelation," *Sciences Religieuses/Studies in Religion* 12 (1983): 27-33.

[43] John J. Collins, *The Apocalyptic Imagination* (2nd ed.; Grand Rapids: Eerdmans, 1998 [orig. pub., 1984]), 5.

[44] The topics of the final judgment and one's fate after death are treated in Chapter 5.

consequence of the reception of older wisdom in the late Second Temple period in light of perspectives and traditions common to this era.

To explicate the theme of revelation in 4QInstruction, in this chapter I will first discuss the epistemology of traditional wisdom and apocalypticism. For the latter tradition I will examine primarily Daniel and *1 Enoch*. An understanding of the conception of knowledge in these traditions will provide a context with which to understand the transmission of knowledge in 4QInstruction. I will then analyze how the mystery that is to be influences several major themes of 4QInstruction. They are broken down into the categories presented below. Each of the following will be discussed in turn:

- Temporal Dominion
- Eschatology
- Creation
- Determinism
- Torah
- Instruction for Daily Life
- Ethical Dualism

2. THE EPISTEMOLOGY OF BIBLICAL WISDOM

Biblical wisdom literature contains different forms of intellectual inquiry. Some texts focus on practical ethics while others concentrate on more speculative matters such as theodicy and creation. James Crenshaw has offered a helpful definition of biblical wisdom:

> thematically, wisdom comprises self-evident intuitions about mastering life for human betterment, gropings after life's secrets with regard to innocent suffering, grappling with finitude, and quest for truth concealed in the created order and manifested in Dame Wisdom.[45]

Despite the variety of biblical wisdom, wisdom is generally understood in this material as the ability to understand the world and be successful in it. It is a way of describing human intelligence. When Solomon asks God for wisdom, he beseeches him for the cerebral prowess and ethical aptitude required to be a good ruler: "Give your servant therefore an understanding mind to govern your people, able to discern between good and evil" (1 Kgs 3:9). The Book of Proverbs likewise understands wisdom as the ability to base actions on an astute perception of the natural order, a talent that results in worldly success: "Wisdom is a fountain of

---

[45] *Old Testament Wisdom: An Introduction* (Atlanta: John Knox Press, 1981), 19.

life to one who has it, but folly is the punishment of fools" (16:22; cf. 3:16-18). Although Qoheleth despairs that he cannot overcome his own finitude with his wisdom, it allows him to understand the world and have prosperity, as evidenced by his material wealth (2:3-8).

The acquisition of wisdom in Proverbs is the product of human reflection on nature and society. Crenshaw writes "In a word, knowledge (in biblical wisdom) resulted from human inquiry rather than from divine initiative."[46] Traditional wisdom teaches that knowledge can be acquired through an empirical understanding of reality that fosters a clear understanding of how consequences result from actions.[47] This allows outcomes to be anticipated and helps one decide upon the appropriate action in a given situation. Following Klaus Koch, scholars often assert that in biblical wisdom reality is structured by a Tat-Ergehen-Zusammenhang (a deed-consequence relationship).[48] In the worldview of Proverbs the wicked will be punished and the righteous rewarded in this world as a result of their actions. In contrast to prophetic literature, in which retribution is meted out by divine intervention, biblical wisdom affirms that the wicked person punishes himself. A good example of this perspective is in Proverbs 26:27: "Whoever digs a pit will fall into it, and a stone will come back on the one who starts it rolling."

The creation theology of Proverbs 8 makes explicit what is implicit in chapters 10-31—that God made the world with a sense of order. This explains why the correlation between action and consequence can be understood and predicted. Lady Wisdom represents a mythological way to teach the wisdom of Proverbs.[49] Like the wisdom of Proverbs 10-31, Lady Wisdom is available to everyone who is interested: "To you, O

---

[46] James Crenshaw, *Education in Ancient Israel* (ABRL; New York: Doubleday, 1998), 120.

[47] There are, however, disclosures of knowledge in biblical wisdom that would not be otherwise available. The mythological details of Lady Wisdom provided in Proverbs 1-9, such as the image of her rejoicing before God (8:31), represent the revelation of information that is not apparent through observation of the natural order. Ben Sira also unveils knowledge about Lady Wisdom that his students would not be able to deduce on their own. They would not otherwise be able to know, for example, that her "throne (in heaven) was a pillar of cloud" (24:4). Ben Sira's access to divine knowledge may be why he understands his teaching as a form of prophecy (24:33). See Alexander Di Lella and Patrick W. Skehan, *The Wisdom of Ben Sira* (AB 39; New York: Doubleday, 1987), 338.

[48] Klaus Koch, "Gibt es ein Vergeltungsdogma im Alten Testament?" *Zeitschrift für Theologie und Kirche* 52 (1955): 1-42. This is available in English as "Is There a Doctrine of Retribution in the Old Testament?" in *Theodicy in the Old Testament* (ed. J.L. Crenshaw; Philadelphia: Fortress, 1983), 57-87.

[49] Carol R. Fontaine, "Wisdom in Proverbs," in *In Search of Wisdom: Essays in Memory of John G. Gammie* (ed. L.G. Perdue et al.; Louisville: Westminster/John Knox, 1993), 114.

people, I call, and my cry is to all that live" (8:4; cf. 1:20-21). She does
not address a visionary or even Israel by name. Those who find her find
life (8:35; 9:11). This is also promised to those who heed the book's
proverbial wisdom, as in, for example, Proverbs 19:23: "The fear of the
Lord is life indeed; filled with it one rests secure and suffers no harm."[50]
In Proverbs wisdom is available to all, although not everyone is interested in acquiring it.

Although wisdom has a human focus, it has a divine provenance. In
the fable of the dispute between two women regarding the custody of a
young boy, the wisdom Solomon displays in his judgment is presented as
divine: "All Israel heard of the judgment that the king had rendered; and
they stood in awe of the king, because they perceived that the wisdom of
God (חכמת אלהים) was in him, to execute justice" (1 Kgs 3:28). Proverbs 2 portrays the worldly success of the wise as a consequence of wisdom coming from God into the heart, where it stands guard: "For the
Lord gives wisdom; from his mouth come knowledge and understanding
... he is a shield to those who walk blamelessly, guarding the paths of
justice and preserving the way of his faithful ones" (vv. 6-8). Some
proverbs assert that divine stewardship explains the functionality of practical wisdom: "The human mind plans the way, but the Lord directs the
steps" (16:9; cf. 19:21; 20:24). Most of Proverbs, however, simply assumes that the world makes sense without elaborate theological speculation. Although wisdom is praised as divine its orientation is anthrocen-
tric.[51]

---

[50] See also 10:11, 16-17, 27; 12:28; 13:14; 14:27; 15:4, 24; 16:22; 21:21; 22:4; 28:16.
The parity between Lady Wisdom and the wisdom of Proverbs 10-31 is also demonstrated
by the fact that both collections, chapters 1-9 and 10-31, conclude with an image of a
woman. There are important similarities between the divine wisdom represented by Lady
Wisdom and the worldly wisdom represented by the phrase אשת־חיל (the "capable wife") of
Proverbs 31:10-31. Both are more valuable than jewels (מפנינים; 3:15; 8:11; 31:10; cf. Job
28:18). Both women are strong (8:14; 31:17), and are portrayed as "rejoicing" (8:30, משחקת
לפניו בכל־עת; 31:25, תשחק ליום אחרון). Their "rejoicing" seems to be a consequence of the
wisdom that makes them successful and allows them to appreciate the nature of God's
created order. The parity between Lady Wisdom and the capable wife underscores the
basic compatibility of worldly and divine wisdom.

[51] At times Proverbs de-emphasizes its normative view that wisdom is a product of
human reflection in order to stress the role of God. Prov 3:5-6, for example, reads "Trust
in the Lord with all your heart, and do not rely on your own insight. In all your ways
acknowledge him, and he will make straight your paths." This serves as a reminder that
God is in control of events. It does not conflict with the basic principle that wisdom is a
product of human contemplation. Rather it highlights an ambiguity inherent in the wisdom tradition. On the one hand Proverbs describes wisdom as worldly knowledge produced by human thought without appeal to the divine realm, and, on the other, praises
wisdom as having a divine provenance. Proverbs 3:5 qualifies the this-worldly focus of
biblical wisdom and helps prevent the conclusion that wisdom is 'secular' and can be

The worldly focus of biblical wisdom also encourages the pursuit of natural analogies. Lessons are deduced from perception of the natural world and applied to one's practical life.[52] For example, Proverbs 6:6 reads: "Go to the ant, you lazybones; consider its ways, and be wise" (cf. 25:23; 27:17). This reliance on natural analogies is continued in Ben Sira and Qoheleth. Both draw analogies from observation of nature in order to assess the human condition: "Like abundant leaves on a spreading tree that sheds some and puts forth others, so are the generations of flesh and blood: one dies and another is born" (Sir 14:18; cf. 17:1; 41:4; Qoh 8:8).

Aside from observation of the natural world, wisdom can also be imparted from a teacher.[53] Proverbs praises the benefits that one can acquire from listening to a teacher: "Hear, my child, your father's instruction, and do not reject your mother's teaching; for they are a fair garland for your head, and pendants for your neck" (1:8-9; cf. Sir 6:32-37). While Qoheleth does not emphasize the benefits of heeding a teacher, he himself is revered as a teacher who imparts wisdom (12:9-10).[54] The belief that a teaching is ancient lends itself to the view that it contains wisdom. Although Solomon is not called a teacher in the Hebrew Bible, people came from around the world to hear his wisdom (1 Kgs 4:34 [5:14]), and the Book of Proverbs is presented as the repository of his instruction. The rabbis continued the tradition that teachings from revered wise men were to be handed down and developed it to a degree unknown in the biblical period.

---

divorced from God. Although one may be wise, one must trust that God will give him success in this world. In 3:5-6 (see also 20:24 and 21:31) Proverbs seems to acknowledge that a human, even one with wisdom, will not necessarily have prosperity. Michael Fox writes "3:5 cautions against the presumption that a man can predict the outcome of his deeds." See his *Proverbs 1-9* (AB 18a; New York: Doubleday, 2000), 149. While there is no Joban-style theodicy in Proverbs, the book shows some awareness of the issue.

[52] Von Rad, *Wisdom in Israel*, 115-24.

[53] James Crenshaw, "Wisdom and Authority: Sapiential Rhetoric and its Warrants," in *Congress Volume: Vienna, 1980* (VTSup 32; Leiden: Brill, 1981), 10-29. See also Collins, *Jewish Wisdom*, 3. Philip Nel has questioned the view that the authority of a wisdom teaching can reside in the figure of the teacher. See his "Authority in the Wisdom Admonitions," *Zeitschrift für die alttestamentliche Wissenschaft* 93 (1981): 418-26. He argues that since the Sitz-im-Leben of wisdom texts cannot be reconstructed, the basis of their authority cannot reside in a teacher. While it is true that the social setting of Proverbs cannot be fully reconstructed, the presence of the figure of the teacher in the pedagogical conceit of the work is clear from Proverbs 1. Although one cannot with confidence determine whether most of Proverbs derives from a school setting or not, the book as a whole is shaped in light of a conviction that a student can learn wisdom from a teacher.

[54] Whereas the praise of Qoheleth as a teacher was probably written by one of his students, Ben Sira extols his own abilities as a teacher (24:33-34).

An important feature of the sapiential tradition in the late Second
Temple period is the incorporation of Torah piety. The parade example
of this is Ben Sira, who praises the Torah as the result of Lady Wisdom's
descent from heaven to Israel: "All this (Lady Wisdom's bounty) is the
book of the covenant of the Most High God, the law that Moses commanded us as an inheritance for the congregations of Jacob" (24:23).
The Torah is an important source of his instruction, and he equates the
acquisition of wisdom with Torah obedience: "If you desire wisdom,
keep the commandments, and the Lord will lavish her upon you" (1:26).
Ben Sira develops antecedent traditions, one of which is the Book of
Deuteronomy.[55] It presents itself as a source of wisdom for Israel:

> I now teach you statutes and ordinances ... You must observe them dili-
> gently, for this will show your wisdom and discernment to the peoples,
> who, when they hear all these statutes, will say, "Surely this great nation is
> a wise and discerning people!" (Deut 4:5-6).[56]

Deuteronomy is concerned with teaching Israel about its past and with
giving ethical guidelines for the management of daily affairs. Its content
is grounded in the revelation at Sinai (29:29). Although its teachings are
based on revelation from heaven, they are available on earth:

> Surely, this commandment that I am commanding you today is not too hard
> for you, nor is it too far away. It is not in heaven, that you should say,
> "Who will go up to heaven for us, and get it for us so that we may hear it
> and observe it?" ... No, the word is very near to you; it is in your mouth
> and in your heart for you to observe (30:11-14).

Although traditional wisdom does not share Deuteronomy's use of the
Sinai event, both agree that wisdom is readily available and is oriented
toward the human realm, even though it has a divine source. Wisdom
may come from heaven, but it is not necessary to go there to acquire it.

---

[55] The Torah is also understood as a kind of wisdom in Ezra 7, where "the law of your
God" (v. 14) and "wisdom" (v. 25) operate as interchangeable terms. There is a similar
perspective in the Torah piety of several psalms, such as Psalm 119. See Michael
Fishbane, "From Scribalism to Rabbinism: Perspectives on the Emergence of Classical
Judaism," in *The Sage in Israel and the Ancient Near East* (ed. J.G. Gammie and L.G.
Perdue; Winona Lake: Eisenbrauns, 1990), 442-43. See also Collins, *Jewish Wisdom*, 54-
56; Anderson, *Contours of Old Testament Theology*, 253-59; Jon D. Levenson, "The
Sources of Torah: Psalm 119 and the Modes of Revelation in Second Temple Judaism," in
Ancient Israelite Religion: Essays in Honor of Frank Moore Cross (ed. P.D. Miller, Jr.,
P.D. Hanson, and S.D. McBride; Philadelphia: Fortress, 1987), 559-74.

[56] Moshe Weinfeld, *Deuteronomy and the Deuteronomic School* (Oxford: Oxford University Press, 1972).

3. THE DISCLOSURE OF KNOWLEDGE IN THE APOCALYPTIC TRADITION

Both biblical wisdom and apocalyptic literature claim to contain wisdom (e.g., *1 En.* 5:8; 49:1-4; 93:10).[57] Yet the epistemology of apocalyptic literature is markedly different from that of biblical wisdom.[58] Whereas the wisdom of Proverbs is produced by human contemplation, Daniel and *1 Enoch* claim to contain revealed wisdom. Daniel, for example, praises God as a "revealer of mysteries" (2:29).[59] In Proverbs one who discloses secrets is condemned as a gossip.[60] The term "raz" represents a crucial difference between biblical wisdom and apocalypticism.[61] It is key for the acquisition of knowledge in Daniel and *1 Enoch* and has no analogue in biblical wisdom.

The Book of Daniel provides the best example of how the term רז functions in apocalyptic literature.[62] In the Hebrew Bible, the word only occurs in Daniel, where it is used nine times (2:18-19, 27-30, 47 [2x]; 4:6), in reference to knowledge given to Daniel by God. The term appears most frequently in the story of Nebuchadnezzar's dream in Daniel 2.[63] In this tale Nebuchadnezzar has a troubling dream that he wishes to understand. The Babylonian wise men are unable to interpret it for him. They defend their inability to provide sufficient explanation by claiming that such knowledge is not attainable by any human: "The thing that the

---

[57] Marie-Theres Wacker, "'Rettendes Wissen' im äthiopischen Henochbuch," in *Rettendes Wissen: Studien zum Fortgang weisheitlichen Denkens im Frühjudentum und im frühen Christentum* (ed. K. Löning; AOAT 300; Münster: Ugarit-Verlag, 2002), 115-54.

[58] Annette Schellenberg, *Erkenntnis als Problem: Qohelet und die alttestamentliche Diskussion um das menschliche Erkennen* (OBO 188; Fribourg: Fribourg University Press, 2002), 273-300; Paolo Sacchi, *Jewish Apocalyptic and Its History* (JSPSup 20; Sheffield: Sheffield Academic Press, 1990), 168-99.

[59] Shannon Burkes, *God, Self, and Death: The Shape of Religious Transformation in the Second Temple Period* (JSJSup 79; Leiden: Brill, 2003), 131-37.

[60] Prov 11:13, "A gossip goes about telling secrets (מגלה־סוד), but one who is trustworthy in spirit keeps a confidence"; 20:19, "A gossip reveals secrets (גולה־סוד); therefore do not associate with a babbler"; 25:9, "Argue your case with your neighbor directly, and do not disclose another's secret (וסוד אחר אל־תגל)." See also Sir 19:6, 12.

[61] For surveys of mystery language in the Second Temple period, see Raymond E. Brown, *The Semitic Background of the Term "Mystery" in the New Testament* (Biblical Series 21; Philadelphia: Fortress Press, 1968); Bockmuehl, *Revelation and Mystery*, 1-126; Rigaux, "Révélation des Mystères," 237-48.

[62] Martin Hengel, *Judaism and Hellenism* (2 vols.; Philadelphia: Fortress, 1973), 1.203, 2.135-36.

[63] For fuller discussions of this story, see Collins, *The Apocalyptic Imagination*, 90-98; idem, *Daniel* (Hermeneia; Minneapolis: Fortress, 1993), 152-75; Peter von der Osten-Sacken, *Die Apokalyptik in ihrem Verhältnis zu Prophetie und Weisheit* (München: C. Kaiser, 1969), 13-34. See also H.-P. Müller, "Mantische Weisheit und Apokalyptik," *Congress Volume: Uppsala 1971* (VTSup 22; Leiden: Brill, 1972), 268-93; Larsen, "Visdom og apokalyptik," 9.

king is asking is too difficult, and no one can reveal it to the king except the gods, whose dwelling is not with mortals" (2:11; cf. 4:9). Deeply unsatisfied by this explanation, the king demands that all the wise men of the realm be executed. Daniel learns of the decree and beseeches God to disclose "this mystery" (רזה דנה; 2:18), in order to save his own life and that of his colleagues (Hananiah, Mishael, and Azariah). Daniel prays to God and praises him as a deity who reveals secrets and provides wisdom to the wise (2:20-23). He does not come upon the "raz" of the dream's interpretation by means of his own perspicuity. It is given to him by God: "there is a God in heaven who reveals mysteries (גלא רזין), and he has disclosed to King Nebuchadnezzar what will happen at the end of days" (2:28). The four kingdoms interpretation of Nebuchadnezzar's dream has attracted a great deal of scholarly interest.[64] Yet Daniel emphasizes not the content of the dream but that God revealed its interpretation (2:27-30).[65]

In the Enochic literature available in Aramaic, רז is used to describe knowledge transmitted from the heavenly realm.[66] In chapter 106 Enoch reveals knowledge about the eschatological judgment to his father Lamech.[67] Enoch concludes the account by affirming that this information was disclosed to him through divine revelation: "For I know the mysteries (רזי) of the holy ones, for that Lord showed (them) to me and made (them) known to me, and I read (them) in the tablets of heaven"

---

[64] A statue of four different sections, each made of a different metal, is interpreted as signifying four successive kingdoms. It relates to a tradition where different world epochs are associated with different metals. Generally the sequence of metals begins with gold and proceeds to progressively lower grade metals. The metals are arranged so that the sequence of historical periods describes a descent. For other attestations of this tradition, see Hesiod, *Works and Days* 109-20; Ovid, *Metamorphoses* 89-150; *Sib. Or.* 4:49; *Bahman Yasht* (*Zand-i Vohuman Yasn*) chapter 1. See further Collins, *Daniel*, 162-70. Later writers occasionally add a fifth empire that is a cipher for Rome, such as Tacitus (*Histories* 5:8-9) and Appian (*Preface* 9). See D. Flusser, "The Four Empires in the Fourth Sibyl and in the Book of Daniel," *Israel Oriental Studies* 2 (1972): 148-75; G. Widengren, "Les quatre Âges du monde," in *Apocalyptique iranienne et dualisme qoumrânien* (ed. G. Widengren, M. Philonenko, and A. Hultgård; Paris: Maisonneuve, 1995), 23-62.

[65] Collins, *The Apocalyptic Imagination*, 92; Burkes, *God, Self, and Death*, 122-23.

[66] The standard edition of this material is J.T. Milik, *The Books of Enoch: Aramaic Fragments from Cave 4* (Oxford: Clarendon, 1976). See further James C. VanderKam, "Some Major Issues in the Contemporary Study of 1 Enoch: Reflections on J.T. Milik's *The Books of Enoch: Aramaic Fragments from Cave 4*," in *From Revelation to Canon: Studies in the Hebrew Bible and Second Temple Literature* (JSJSup 62; Leiden: Brill, 2000), 354-65; M.E. Stone, "The Books and Traditions of Enoch," in *Selected Studies in Pseudepigrapha & Apocrypha* (SVTP 9; Leiden: Brill, 1991), 212-27. See also Florentino García Martínez, *Qumran and Apocalyptic* (STDJ 9; Leiden: Brill, 1992), 45-96.

[67] See, for example, 106:15: "And there will be great destruction over the whole earth, and there will be a deluge and there will be great destruction for one year."

(106:19; 4QEnᶜ 5 ii 26-27; cf. 93:2; 103:1).⁶⁸ The word רז is also used in 4QEnᵃ 1 iv 5 (cf. *1 En.* 8:3), in which the Watchers reveal "secrets (רזין) to their wives."⁶⁹ Milik also claimed that in the Book of Giants God is praised for knowing all mysteries: "for [you] know all mysteries (רזיא)" (4QEnGiantsᵃ 9 3).⁷⁰

There are numerous other "mysteries" in *1 Enoch* for which an Aramaic text is not extant. These mysteries purportedly provide knowledge with a heavenly provenance, as in Daniel 2 and *1 Enoch* 106. Information regarding numerous topics, such as cosmology, angelology, and eschatology, is presented as "mysteries." For example, *1 Enoch* 104:10-13 uses mystery language in reference to eschatological events:

> And now I know this mystery, that many sinners will alter and distort the words of truth ... I know another mystery (μυστήριον), that books will be given to the righteous and the wise (which will be the source of) joy and truth and much wisdom (cf. 103:2).⁷¹

1 Enoch 41:3 describes secret knowledge of the physical universe: "And there my eyes saw the secrets of the flashes of lightning and of the thunder ... and the secrets of the clouds and of the dew ..." (cf. 59:1; 69:16-25; 71:3).⁷² Similarly, *1 Enoch* 52:2 reads "there (in the west) my eyes saw the secrets of heaven, everything that will occur on earth ..." (cf. 5:8; 48:1; 49:1).⁷³ Knowledge is understood as "mysteries" elsewhere in

---

⁶⁸ Michael Knibb, *The Ethiopic Book of Enoch* (2 vols.; Oxford: Clarendon, 1978), 2.248. See also George W.E. Nickelsburg, *1 Enoch: A Commentary on the Book of 1 Enoch, Chapters 1-36, 81-108* (Hermeneia; Minneapolis: Fortress, 2001), 549.

⁶⁹ This text is not in the Ethiopic manuscripts, but it is found in the Greek version of *1 Enoch* 8:3 preserved in Syncellus. See Knibb, *The Ethiopic Book of Enoch*, 2.83.

⁷⁰ This is similar to *1 Enoch* 9:4-11; 63:2-4; and 84:2-6. See Milik, *The Books of Enoch*, 316-17. He also reconstructed the word רז based on a visible *rēš* in 1Q23 9+14+15 2, which is generally considered a manuscript of the Book of Giants (1Q23-24, 2Q26, 4Q203, 4Q531-32, 4Q533?, 4Q556, 6Q8). See ibid., 302. Loren T. Stuckenbruck does not follow this reconstruction in his edition of this text. See his *The Book of Giants from Qumran* (TSAJ 63; Tübingen: Mohr-Siebeck, 1997), 58.

⁷¹ For the Greek text of this passage, see Campbell Bonner, ed., *The Last Chapters of Enoch in Greek* (Darmstadt: Wissenschaftliche Buchgesellschaft, 1968), 75. The word μυστήριον is used to translate רז in Daniel 2:19, 27, 30, and 47.

⁷² Also note *1 En.* 16:3: "You were in heaven but (its) secrets had not yet been revealed to you and a worthless mystery you knew. This you made known to the women in the hardness of your hearts, and through this mystery the women and the men cause evil to increase on earth" (cf. 9:6; 10:7).

⁷³ The translation by E. Isaac reads "my eyes saw there (in the west) all the secret things of heaven and the future things." See James H. Charlesworth, ed., *The Old Testament Pseudepigrapha* (2 vols.; New York: Doubleday, 1983), 1.37. According to Isaac, the Ethiopic for the phrase "the future things" literally means "that which is to become." A good project for a scholar trained in Ge'ez would be to determine if this term bears any relation to the mystery that is to be.

apocalyptic literature.[74] The use of the term "mystery" as signifying the content of an esoteric teaching is more fully developed in texts from later periods.[75] Although 4QInstruction does not have the phrase "Let me tell you a mystery" in the manner of these texts, it presents its teachings as "mysteries" (e.g., 4Q418 177 7a), as does *1 Enoch* and later material.

Daniel and Enoch are sages who have access to higher wisdom.[76] The wisdom that these figures possess is not a product of their own intellec-

---

[74] See, for example, *2 Bar.* 81:4, "he (the Most High) ... made known to me the mysteries of the times, and showed me the coming of the periods" (cf. 44:14; 85:8); *4 Ezra* 14:5, "I (the Lord) told him (Ezra) many wondrous things, and showed him the secrets of the times and declared to him the ends of the times." See also Wis 2:22, "they did not know the secret purposes of God (μυστήρια θεοῦ), nor hoped for the wages of holiness, nor discerned the prize for blameless souls"; 8:3-8, "Indeed, she (Wisdom) shares the secrets of God's knowledge ... she has foreknowledge of signs and wonders, and of the unfolding of the ages and the times" (cf. *T. Levi* 2:10; *Apoc. Ab.* 9:6). The Book of Revelation uses mystery language to refer to the fact that creation is unfolding according to a divine plan. In 10:5-7 an angel swears in the name of God "who lives forever and ever, who created heaven and what is in it, the earth and what is in it, and the sea and what is in it" that when the seventh angel blows his trumpet "the mystery of God will be fulfilled (ἐτελέσθη τὸ μυστήριον τοῦ θεοῦ)."

[75] 1 Cor 15:51-52, "Listen, I will tell you a mystery (μυστήριον)! We will not all die, but we will all be changed, in a moment, in the twinkling of an eye, at the last trumpet. For the trumpet will sound, and the dead will be raised imperishable, and we will be changed"; Rev 1:20, "As for the mystery of the seven stars that you saw in my right hand, and the seven golden lampstands: the seven stars are the angels of the seven churches, and the seven lampstands are the seven churches"; 17:10, "and on her forehead was written a name, a mystery: 'Babylon the great, mother of whores and of earth's abominations'"; 2 Thess 2:7, "For the mystery of lawlessness is already at work"; Rom 11:25, "I want you to understand this mystery (τὸ μυστήριον τοῦτο): a hardening has come upon part of Israel, until the full number of the Gentiles has come in"; *Odes Sol.* 8:10, "Keep my mystery, you who are kept by it"; *Trimorphic Protennoia* 42:29-30, "For I shall tell you a mystery [of] this Aeon that is, and tell you about the forces that are in it" [James M. Robinson, ed., *The Nag Hammadi Library* (San Francisco: Harper & Row, 1981), 466]; *Gospel of Philip* 71:4, "Is it permitted to utter a mystery?" [*Nag Hammadi Library*, 143]; *Gospel of Bartholomew* 2:5, "But Mary answered: Do not ask me concerning this mystery. If I begin to tell you, fire will come out of my mouth and consume the whole earth" [Wilhelm Schneemelcher, ed., *New Testament Apocrypha* (rev. ed.; 2 vols.; Louisville/Cambridge: Westminster/James Clarke & Co Ltd, 1991), 1.543]; *Two Books of Jeu* 43, "These mysteries (μυστήρια) which I shall give you, preserve, and give them to no man except he be worthy of them" [*New Testament Apocrypha*, 1.372]; see also *Acts of John* 101 [*New Testament Apocrypha*, 2.185]. Mystery language is also prominent in Colossians (1:26-27; 2:2; 4:3) and Ephesians (1:9; 3:3-5, 9; 5:32; 6:19). While some of the texts mentioned above undoubtedly reflect the influence of Hellenistic esoteric traditions, they nevertheless use the term "mystery" in a way that is similar to *1 Enoch*. Also note the parallel in Tablet 11 of Gilgamesh: "I will disclose, O Gilgamesh, a hidden thing, And [a secret of the gods I will] tell thee ... If thy hands obtain the plant, [thou wilt find new life]." For this translation, see J.B. Pritchard, *The Ancient Near East* (2 vols.; Princeton: Princeton University Press, 1958), 1.73.

[76] John J. Collins, "The Sage in Apocalyptic and Pseudepigraphic Literature," in *The Sage in Israel and the Ancient Near East* (ed. J.G. Gammie and L.G. Perdue; Winona

tual capacity. It is knowledge that is revealed to them. This form of wisdom acquisition is common in apocalyptic literature. Its epistemology is in stark contrast to the normative sapiential perspective that wisdom comes from contemplation of the observable world.[77]

Neither Daniel nor *1 Enoch* include the phrase *raz nihyeh*. But they both use the term *raz* to refer to revealed knowledge. The mystery that is to be is similar to the language of revelation in these apocalypses. 4QInstruction's רז language attests an esoteric tradition, also evident in Daniel and *1 Enoch*, that claims that some individuals have access to revealed wisdom.[78]

4. REVELATION IN 4QINSTRUCTION: THE רז נהיה

The epistemology of 4QInstruction is closer to that of apocalypticism than biblical wisdom. In this text wisdom is acquired through the contemplation of revealed mysteries rather than from knowledge the addressee can acquire on his own.[79] For example, 4Q417 1 i 25-27 exhorts

---

Lake: Eisenbrauns, 1990), 343-54; Karl Löning, "Die Konfrontation des Menschen mit der Weisheit Gottes: Elemente einer sapientialen Soteriologie," in *Rettendes Wissen: Studien zum Fortgang weisheitlichen Denkens im Frühjudentum und im frühen Christentum* (ed. K. Löning; AOAT 300; Münster: Ugarit-Verlag, 2002), 16-22.

[77] Job represents an exception in the biblical wisdom corpus. Like Daniel and *1 Enoch*, Job depicts God as a revealer of secrets, although this is not a major theme of the book. For example, 12:22 reads: "He (God) uncovers the deeps out of darkness, and brings deep darkness to light." Elgvin, "An Analysis of 4QInstruction," 62, compares this text to Daniel 2:22: "He reveals deep and hidden things (עמיקתא ומסתרתא)." In Job 4:12-20 Eliphaz's understanding of the sinfulness of humanity is presented as disclosed knowledge from a theophanic vision (cf. 33:15-16). But, as with Qoheleth, in Job there is a greater sense of humanity's epistemological limits than in apocalyptic literature: "But oh, that God would speak, and open his lips to you, and that he would tell you the secrets of wisdom (תעלמות חכמה)!" (11:5-6; cf. Qoh 7:24; Deut 29:28). See Bockmuehl, *Revelation and Mystery*, 14. The God of Job is portrayed as a revealer of secrets. Unlike God in *1 Enoch*, however, there is a great deal of knowledge that Job's God does not want to reveal. (Compare the recital of aspects of the natural world that God will not disclose in Job 38 with the extensive tours in *1 Enoch* of realms in this world and the heavens that humans are not normally permitted to see.) Ben Sira also depicts God as revealing secrets but these are not understood as revelation in the same sense as is often the case in apocalyptic literature. This is discussed in section 3.5 of Chapter 1.

[78] Some have argued that 4QInstruction's frequent use of the enigmatic term אז, which has been translated as "secret," is another example of mystery language in 4QInstruction. Elgvin is probably right, however, to suggest that its meaning is closer to "resources" or "assets." For a fuller discussion, see section 3.3 of Chapter 4.

[79] Cf. 4Q299 8 6, "With great intelligence he opened our ear, so that we would h[ear] the inclination of understanding for all who pursue knowledge ... all intelligence is from eternity"; 4Q301 1 2, "those who search the roots of understanding with those who hold

the addressee: "O wise son, understand your mysteries ... you shall not search out afte[r] you[r] own heart, and ^{after} your own e[y]es."[80]

The prominence of revelation in 4QInstruction invites comparison with apocalyptic literature. It has been suggested that *1 Enoch* represents the kind of esoteric wisdom speculation that Ben Sira dismisses in 3:21-24:

> Neither seek what is too difficult for you, nor investigate what is beyond your power. Reflect upon what you have been commanded, for what is hidden is not your concern. Do not meddle in matters that are beyond you, for more than you can understand has been shown you. For their conceit has led many astray, and wrong opinion has impaired their judgment.[81]

He also dismisses mantic wisdom: "Divinations and omens and dreams are unreal, and like a woman in labor, the mind has fantasies" (34:5). 4QInstruction can also be reasonably understood as the type of wisdom that Ben Sira rejects.[82] Like *1 Enoch*, the Qumran wisdom text claims to disclose divine mysteries, and appeals to revelation beyond that of Sinai.

Although the epistemology of 4QInstruction is apocalyptic, there are important differences between its use of revelation and that of the apocalypses. 4QInstruction has no otherworldly journeys or angels disclosing secrets to a visionary. It has no lengthy accounts of visions. There is minimal description of the content of the vision of Hagu. The teachings

---

fast to [the wondrous] se[crets." See *DJD 20*, 50, 115. For claims of revelation in the uncontested sectarian literature, see 1QpHab 7:4-5; CD 3:13-14; 1QS 11:3-4; 1QH 12:27; 13:25; 15:27; 20:11-13. See further Collins, *The Apocalyptic Imagination*, 150-52; Eckhard J. Schnabel, *Law and Wisdom from Ben Sira to Paul* (WUNT 2/16; Tübingen: J.C.B. Mohr [Paul Siebeck], 1985), 172-74; Florentino García Martínez, "Wisdom at Qumran: Worldly or Heavenly?" in *Wisdom and Apocalypticism in the Dead Sea Scrolls and in the Biblical Tradition* (ed. F. García Martínez; BETL 168; Leuven: Peeters-Leuven University Press, forthcoming).

[80] The phrase "you shall not search out ..." from 4Q417 1 i 27 is found verbatim in Numbers 15:39. See *DJD 34*, 168. The supralinear word "after" suggests that the manuscript was corrected in light of the biblical text. The second hand could have been from the circles responsible for the composition of 4QInstruction or from later scribes. In any case, this line demonstrates that the author used the Torah as a source for his teaching. See further section 4.4 of this chapter. Also note the parallel to 4Q417 1 i 25-27 in 4Q413 1-2 2-3: "and as he despised every wicked individual [who would follow what] his ears hear and what his eyes see (that wicked individual) would not survive."

[81] R.A. Argall, *1 Enoch and Sirach* (SBLEJL 8; Atlanta: Scholars Press, 1995). Some scholars understand Ben Sira 3:21-24 as polemic against Greek wisdom. See, for example, Di Lella and Skehan, *The Wisdom of Ben Sira*, 160; Hengel, *Judaism and Hellenism*, 1.139. See also Benjamin G. Wright III, "Putting the Puzzle Together: Some Suggestions Concerning the Social Location of the Wisdom of Ben Sira," in *Society of Biblical Literature Seminar Papers 1996* (SBLSP 35; Atlanta: Scholars Press, 1996), 133-49.

[82] Elgvin, "An Analysis of 4QInstruction," 172.

of 4QInstruction are not presented as revelatory discourses from the mouth of an angel. Its instruction is not inspired speech.[83]

4QInstruction also describes the bestowal of revelation in a way that is quite different from that commonly found in the apocalypses. In Daniel and the *Book of the Watchers* the revelation of visions and the transmission of divine knowledge are narrated to the reader. One can look over the shoulders, as it were, of Daniel and Enoch as they receive revelations. In the case of 4QInstruction the situation is somewhat different. The *raz nihyeh* has already been given (e.g., 4Q418 123 ii 3-4). Like the *Epistle of Enoch*, 4QInstruction does not give revelation directly. Rather it has already been disclosed.[84] 4QInstruction also relates revealed knowledge to the addressee's ordinary and ethical life to an extent that is more reminiscent of the testaments than the apocalypses. Whereas Daniel is often understood to contain a form of "mantic wisdom" by which understanding is obtained through dream interpretation and divination, 4QInstruction has no interest in acquiring knowledge through these means.[85]

4QInstruction is also more inconsistent in its use of revelation than is generally the case in apocalyptic literature. While 4QInstruction grounds practical advice in revelation, the composition also provides instruction on mundane topics without recourse to revelation. For example, 4Q416 2 iii 15-19 connects the observance of filial piety with the mystery that is to be, whereas 4Q416 2 ii 14-21 contains a string of ten vetitives regarding social relations and financial affairs that never appeals to revelation. Such instruction may presume the revelatory authority established elsewhere in the text. But the vetitives themselves are grounded in common sense and are reminiscent of biblical wisdom. 4QInstruction also provides eschatological knowledge without recourse to revelation. The extant portions of 4Q416 1 and 4Q418 69 ii, which provide the work's most elaborate descriptions of the final judgment, never appeal to the mystery that is to be.

There are notable differences between the form of revelation in 4QInstruction and that commonly found in the apocalyptic tradition. With these differences in mind, the theme of revelation in 4QInstruction can be examined in fuller detail.

---

[83] Elgvin, "The Mystery to Come," 131.

[84] Cf. *1 En.* 103:2: "I have read the tablets of heaven and seen the writings of the holy ones" (cf. 93:2). See Collins, *The Apocalyptic Imagination*, 62.

[85] James C. VanderKam, "Mantic Wisdom in the Dead Sea Scrolls," *Dead Sea Discoveries* 4 (1997): 336-53; ·idem, "The Prophetic-Sapiential Origins of Apocalyptic Thought," in *From Revelation to Canon*, 241-54; Collins, *The Apocalyptic Imagination*, 21; Müller, "Mantische Weisheit und Apokalyptik," 268-93.

4.1. Temporal Dominion

The "mystery" of the mystery that is to be refers to the total scope of God's mastery over the created order. The Niphal participle נהיה is more difficult to assess than the word רז. As discussed in section 1, the temporal meaning of נהיה is not fully evident from the word's grammatical form and cannot be expressed adequately in translation. The Niphal participle of the phrase רז נהיה underscores the temporal totality of God's dominion, from the beginning of the historical order to its end. Assessing the contribution of this participle demands surveying the use of היה in the Niphal.[86]

In the Hebrew Bible the verb היה in the Niphal normally takes the meaning of "to happen" in the past tense.[87] This is even the case in relatively late biblical texts.[88] Because of this semantic background de Vaux, one of the first modern scholars to study the רז נהיה, translated it as "le mystère passé."[89] The verb היה in the Niphal is also used in the Hebrew Bible in reference to the past to make a point that is valid for the totality of the temporal order.[90]

Late Second Temple attestations of the verb היה in the Niphal, unlike the biblical examples, often refer to either the future or the entire scope

---

[86] See also Matthew J. Goff, "The Mystery of Creation in 4QInstruction," *Dead Sea Discoveries* 10 (2003), 3-7.

[87] Deut 4:32, "For ask now about former ages, long before your own, ever since the day that God created human beings on the earth; ask from one end of heaven to the other: has anything so great as this ever happened (הנהיה) or has its like ever been heard of?"; 27:9, "Keep silence and hear, O Israel! This very day you have become (נהיית) the people of the Lord your God"; Judg 20:3, "And the Israelites said, 'Tell us, how did this criminal act come about (נהיתה)?'"; Prov 13:19, "A desire realized (נהיה) is sweet to the soul, but to turn away from evil is an abomination to fools." See also Judg 19:30; Jer 5:30; 48:19.

[88] Neh 6:8, "No such things as you say have been done (נהיים); you are inventing them out of your own mind"; Dan 8:27, "So I, Daniel, was overcome (נהייתי) and lay sick for some days; then I arose and went about the king's business." The word נהייתי of Daniel 8:27 may, however, be derived from הוה, "to ruin," as proposed by Rashi. There is a similar problem in 2:1. See Collins, *Daniel*, 155, 342.

[89] "La Grotte des manuscrits hébreux," 605.

[90] Exod 11:6, "Then there will be a loud cry throughout the whole land of Egypt, such as has never been (נהיתה) or will ever be again"; Joel 2:1-2, "for the day of the Lord is coming, it is near—a day of darkness and gloom ... Like blackness spread upon the mountains a great and powerful army comes; their like has never been from of old (נהיה מן העולם), nor will be again after them in ages to come"; Dan 12:1, "There shall be a time of anguish, such as has never occurred (נהיתה) since nations first came into existence. But at that time your people shall be delivered, everyone who is found written in the book."

of the historical order. This usage forms the philological background against which the רז נהיה of 4QInstruction should be understood.[91]

The Community Rule uses היה in the Niphal several times, generally to emphasize that God's dominion extends throughout history. The Treatise on the Two Spirits employs this word in reference to the future in order to affirm God's eternal supremacy: "From the God of Knowledge stems all there is and all there will be (כול הויה ונהייה)" (1QS 3:15).[92] The Niphal participle of היה is used in 1QS 10 to refer to the entirety of the temporal order. The column begins by describing the orderly regulation of astral bodies. It emphasizes that throughout the entire chronological order their movements have been established by God:

> With the offering of lips I shall bless him, in accordance with the decree recorded for ever. At the commencement of the years and in the turning of their seasons, when the decree of their disposition is carried out, on its prescribed day, one after another (10:6-7).

The participle נהיה is employed to affirm that this natural order shows God's dominion throughout all of history: "It is a great day for the holy of holies, and a sign of the opening of his everlasting mercies for the beginnings of the seasons in every age that exists (בכול קץ נהיה)" (10:4-5; cf. 11:8-9).[93]

The Community Rule's concluding hymn attests a similar use of היה in the Niphal. This text uses the mystery that is to be to describe the revelation of God's mastery throughout history (11:3-4). This eternal knowledge is a source of support for the speaker: "What always is (הויא עולם), is support for my right hand" (11:4). The רז נהיה is in parallel with הויא עולם. The mystery that is to be refers to the revelation of God's eternal dominion. 1QS 11:11 uses היה in the Niphal to refer to all of history: "By his knowledge everything comes into being (נהיה) and all that exists (כול הויה) he establishes with his calculations." While נהיה could have a future designation in this phrase, the above translation is used since נהיה is in parallelism, in a manner similar to line 4 of this

---

[91] Larsen, "Visdom og apokalyptik," 11-12; Schoors, "The Language of the Qumran Sapiential Works," 86-87.

[92] Hengel, *Judaism and Hellenism*, 1.219. This use of the Niphal in 1QS 3 is similar to that of 4Q180 (4QAges of Creation A): "God made a time to bring to perfect accomplishment [all that is] and is to come (כול הויה] ונהיה)" (1 1-2). For this translation, see John Strugnell, "Notes en marge du volume V des 'Discoveries in the Judaean Desert of Jordan,'" *Revue de Qumran* 7 (1970), 252. See also John M. Allegro, *Qumrân Cave 4.I (4Q158-4Q186)* (DJDJ 5; Oxford: Clarendon, 1968), 77-78.

[93] García Martínez and Tigchelaar, *The Dead Sea Scrolls Study Edition*, 1.95, translate the final phrase as "every future age." 1QS 10:4-5 certainly asserts that the normal flow of the seasons will occur in the future, but it also underscores that this reflects a regulation of the seasons that extends throughout all time.

column, with כול הויה. The word היה in the Niphal also denotes all moments of the created order in 1QS 11:17-18: "You have taught all knowledge and all that exists (כול הנהיה) is so by your will."[94]

The Damascus Document employs היה in the Niphal in ways that are analogous to its usage in the Community Rule. This is evident in CD 2:9-10. This passage's use of the word היה in the Niphal is ambiguous, but is best understood as referring to the entire chronological order: "And he (God) knew the years of existence, and the number and detail of their ages, of all those who exist over the centuries (כל הוי עולמים ונהיות)." The word נהיות could be understood as having a future sense.[95] However, since it is in parallel with כל הוי עולמים, the meaning of the phrase appears similar to the Niphal attestation of היה in 1QS 11. The term נהיות in CD 2 seems to refer to all of history. This option fits well with the deterministic sense of the passage. CD 2:10 asserts that God knows the deeds and lives of all people, including those who have lived and those who have not been born. נהיות helps establish the claim that God's dominion is firmly in place throughout all time. Another example of היה in the Niphal is in CD 13:7-8. While this passage is vague, it refers either to future events or things which exist forever: "He (the Inspector) shall instruct the Many in the deeds of God, and shall teach them his mighty marvels, and recount to them the eternal events (נהיות עולם) with their explanations."[96]

Other Qumran texts also utilize the Niphal of the word היה as a way to describe the entire scope of history. The Songs of the Sabbath Sacrifice uses היה in the Niphal to refer to all things that exist: "For from the God of Knowledge came into being everything [which exists for ever] (נהיו [הוי עד] כול)" (4Q402 4 12).[97] Even though the word נהיו is translated in the past tense, it stresses that God created all things and underscores the eternal nature of the cosmos. A Niphal participle is used similarly in 1QH 5:17-18 to affirm that God makes things that are eternal: "... creating new things, demolishing ancient things and [erec]ting what exists for

---

[94] The word, however, seems to refer to the future in 11:8-9, which describes the community as an "eternal planting throughout all future ages (כול קץ נהיה)."

[95] J.M. Baumgarten translates נהיות as "(including) what will come to be." See his *Qumran Cave 4.XIII: The Damascus Document (4Q266-273)* (DJD 18; Oxford: Clarendon, 1996), 38.

[96] Elgvin, "An Analysis of 4QInstruction," 81, translates the final portion of the phrase as "and recount to them what ever came into being." He also uses the phrase נהיות עולם of CD 13:8 to reconstruct the fragmentary text נהיי ע̇ל] of 4Q418 238 3 (cf. 1QM 17:5). He translates the word נהיות of CD 13:8 as past tense. Strugnell and Harrington, *DJD 34*, 448, reconstruct נהיי ע̇ל] in 4Q418 238 3 as Elgvin does, but understand it as having a future orientation.

[97] *DJD 11*, 228-29.

ever (נהיות עולם)."⁹⁸ 1QH 19:13-14 also uses the Niphal: "he can take his place in your presence with the perpetual host and the spirits … to renew him with everything that exists forever (כול נהיה)." The Niphal in this passage may have a future orientation. In this case it would signify that the heavenly host, and the elect with whom it is associated, will live forever. But this underscores the fact that the angels exist forever, and thus throughout the historical order and not exclusively the future.

Ben Sira employs היה as a Niphal participle in reference to the future. But the word nevertheless establishes the totality of God's knowledge of the universe throughout the entire temporal order:

> He searches out the abyss and the human heart; he understands their in-nermost secrets. For the Most High knows all that may be known; he sees from of old the things that are to come. He discloses what has been and what is to be (נהיות/τὰ ἐσόμενα), and he reveals the traces of hidden things (נסתרות/ἀποκρύφων) (42:19; cf. 39:19-20).⁹⁹

Ben Sira uses נהיות in relation to the future in his praise of Isaiah, as well as the past: "He revealed what was to occur (נהיות/τὰ ἐσόμενα) to the end of time, and the hidden things (נסתרות/τὰ ἀπόκρυφα) before they hap-pened" (48:25; cf. Isa 42:9).¹⁰⁰ Both times that Ben Sira utilizes the verb היה in the Niphal to describe things that are to happen, he includes lan-guage of concealment (נסתרות; cf. 4Q418 126 ii 5). Ben Sira does not agree with the esoteric type of teaching that 4QInstruction represents (cf. 3:21-24). But, like the author of the Qumran wisdom text, he combines the Niphal participle of היה with mystery language.

The Niphal of היה has a future orientation in the War Scroll: "It will be a time of suffering fo[r al]l the nation redeemed by God. Of all their sufferings, none will be (נהיתה) like this, hastening till eternal redemp-tion is fulfilled" (1:11-12). 1QM 17:4-5 uses two Niphal participles, the first to refer to the future; the second, while fragmentary, seems to denote all aspects of the temporal scheme: "Not [do they know that from the God of] Israel everything is and will be (הויה ונהיה) … in all that will happen eternally (נהיי עולמים)."

The examples that have been surveyed fall into two general groups: 1) texts that use היה in the Niphal exclusively in the future tense (1QM 1:12; 17:5; 1QS 11:9) and 2) texts that use the verb to denote the entirety of the chronological scheme (1QS 10:5; 11:11, 18; 4Q402 4 12; 1QM

---

⁹⁸ García Martínez and Tigchelaar, *The Dead Sea Scrolls Study Edition*, 1.151, trans-late "what would exist for ever."

⁹⁹ Also note *Jub.* 4:19, "he (Enoch) saw what was and what will be in a vision of his sleep" and Wis 8:8, "she (Wisdom) knows the things of old, and infers the things to come."

¹⁰⁰ Di Lella and Skehan, *The Wisdom of Ben Sira*, 539.

17:5; CD 2:9-10; 1QH 5:17-18; 4Q180 1 1-2). Ben Sira 42:19, 48:25, 1QS 3:15, and 1QH 19:13-14 use the word to refer to the future, but do so in a way that expresses God's dominion throughout all of history. CD 13:8 is ambiguous, and can plausibly be read with the verb having a future sense or as referring to the totality of the temporal order. In complete contrast to the use of the verb in the Niphal in the Hebrew Bible, it is rarely used in the past tense in the Dead Sea Scrolls (but see 1Q27 1 i 3).[101] The evidence demonstrates that in late Second Temple literature היה in the Niphal is more likely to express the entire scope of history rather than just the future.

4QInstruction accords with the tendency in late Second Temple sources to employ היה in the Niphal to refer to the total temporal order. Aside from the mystery that is to be, the composition uses this verb to signify eternity in other ways. 4Q418 69 ii 7 seems to refer to angels who exist eternally: "All who exist forever (כול נהיה עולם), those who seek truth, will rouse themselves for yo[ur] judgment" (cf. 4Q418 190 3).[102] 4Q418 238 3 is fragmentary but includes the phrase "understa]nd what exists fo[ever (עֹ]ולם בנהיי נֹן[התבו)."[103] In 4Q418 126 ii 4-5 the verb is vague, but seems to refer to all aspects of the created order: "He has spread them out; truthfully he has established them ... everything is hidden. Furthermore, they do not exist (נהיו) without his good will." The participle could be translated as having a future sense, but the stress of the passage on all of creation suggests the verb is intended to signify the creation of things throughout all of history.[104]

Like other Second Temple texts, 4QInstruction uses היה in the Niphal to establish that God exerts dominion throughout the totality of the temporal order. A clear example of this is 4Q417 1 i 3-4. This fragmentary passage employs היה in the Niphal three times. It occurs once in the mystery that is to be. The other two attestations probably refer, respec-

---

[101] היה as a Niphal participle rarely refers to the present in the Dead Sea Scrolls. 1QH 11:32-33 could be understood this way: "The earth cries out at the calamity which overtakes (ההווה הנהיה) the world."

[102] Elgvin has argued that 4Q418 69 ii 7 uses נהיה in reference to the past. He translates "everything that ever came into being." See his "An Analysis of 4QInstruction," 79. Strugnell and Harrington, however, translate the phrase "all those who will endure forever." See *DJD 34*, 283. Since the angels live forever, the verb נהיה refers not to the past or the future exclusively but to the entire range of history. This argument is made in section 2.1 of Chapter 5.

[103] Tigchelaar, *To Increase Learning*, 183, reconstructs the phrase נהיה עולם in 4Q416 1 1. He makes the hypothetical suggestion that material from 4Q418 238 should be incorporated into this line.

[104] The translation in *DJD 34*, 352, awkwardly captures the temporal ambiguity of the passage: "And furthermore they have (will) not come into being without His good pleasure."

tively, to the past and present to help form a tripartite division of time: "Gaze [upon the mystery that is to be and the deeds of old, from what has been to what exists through what] [will be] ... [for]ever (ברז נהיה וֹהֹבֹטֹ] (ומעשי קדם למה נהיה ומה נהיה // במה] [יהיה] ... [עו]לֹם)."[105] This passage attests, as suggested by Elgvin, a three-fold division of time.[106] This claim is made on the basis of 4Q418 123 ii 3-4, which associates a three-fold division of time with the mystery that is to be:

> Everything that exists in it, from what has been to what will be in it (כול הנהיה בה למה היה ומה יהיה בו] ... His period which God revealed to the ear of the understanding ones through the mystery that is to be.[107]

4Q417 1 i appears to also preserve a three-part division of time in lines 4-5: "[with what] [exists, what has been, and what] [will be?] ... ([למה] [הויא ולמה נהיה במה] //)."[108] The fragmentary second line of 4Q418 123 ii seems to attest a merism covering the beginning and end of history: "for the entering-in of years and the going-out of times."[109] This demonstrates further that a main theme of this fragment is the full scope of history.

4Q417 1 i 3-4 and 4Q418 123 ii 3-4 demarcate the entire historical order into three large blocs. It is a periodization of time without systematic elaboration. 4QInstruction is more interested in the totality of time than describing each period in the manner of the *Apocalypse of Weeks*. Both 4Q417 1 i 3-4 and 4Q418 123 ii 3-4 use היה in the Niphal to refer to all of time—the past, present, and future. Both texts also connect this tripartite division of time to the mystery that is to be. This clarifies the

---

[105] The supplement [במה] // נהיה ומה נהיה למה קדם] is guaranteed by 4Q418 43 2-3.

[106] Elgvin, "An Analysis of 4QInstruction," 259. The Book of Revelation also divides time into past, present and future: "Grace to you and peace from him who is and who was and who is to come (ὁ ὢν καὶ ὁ ἦν καὶ ὁ ἐρχόμενος)" (1:4; cf. 1:8; 4:8). See *DJD 34*, 157. The bipartite division of time is better attested than the tripartite in Second Temple literature. See, for example, 1QS 3:15; 1QM 17:4-5; CD 2:10; and Sir 42:19. The tripartite division of time is also attested in Greek literature. See, for example, *Timaeus* 37D: "For we say that it (Eternal Being) was and is and will be (ἦν ἔστιν τε καὶ ἔσται)." A similar division can be found in *Pausanias* 10.12.10 and *Iliad* 1.80-81. See further David Aune, *Revelation 1-5* (WBC 52a; Dallas: Word Books, 1997), 30-33.

[107] The use of the word יהיה in 4Q418 123 ii 3 is the basis for supplementing 4Q417 1 i 4 with this word. It forms the third leg of the tripartite division of time in 4Q418 123 ii. Although Strugnell and Harrington, *DJD 34*, 157, consider the form of the verbs unknown in 4Q417 1 i 3-4, they recognize in the passage remnants of a tripartite division of time. They do not attempt, unlike Elgvin, to reconstruct the phrase following במה in 4Q417 1 i 4, which forms the third segment of the division. This is also the case in Tigchelaar, *To Increase Learning*, 52, and Jefferies, *Wisdom at Qumran*, 265.

[108] This line should perhaps also be supplemented, like 4Q417 1 i 3-4, with יהיה after the phrase במה. The presence of this stich in 4Q417 1 i is clear from 4Q418 43 2-3.

[109] *DJD 34*, 347.

temporal sense of the mystery that is to be. The Niphal participle נהיה helps establish that the "mystery" of the mystery that is to be extends throughout the entire chronological scheme. The Niphal of היה also conveys this sense in texts such as 1QS 11:18 and 4Q402 4 12 (the second category of the above schema).[110]

The mystery that is to be pertains to the future, although 4QInstruction does not associate it with eschatological judgment to the extent found in the Book of Mysteries (1Q27 1 i 3-4). Nevertheless the mystery that is to be is associated with eschatological events.[111] For example, 4Q417 2 i 10-11 promises that contemplation of this mystery will allow the addressee to know who will receive eschatological salvation: "[Gaze upon the mystery] that is to be, and grasp the birth-times of salvation and know who is inheriting glory and who ini[qu]ity (דע מי נוחל כבוד וע[ו]ל)."[112] 4Q416 2 iii 9-10 similarly exhorts the addressee: "If he restores you to glory, walk in it, and with the mystery [that] is to be examine one's origins (דרוש מולדיו). Then you will know his inheritance."[113] The mystery that is to be is also related to judgment in 4Q417 1 i: "[Day and night meditate upon the mystery that is] to be ... in all their ways with their reckoning for all the periods of eternity, and the eternal reckoning (עם עד // פקודת ופקודם עולם קצי לכול פקודתם)" (ll. 6-8). In a fragmentary passage, 4Q423 5 1-2, the phrase occurs along with Korah, the figure from Numbers 16 who was struck down for his rebelliousness: "... the judgment of Korah. And as he opened your ear [to the mystery that is to be]

---

[110] Elgvin speculates that in 4QInstruction נהיה may be a play on the Niphal perfect and participle. The word would then have intentional temporal ambiguity. See his "An Analysis of 4QInstruction," 78; idem, "The Mystery to Come," 133. The mystery that is to be has temporal ambiguity in that it does not refer exclusively to the past, present, or future. However, it is more likely that both attestations are Niphal participles, rather than a "play" between a Niphal perfect and a participle. See Harrington, "The Raz Nihyeh in a Qumran Wisdom Text," 551; *DJD 20*, 37.

[111] The eschatology of 4QInstruction is given fuller treatment in Chapter 5.

[112] There is some dispute regarding the proper transcription of the word וע[ו]ל. Strugnell and Harrington, *DJD 34*, 182, tentatively suggest that the most likely reading is either אבל or עמל. In their transcription of 4Q417 2 i the word is recorded as ועמל. This reading has support from the word תעמל in line 10. "Toil," following this reading, is what those who will not inherit glory will experience. However the ועמל reading cannot be supported. According to PAM 43.516, no traces of the letter *mêm* are visible. Moreover, there does not seem to be enough space between the *'ayin* and the *lāmed* for a *mêm*. There is, however, enough room for a *wāw*. Elgvin, "An Analysis of 4QInstruction," 196, and Tigchelaar, *To Increase Learning*, 55, transcribe this word as וע[ו]ל, "iniquity." (Elgvin translates it as "corruption.") This option works since the word in question is dualistically opposed to "glory" and refers to those who will be punished at the final judgment. Materially it is also to be preferred. Semantically, however, there is little difference between the readings of Elgvin, Tigchelaar and the editors of *DJD 34*.

[113] 4Q418 9 8 has the variant מו[ל]דו for מולדיו. See Tigchelaar, *To Increase Learning*, 152; *DJD 34*, 111.

..." The mystery that is to be, however, never occurs in 4Q416 1 or 4Q418 69 ii, the most extensive eschatological texts of 4QInstruction. Nevertheless the phrase is clearly associated with future judgment.

4.2 The רז נהיה and the Theme of Creation

The mystery that is to be is associated not only with the eschatological future but also with the beginning of creation: "By means of the mystery that is to be (ברז נהיה) he has laid out its foundation and its works ..." (4Q417 1 i 8-9).[114] Creation is portrayed as a *raz*, a mystery. The interpretation of 4QInstruction's depiction of creation has been disputed. Elgvin and Lange present different ways to understand 4Q417 1 i 8-9. Lange relates the mystery that is to be to Proverbs 3:19.[115] He understands the mystery that is to be as a "Schöpfungsinstrument" which represents "die präexistente Ordnung des Seins."[116] For him the mystery that is to be signifies, in the form of revelation, the traditional sapiential assertion that God endowed the world with order at the moment of creation.[117] Elgvin understands the phrase ברז נהיה of 4Q417 1 i 8 as an apocalyptic appropriation of the tradition that God made the world by wisdom (בחכמה). The mystery that is to be, not wisdom, has the instrumental *bet*. He writes:

> While חכמה, ערמה, and בינה are portrayed as accompanying attributes of God, *raz nihyeh* is the plan by which he designed the world and its foundations ... *Raz nihyeh* is clearly a reinterpretation of the divine Wisdom of Proverbs 1-9.[118]

Elgvin argues that in 4QInstruction "'Lady Wisdom' has been replaced by the apocalyptic concept *raz* or *raz nihyeh*, the unfolding mystery of God."[119] He acknowledges that Lady Wisdom "does not figure clearly" in 4QInstruction. There is no explicit mention of her in the text.[120] The

---

[114] See also Goff, "The Mystery of Creation," 8-12.

[115] Prov 3:19 reads: "The Lord by wisdom (בחכמה) founded the earth; by understanding he established the heavens." That God made the world בחכמה is also found in Jeremiah 10:12; 51:15; and Psalm 104:24. See also Harrington, "Wisdom at Qumran," 149-51.

[116] *Weisheit und Prädestination*, 62.

[117] See section 3.1 of Chapter 1 for an overview of A. Lange's perspective. See also Bilha Nitzan, "The Idea of Creation and Its Implications in Qumran Literature," in *Creation in Jewish and Christian Tradition* (ed. H.G. Reventlow and Y. Hoffman; Sheffield: Sheffield Academic Press, 2002), 240-64.

[118] Elgvin, "Wisdom and Apocalypticism," 235.

[119] "An Analysis of 4QInstruction," 61.

[120] It is reasonable to assume that 4QInstruction is familiar with the Lady Wisdom tradition. Traditional wisdom has been handed down to the author of this text, and there is no reason to posit that this transmission did not include Lady Wisdom since she is an

mystery that is to be for Elgvin represents 4QInstruction's break from the traditional creation theology of Proverbs. Lange's view, by contrast, emphasizes the continuity between Proverbs and 4QInstruction, since both declare that God created the world with an inherent sense of order.

The main text for assessing the theme of creation in 4QInstruction is 4Q417 1 i 6-9. This passage reads:

> [Day and night meditate upon the mystery that is] to be. Inquire constantly. Then you will know truth and iniquity, wisdom and [foll]y you will [recognize] ... Then you will distinguish between [goo]d and [evil according to their] works, for the God of Knowledge is a foundation of truth. By means of the mystery that is to be he has laid out its foundation and its works
> ...[121] (ברז נהיה // פרש את אושה ומעשיה)

According to this pericope, the addressee is to contemplate the mystery that is to be constantly. From this study he will acquire the knowledge of good and evil. The possibility of obtaining this knowledge is established by the fact that God is a "foundation of truth." God created "its foundation and its works." The antecedent of the feminine suffix of "foundation" and "works" is most likely "truth."[122] The act of creation was carried out by means of the mystery that is to be. By associating creation with the mystery that is to be, 4QInstruction implies that creation is under divine control. God endowed the world with an overarching framework by means of the mystery that is to be.

The relationship between the divine control of the world and the mystery that is to be helps clarify why the latter is presented as the source of the knowledge of good and evil (cf. 1QH 5:9). In 4QInstruction knowing good and evil is not simply a capacity for moral conduct. It denotes the acquisition of wisdom about the divine framework in which the human realm should be understood.[123] In the Treatise on the Two Spirits

---

important figure in the sapiential tradition. One can speculate that 4QInstruction avoids this allegory in order to highlight that God alone made the world, without the assistance of any intermediary figure. Ben Sira 42:21 makes this viewpoint explicit: "He has set in order the splendors of his wisdom; he is from all eternity one and the same. Nothing can be added or taken away, and he needs no one to be his counselor." Proverbs 8:30 has been interpreted as depicting Lady Wisdom as an "artisan" (אמון) and co-creator. See Fox, *Proverbs 1-9*, 285-87; Richard Clifford, *Proverbs* (OTL; Louisville: Westminster John Knox, 1999), 99-101. For more on the figure of Lady Wisdom in the Dead Sea Scrolls, see S.W. Crawford, "Lady Wisdom and Dame Folly at Qumran," *Dead Sea Discoveries* 5 (1998): 355-66. See also Daniel J. Harrington, "Ten Reasons Why the Qumran Wisdom Texts are Important," *Dead Sea Discoveries* 4 (1997): 245-55.

[121] *DJD 34*, 151; Tigchelaar, *To Increase Learning*, 52.

[122] *DJD 34*, 158.

[123] The importance of the theme of the knowledge of good and evil in 4QInstruction is also clear in 4Q417 1 i 17-18. In this text the vision of Hagu is not given to the "fleshly

attaining knowledge of good and evil is also associated with an awareness of the world's overarching framework: "He knows the result of their
deeds for all times [everlas]ting and has given them as a legacy to the
sons of man so that they know good [and evil] ([לדעת טוב [ורע])" (1QS
4:25-26).[124] In 4QInstruction the mystery that is to be enables one to
understand the natural order in a more comprehensive way because God
used it to create the world.

Creation by means of the mystery that is to be implies the goodness
and rational structure of the natural order. After the affirmation in
4Q417 1 i 8-9 that God created the world with the mystery that is to be,
the text reads: "[with all wisd]om and all [clever]ness he has fashioned it
([לכל חכ]מה ולכל[ער]מה יצרה)" (l. 9).[125] 4Q417 1 i 8-9 uses the phrase
ברז נהיה in conjunction with a verb that refers to divine creation (פֿרֹשׁ).
Immediately following is the phrase [לכל חכ]מה in conjunction with a
verb that refers to divine creation (יצרה). The role of divine wisdom in
creation is also clear in 4Q418 126 ii 4-5: "He has spread them out
(פֿרשׂם); truthfully he has established them ... Furthermore, they do not
exist without his good will, and apart from [his] wis[dom (וגם לוא

<hr/>

spirit" because it does not know the difference between good and evil. This issue is examined in Chapter 3. See also section 4.5 of this chapter.

[124] The Book of Mysteries also combines the knowledge of good and evil with revelation. 4Q300 3 2 (par 1Q27 1 i 2) has been reconstructed as reading "in order that they
would know (the difference) between g[ood and evil ... that they might understand the
mysteries of transgression (רזי פשע)]." Line 3 suggests that the group referred to in line 2
did not attain this knowledge: "But [they] did not know [the mystery that is to be, and the
former things they did not consider]." See DJD 20, 105. In 1QH 6:11-12 the speaker's
understanding of good and evil is associated with the "spirits of man" and presented as a
revelation: "You teach your servant [... of the spirit]s of man, for corresponding to the
spirits ... between good and evil (בין טוב לרשע), and set over them [... to sho]w them their
actions" (cf. 5:6).

[125] The phrase [לכל חכ]מה ולכל[ער]מה has been reconstructed text-critically. This portion of 4Q417 1 i has substantial ink erosion. Crucial for understanding this poorly preserved phrase is recognizing its use of poetic parallelism. See DJD 34, 158. The second
section of the portion to be reconstructed, ולכל[ ]מה, includes a noun ending in מה- that is
preceded by ולכל. Before it occurs another noun that ends in מה-. Given the parallelism of
this stich, it is likely that the first word of the first section to be reconstructed is לכל, as in
the second portion, or its semantic equivalent. Therefore the line has two nouns that end
in [ ]מה, each of which is modified by לכל. The theme of creation suggests that the second
word ending in מה- is ערמה and that the first is חכמה (or vice versa). Several scholars have
reconstructed the text in this way. See DJD 34, 151; Elgvin, "An Analysis of
4QInstruction," 256. Tigchelaar, To Increase Learning, 52-53, agrees with the reconstruction חכמה but not with ערמה. He points out that the editors of DJD 34 consider the rēš
to be visible in the fragment, and argues that the transcription ולכל[ ]רמה would leave a
gap that is too large for only one letter ('ayin). There is indeed no visible rēš in the fragment. Nevertheless the reconstruction ער[ ]מה is to be favored on thematic grounds. The
lacuna in question is large enough for two letters. According to PAM 41.942, the line
immediately above the gap in question has two letters, the hē and dālet of the word הדעות.

נהיו בלוא רצונו ומחוכ̇]מתו) ...‏" The phrase "apart from [his] wis[dom]" could be understood as either the end of the sentence, or as the beginning of a sentence that has not fully survived. In either case the phrase is in parallelism with "without his favor." God's wisdom is mentioned to underscore that the natural order was fashioned according to his will and intelligence.

The epithet "the God of Knowledge" (אל הדעות) also underscores the goodness of creation in 4QInstruction.[126] According to 4Q417 1 i 8, "the God of Knowledge" is "a foundation of truth" (cf. 1 Sam 2:3). 4Q418 55 5-6 is a fragmentary passage that connects the epithet "God of Knowledge" to the claim that the world was made with a foundation of truth: "Is [he] not [the] God of Knowledge (אל ה]ד̇עות)? ... upon truth, in order to establish all [of their ways upon und]erstanding (ב]ינה)?"[127] The epithet is used elsewhere in the Dead Sea Scrolls to praise God's role in creation.[128] The "God of Knowledge" is praised for having made a created order that reflects his mastery and dominion. The epithet also emphasizes that God used his wisdom when establishing the created order.

Divine creation of the natural order has deterministic implications.[129] 4Q417 1 i 11-12 reads: "in proper understanding were made [known the secr]ets of his plan." 4QInstruction affirms that there is a divine plan guiding events that has been revealed to the addressee. This helps explain why the text presents the act of creation as a "mystery." Since the nature of the created order is a revealed truth, it follows that the way in which it was formed also requires revelation. Claiming that the act of creation is a revealed "mystery" helps promotes the view that the natural order bears the stamp of a transcendent deity. Contra Lange, there is no evidence that this is in reaction to the skepticism of Job or Qoheleth.[130] But, as Lange suggests, the view that creation is a revealed "mystery"

[126] Elgvin, "An Analysis of 4QInstruction," 260; *DJD 34*, 158; Tigchelaar, *To Increase Learning*, 197.

[127] *DJD 34*, 265; Tigchelaar, *To Increase Learning*, 89.

[128] The hymns of the Hodayot employ the phrase in relation to creation: "For the God of Knowledge has established it (the created order) and no one else with him" (1QH 20:10-11). 1QH 9:26-27, like 4Q417 1 i 8, connects the "God of Knowledge" to the "foundation of truth": "To you, you God of Knowledge, belong all the works of justice and the foundation of truth (סוד אמת)." See also 22:15. For the phrase סוד אמת, see further 4:19; 10:10; 18:4; and 19:9. It may also occur in 4Q418a 12 2. For the phrase אל הדעות, see also 4Q504 4 4. For the phrase אלוהי דעת, see 4Q402 4 12 and 4Q510 1 2. Cf. 4Q400 2 8; 4Q405 23 ii 12; 4Q511 1 7-8; 4Q299 35 1; and 4Q299 73 3. See further Elgvin, "An Analysis of 4QInstruction," 261; *DJD 34*, 158.

[129] The determinism of 4QInstruction is more fully examined in the following section (4.3).

[130] Lange, *Weisheit und Prädestination*, 92.

implies that human observation alone is not sufficient to perceive fully the nature of the created order.

Elgvin and Lange both identify key factors when relating 4QInstruction's creation theology to Proverbs. Lange is surely right to argue that 4QInstruction uses the mystery that is to be to put forward the view that the world has an inherent sense of order, as does Proverbs. Yet whereas Lady Wisdom wants to describe to all passers-by the first moments of creation, in 4QInstruction creation is presented as a mystery that is disclosed to the addressee. This is a departure from traditional wisdom, as Elgvin has stressed.

Elgvin understands the theme of creation in 4QInstruction in relation to apocalypticism and Lange in relation to the sapiential tradition. The two traditions are complementary influences. It is more important to understand how these traditions are combined than to argue that one should be emphasized at the expense of the other.[131] Despite its reliance on revelation, 4QInstruction's creation theology should not be viewed solely in terms of apocalypticism, without recourse to traditional creation theology. 4QInstruction shows no interest in Lady Wisdom, but there is continuity between its presentation of creation and that of Proverbs. In Proverbs 1-9 divine creation explains why the world makes sense, an idea assumed by Proverbs 10-31. Creation theology undergirds a perspective about the world basic to Proverbs. This is also the case in 4QInstruction. As in Proverbs, 4QInstruction's understanding of the world is related to creation. The world is the way it is because of how it was made. God used the mystery that is to be to create the world, and therefore it can be employed by the addressee to understand the natural order. Appealing to creation as a way to understand the natural order reflects the influence of the sapiential tradition. Apocalyptic texts generally do not turn to creation to argue that the world has a sense of order. One notable exception is the Enochic *Astronomical Book*.[132] It is more common in apocalyptic literature to affirm the deterministic nature of reality by claiming that history unfolds according to ordained stages (i.e., the *Apocalypse of Weeks*; Dan 9), and that it is ordained to end at a specific point.

Both the author of 4QInstruction and the sages of ancient Israel reflected on the nature of creation and its beginning. 4QInstruction comes down on this issue in a way that is very different from the sages who produced Proverbs 1-9. 4QInstruction does not appeal to Lady Wisdom.

---

[131] Larsen, "Visdom og apokalyptik," 1-14.

[132] For more on this text, see James C. VanderKam, *Calendars in the Dead Sea Scrolls: Measuring Time* (London/New York: Routledge, 1998), 17-27.

It does not claim, in complete contrast to Proverbs, that everyone can understand the structure of creation. It is a revealed mystery given to the elect (cf. 1QH 5:19). In a departure from biblical wisdom, the text's reflection on creation is influenced by its apocalyptic worldview. 4QInstruction illustrates that in the second century BCE a wisdom text could have an apocalyptic worldview.

4.3 The נהיה רז and Determinism

The mystery that is to be explains the deterministic mindset of 4QInstruction. Determinism is a natural expression of 4QInstruction's emphasis on God's dominion throughout history. 4Q417 1 i 10-11 reads: "He has [ex]pounded for their un[der]standing every d[ee]d (פֿר[שׁ] לֹ[מֹ]נֹ[ב]ֹנתם לכול מ[עשֹ]ֹה[133) so that one may walk in [the inclination] of their understanding."[134] God has arranged in advance every deed as part

---

[133] Strugnell and Harrington, *DJD 34*, 151, transcribe this word as מֹ[עשׁי]ֹה. They translate it as "d[ee]d." The word, if reconstructed in this way, could be understood as having a suffix. But it is not clear what the antecedent would be if the word were understood in this fashion. For this reason the transcription used here does not supplement a *yôd*, following Elgvin, "An Analysis of 4QInstruction," 256. See also Tigchelaar, *To Increase Learning*, 52.

[134] 4Q417 1 i has a nice word play between פרש and פֿרשׁ. The former is used in line 9 with the meaning "to lay out; to spread out" to describe God's act of creation ("he has laid out [פֹֿרֹשׁ] its foundation and its works"). Line 10 uses the verb פרש in relation to God providing understanding. The text makes an important link between God's creation and his revelation of the deterministic nature of reality. Note also the incomplete expression]ֹיפרש לֹאׁ of 4Q417 1 i 11. The segment]לֹאׁ can be reconstructed as]לֹאׁנוש, as suggested in *DJD 34*, 154. If this is the proper reconstruction, the original text of 4Q417 1 i 11 may have affirmed that God revealed knowledge to אנוש, the same term used in 4Q417 1 i 16. The word אנוש in this line is discussed more fully in the next chapter. The]לֹאׁנוש reading is tentatively endorsed here. The fragmentary nature of the text forces this interpretation to remain tentative.

There is some disagreement regarding the transcription of the final phrase of the portion of 4Q417 1 i 10-11 that is cited above, "their understanding" (מבינתם). The issue is whether this word should have a singular or plural suffix. Most transcriptions include a singular masculine suffix. See Elgvin, "An Analysis of 4QInstruction," 256; Tigchelaar, *To Increase Learning*, 52; Lange, *Weisheit und Prädestination*, 51; Jefferies, *Wisdom at Qumran*, 265. Strugnell and Harrington, *DJD 34*, 153, however, prefer a plural suffix, transcribing a final *mêm*. They grant that a singular suffix is possible and translate "their/his." The final *mêm* reading derives support from the phrase לֹמֹ[ב]ֹנֹתם of l. 10. It is also likely because of faint letter traces slightly lower than one would expect with most other letters. (Final *mêm*s in this fragment are much lower on the line than other letters.) According to this reading, God made clear all deeds for *their* understanding so that they may act according to the inclination of *their* understanding. A singular suffix reading would produce a line that is semantically similar. The sense of such a reading would be that *each* may act according to the inclination of *his* understanding. Unlike the reading

of the divine plan governing reality that is revealed to the addressee. 4Q417 1 i 11-12 continues by emphasizing the revelation of the divine framework: "... in proper understanding were made [known the secr]ets of his plan (מחשבתו // נס[תרי נוד]עו), along with his walking [perfe]ctly [in all] his [de]eds." The behavior of the addressee is expected to be in accordance with his knowledge of the determined nature of the world. 4Q417 1 i 18-19 declares that one who studies the mystery that is to be will know how God's predetermined plan unfolds: "And you, under-standing son, gaze into the mystery that is to be and know [the path]s of all life. The way that one conducts himself he appoints over [his] deed[s]." The deterministic theology of 4QInstruction is similar to that of the Treatise of the Two Spirits:

> From the God of Knowledge stems all there is and all there will be. Before they existed he established their entire design. And when they have come into being, at their appointed time, they will execute all their works accord-ing to his glorious design, without altering anything (1QS 3:15-16).

The determinism of 4QInstruction is evident in its use of the term "in-heritance" (נחלה). Everyone has an allotment from God, an "inheri-tance": "For God has distributed the inheritance of [eve]ry [living being] (אל פלג נחלת כו[ל חי])" (4Q418 81 20).[135] This point is reiterated in 4Q416 3 2, 4Q418 81 2-3, and 4Q423 5 3.[136] The Treatise on the Two Spirits uses related language to express a similar idea:

> In these (the two spirits) (lies) the history of all men; in their (two) divi-sions all their armies have a share (ינחלו) for their generations ... every deed they do (falls) into their divisions, dependent on what might be the birthright of man (נחלת איש), great or small, for all eternal times (1QS 4:15-16; cf. 4:24; 11:7).[137]

---

with the final *mêm*, however, it would be open to the interpretation that each may act according to God's understanding.

[135] Strugnell and Harrington, *DJD 34*, 301, supplement נחלת with a final *mêm* whereas Elgvin, "An Analysis of 4QInstruction," 268, does not include a suffix. The latter is also the reading in Tigchelaar, *To Increase Learning*, 94. The editors of *DJD 34* argue that a singular suffix is possible, rendering the word as "[their/his/His] inheritance." They also reconstruct כו[ל rather than simply כו]ל. Tigchelaar, *To Increase Learning*, 96, argues that the reconstruction נחלת[ם בכו]ל proposed by the editors of *DJD 34* is "completely impossible" because there is not enough space between the visible material to insert this many letters. For this reason the phrase נחלת כו[ל that is proposed by Tigchelaar and Elgvin is to be preferred.

[136] Note that the term "inheritance" in 4Q417 2 i 17-18 refers to what one receives in exchange for trading agricultural surplus. See section 3.4 of Chapter 4. See also the fragmentary text 4Q418 234 1, "inheritance of holin[ess" (נחלת קוד[ש). Tigchelaar, *To Increase Learning*, 119, suggests that this fragment overlaps with 4Q415 1 ii-2 i.

[137] A. Lange, "Die Weisheitstexte aus Qumran: Eine Einleitung," in *The Wisdom Texts from Qumran*, 25.

The gifts of the elect are portrayed as an "inheritance" elsewhere in late
Second Temple literature.[138]

Not only righteous humans have an "inheritance." 4QInstruction affirms that "according to his inheritance (נחלתו) in it he (a wicked person)
will be tr[eated as wicked]" (4Q417 1 i 24; cf. *1 En.* 45:2). The angels
also have an inheritance: "the so[ns of] heaven, whose inheritance is
eternal life (חיים עולם נחלתם)" (4Q418 69 ii 12-13).[139]

The addressee's "inheritance" is much greater than that which is allotted to most people. 4QInstruction affirms that he has affinity with the
angels. This is presented as a feature of God's divine plan. This is clear
in 4Q418 81 4-5: "With all the [div]ine being[s] he has cast your lot
(בכול [א]ל[ים] // הפיל גורלכה). Your glory he has magnified greatly" (cf.
1QS 11:7-8; 1QH 19:11-12).[140] 4Q418 81 3 makes explicit that the addressee's inheritance includes a special relationship with God: "He is
your portion and your inheritance among the sons of Adam. [And over]
his [in]heritance he has set you in authority." 4Q423 4 3 reformulates
this line so that God himself declares that he is the addressee's portion
and inheritance. 4Q418 81 3 alludes to the stipulation of priestly enti-

---

[138] See, for example, 1QH 18:27-29, "But to the sons of your truth you have given intelligence ... And so for the son of [your] maid-[servant ...] you have increased his legacy
in the knowledge of your truth (הרביתה נחלתו בדעת אמתכה) ..." (cf. 6:19; 14:8); *1 En.* 58:2,
"Blessed (are) you, the righteous and chosen, for your lot (will be) glorious!" (cf. 67:1-2;
Sir 45:25). Elect status is also described in terms of a promised inheritance in the New
Testament. See Eph 1:17-18: "I pray that the God of our Lord Jesus Christ, the Father of
glory, may give you a spirit of wisdom and revelation (πνεῦμα σοφίας καὶ ἀποκαλύψεως)
as you come to know him, so that ... you may know what is the hope to which he has
called you, what are the riches of his glorious inheritance among the saints ..." Cf. also
Col 1:12; 3:24; Eph 5:5; Heb 9:15; 1 Pet 1:4. See Eduard Lohse, *Colossians and Philemon* (Hermeneia; Philadelphia: Fortress, 1971), 18, 161.

[139] According to *1 Enoch* 37:4, Enoch is likewise given "the lot of eternal life." See
also *1 En.* 103:3: "Much good will be given to you in recompense for your toil, and (that)
your lot (will be) more excellent than the lot of the living."

[140] The material reconstruction of [א]ל[ים] is not fully certain. Elgvin does not attempt
to reconstruct this word, although he grants that part of a *lāmed* is visible. See his "An
Analysis of 4QInstruction," 268. I use the reconstruction of Strugnell and Harrington.
See *DJD 34*, 305. Their reconstruction is suggested by the fact that 4Q418 81 1-5 explains that the addressee has a special relationship with God and the angels. Tigchelaar,
To Increase Learning, 94, reconstructs [מ]ל[אכיו], "his angels," which is semantically
equivalent to the proposal in *DJD 34*. For more discussion, see section 2.4.3 of Chapter 3
and section 3 of Chapter 5. Note also that גורל is used in reference to the elect in
11QMelchizedek: "atonement shall be made for all the sons of [light and for] the men [of]
the lot of (גורל) Mel[chi]zedek" (11Q13 2 8). See Florentino García Martínez et al., *Qumran Cave 11.II (11Q2-18, 11Q20-31)* (DJD 23; Oxford: Clarendon, 1998), 229. See also
Armin Lange, "The Determination of Fate by the Oracle of the Lot in the Dead Sea
Scrolls, the Hebrew Bible and Ancient Mesopotamian Literature," in *Sapiential, Liturgical and Poetical Texts from Qumran*, 39-48.

tlements in Numbers 18:20.[141] The phrase "He is your portion and your inheritance" utilizes a levitical tradition that all twelve tribes received an allotment of land except for the Levites. In Numbers 18 this tradition is used to justify Aaronid dominion over the Temple cult.[142] In 4QInstruction this tradition is used to legitimate the addressee's elect status.

The privileged status of the addressee is described elsewhere in 4QInstruction as his "inheritance."[143] In 4Q416 4 3 the addressee is exhorted to "rejoice in the inheritance of truth (שמחה בנחלת אמת)" (cf. 4Q418 102 5). 4Q418 88 8 proclaims: "Truly your in[her]itance will be fulfilled (באמת תמלא נ[ח]לתכה)." 4Q418 162 is fragmentary but may indicate that the addressee's inheritance will spare him from punishment at the moment of God's judgment. Lines 3-4 read "... will increase his inheritance (נחלתו) ... eternal destruction (שׂחת עולם), and you will have glo[ry] ..." Since the addressee is promised glory, it is reasonable to assume a phrase such as "you will be spared from" came before "eternal destruction."[144] The phrase "inheritors of the land" (נוחלי ארץ) of 4Q418 81 14, the immediate context of which has not fully survived, may also refer to the elect status of the addressee (cf. 1 En. 5:7; Matt 5:5; m. Sanh. 10:1; m. Qidd. 1:10).[145]

4.4 The נהיה רז and the Torah

The mystery that is to be is used to encourage the addressee to acquire knowledge. In that sense it is a source of wisdom. Since the Torah was also understood to be a source of wisdom in the Second Temple period

---

[141] DJD 34, 305, 517; Elgvin, "An Analysis of 4QInstruction," 117; idem, "Wisdom and Apocalypticism," 245.

[142] See also Deut 10:9; 12:12; 18:1; Josh 13:14, 33. Numbers 18 stipulates priestly entitlements such as tithes and first fruits. See Baruch Levine, Numbers 1-20 (AB 4A; New York: Doubleday, 1993), 436, 450. The Aaronic grant of Numbers 18:20 is affirmed in Ben Sira 45:22: "But in the land of the people he (Aaron) has no inheritance, and he has no portion among the people; for the Lord himself is his portion and inheritance." Cf. Sir 45:25: "the inheritance of Aaron is for all his offspring (נחלת אהרן לכל זרעו)."

[143] The word "inheritance" also occurs in 4Q415 2 i + 1 ii 6; 4Q415 15 1; 4Q416 2 iv 11-12; 4Q416 3 1; 4Q418 138 2; 4Q418 172 5; 4Q418 185 2; 4Q418 201 1 (reconstructed); 4Q418 251 1 (reconstructed); and 4Q423 12 2. Many of these attestations are in contexts too fragmentary to interpret properly.

[144] DJD 34, 386.

[145] The entire line reads "... world, in it all the inheritors of the earth shall walk." See Stuckenbruck, "4QInstruction and the Possible Influence of Early Enochic Traditions," 247-49; Elgvin, "An Analysis of 4QInstruction," 116, 133-34. See also section 2.4.3 of Chapter 3.

(e.g., Sir 1:25-27), it is reasonable to ask how the mystery that is to be should be understood in relation to it.

Elgvin and Lange present opposite ways to understand the issue.[146] Lange argues that the mystery that is to be indicates that 4QInstruction exhibits "eine Verbindung von Weisheit und Thora."[147] 4QInstruction is thus seen as thematically similar to Ben Sira 24 and Baruch 3:9-4:4. He presents the mystery that is to be as typologically similar to the rabbinic understanding of the Torah. *Bereshit Rabbah* 1 interprets Proverbs's declaration that God made the world with wisdom as a prooftext for the view that God used the Torah to create the world. The Torah is the template according to which the created order was fashioned. Lange contends that 4QInstruction's mystery that is to be as a divine ordering principle is compatible with the rabbinic understanding of the Torah.[148]

Lange's reading of 4Q417 1 i 6 exemplifies his assessment of the status of Torah in 4QInstruction.[149] The relevant portion of the line reads "[Day and night meditate upon the mystery that is] to be (יומם ולילה] הגה ברז נ[היה)."[150] He claims that this "handelt es sich um ein Zitat von Ps 1,2."[151] Psalm 1:2 utilizes the phrase "day and night" in relation to the

---

[146] The issue has also been examined by Jack T. Sanders. See his "When Sacred Canopies Collide: The Reception of the Torah of Moses in the Wisdom Literature of the Second-Temple Period," *Journal for the Study of Judaism* 32 (2001): 121-36. Giving minimal treatment to 4QInstruction, he claims that the Qumran wisdom texts "go somewhat further" than Ben Sira's incorporation of Torah piety into the wisdom tradition. 4QInstruction, however, does not support this conclusion. Nickelsburg contrasts *1 Enoch*, The Wisdom of Solomon, and 4QInstruction with Ben Sira, Baruch, and Tobit. The latter group thematizes Torah and emphasizes its authoritative status. The former group is characterized by a "disjunction with the Mosaic tradition." See his *1 Enoch*, 59-60. See also G. Sauer, "Weisheit und Tora in qumranischer Zeit," in *Weisheit ausserhalb der kanonischen Weisheitsschriften* (ed. B. Janowski; Gütersloh: Kaiser, 1996), 107-27.

[147] *Weisheit und Prädestination*, 48. See also his "Die Endgestalt des protomasoretischen Psalters und die Toraweisheit," in *Der Psalter in Judentum und Christentum* (ed. E. Zenger; Herders Biblische Studien 18; Freiburg: Herder, 1998), 101-36. Lange argues that 4QInstruction, the Book of Mysteries, and the proto-MT Psalter all share a kind of Torah wisdom that is dualistic with historical and cosmic dimensions. This view magnifies the importance of the Torah in 4QInstruction by connecting it to circles that redacted biblical texts. There is a similar approach to 4QInstruction in his "In Diskussion mit dem Tempel: zur Auseinandersetzung zwischen Kohelet und weisheitlichen Kreisen am Jerusalemer Tempel," in *Qohelet in the Context of Wisdom* (ed. A. Schoors; BETL 136; Leuven: Leuven University Press/Peeters, 1998), 113-60. This article is discussed in section 3.1 of Chapter 1.

[148] *Weisheit und Prädestination*, 90.

[149] This topic is also discussed in section 2.2 of Chapter 3.

[150] The segment [לילה הגה ברז נ] is taken from the parallel text 4Q418 43 4. The word "day" is a supplement endorsed in *DJD 34*, 151; Elgvin, "An Analysis of 4QInstruction," 256; and Tigchelaar, *To Increase Learning*, 52.

[151] *Weisheit und Prädestination*, 62.

Torah.[152] Both Psalm 1:2 and 4Q417 1 i 6 use the expression "day and night" to refer to the act of constant study. It does not necessarily follow from this that the mystery that is to be should be identified with the Torah. The idiom "day and night" is well known in the Hebrew Bible as a term that expresses continuous action.[153] The phrase is too common to identify a citation of Psalm 1:2 in 4Q417 1 i 6. The expression occurs in 4Q417 2 i 21-22 in the context of worrying constantly about paying off debts: "there will be no [sleep for y]ou day or night (יומם ולילה), and there will be no rest for your soul [until] you pay back [your] credit[or his loan]." No one would suggest this is a citation of Psalm 1:2.

Lange also argues that 4Q416 2 iii 18-19, which alludes to the fifth commandment, allows one to identity the mystery that to be with the Torah: "honor them (one's parents) for the sake of your glory and with [reverence] honor them for the sake of your life and the length of your days."[154] It is not disputed that 4QInstruction displays an awareness of Pentateuchal traditions.[155] 4Q416 2 iii 18-19 indicates that the author of 4QInstruction understood the Torah to be a source of wisdom. 4Q416 2 ii 8-9 may understand the Torah and "mysteries" as both important to the addressee: "And do not let go of your statutes. Carefully observe your mysteries." In 4Q418 184, an unfortunately fragmentary passage, line 1 reads ביד משה, "through the hand of Moses," with the mystery that is to be mentioned in line 2 (cf. 4Q423 11 2). This suggests that the revelation of the mystery that is to be may be somehow associated with the Torah, as does 4Q416 2 ii 8-9, but the evidence is by no means conclu-

---

[152] Ps 1:2: "but their delight is in the law of the Lord, and on his law they meditate day and night (יומם ולילה)."

[153] For the biblical phrase יומם ולילה and its variants, see, for example, Isa 34:10; 60:11; 62:6; Jer 9:1; 14:17; 16:13; Lam 2:18. The phrase is also used in New Testament texts to refer to constant prayer. See Luke 2:37; 18:7; 1 Thess 3:10; 1 Tim 5:5.

The phrase "day and night" is used elsewhere in reference to constant Torah study. See Josh 1:8, "This book of the law shall not depart out of your mouth; you shall meditate on it day and night (יומם ולילה), so that you may be careful to act in accordance with all that is written in it"; 1QS 6:6-7, "in the place in which the Ten assemble there should not be missing a man to interpret the law day and night, always (יומם ולילה תמיד), one relieving another."

[154] *Weisheit und Prädestination*, 58. See also section 4.5 of this chapter.

[155] See, for example, the allusion to Numbers 18:20 in 4Q418 81 3, the mention of Korah in 4Q423 5, the citation of Numbers 15:39 in 4Q417 1 i 27, and the dependence of 4Q416 2 iv 7-13 on Numbers 30 in its treatment of vows. Perhaps the most important use of Torah traditions in 4QInstruction is its use of Genesis texts in its presentation of Adam and Eden traditions examined in Chapter 3. See also Harrington, "Ten Reasons Why the Qumran Wisdom Texts are Important," 249.

sive.[156] The Torah is not a major theme of 4QInstruction. The word "Torah" never occurs in the text.[157] It has nothing comparable to the laudatory descriptions of the Torah in Ben Sira. Lange observes that the function of the mystery that is to be as an ordering principle is compatible with rabbinic conceptions of the Torah. But, unlike the rabbis, the author of 4QInstruction does not thematize the Torah.[158] It is not clear that it should be associated with the mystery that is to be to the extent suggested by Lange.

Elgvin is critical of Lange's view that the mystery that is to be should be associated with the Torah.[159] Elgvin holds that the mystery that is to be is an esoteric source of wisdom that is an alternative to the public wisdom of the Torah. The two options are, Elgvin argues, in tension with one another. The mystery that is to be, for him, displaces the Torah as a source of wisdom. This argument is based in part on a fragmentary text, 4Q423 3 1-2: "And your st]rength will be s[pent] in vain ... [through the mystery] that is to be (נֹהיה] ברז // ... חכה]כֹוֹן לריק וֹתֹ]ם)." The first portion of this line alludes to Leviticus 26:20.[160] 4Q423 3 2 urges the listener to "walk." Leviticus 26:3 encourages one to walk according to God's laws, whereas the exhortation to walk in 4Q423 is in the context of the mystery that is to be. Elgvin concludes that in 4QInstruction "true wisdom is not found in the Torah but in *raz nihyeh.*"[161] In a reversal of Lange, Elgvin distinguishes 4QInstruction from the Torah wisdom of texts such as Ben Sira 24 and Baruch 3:9-4:4. Elgvin is correct to point out that the mystery that is to be is a more central theme in 4QInstruction than the Torah. It is not clear, however, that for 4QInstruction "true wisdom is not found in the Torah."

---

[156] Harrington, "The Raz Nihyeh," 552; George J. Brooke, "Biblical Interpretation in the Wisdom Texts from Qumran," in *The Wisdom Texts from Qumran*, 215; Murphy, *Wealth in the Dead Sea Scrolls*, 171.

[157] *DJD 34*, 27.

[158] Sanders, "When Sacred Canopies Collide," 127, cites 4Q416 2 iii 18-19, which alludes to the fifth commandment, and 4Q418 103 ii 6-7, which is reliant on Leviticus 19 and Deuteronomy 22, to claim that 4QInstruction, like other Qumran wisdom texts, points "to a closer adherence to the Mosaic Torah among the DSS wisdom texts than we saw in ben Sira." It is misleading to suggest that the Torah plays a more central role in 4QInstruction than Ben Sira. The central concept for 4QInstruction is the mystery that is to be, not the Torah.

[159] Elgvin, "An Analysis of 4QInstruction," 81; idem, "Wisdom and Apocalypticism," 237.

[160] This verse reads: "Your strength shall be spent to no purpose (כחכם לריק ותם): your land shall not yield its produce, and the trees of the land shall not yield their fruit." 4QInstruction changes the pronoun of the word "strength" from plural to singular. See Elgvin, "An Analysis of 4QInstruction," 78; *DJD 34*, 512.

[161] Elgvin, "Wisdom and Apocalypticism," 237.

4QInstruction uses the Torah as a source for its teaching, as is evident in 4Q423 3 itself. Its allusion to Leviticus 26 suggests not that the composition displaces Torah wisdom with apocalypticism but that its reception of the Torah is colored by an appeal to revelation beyond that of Sinai.

The author of 4QInstruction was familiar with the Torah and understood it to be a source of wisdom. However 4QInstruction includes no elaborate poetry praising the virtues of Torah. 4QInstruction does not celebrate the Torah as the fruit of Lady Wisdom's descent from heaven in the style of Ben Sira 24. It does not exhibit the Torah piety of Psalm 1. It does not use biblical material as prooftexts in the manner of 1QS and CD. The mystery that is to be should not be identified as the Torah in 4QInstruction à la Lange. Nor should it be portrayed as an alternative to the Torah in the manner of Elgvin. The mystery that is to be is designed to encourage the addressee to acquire knowledge. Some of the wisdom 4QInstruction offers is dependent on the Torah.

4.5 The רז נהיה and Daily Life

4QInstruction expects more of its addressee than simply to be aware of the extent of God's dominion. It wants him to live his ordinary life with this in mind. The mystery that is to be affects the addressee's ethical conduct and the way he handles his daily affairs.[162] To accomplish this 4QInstruction combines the mystery that is to be with specific teachings that are similar to traditional wisdom.

Filial piety is combined with the mystery that is to be.[163] 4Q416 2 iii 15-19 reads:

---

[162] Cana Werman's analysis of the mystery that is to be acknowledges that it includes a practical and ethical component. She claims that the term signifies "the ways (conduct of people) and their rewards and punishment during every period of the world." See her "What is the Book of Hagu?" in *Sapiential Perspectives: Wisdom Literature in Light of the Dead Sea Scrolls. Proceedings of the Sixth International Symposium of the Orion Center, 20-22 May 2001* (ed. G. Sterling and J.J. Collins; Leiden: Brill, forthcoming). She is certainly right to depict the *raz nihyeh* as the "unfolding of history as planned by God." Werman, however, does not emphasize the pivotal role of supernatural revelation for understanding the phrase. Puech has stressed that the function of the mystery that is to be is to encourage "les membres du peuple à persévérer dans la fidélité à l'alliance afin d'être inscrits au nombre des élus." See his "Apports des textes apocalyptiques et sapientiels de Qumrân à l'eschatologie du judaïsme ancien," in *Wisdom and Apocalypticism in the Dead Sea Scrolls and in the Biblical Tradition.* See also Hempel, "The Qumran Sapiential Texts and the Rule Books," 283; Cana Werman "'The תורה and the תעודה' Engraved on the Tablets," *Dead Sea Discoveries* 9 (2002), 91.

[163] Elgvin, "An Analysis of 4QInstruction," 156-57; Crispin H.T. Fletcher-Louis, *All the Glory of Adam: Liturgical Anthropology in the Dead Sea Scrolls* (STDJ 42; Leiden: Brill, 2002), 121-22; Murphy, *Wealth in the Dead Sea Scrolls*, 191-92.

Honor your father with your poverty (כבד אביכה ברישכה) and your mother with your lowly status (במצעריכה). For as God is to a man, so is his father, and as the Lord is to a person, so is his mother, for they are the crucible (i.e., womb) that bore you. And as he gave them authority over you, and the inclination over the spirit, so serve them; and as he revealed to you through the mystery that is to be, honor them for the sake of your glory and with [reverence] honor them for the sake of your life and the length of your days.[164]

Filial piety is a commonplace in the sapiential tradition. A representative expression of this is Proverbs 23:22: "Listen to your father who begot you, and do not despise your mother when she is old."[165] That the addressee should honor his father with "poverty" is not found in the promotion of filial piety in the sapiential and covenantal traditions. The statement "For as God is to a man, so is his father, and as the Lord is to a person, so is his mother" provides a theological basis for filial piety. One should look at his parents as if they were God because they gave him

---

[164] There are several text-critical issues in this passage that deserve comment. One is the word כבד. 4Q416 2 iii 15 reads כבוד. This should be read as כבד, following the variant text of 4Q418 9 17. All critical editions agree on this. See *DJD 34*, 120; Elgvin, "An Analysis of 4QInstruction," 222; Jefferies, *Wisdom at Qumran*, 211. An imperative reads better than the noun "glory" or a passive participle.

The word מצעריכה of 4Q416 2 iii 16 could be read as מצעדיכה ("your steps"). *Dālet* and *rêš* are hard to distinguish in 4Q416. The variant text of 4Q418 9 17 appears to read מצעריכה ("your lowly status"), although the *rêš* of this word is not entirely certain. This is how Tigchelaar, *To Increase Learning*, 152, transcribes the text. In both texts *dālet* and *rêš* are materially possible, forcing the interpreter to decide between the two semantically. The editors of *DJD 34* prefer the "lowly status" reading. See *DJD 34*, 120. Harrington, *Wisdom Texts*, 44, translates the word as "low estate." Elgvin, "An Analysis of 4QInstruction," 230, prefers the "your steps" reading on the grounds that מצער is never attested in the plural. The במצעריכה option grants that this is an otherwise unattested occurrence of the word in the plural. This should not be considered impossible. The במצעריכה reading is favored because of the parallelism with ברישכה. It is also supported by 4Q417 2 i 10: כיא מה צעיר מרש, "for what is more lowly than a poor person!"

The phrase translated "as God" in 4Q416 2 iii 16 actually reads כאב, "as a father." This yields a phrase that literally reads "For as a father is to a man, so is his father, and as the Lord is to a person, so is his mother." 4Q418 9 17 has an important variant, reading כאל for כאב. The "God" reading avoids tautology and makes for good parallelism. The כאל reading is generally regarded as superior.

[165] See Prov 20:20; 23:25; 28:24; 29:15; 30:17; Sir 3:1-16. Note also the Egyptian *Instruction of Any* 7:17-18: "Double the food your mother gave you, support her as she supported you; she had a heavy load in you, but she did not abandon you." See Miriam Lichtheim, *Ancient Egyptian Literature* (3 vols.; Berkeley: University of California Press, 1973-80), 2.141.

life.[166] Proverbs 23:25 puts forward a similar perspective: "Let your father and mother be glad, let her who bore you rejoice."[167]

4Q416 2 iii 18-19 promises long life to those who practice filial piety: "with [reverence] honor them for the sake of your life and the length of your days (למען חייכה וארוך ימיכה)." Long life is a classic goal of the sapiential tradition.[168] Filial piety is also associated with long life in the covenantal tradition. 4QInstruction reformulates the fifth commandment.[169] The language of 4Q416 2 iii 18-19 is apparently influenced by the call to choose life in Deuteronomy 30:20.[170] Elgvin observes that Ben Sira, like 4QInstruction, connects filial piety to God and proclaims it will result in long life: "Those who respect their father will have long life, and those who honor their mother obey the Lord; they will serve their parents as their masters (ὡς δεσπόταις)" (3:6-7).[171] Kugel has suggested that both Ben Sira 3 and 4Q416 2 iii 18-19 attest an exegetical tradition based on an understanding of the Ten Commandments being written on two tablets.[172]

4QInstruction's encouragement of filial piety concludes with an admonition that capstones its instruction on this subject: "as he revealed to

---

[166] For the Second Temple tradition of construing God as a father, see Isa 63:16; 64:7; Sir 23:4; Tob 13:4; Wis 2:16. Cf. 4Q418 86 1 and 4Q423 7 3. See further Elgvin, "An Analysis of 4QInstruction," 142-43.

[167] Cf. Sir 7:27; Tob 10:12.

[168] A representative expression of this is Proverbs 3:1-2: "My child, do not forget my teaching, but let your heart keep my commandments; for length of days and years of life (ארך ימים ושנות חיים) and abundant welfare they will give you." See also, for example, 3:16, 22; 4:13, 22; 8:36; 10:16, 27; 14:27; 19:23; and Sir 4:12. Long life as a reward for obedience can also be found, for example, in Job 12:12; Pss 21:4; 91:5; and Bar 3:14.

[169] "Honor your father and your mother, so that your days may be long in the land that the Lord your God is giving you" (Exod 20:12; cf. Deut 5:16). See DJD 34, 122; Elgvin, "An Analysis of 4QInstruction," 231.

[170] "Choose life so that you and your descendants may live, loving the Lord your God, obeying him, and holding fast to him; for that means life to you and length of days (כי הוא חייך וארך ימיך) ..."

[171] Elgvin, "An Analysis of 4QInstruction," 230.

[172] See James L. Kugel, "Some Instances of Biblical Interpretation in the Hymns and Wisdom Writings of Qumran," in Studies in Ancient Midrash (ed. J.L. Kugel; Cambridge: Harvard University Center for Jewish Studies, 2001), 166-67. He argues that associating filial piety with God is an exegetical attempt to explain why the Ten Commandments, which do not include a large amount of text, are written on two tablets rather than one. It was rationalized that the first five deal with affairs between humans and God, whereas the second five were only concerned with conduct among humans. Thus each division is written on its own tablet. If one posits such a distinction, the fifth commandment to honor one's parents becomes a difficulty. Hence there would have been an incentive to associate filial piety with God, even though it is solely an act between humans. Philo presents filial piety in this way in On the Decalogue 106-07. It cannot be proven, but Kugel may be correct that Ben Sira and 4QInstruction attest a similar exegetical tradition regarding the Decalogue.

you through the mystery that is to be, honor them for the sake of your glory ..." (4Q416 2 iii 17-18). This is a good example of 4QInstruction grounding practical wisdom in an appeal to revelation.[173] Filial piety should be practiced because it will provide long life. Knowledge of the mystery that is to be helps one attain this goal.

4QInstruction also employs the mystery that is to be in its instruction on marriage. 4Q416 2 iii 20-21 reads: "you have married a woman in your poverty, get [her] birth-times ([ה]ׄמׄולדיׄ) ... from the mystery that is to be when you associate yourself together (with her)" (cf. 4Q416 2 iv 1-13).[174] Although the fragmentary nature of this text makes interpretation difficult, the addressee is told to marry while keeping the mystery that is to be in mind. Like biblical wisdom, 4QInstruction provides advice that enables the addressee to have a successful marriage (e.g., Prov 18:22; 19:14; 31:10; Qoh 9:9). In 4QInstruction this requires knowledge of the mystery that is to be.

The mystery that is to be is also associated with raising a successful harvest. Knowledge of the mystery of divine dominion results in living a life in accordance with it, producing worldly success. 4Q418 103 ii assumes the addressee is a farmer.[175] 4Q423 5 5 calls the addressee a farmer (lit. "man of the soil"), possibly alluding to Noah.[176] 4Q423 3 2 is a fragmentary passage that connects the mystery that is to be to a successful harvest: "... [through the mystery] that is to be. Thus you will walk, and al[l your] c[rops will multiply]." "Walking" (הלך) signifies conduct elsewhere in 4QInstruction.[177] A connection between the raising of crops and the mystery that is to be is also made in 1Q26 1 4-6 (cf. 4Q423 4 1-2), which reads in part: "... As he revealed to your ear through the mystery that is to [be] ... Take care lest she honor you more than him ... and (lest) you be cursed in all your crops, and be [asha]med for all your deeds ..."[178] The meaning of this line is obscure. If the ad-

---

[173] The phrase "for the sake of your glory" is a rationale for filial piety that is similar to Ben Sira 3:11: "The glory of one's father is one's own glory (כבוד איש כבוד אביו)."

[174] Strugnell and Harrington translate [ה]ׄמׄולדיׄ as her "offspring." See *DJD 34*, 113. However, in light of the use of the phrase מולדי ישע in 4Q417 2 i 10-12 and similar terms in the Book of Mysteries and 4Q186 (see section 2.4 of Chapter 5), it is better to suggest, with Elgvin, that מולדי[ה] refers to the wife's time of birth. If elect status were understood as to some extent determined by the time of birth, this would suggest that one should marry a person who also has elect status. See his "An Analysis of 4QInstruction," 231.

[175] See section 3.2 of Chapter 4.

[176] See Gen 9:20; *DJD 34*, 521.

[177] 4Q417 1 i 10; 4Q417 2 i 8; 4Q418 81 6, 14; and 4Q418 126 ii 11. See also Elgvin, "Wisdom and Apocalypticism," 236.

[178] *DJD 34*, 536. Tigchelaar, *To Increase Learning*, 146, has proposed that 4Q418 244 2 be joined to the beginning of 1Q26 1 6. Before the phrase "and (lest) you be cursed (ונארותה)" there is a *he* which, according to Tigchelaar, is the last letter of the phrase

dressee is considered a farmer, this text may be in reference to his wife. If this interpretation is correct, the fragment warns him to make sure that his wife understands, under threat of crop failure, that agricultural success is to be attributed to God rather than the labor of her husband.[179] This knowledge is available through the mystery that is to be. 4Q423 5 5-6 urges the addressee to "observe the appointed times of the summer, gather your crops in their time, and the season [of harvest in its appointed time]."[180] This advice is not combined with the mystery that is to be directly, although it has been safely reconstructed in 4Q423 5 2.[181] This fragment also associates raising crops with the knowledge of good and evil: "[Un]derstand all your crops. In your labor pay attentio[n to the knowledge of] good and evil" (l. 6). Since the knowledge of good and evil is related to the divine framework guiding events, this wisdom is, like the mystery that is to be, associated with the addressee's agricultural work. Having a successful harvest is portrayed as a result of understanding the regular functioning of the natural world. Proverbs also provides instruction for people in an agricultural setting, and, like 4Q423 5 5-6, uses the regular functioning of nature as a basis for instruction.[182] The agricultural teaching in 4QInstruction may reflect an awareness of traditional wisdom on the subject. But its interest in the larger macrocosm in relation to the addressee's ordinary life is closer to *1 Enoch* 2-5 than the agricultural wisdom of Proverbs.[183]

The addressee's daily life should also include constant praise of the divine. As with Ben Sira, in 4QInstruction praise is a natural response to the acknowledgement of God's grandeur.[184] Although the call to praise is never directly connected to the mystery that is to be, the addressee is encouraged to praise God because of his splendor and might which he learns about through the mystery that is to be. 4Q416 2 iii 11 reads

---

בעבורתכה from 4Q418 244 2. This is possible but cannot be confirmed. If granted, this join does not significantly change the sense of the passage.

[179] *DJD 34*, 517.

[180] See also 4Q418 123 ii 6, שקול מעשיכה עם קצ[ים, "Weigh your deeds with the tim[es." Cf. 1QS 8:4.

[181] The end of 4Q423 5 1 reads ואשר גלה אוזנכה, "And as he opened your ear ..." This phrase occurs in 4QInstruction with the mystery that is to be (e.g., 4Q418 123 ii 4; 4Q418 190 2); it is safe to assume that this is also the case with 4Q423 5. The mystery that is to be can be read as the first phrase of line 2.

[182] See, for example: "Like snow in summer or rain in harvest, so honor is not fitting for a fool" (26:1). See also 12:10; 14:4; 25:14; 27:23-27; Clifford, *Proverbs*, 131, 143.

[183] R. Argall has written that the authors of *1 Enoch* 2-5 "regard observable reality as a kind of cosmic parable and exhort their readers to draw the appropriate lesson." See his *1 Enoch and Sirach*, 101. See also Nickelsburg, *1 Enoch*, 150-64; L. Hartman, *Asking for a Meaning: A Study of 1 Enoch 1-5* (Lund: Gleerup, 1979).

[184] See, for example, Sir 17:10; 39:15; and 43:30.

"Praise his name constantly (שמו הלל תמיד)." 4Q417 1 ii 9 also encourages divine praise.[185]

Along with practical instruction on specific topics, 4QInstruction also provides general ethical principles that shape conduct. For example, the knowledge of truth and iniquity is emphasized in 4Q416 2 iii 14-15: "Examine the mystery that is to be, have understanding in all the ways of truth (כל דרכי אמת), and perceive all the roots of iniquity (כל שורשי עולה)."[186] The column continues with another set of opposing terms that describe what the addressee should learn: "then you will know what is bitter for a man and what is sweet for a person (מה מר לאיש ומה מתוק לגבר)" (l. 15).[187] The word pair "bitter" and "sweet" occurs in the Hebrew Bible. Isaiah 5:20 reads: "Ah, you who call evil good and good evil, who put darkness for light and light for darkness, who put bitter for sweet and sweet for bitter (מר למתוק ומתוק למר)!"[188] Isaiah presents "bitter" and "sweet" as a polarity analogous to good and evil. This suggests that the phrase in 4Q416 2 iii 15 should be read the same way.

The addressee's ability to choose good and avoid evil is not presented as a fait accompli. He is in control of his own ethical conduct and the author of 4QInstruction wants him to handle this appropriately. Nevertheless, the knowledge of good and evil is related to the addressee's elect status, since he learns it through the mystery that is to be (4Q417 1 i 6-8). His acquisition of the knowledge of good and evil is a sign that he has fulfilled the role that God has established for him. In 4QInstruction the modern categories of free will and determinism are not fully distinct. Although living ethically is the responsibility of the addressee, 4QInstruction's ethical dualism is an aspect of its deterministic mindset.

The ethical dualism of 4QInstruction has some similarities with that of the Treatise of the Two Spirits. The Treatise uses the term "ways of truth": "Deeds of injustice are an abhorrence to truth and all the ways of truth (דרכי אמת) are an abhorrence to injustice (תועבת עולה)" (4:17; cf. 4:2; 1QH 5:9; 1 En. 104:13).[189] As in 4Q416 2 iii 14, the "ways of truth" are presented as the polar opposite of עולה. In the Treatise the two opposing forces of light and darkness, which represent good and evil, are engaged in an eternal struggle that is played out in the human psyche.

---

[185] This topic is discussed further in section 2.4.3 of Chapter 3.

[186] The addressee is associated with "truth" elsewhere in 4QInstruction. In 4Q418 55 6 God gives an allotment to "the inheritors of truth" (נוחלי אמת). 4Q418 69 ii 10 encourages the "truly chosen ones" (בחירי אמת) not to tire of study (cf. 1QS 4:6).

[187] Note the parallel in Ahiqar 148: "Do not be too sweet lest you be [swallowed]; do not be too bitter [lest you be spat out]."

[188] The pair is also found in Proverbs 27:7: "The sated appetite spurns honey, but to a ravenous appetite even the bitter is sweet (ונפש רעבה כל־מר מתוק)." Cf. Exod 15:23-25.

[189] Tigchelaar, To Increase Learning, 198.

4QInstruction, by contrast, shows no interest in a mythological struggle between good and evil. It emphasizes instead that the addressee should know the difference between the two. Despite their differences, both texts present knowledge of good and evil in relation to a larger deterministic framework (1QS 4:25-26).[190] The imagery of light and darkness is absent in 4QInstruction, whereas it is central to the dualism of the Treatise. Since the wisdom text was well known at Qumran, it is possible that it was a source for the Treatise, whose author developed a form of dualism that was more absolute than that of 4QInstruction.[191]

5. CONCLUSION

4QInstruction presents its teachings as "mysteries." They are often connected to the mystery that is to be. God created the world with the mystery that is to be. This was a mighty act that displays his power and explains the dominion that he exerts over the natural order. Acquiring wisdom entails learning the divine plan that orchestrates reality. By combining teachings on various topics with the mystery that is to be, 4QInstruction urges the addressee to comprehend the deterministic framework of creation in a way that shapes his conduct. Unlike traditional wisdom, in 4QInstruction the divine plan is a hidden truth. 4QInstruction purports, like Daniel and *1 Enoch*, to disclose heavenly wisdom that would not be otherwise available. The epistemology of 4QInstruction and that of the Book of Proverbs are quite different. Yet despite differences in worldview, the form and content of many of 4QInstruction's teachings are similar to the traditional wisdom preserved in Proverbs. 4QInstruction encourages the addressee to live his ordinary life in a way that befits the knowledge that has been revealed to him.

---

[190] Lange has used the similarities between the two works to claim that they stem from a common milieu. See *Weisheit und Prädestination*, 168-70.

[191] Tigchelaar, *To Increase Learning*, 200-03, has argued that part of the Treatise reflects familiarity with 4QInstruction.

CHAPTER THREE

THE "SPIRITUAL PEOPLE" AND THE "FLESHLY SPIRIT":
THE INSTRUCTION OF 4Q417 1 i 13-18

1. INTRODUCTION

4Q417 1 i 13-18 is comprised of several enigmatic details.[1] One of the
most intriguing is a reference to the "vision of Hagu" (חזון ההגוי).[2]
While Daniel and *1 Enoch* provide explicit accounts of visions unfolding
to seers, 4QInstruction offers little information about this vision. 4Q417
1 i 13-18 is the only passage of the composition that attests the vision of
Hagu. It is associated with a "book of remembrance"—a heavenly book
in which is inscribed the judgment of the "sons of Sheth." The "spiritual
people" are given the vision of Hagu and the "fleshly spirit" is not. It is
also given to אנוש, a term that is open to several interpretations—
humankind, Enosh, or Adam. The vision of Hagu is made available to

---

[1] This passage has been a focal point of 4QInstruction scholarship. See, for example,
DJD 34, 162-66; Torleif Elgvin, "An Analysis of 4QInstruction" (diss.; Hebrew Univer-
sity of Jerusalem, 1997), 85-94; idem, "The Mystery to Come: Early Essene Theology of
Revelation," in *Qumran between the Old and New Testaments* (ed. F.H. Cryer and T.L.
Thompson; JSOTSup 290; Sheffield: Sheffield Academic Press, 1998), 139-47; Armin
Lange, *Weisheit und Prädestination: Weisheitliche Urordnung und Prädestination in den
Textfunden von Qumran* (STDJ 18; Leiden: Brill, 1995), 80-90; Daniel J. Harrington,
Wisdom Texts from Qumran (London: Routledge, 1996), 55-56; John J. Collins, "In the
Likeness of the Holy Ones: The Creation of Humankind in a Wisdom Text from Qumran,"
in *The Provo International Conference on the Dead Sea Scrolls* (ed. D.W. Parry and E.
Ulrich; STDJ 30; Leiden: Brill, 1999), 609-19; André Caquot, "Les textes de sagesse de
Qoumrân (Aperçu préliminaire)," *Revue d'histoire et de philosophie religieuses* 76
(1996), 17-19; Crispin H.T. Fletcher-Louis, *All the Glory of Adam: Liturgical Anthropology in the Dead Sea Scrolls* (STDJ 42; Leiden: Brill, 2002), 113-18; Stefan Beyerle,
"Und dann werden die Zeichen der Wahrheit erscheinen ..." (Habilitationsschrift;
Rheinischen Friedrich-Wilhelms-Universität, 2001), 531-33; Jörg Frey, "Flesh and Spirit
in the Palestinian Jewish Sapiential Tradition and in the Qumran Texts: An Inquiry into
the Background of Pauline Usage," in *The Wisdom Texts from Qumran and the Development of Sapiential Thought* (ed. C. Hempel, A. Lange, and H. Lichtenberger; BETL 159;
Leuven: Leuven University Press/Peeters, 2002), 392-97.

[2] This study uses the spelling "Hagu." Scholars also use "Hagi" or "Hago." See
Elgvin, "An Analysis of 4QInstruction," 92. The different spellings have no impact on the
interpretation of the text.

the "spiritual people" because they were created "according to the likeness of the holy ones" (כתבנית קדושים) (4Q417 1 i 17). 4Q417 1 i 17-18
claims that the "fleshly spirit" does not possess the knowledge of good or
evil. This suggests that the author had Genesis 2-3 in mind. The statement that אנוש is fashioned in likeness of the holy ones can be read as an
allusion to Genesis 1, in which Adam is created in the image of God.

There have been several efforts to understand the vision of Hagu. The
editors of *DJD 34* argue that it refers to a theurgic act that provides access to the book of remembrance. Their translation of 4Q417 1 i 16
reads: "And that is the appearance/vision of the meditation on a book of
memorial."[3] This interpretation is possible but 4QInstruction provides no
information about any praxis associated with the vision. One can only
speculate on this point. Elgvin argues that the vision of Hagu "is an
apocalyptic, visionary book which reveals salvation history from creation
to the last days."[4] He understands the vision of Hagu to be similar to the
mystery that is to be. Elgvin also suggests that the vision could be a
reference to an Enochic text, such as the *Apocalypse of Weeks* or the
Animal Apocalypse, since both are portrayed as visions. But in
4QInstruction the vision of Hagu is never treated as an actual document.
Lange associates the vision of Hagu with a heavenly book that contains
the "Ordnung von Sein und Welt" that is at the core of his understanding
of the mystery that is to be.[5] The vision of Hagu is also for him a heavenly version of the Torah, a view that is based on his understanding of
the phrase "engraved is the statute" of 4Q417 1 i 14.[6] As reviewed in the
previous chapter, the Torah is not a major theme of 4QInstruction. This
suggests that the vision of Hagu should not be understood as a type of
heavenly template for the Torah. Lange and Elgvin, like others, understand the vision of Hagu as a form of revelation that is broadly compatible with the mystery that is to be.[7] 4QInstruction itself provides relatively few details about the content of this vision. It offers information

---

[3] *DJD 34*, 155.

[4] Elgvin, "An Analysis of 4QInstruction," 94.

[5] Lange, *Weisheit und Prädestination*, 62.

[6] Ibid., 85.

[7] Elgvin, "An Analysis of 4QInstruction," 93; Lange, *Weisheit und Prädestination*, 83;
John J. Collins, *Jewish Wisdom in the Hellenistic Age* (OTL; Louisville: Westminster
John Knox, 1997), 123. Cana Werman has argued that the vision of Hagu refers to the act
of the addressee meditating on his life and history. She minimizes its association with
supernatural revelation. It is important, however, to acknowledge that the vision of Hagu,
like the mystery that to be, refers to the revelation of heavenly wisdom. See her "What is
the Book of Hagu?" in *Sapiential Perspectives: Wisdom Literature in Light of the Dead
Sea Scrolls. Proceedings of the Sixth International Symposium of the Orion Center, 20-
22 May 2001* (ed. G. Sterling and J.J. Collins; Leiden: Brill, forthcoming).

about who possesses it and who does not—the "spiritual people" and the "fleshly spirit," respectively. Access to the vision of Hagu is an important feature of 4Q417 1 i 13-18 that warrants fuller investigation.

Knowing the difference between the "spiritual people" and the "fleshly spirit" is an important lesson for the addressee of 4QInstruction. He is to identify with the "spiritual people." He has access to revelation in the form of the mystery that is to be, just as the "spiritual people" are given revelation through the vision of Hagu. He is distinguished from the "fleshly spirit," as are the "spiritual people" (4Q418 81 1-2). The addressee is urged to be moral and acquire wisdom. The author of 4QInstruction acknowledges that he might not act in the way. He is warned of the evil inclination, implying that he could turn to a life of wickedness (4Q417 1 ii 12; cf. 4Q423 9 3). 4QInstruction puts forward two very different ways of being human. The "fleshly spirit" represents a way of living that is to be avoided, while the "spiritual people" signify an ideal to which the addressee is to aspire.

In this chapter I will explicate the pericope which discusses the vision of Hagu, 4Q417 1 i 13-18. I will argue that this vision refers to a type of revelation that teaches the addressee that there are two contrasting types of humankind. I will also contend that 4QInstruction's interpretation of Genesis 1-3 is important for its understanding of humanity. To examine these themes 4Q418 81 and 4Q423 1 require consideration. I will also compare 4QInstruction with other Second Temple instructional texts— Ben Sira, the Treatise on the Two Spirits, and the writings of Philo—that draw on Genesis 1-3.

Before proceeding with these tasks, there is one other point that demands attention. While the vision of Hagu is unattested elsewhere in Second Temple literature, scholarship has long been aware of a "Book of Hagu."[8] This book is mentioned in the Damascus Document and the

---

[8] This book has received a large amount of scholarly attention. Louis Ginzberg understood it as a kind of sectarian Mishnah and took the Book of Hagu to mean literally "the book of interpretations." See his *An Unknown Jewish Sect* (New York: Ktav, 1976), 50. This book was originally published as *Eine unbekannte jüdische Sekte* (New York: privately published, 1922). I. Rabinowitz identified the Book of Hagu as the books of the Torah regarded as holy by the Qumran sect. See his "The Qumran Author's *spr hhgw/y*," *Journal of Near Eastern Studies* 20 (1961): 109-14. A. Dupont-Sommer identified the Book of Hagu as the Community Rule. See his *The Essene Writings from Qumran* (trans. G. Vermes; Cleveland: Meridian, 1962), 70. Yigael Yadin argued that the Book of Hagu was a reference to the Temple Scroll. See his *The Temple Scroll* (New York: Random House, 1985), 226. See also Elgvin, "An Analysis of 4QInstruction," 93, note 131; Devora Steinmetz, "Sefer HeHago: The Community and the Book," *Journal of Jewish Studies* 52 (2001): 40-58. Steinmetz suggests that the term "Hagu" is derived from Proverbs 25:4-5. Werman, "What is the Book of Hagu?" has argued that this book, like the vision of Hagu, contains "meditations on creation and history."

Rule of the Congregation (1QSa). In CD 10:6 the judges of the congregation are required to learn the Book of Hagu and the "principles of the covenant." Similarly, 1QSa 1:6-7 asserts that group members are to be trained in the Book of Hagu and "the statutes of the covenant."[9] CD 13:2-3 stipulates that only a priest trained in the Book of Hagu can be a leader in the "camps." CD 14:6-8, in similar fashion, declares that a priest must be trained in Hagu to be a leader of the "Many."[10] The Book of Hagu is associated with the education of group members by priestly leaders. Since both a "covenant" and the Book of Hagu are mentioned in 1QSa 1:7 and CD 10:6, they might refer, respectively, to the Torah and a parallel but distinct revelatory tradition. Elgvin understands the "covenant" not as the Torah but the halakhah of the community.[11]

The content of the Book of Hagu remains enigmatic, like the vision of Hagu. This prevents a confident assessment of the relationship between them. However, it is reasonable to speculate that the vision of Hagu of 4QInstruction has some connection to the Qumran sect's Book of Hagu. Given 4QInstruction's pedagogical ethos, it is significant that this book is a requirement for sect leaders who provide instruction. The vision of Hagu, which is associated with the book of remembrance, may have inspired the title of the Book of Hagu.[12] The main difference between the two is that the Book of Hagu is discussed as if it were an actual document, whereas this is never the case for the vision of Hagu.

2. THE VISION OF HAGU PERICOPE

The vision of Hagu pericope, 4Q417 1 i 13-18, reads as follows:

[9] In an opinion similar to Rabinowitz, L.H. Schiffman argues that the Book of Hagu should be understood as a reference to the Torah. See his *The Eschatological Community of the Dead Sea Scrolls: A Study of the Rule of the Congregation* (SBLMS 38; Atlanta: Scholars Press, 1989), 15.

[10] Elgvin has argued that the Book of Hagu is mentioned in the Cave 11 manuscript of the War Scroll. He reconstructs 11Q14 2 1 as reading "the command]ments of Haguy, the discer[ning ones (?)." See "An Analysis of 4QInstruction," 94. His reconstruction of this text is not endorsed in its official edition. In this version the Hebrew of the line is reconstructed, on the basis of Ben Sira 50:26, as מ[שי הגוי הנב]ל, which is translated "of the stup[id] nation." See Florentino García Martínez et al., *Qumran Cave 11.II (11Q2-18, 11Q20-31)* (DJD 23; Oxford: Clarendon, 1998), 249-50. See also 1QH 19:2, 21-22. Rabinowitz, "The Qumran Author's *spr hhgw/y*," 109, has speculated that this column may contain a reference to the Book of Hagu.

[11] "An Analysis of 4QInstruction," 94.

[12] Elgvin, "An Analysis of 4QInstruction," 93, argues that the Book of Hagu "is a strong indication of some kind of sectarian provenance for 4QInstruction." This topic is addressed in section 2 of Chapter 6.

ואתה 13

מבין ריש פעלתכה בזכרון הע[ו]ז כי]בא חֹרֹוֹת ֿחוק{כה} וֿחקוק כֹול 14
הפקֹודֹה

כי חרות מחוקק לאל על כול ע[וֹלות] בני שֿיֿח וספר זכרון כתוב לפניו 15

לשמרי דברו והוֹאה חזון ההגֹוֹי לֿספר זכרון וינחילנֹוֹ לאנוש עם ֿֿֿרוח 16
כֹ[י]א

כתבנית קדושים יצרו ועוד לוא נתן הגֹוֹי לרוח בשר כי לא ידע בין 17

[טו]ֹב לרע כמשפט [ר]וֿחֹוֹ *vacat* 18

13. And you,

14. understanding one, inherit your reward by remembering the mi[ght because] it is coming. Engraved is the statute, and ordained is all the punishment,

15. because engraved is that which has been ordained by God against all the in[iquities of] the sons of Sheth. The book of remembrance is written before him

16. for those who keep his word—that is, the vision of Hagu for the book of remembrance. He bequeathed it to אנוש together with a spiritual people, be[cau]se

17. he fashioned him according to the likeness of the holy ones. Moreover, he did not give Hagu to the fleshly spirit because it did not distinguish between

18. [go]od and evil according to the judgment of its [sp]irit.

2.1 Text-Critical Issues in the Vision of Hagu Pericope

Several portions of this text are difficult to reconstruct. Before interpretation of this pericope can proceed, there are several instances where it is necessary to explain my transcription and translation.

L.14 ריֿש. This word can also be transcribed as רֹוֹש. Lange reads the word as ריֿש, translating it as "Armselig."[13] Elgvin transcribes רֹוֹש and understands the word as equivalent to ראֿש. He thus translates מבין רֹוֹש פעלתכה as "understand the origin of your own doing."[14] This translation does not understand the word מבין in the vocative sense, although this is normally how it is used in 4QInstruction. Strugnell and Harrington tran-

---

[13] *Weisheit und Prädestination*, 51.

[14] "An Analysis of 4QInstruction," 256. He has elsewhere argued for the "poverty" reading advocated by Lange. See Elgvin, "The Mystery to Come," 140.

scribe the word as רוֹשׁ, understanding it as the imperative of "inherit."[15]
In biblical Hebrew רֵשׁ or רְשׁ is expected for I-*yôd* imperatives. The word
in question could be read with a *yôd*, in which case it would be a *plene*
spelling, רִישׁ. Whether the word has a *yôd* or a *wāw*, reading it as an
imperative of "inherit" makes sense. The "inherit" reading accords with
4QInstruction's interest in explaining to the addressee his "inheritance"
(נחלה).[16] Reading רוֹשׁ as an imperative is also supported by the fact that
the vocative "O understanding one" is often followed by an admonition
in 4QInstruction.

L.14 הֹעַ[ו]ז. Nobody agrees on how to reconstruct the traces after בזכרון.
Strugnell and Harrington reconstruct the word in question as הֹשׁ[לום.[17]
They grant that an *'ayin*, instead of a *śin*, is possible.[18] They translate the
relevant phrase as: "Remembering the re[quital for] it comes." The transcription השלום is supported by the fact that the line refers to the final
judgment, which the addressee is encouraged to keep in mind.[19]   However, this reconstruction is not likely. According to PAM 41.942, *'ayin*
rather than *śin* seems to be the preferable reading, although this is not
entirely certain. Tigchelaar reads the disputed letter in this way but does
not attempt to reconstruct the word.[20] Elgvin reads the traces after בזכרון
as הֹעַ[ט, "stylus."[21] To support this reading, he understands the word בא
of line 14 as a scribal error for בו. His translation reads: "And you understand the origin of your own doing when you remember the st[ylus.
For] with it was the decree engraved ..." The "stylus" reading fits nicely
with the phrase "engraved is the decree" of the following stich.   1QH
9:23-24 provides support for this reconstruction: "Everything has been
engraved before you with the stylus of remembrance (בחרת זכרון)."[22]

---

[15] *DJD 34*, 161-62. This is also how D. Jefferies translates the term. See his *Wisdom at Qumran: A Form-Critical Analysis of the Admonitions in 4QInstruction* (Gorgias Dissertations, Near Eastern Studies 3; Piscataway: Gorgias Press, 2002), 266, 271.
[16] See section 4.3 of Chapter 2.
[17] *DJD 34*, 162.
[18] Ibid., 154.
[19] See section 2.7 of Chapter 5.
[20] *To Increase Learning*, 52.
[21] "An Analysis of 4QInstruction," 256.
[22] There is a tradition of mentioning a writing utensil to emphasize that a decree has been ordained. For example, Jer 17:1 reads: "The sin of Judah is written with an iron pen (בעט ברזל); with a diamond point it is engraved (חרושה) on the tablet of their hearts" (cf. Isa 30:8). In 1QM 12:3 God is praised for having written "the covenant of your peace" that is "engraved (חרתה) for them with the chisel of life (בחרט חיים)." A "gold stylus" (חרט זהב) is found in a fragmentary passage in 4Q382 (4Qpap paraKings et al.) 25 4. See Harold Attridge et al., *Qumran Cave 4.VIII: Parabiblical Texts, Part 1* (DJD 13; Oxford: Claren-don, 1994), 376. While not in the context of a decree from God, Job wishes that his plight

However, if one understands רִישׁ as the imperative of "inherit," it is not clear what it would mean to "inherit your doing when you remember the stylus." In an earlier publication, Elgvin did not reconstruct הֵ]עֹט but הֵ]עֵת, "time."[23] The word הֵעֵת is excluded by the fact that it is a feminine noun, while the following phrase, כי בא, requires a masculine subject. (This also excludes reading פעלתכה as the subject of this phrase.) None of the available reconstructions of this phrase is to be favored.

I tentatively propose the reconstruction בזכרון הֵ]עֹוז. The narrow letters *wāw* and *zayin* would fit the lacuna physically. This supplement is also supported by Strugnell and Harrington's reconstruction of the phrase בכבוד עֹ]וזו in line 13. According to this line, the addressee will understand the glory of God's might if he heeds the call to acquire knowledge. The importance of knowing God's strength is also emphasized by the phrase גבורות מעשיו (cf. 1QS 1:21). Following this thought, it is likely that in line 14 he is exhorted to inherit his reward by remembering the power of God. Line 14 seems to offer additional encouragement to the addressee to perceive God's might and dominion. Although the exact transcription of the word understood here as העוז is disputed, it clearly relates to the theme of judgment.

L.15 [ע]ולות. There is no real dispute about this word, although there is some confusion. The word is damaged from ink erosion. Only the *'ayin* is visible. Strugnell and Harrington do not provide a reconstruction of this word in their transcription of 4Q417 1 i.[24] But they include the phrase "ini[quities of]" in their translation of line 15. In their comments on this line they grant that the word could be reconstructed as עוונות.[25] Elgvin reconstructs [ע]ולת, which is semantically equivalent to the reconstruction in *DJD 34*.[26] Lange similarly proposes [ע]ולות.[27] Lange's reading is adopted here. There is no major difference in any of the reconstructions scholars have provided. Since the word beginning with *'ayin* precedes the "sons of Sheth" who are to be judged, it is reasonable to

---

would be remembered forever: "O that my words were written down! O that they were inscribed in a book! O that with an iron pen and with lead they were engraved (יחצבון) on a rock forever!" (19:23-24).

[23] See his "The Mystery to Come," 140. There the translation is given as "And you, understand the poverty of your deed when you remember the ti[me. For] the engraved law has come." This is similar to the reconstruction of Lange, *Weisheit und Prädestination*, 51.

[24] *DJD 34*, 151.

[25] Ibid., 163.

[26] "An Analysis of 4QInstruction," 257.

[27] *Weisheit und Prädestination*, 51.

posit that the word has a negative valence, as all the available options do.[28]

L.16 לֵספֶר זכרון. The main issue regarding this phrase involves the *lāmed* preceding ספר. Disputing the presence of this letter impacts how the vision of Hagu should be understood vis-à-vis the book of remembrance. The *lāmed* is given in *DJD 34* as possible but not certain.[29] Elgvin transcribes a *wāw* before ספר. This produces the reading "It is the Vision of Hagi and a book of memory."[30] Tigchelaar disputes the presence of traces of a *lāmed*, transcribing simply ספר.[31] Tigchelaar grants, however, that "the area above the ceiling-line is indeed darker than average." To my eye this dark "area," according to Plate VIII in *DJD 34*, seems to be the upper stroke of a *lāmed*. Also the gap between ספר and the preceding word ההגוֹי is too large to be only the expected lacuna between words. This suggests that ספר is preceded by a letter, the traces of which appear to be visible. I use the reading in *DJD 34* because the upper stroke of a *lāmed* appears to be visible in PAM 41.942.

L.16 יָנחילֶנוֹ. The proper transcription of יָנחילנו is disputed. Several commentators favor יָנחילה.[32] The problem with this reading is that both possible antecedents for the suffix of this verb, ספר and חזון, are masculine nouns. Strugnell and Harrington argue that this was the original reading, but that a second hand changed it to יָנחילֶנוֹ, putting the verb into the plural while giving it a masculine suffix.[33] While the motivation to change the suffix from feminine to masculine is clear, the editors of *DJD 34* grant that if the verb is understood as plural its subject is unclear. It is possible that the *wāw* they understand as a plural marker was intended to mark the *segōl* of the third person masculine singular suffix for an imperfect (נּוּ-) in Tiberian Hebrew.[34] In the translation of *DJD 34* the verb is tentatively given in the singular, indicating that the plural

---

[28] Tigchelaar, *To Increase Learning*, 52, does not provide any reconstruction of]ע. Jefferies, *Wisdom at Qumran*, 266, leaves the entire word blank.

[29] *DJD 34*, 151.

[30] Elgvin, "An Analysis of 4QInstruction," 258; idem, "The Mystery to Come," 140.

[31] *To Increase Learning*, 54. Lange, *Weisheit und Prädestination*, 51, also transcribes ספר without a *lāmed*.

[32] See Elgvin, "An Analysis of 4QInstruction," 256; Lange, *Weisheit und Prädestination*, 51; Jefferies, *Wisdom at Qumran*, 266; Beyerle, "Und dann werden die Zeichen der Wahrheit erscheinen …," 533.

[33] *DJD 34*, 163.

[34] This seems to be the case, for example, with the word פוחי in 1QSa 1:19. See also Elisha Qimron, *The Hebrew of the Dead Sea Scrolls* (HSS 29; Atlanta: Scholars Press, 1986), 17.

transcription is a problem. Tigchelaar understands the word as יַנחילֻנֹו.[35]
I prefer his transcription. Common sense demands a singular verb (with
God as the antecedent; "he bequeathed it") and a singular masculine
suffix, referring to the vision of Hagu that is equated with the book of
remembrance. Tigchelaar acknowledges, however, that the letter he
understands as a *nûn* does not include the base-stroke that one would
expect for this letter.[36] This is admittedly a problem. There is no option
regarding the transcription of this word that is entirely free of problems.
This situation is likely a consequence of the scribal reworking of the line,
as suggested by Strugnell and Harrington.

2.2 The Inevitability of Judgment against the Wicked

The first item of the vision of Hagu pericope that requires interpretation
is its characterization of judgment. 4Q417 1 i 13-15 proclaims the inevitability of judgment against the wicked. The phrase "by remembering
the mi[ght because] it is coming" is parallel to the rhetoric of judgment
following it: "Engraved is the statute (חָרוֹת החוק), and ordained is all the
punishment."[37] The phrase חָרוֹת החוק has been understood as an allusion
to the Mosaic tablets of the Torah on the basis of Exodus 32:16: "The
tablets were the work of God, and the writing was the writing of God,
engraved upon the tablets (חרות על־הלחת)."[38] Lange understands the
phrase חָרוֹת החוק as a reference to the Sinai event.[39] This forms part of
his argument that the vision of Hagu is a heavenly version of the Torah.
Similar phrases, such as חוק חרות, however, are used elsewhere in the
Dead Sea Scrolls without relation to the Torah.[40] Even if one were to
grant a connection to Exodus 32, the view of Lange cannot be supported.
In 4QInstruction the Torah is not praised or thematized in the manner of
Ben Sira or Baruch.[41] If there is a reference to Exodus 32, it is used to
assert that punishment is ordained to come. Judgment is not invoked to
remind one of the importance of Torah. Rather the Torah is invoked to
remind one of the importance of judgment. The ordained punishment of

---

[35] *To Increase Learning*, 52.

[36] Ibid., 54.

[37] At one point a copyist deleted a second person suffix from the word חוק. See *DJD 34*, 162.

[38] *DJD 34*, 162; Elgvin, "An Analysis of 4QInstruction," 263.

[39] *Weisheit und Prädestination*, 83.

[40] The phrase חוק חרות, for example, occurs in 1QS 10:1, 6, and 8 as a way to describe the harmony of the created order and the subsequent regularity with which the speaker will give divine praise (cf. 4Q511 63-64 ii 3). In 1QS 10:11 the phrase is used to describe the speaker's awareness of his sin. Cf. 4Q400 1 i 5; 1QH 9:24; 4Q180 1 3.

[41] See section 4.4 of Chapter 2.

the wicked is also emphasized by the phrase "because engraved is that which has been ordained by God (כי חרות מחוקק לאל)" in line 15. The "statute" that is engraved is the judgment God has written against the wicked, as God writes out a decree against the Amalekites in Exodus 17:14.[42] Judgment is understood as written down in heaven as a way to emphasize its inevitability.

Elgvin interprets the phrase "engraved is the statute" as a reference to the vision of Hagu, which is understood to be written on heavenly tablets. The vision "deals with God's preordination of cosmic history and the ways of men."[43] Given the prominence of the vision in 4Q417 1 i, it is likely that the "statute" that is engraved is a reference to the vision of Hagu. But it can also be understood as a reference to the Torah, as previously discussed.[44] The phrase is ambiguous, but Elgvin's reading is more likely. The vision of Hagu clearly signifies a divine plan that is revealed to the "spiritual people."[45] In 4QInstruction an overarching divine framework is normally associated with the mystery that is to be. In this regard the vision of Hagu is similar to the mystery that is to be. 4Q417 1 i 13-15 emphasizes that the judgment of the wicked is an ordained feature of the divine plan. This is emphasized by the word "statute" whether one understands it as an allusion to the Torah or the vision of Hagu.

4Q417 1 i 14-15 calls a group that is destined to be punished the "sons of Sheth" (בני שית). The interpretation of this phrase is a matter of debate. It has been read as a reference to the patriarch Seth. It can also be understood as an allusion to Numbers 24:17. Lange argues that the prediluvian patriarch is intended.[46] He considers the בני שית a reference to the myth of the fall of the angels and the first wicked generation,

---

[42] Note the parallel in the Book of Giants: "And behold, [book]s were opened and judgment was spoken; and the judgment of [the Great One] was [wr]itten [in a book] and sealed in an inscription ... for every living being and (all) flesh" (4Q530 2 18-19). This translation is from Loren T. Stuckenbruck, *The Book of Giants from Qumran* (TSAJ 63; Tübingen: Mohr-Siebeck, 1997), 120. See also Émile Puech, *Qumrân Grotte 4.XXII: Textes Araméens, Première Partie (4Q529-549)* (DJD 31; Oxford: Clarendon, 2001), 28, 36.

[43] Elgvin, "An Analysis of 4QInstruction," 86.

[44] Earlier Elgvin understood 4Q417 1 i 13-15 as referring to the Torah. See his "The Mystery to Come," 140. See also Loren T. Stuckenbruck, "4QInstruction and the Possible Influence of Early Enochic Traditions: An Evaluation," in *The Wisdom Texts from Qumran*, 260.

[45] Caquot has written that 4Q417 1 i "semble être à l'éloge d'une connaissance reposant sur une révélation." See "Les textes de sagesse de Qoumrân," 19.

[46] *Weisheit und Prädestination*, 87. See also Caquot, "Les textes de sagesse de Qoumrân," 18; H. Niehr, "Die Weisheit des Achikar und der *musar lammebin* im Vergleich," in *The Wisdom Texts from Qumran*, 186.

which in rabbinic tradition is associated with the wicked "generation of Enosh."[47] However, that the בני שית have not yet been judged suggests that they should not be situated in the primeval period. It is not clear that this passage should be interpreted in light of the Watchers myth. I am not aware of an instance in Second Temple literature where the fallen angels, or the humans with whom they mingle, are designated the "sons of Seth."

The phrase בני שית should not be understood in relation to the patriarch Seth. He is typically portrayed in positive terms, whereas the בני שית are clearly the wicked who will be judged. Aside from Adam, the only patriarch with whom the divine "image" is associated is Seth. Genesis 5:1 reiterates, using different terminology, the assertion of 1:27 that Adam was made in the image of God: "When God created humankind (אדם), he made them in the likeness of God (בדמות אלהים)." Genesis 5:3 maintains that the divine image stayed in Adam's line when he sired Seth: "When Adam had lived one hundred thirty years, he became the father of a son in his likeness, according to his image (בדמותו כצלמו), and named him Seth." The depiction of Seth in Genesis affects his interpretation in the late Second Temple period. Josephus, for example, declares that Seth "strove after virtue" (ἀρετὴν ἐπετήδευσε), a righteous patriarch placed between the murderous Cain and the generation tainted by fallen angels (J.A., 1.68).[48] Philo in the Posterity and Exile of Cain also praises Seth's "virtue": "Seth, inasmuch as he is sprung from human virtue (ἀνθρωπίνης ἀρετῆς), will never relinquish the race of men, but will obtain enlargement" (173; cf. 169).[49] Klijn has observed that some of the cows in the Animal Apocalypse correspond to the primeval patriarchs, with Seth represented by a white bull (1 En. 85:9).[50] Drawing on Genesis 5, both the Apocalypse of Moses (10:3; 12:2; cf. 38:4) and the Life of Adam and Eve (37:3; 39:2) call Seth the "image of God." Seth is also connected to Adam in genealogies in 1 Enoch 37:1, Ben Sira 49:16,

---

[47] Lange, Weisheit und Prädestination, 88, writes that the passage "liegt demzufolge ein Mythos zugrunde, der den Engelfall und den Beginn des Frevels zur Zeit der Söhne Seths geschehen läßt." See also Collins, "In the Likeness of the Holy Ones," 611-12; Steven D. Fraade, Enosh and His Generation: Pre-Israelite Hero and History in Postbiblical Interpretation (SBLMS 30; Chico: Scholars Press, 1984), 173-78; A.F.J. Klijn, Seth in Jewish, Christian and Gnostic Literature (NovTSup 46; Leiden: Brill, 1977), 7.

[48] This translation is from Louis H. Feldman, Flavius Josephus: Translation and Commentary. Volume 3: Judean Antiquities 1-4 (Leiden: Brill, 2000), 24. See also J.R. Levison, Portraits of Adam in Early Judaism from Sirach to 2 Baruch (Sheffield: JSOT, 1988), 108-09; Klijn, Seth, 23-25.

[49] Ibid., 25-27; Feldman, Flavius Josephus, 24.

[50] Klijn, Seth, 21.

and Luke 3:38.[51]   The positive valuation of Seth is continued in rabbinic literature.[52]   Second Temple exegetes often viewed Seth favorably.   He possessed the image of God and served as a foil to Cain, presumably because he replaces the slain Abel (Gen 4:25).   I have been unable to discover any Second Temple source that depicts Seth in negative terms. The wicked בני שׁית of 4QInstruction should not be understood in relation to the patriarch Seth.

The "sons of Sheth" should be considered a general designation for the wicked through its allusion to Numbers 24:17.[53]   4Q417 1 i 14-15 proclaims that they have iniquities and that God will give them their due recompense.   In Numbers 24:17 the "Shethites" (or "sons of Sheth") are a Moabite tribe whose destruction is ordained: "a star shall come out of Jacob, and a scepter shall rise out of Israel; it shall crush the borderlands of Moab, and the territory of all the Shethites (כל־בני־שׁת)" (cf. 21:18).[54] This verse is interpreted in the War Scroll to refer to the destruction of Gentiles in general.[55]   CD 7:21 uses the phrase "sons of Sheth" after

---

[51] See *DJD 34*, 163. S. Fraade reminds one that Isho'dad of Merv, a 9th century Nestorian bishop, wrote that the divine image continued through Seth. See his *Enosh and His Generation*, 99.

[52] *Pirke de Rabbi Eliezer* 22 claims "from Seth arose and were descended all the generations of the righteous. From Cain arose and were descended all the generations of the wicked." In *Abot de Rabbi Nathan* 2, Seth, along with Adam and Moses and other revered figures, is said to have been born circumcised. Cf. *b. Sukkah* 52b; *Song Rab.* 8.9.3. See Klijn, *Seth*, 8, 12; Judah Goldin, *The Fathers According to Rabbi Nathan* (YJS 10; New York/London: Yale University Press, 1983 [orig. pub., 1955]), 23.

[53] Harrington, *Wisdom Texts from Qumran*, 55. Elgvin also understands this phrase as a reference to the wicked, translating שׁית as "perdition." See his "The Mystery to Come," 141; idem, "An Analysis of 4QInstruction," 88.

[54] Cf. the בני שׁאון of Jer 48:45, who are mentioned in connection with Moab, as in Numbers 24:17: "In the shadow of Heshbon fugitives stop exhausted; for a fire has gone out from Heshbon, a flame from the house of Sihon; it has destroyed the forehead of Moab, the scalp of the people of tumult (בני שׁאון)." Strugnell and Harrington grant that a Transjordanian tribe was originally addressed in Numbers 24:17. They remain unclear, however, as to the identity of the בני שׁית of 4QInstruction. They write that if they are not the "Suteans (the Moabite tribe of Numbers 24), admittedly an antiquarian suggestion, it remains obscure who they are." See *DJD 34*, 163.

[55] Numbers 24:17-19 is quoted in 1QM 11:6-7. 1QM 11:1-3 recounts God's destruction of the Philistines, and 1QM 11:11 cites the mention of "Ashur" in Isaiah 31:8 to demonstrate God's power "against the Kittim." In 1QM 1:1-7 the final eschatological war is envisioned as a battle against Gentiles in general rather than one ethnic group in particular. For discussion of the War Scroll's use of Numbers 24, see Joseph A. Fitzmyer, "The use of explicit Old Testament quotations in Qumran literature and in the New Testament," in *The Semitic Background of the New Testament* (Grand Rapids/Livonia: Eerdmans/Dove, 1997), 43; John J. Collins, *The Scepter and the Star: The Messiahs of the Dead Sea Scrolls and Other Ancient Literature* (ABRL; New York: Doubleday, 1995), 63-67; Kevin J. Cathcart, "Numbers 24:17 in Ancient Translations and Interpretations," in

citing part of Numbers 24:17.[56] This verse is cited along with several others (Isa 7:17; Amos 5:26-27; 9:11) to argue that God will punish the wicked (CD 7:9). The phrase "sons of Sheth" refers not to Gentiles in general or a specific Transjordanian tribe but those who "escaped at the time of the first visitation while the renegades were delivered up to the sword" (7:21-8:1). The "sons of Sheth" in CD is not an ethnic designation but a moral and eschatological one—it refers to the wicked who have not yet been punished. This is also, I suggest, how the phrase should be understood in 4QInstruction. The expression "sons of Sheth" in 4Q417 1 i 15, as in CD 7, signifies the wicked whose punishment is determined but not yet realized. Although Numbers 24:17 originally referred to the destruction of a Moabite tribe, in later interpretation this group was not necessarily in mind. The Damascus Document, the War Scroll, and 4QInstruction all attest a tradition of using this verse to proclaim the downfall of the wicked, although they do not agree on who should be included in this group.

The wickedness of the בני שׁית is also suggested by their compatibility with the "fleshly spirit." They too will be punished at the moment of judgment. The sons of his truth will please God but "every fleshly spirit will be laid bare (יתערערו כל רוח בשׁר)" at the moment of judgment (4Q416 1 12; cf. 4Q416 2 ii 2-3; 4Q418 69 ii 8).[57] The "fleshly spirit" and the "sons of Sheth" should both be understood as terms for the wicked who are destined to be destroyed at judgment.

2.3 The Vision of Hagu and the Book of Remembrance

Scholars have observed that the vision of Hagu is equated with the book of remembrance: "The book of remembrance is written before him for those who keep his word—that is (והואה), the vision of Hagu for the book of remembrance" (4Q417 1 i 15-16).[58] The pronoun of the expres-

---

The Interpretation of the Bible: The International Symposium in Slovenia (ed. J. Krasovec; JSOTSup 289; Sheffield: Sheffield Academic Press, 1998), 511-20.

[56] See Fitzmyer, "The use of explicit Old Testament quotations," 25-26; Collins, The Scepter and the Star, 63-64. Numbers 24:17 is cited in 4QTestamonia without interpretation (4Q175 13). Cf. T. Levi 18:3; T. Jud. 24:1. It has also been claimed that 2 Peter 1:19 alludes to Numbers 24:17. See Duane F. Watson, "The Oral-Scribal and Cultural Intertexture of Apocalyptic Discourse in Jude and 2 Peter," in The Intertexture of Apocalyptic Discourse in the New Testament (ed. D.F. Watson; SBLSymS 14; Atlanta: Society of Biblical Literature, 2002), 200.

[57] The obscure verb יתערערו is discussed in section 2 of Chapter 5.

[58] Collins, Jewish Wisdom, 125; Lange, Weisheit und Prädestination, 51; Elgvin, "An Analysis of 4QInstruction," 258.

sion והואה is probably deictic.⁵⁹ Given the *lāmed* in the phrase לספר זכרון of line 16, this is the best way to make sense of the word. The phrase beginning with *lāmed* establishes that the book of remembrance mentioned in line 15 should be understood as the vision of Hagu.⁶⁰

4QInstruction's book of remembrance has been associated with the heavenly books and tablets in *1 Enoch* and *Jubilees*. The tablets of *1 Enoch* contain angelic knowledge: "I will speak these things … according to that which appeared to me in the heavenly vision, and (which) I know from the words of the holy angels, and understand from the tablets of heaven" (93:2).⁶¹ 4QInstruction's book of remembrance is with God in heaven (4Q417 1 i 15). It is a heavenly book to which the elect have access. The phrase "book of remembrance" is borrowed from Malachi 3:16: "The Lord took note and listened, and a book of remembrance (ספר זכרון) was written before him of those who revered the Lord and thought on his name."⁶² 4QInstruction's "book of remembrance" emphasizes that judgment will not be forgotten and is a basic feature of the divine plan.

---

⁵⁹ This type of pronoun introduces a nominal phrase that gives further elaboration on the noun immediately preceding it. This use of הוא or היא is well known from the Bible, although it is generally not preceded by a *wāw*, as in 4Q417 1 i 16. A good biblical example of a deictic pronoun is in Genesis 35:6: "Jacob came to Luz (that is, Bethel) (הוא בית־אל)." Strugnell and Harrington reject the deictic understanding of והואה on the grounds that it would make the description of the vision and the book repetitive. See *DJD 34*, 164.

⁶⁰ For this use of the letter *lāmed*, see, for example, Num 22:22.

⁶¹ Collins, *Jewish Wisdom*, 123. See Dan 7:10; 10:21; 12:1; *1 En.* 47:3; 81:3; 89:70; 90:20; 103:1; 108:3; *Jub.* 4:32; 6:30; 15:25; 16:3, 30; 18:19; 28:6; 30:9; 31:32; 32:16; 33:10. For the Mesopotamian tradition of heavenly books, see Elgvin, "An Analysis of 4QInstruction," 88; Lange, *Weisheit und Prädestination*, 69-79; Shalom Paul, "Heavenly Tablets and the Book of Life," *Journal of the Ancient Near Eastern Society of Columbia University* 5 (1973): 345-53. See also Martin Hengel, *Judaism and Hellenism* (2 vols.; Philadelphia: Fortress, 1973), 1.211, 242; Cana Werman, "'The תורה and the תעודה' Engraved on the Tablets," *Dead Sea Discoveries* 9 (2002): 75-103; Christfried Böttrich, "Frühjüdische Weisheitstraditionen im slavischen Henochbuch und in Qumran," in *The Wisdom Texts from Qumran*, 308-11; Beyerle, "Und dann werden die Zeichen der Wahrheit erscheinen …," 533; George W.E. Nickelsburg, *1 Enoch: A Commentary on the Book of 1 Enoch, Chapters 1-36, 81-108* (Hermeneia; Minneapolis: Fortress, 2001), 478-80.

⁶² On the basis of Esther 6:1, Malachi 3:16 has been understood as a "Persianism," with elements of the heavenly world depicted as analogous to features of the Persian court. Esther 6:1 reads "On that night the king could not sleep, and he gave orders to bring the book of records, the annals (את־ספר הזכרנות דברי הימים), and they were read to the king." See Andrew Hill, *Malachi* (AB 25D; New York: Doubleday, 1998), 340. Elgvin, "An Analysis of 4QInstruction," 258; idem, "The Mystery to Come," 140; Lange, *Weisheit und Prädestination*, 53, 71; Collins, *Jewish Wisdom*, 126; *DJD 34*, 163; James Aitken, "Apocalyptic, Revelation and Early Jewish Wisdom Literature," in *New Heaven and New Earth. Prophecy and the Millennium: Essays in honour of Anthony Gelston* (ed. P.J. Harland and C.T.R. Hayward; VTSup 77; Leiden: Brill, 1999), 185.

Aside from the book of remembrance, there are several other points of
contact between 4Q417 1 i and Malachi 3.[63] Malachi's book of remembrance is granted to the pious. It is given to the ירָאֵי יהוה וּלְחשְׁבֵי שְׁמוֹ,
and the שׁמְרֵי דברוֹ are given the book of remembrance in 4Q417 1 i 16.
Since "those who keep his word" are given this book, the expression is
probably a reference to the "spiritual people." The phrase could also
refer to the group that includes the addressee (cf. 4Q418 81 8-9). After
Malachi 3:16 mentions its heavenly book, it describes the fiery judgment
of the day of the Lord (3:17-4:6 [3:17-24]). The book of remembrance in
4QInstruction is also associated with judgment (4Q417 1 i 14-15).[64]

By appealing to Malachi 3, 4QInstruction claims that the vision of
Hagu contains wisdom inscribed in a heavenly book that is available to
the elect. The vision refers to the revelation of heavenly wisdom. The
content of this vision includes knowledge about the imminent judgment
against the wicked. Although the text does not say so directly, the vision
also seems to provide the knowledge of good and evil. This is implied
by the fact that the "fleshly spirit" does not know good from evil and is
not given the vision of Hagu (4Q417 1 i 18-19). That אנוֹשׁ can be read as
"Adam" also evokes the theme of the knowledge of good and evil.

2.4 The "Spiritual People," the "Fleshly Spirit," and אנוֹשׁ

4Q417 1 i 13-18 hinges on a contrast between the "spiritual people" and
the "fleshly spirit." The "spiritual people" are given the vision of Hagu
and the "fleshly spirit" is not, because it does not have the knowledge of

---

[63] In Malachi 3:6-12 God promises that if Israel returns to God, he will return to Israel.
Israel is accused of stealing offerings from the Temple and is cursed for it (3:8-9). If the
people restore proper cult observance God will reward them with agricultural abundance
(3:10-11). The book of remembrance in 3:16 is mentioned after the "fearers of God"
discuss with each other the proposal offered by God in 3:6-12. God hears them and in
response the heavenly book is written "for the fearers of God." The book helps ratify the
agreement between God and Israel. It gives concrete expression to the renewed covenantal
bond. For this reason Hill, *Malachi*, 340, understands the book of remembrance as a
"divine ledger" that lists the names of the righteous and their words and deeds. If so, it is
an early form of the "Book of Life," a heavenly record of the names of the righteous. The
book ensures that the "fearers" will be spared when the Day of the Lord comes (see 3:20).
For the book of life, see Dan 12:1; 4Q504 1-2 vi 14; 1QM 12:3; Phil 4:3; Rev 3:5; 13:8;
17:8; 20:12, 15; 21:27; 22:19. Elgvin understands 4QInstruction's book of remembrance
in light of this tradition. See "An Analysis of 4QInstruction," 87, note 112.

[64] For other allusions to Malachi 3:16, see, for example, CD 20:17-21. It cites Malachi
3:16 and adds "until salvation and justice are revealed to those who fear God" (20:20). In
CD it is a prooftext for the salvation of the elect. Malachi 3:16-18 is also cited in 4Q253a
(4QCommentary on Malachi) 1 i 1-4. See George J. Brooke et al., *Qumran Cave 4.XVII:
Parabiblical Texts, Part 3* (DJD 22; Oxford: Clarendon, 1996), 214.

good and evil. The former is in the likeness of the angels and the latter is not. Unlike the "spiritual people," the "fleshly spirit" is mentioned elsewhere in 4QInstruction. In 4Q418 81 1-2 the addressee is told that he has been separated from the "fleshly spirit" in order to remove him "from all that he (God) hates" (cf. 4Q417 1 ii 14; 4Q418 126 ii 8; 4Q418 221 4). 4Q416 1 12 affirms that this spirit will be destroyed in the final judgment.

The Hodayot uses the phrase "fleshly spirit" to refer to human beings. 1QH 5:19-20 asks how a "fleshly spirit" can understand the revelation that has been given to him: "In the mysteries of your insight (רזי שכלכה) [you] have apportioned all these things ... [However, what is] the fleshly spirit (רוח בשר) to understand all these matters"?[65] In this text the "fleshly spirit" refers to the base and creaturely aspect of the human condition. The elect speaker considers himself to be a "fleshly spirit" and is painfully aware that this is in tension with his access to revelation. In the concluding hymn of the Community Rule the speaker laments that, even though revelation has been given to him, including the mystery that is to be, he still belongs to the "assembly of unfaithful flesh" (סוד בשר עול) (11:9; cf. ll. 3-4, 6).[66] Unlike these texts, in 4QInstruction the "fleshly spirit" is emphatically not given revelation. In 4Q417 1 i 13-18 the expression should not be understood as a reference to the human condition *per se*, but rather as a designation for people who are not among the elect. Since the "fleshly spirit" cannot distinguish good from evil, it is reasonable to assume that such people are predisposed towards wickedness. But in 4Q417 1 i 13-18 this is never explicitly affirmed. This passage is more interested in distinguishing the "spiritual people" from the "fleshly spirit" than describing what this "spirit" is actually like.

The author of 4QInstruction roots the formation of two distinct types of people in the creation of humankind. This is clear from the text's allusions to Genesis 1-3. The main passage regarding this topic reads: "He bequeathed it (the vision of Hagu) to אנוש together with a spiritual people, be[cau]se he fashioned him according to the likeness of the holy ones" (4Q417 1 i 16-17). Both אנוש and the "spiritual people" have access to the vision of Hagu. Regarding the word אנוש, several interpretive options are possible. It could be understood as referring to humankind.

---

[65] רוח בשר also occurs in a fragmentary passage in 1QH 5:4. Cf. the phrase אנוש בשר of 5:3 and the "fleshly inclination" in 18:23. See also Frey, "Flesh and Spirit," 378-97.

[66] For the negative use of בשר in the main writings of the Qumran community, see Jörg Frey, "The Notion of Flesh in 4QInstruction and the Background of Pauline Usage," in *Sapiential, Liturgical and Poetical Texts from Qumran: Proceedings of the Third Meeting of the International Organization for Qumran Studies, Oslo 1998* (ed. D. Falk et al.; STDJ 35; Leiden: Brill, 2000), 201-08.

Elgvin and others have read it this way.[67] אנוש is a common term for
"man" in the Dead Sea Scrolls. But since 4QInstruction is emphasizing
that this אנוש has been given revelation, it is not clear that it should be
understood as referring to humanity in general.[68] אנוש can also be understood as the patriarch Enosh. The editors of *DJD 34* understand the
word in this way.[69] Their main rationale is that it should not be read as
referring to humankind in general. Lange also reads אנוש as Enosh.[70]
Elgvin rejects the Enosh reading since Second Temple traditions about
him do not depict him as a recipient of revelation.[71] The word אנוש of
4Q417 1 i 16 can be read as referring to humankind in general or Enosh,
although both readings can be criticized.

One valid interpretative option has not received enough attention—
אנוש as a reference to the biblical Adam.[72] Even though 4Q417 1 i 16
does not use the word אדם, the line can be read as referring to Adam.
The Treatise on the Two Spirits uses the word אנוש to allude to Adam in
1QS 3:17-18: "He created Adam (אנוש) to rule the world." The "spiritual
people" were given the vision of Hagu "be[cau]se he fashioned him according to the likeness of the holy ones (כתבנית קדושים יצרו // כֹ[י]אֹ)"
(4Q417 1 i 16-17). This translation understands the word יצרו as a verb
but it can also be considered a noun (cf. 4Q416 2 iii 17). In that case the
line could be rendered "according to the likeness of the holy ones is his
inclination."[73] Either way 4QInstruction claims that the "spiritual peo-

---

[67] Elgvin, "An Analysis of 4QInstruction," 93; idem, "The Mystery to Come,"142-43.
Caquot, Les textes de sagesse de Qoumrân," 18, translates אנוש as "homme." Harrington,
Wisdom Texts, 56, favors the humankind reading but speculates that Enosh might be the
correct interpretation.

[68] The word, however, clearly has this meaning in 4Q418 55 11 and 4Q418 77 3.

[69] *DJD 34*, 165.

[70] *Weisheit und Prädestination*, 87. See also George J. Brooke, "Biblical Interpretation in the Wisdom Texts from Qumran," in *The Wisdom Texts from Qumran*, 213.

[71] Elgvin, "An Analysis of 4QInstruction," 88. Enosh is not explicitly identified as a
recipient of revelation in 4Q369 (4QPrayer of Enosh?), although the text is fragmentary.
If this composition is actually about him, it is significant that the divine grant of dominion,
typically associated with Adam, is here associated with Enosh (cf. 1 ii 6-7). Enosh receives revelation in the Mani Codex, a late source (4th century CE) that attributes an
apocalypse to him. See also Collins, *Jewish Wisdom*, 124; *DJD 13*, 353-62; Fraade,
Enosh and His Generation, 5-28.

[72] Collins, "In the Likeness of the Holy Ones," 610-12; Beyerle, "Und dann werden die
Zeichen der Wahrheit erscheinen ...," 533.

[73] The inclination, or *yēser*, refers to a disposition towards a type of conduct. In Jewish
tradition there is a good and evil *yēser*. The rabbis explained that this was based upon
exegesis of the word ייצר in Genesis 2:7, with each *yōd* signifying one of the two inclina-
tions. See, for example, *Gen. Rab.* 14:4. For more on the wicked *yēser*, see John J.
Collins, "Wisdom, Apocalypticism and the Dead Sea Scrolls," in *Seers, Sibyls and Sages
in Hellenistic Roman Judaism* (JSJSup 54; Leiden: Brill, 1997), 385-404; Roland E.
Murphy, " *Yeser* in the Qumran Literature," *Biblica* 39 (1958): 334-44.

ple" were created in a way that makes them similar to the angels.[74] They have a תבנית, or "form," that is like the angels.[75] Collins has argued that כתבנית קדושים should be understood as a paraphrase of בצלם אלהים from Genesis 1:27, "taking אלהים in its angelic sense."[76] In this reading, the claim that the "spiritual people" are created in the "likeness of the angels" not only establishes similarity between these people and the angels. It also implies that Adam was fashioned like the angels.

Other Second Temple texts associate Adam with angelic wisdom. This supports Collins' reading of 4Q417 1 i 17. *Jubilees* depicts the angels as teaching Adam in the garden (3:15).[77] The Treatise on the Two Spirits associates heavenly revelation with Adam. It affirms that God will make "the wisdom of the sons of heaven" (חכמת בני שמים) available

---

[74] The claim bears some analogy to the assertion in the New Testament that Jesus is a priest "according to the order of Melchizedek" (Heb 7:17).

[75] Collins, "In the Likeness of the Holy Ones," 613, points out that the word תבנית is used in Ezekiel and the Songs of the Sabbath Sacrifice to refer to angels. See Ezek 10:8, "The cherubim appeared to have the form (תבנית) of a human hand under their wings" (cf. 8:3); 11Q17 8 3-4, "... all the figures (תבנית) of the wonder[ful] spirits ... gods, awesome in strength ..." See *DJD 23*, 289. 4Q403 1 ii 3 uses the word תבנית to describe God's glory. Line 16 of this fragment also attests the word תבנית. According to C. Newsom, this occurrence should be understood as a reference to the sanctuary. See Esther Eshel et al., *Qumran Cave 4.VI: Poetical and Liturgical Texts, Part 1* (DJD 11; Oxford: Clarendon, 1998), 279, 284, 286. Cf. 4Q403 1 i 44; 4Q405 20 ii-21-22 8; 1QM 10:14; and Exod 25:40. See also section 2.4.4 of this chapter.

[76] Collins, "In the Likeness of the Holy Ones," 613, 615; *DJD 34*, 166. See also J. Maxwell Miller, "In the 'Image' and 'Likeness' of God," *Journal of Biblical Literature* 91 (1972): 289-304; John F.A. Sawyer, "The Meaning of בצלם אלהים ('In the Image of God') in Genesis I-XI," *Journal of Theological Studies* 25 (1974): 418-26.

[77] *2 Enoch* claims that Adam is angelic: "And on the earth I assigned him to be a second angel" (30:11). *Testament of Abraham* 11 (Recension A) depicts Adam sitting on a throne in heaven, clothed in glory. *3 Baruch* 4:7-15 describes angels planting the garden. Also note that Josephus claims that Adam had eschatological knowledge, writing that the patriarch "predicted a destruction of the universe, at one time by a violent fire and at another time by a mighty deluge of water" (*J.A.*, 1.70). See Feldman, *Flavius Josephus*, 24; Levison, *Portraits of Adam*, 109; R. Scroggs, *The Last Adam: A Study in Pauline Anthropology* (Philadelphia: Fortress Press, 1966), 26; Andrei A. Orlov, "The Flooded Arboretums: The Garden Traditions in the Slavonic Version of *3 Baruch* and the *Book of Giants*," *Catholic Biblical Quarterly* 65 (2003): 184-201. There is also a rabbinic tradition that the angels gave Adam revelation in the form of a heavenly book. The *Sefer Raziel*, a composite work that includes portions of the *Sefer ha-Razim* (the Book of Mysteries), claims to be this book. See Steve Savedow, *Sepher Rezial Hemelach: The Book of the Angel Rezial* (York Beach: Samuel Weiser, 2000); Louis Ginzberg, *The Legends of the Jews* (7 vols.; Philadelphia: Jewish Publication Society of America, 1961 [orig. pub., 1909]), 1.90-93; Gershom Scholem, *Origins of the Kabbalah* (Princeton: Princeton University Press/Jewish Publication Society, 1987 [orig. pub., 1962]), 106-23.

to the elect so that they may obtain the "glory of Adam" (1QS 4:22-23).[78]
Support for the view that Adam acquired angelic wisdom may derive
from Genesis. In Genesis 3:5 the serpent tells Eve "for God (אלהים)
knows that when you eat of it your eyes will be opened, and you will be
like God (כאלהים), knowing good and evil" (cf. v. 22).[79] The expression
כאלהים is translated in the LXX as ὡς θεοί, "like divine beings."[80] The
translator of this verse believed that the knowledge of good and evil
would make Adam like the angels.

In contrast to the god-like Adam of Genesis 1, Adam in chapters 2-3
is creaturely. While Genesis 1:27 emphasizes Adam's affinity with the
divine realm, in 2:7 his base and earthly nature is stressed: "then the Lord
God formed man (האדם) from the dust of the ground, and breathed into
his nostrils the breath of life; and the man became a living being (נפש
חיה)." 4QInstruction stresses the mortality of the "fleshly spirit" (4Q416
1 12). If כתבנית קדושים should be associated with the expression בצלם
אלהים from Genesis 1:27, רוח בשר perhaps paraphrases the phrase נפש
חיה from Genesis 2:7.[81] נפש חיה is used elsewhere in the sense of "crea-

---

[78] This phrase also occurs in CD 3:20 and 1QH 4:14-15. While the expression is enigmatic, it seems to be a designation of elect status that denotes the promise of eternal life.
The "glory of Adam" is also discussed in section 2.5.2 of this chapter. Note also that the
Psalm 37 Pesher proclaims that the descendents of the elect will possess forever the "inheritance of Adam" (נחלת אדם) (4Q171 3 1-2). See also Sir 49:16: "Glorious too were
Shem and Seth and Enosh; but beyond that of any living being was the splendor of Adam
(ועל כל חי תפארת אדם)." This translation is from Di Lella and Skehan, *The Wisdom of Ben
Sira* (AB 39; New York: Doubleday, 1987), 541. Also note *3 Bar.* 4:16, which claims
that Adam lost the "glory of God," and *Apoc. Mos.* 28:4, which promises Adam eternal
life. See Fletcher-Louis, *All the Glory of Adam*, 95-97; James R. Davila, *Liturgical
Works* (ECDSS 6; Grand Rapids: Eerdmans, 2000), 245; Michael Mach, *Entwicklungsstadien des jüdischen Engelglaubens in vorrabbinischer Zeit* (TSAJ 34; Tübingen:
J.C.B. Mohr [Paul Siebeck], 1992), 133-42.

[79] There is a parallel in the Gilgamesh epic. Upon Enkidu's sexual encounter with the
prostitute she says to him: "You have become [profound] Enkidu, you have become like a
god" (1 iv). This translation is from Stephanie Dalley, *Myths from Mesopotamia* (Oxford:
Oxford University Press, 1989), 56. See also Robert Gordis, "The Knowledge of Good
and Evil in the Old Testament and the Qumran Scrolls," *Journal of Biblical Literature* 76
(1957), 135.

[80] LXX Genesis 3:5 renders the first אלהים in the singular and the second in the plural.
There is a similar situation regarding the LXX version of Psalm 8:6. The phrase תחסרהו
מעט מאלהים of this verse is normally rendered as "you have made them a little lower than
God," but the LXX translates it as "You made him a little less than the angels (ἠλάττωσας
αὐτὸν βραχύ τι παρ' ἀγγέλους)."

[81] Elgvin understands the phrase כתבנית קדושים יצרו as a conflation of Genesis 1:27 and
2:7, arguing that 4QInstruction did not interpret Genesis as attesting the creation of two
Adams, but one. See "An Analysis of 4QInstruction," 91. The point, however, is not
whether Genesis 1-3 was understood as having two Adams or one. 4QInstruction describes two different ways of being human by appealing to the two contrasting portrayals
of Adam in Genesis 1-3.

ture." This is the case, for example, in Genesis 9:16: "When the bow is in the clouds, I will see it and remember the everlasting covenant between God and every living creature of all flesh (כל־נפש חיה בכל־בשר) that is on the earth" (see also 9:12; cf. Ezek 47:9). The god-like Adam of Genesis 1 corresponds to the "spiritual people." The Adam made of dust in Genesis 2-3 accords with the "fleshly spirit."[82] 4QInstruction's presentation of two different types of humankind appeals to the two contrasting portrayals of Adam in Genesis 1-3.

It is possible that the author of 4QInstruction did not believe that two separate types of humankind were fashioned at creation but rather that they became two groups later in time. One can read the expression ועוד in 4Q417 1 i 17 as "but no more." This would suggest that at a certain point God stopped giving the vision of Hagu to this spirit: "But no more (ועוד) did he give Hagu to the fleshly spirit."[83] One can speculate that the "fleshly spirit" once enjoyed the vision of Hagu, like the "spiritual people," and that they were originally a single group.[84] In this reading the vision was taken away from the "fleshly spirit" when it failed to distinguish good from evil. This is an interpretive possibility. But it is unlikely, given that 4QInstruction displays no awareness of a fall of humankind rooted in Adam's sin. In my translation above עוד is understood as "moreover." This emphasizes the separation of the two groups without implying that the "fleshly spirit" ever had the vision of Hagu.

---

[82] With the "spiritual people" similar to the Adam of Genesis 1 and the "fleshly spirit" like the Adam of Genesis 2-3, it is possible to contend, with Collins, that 4QInstruction attests a 'double creation of man' in the manner of Philo. See Collins, "In the Likeness of the Holy Ones," 617. See further section 2.5.3 of this chapter.

[83] Strugnell and Harrington, *DJD 34*, 166, favor this translation of the phrase. See also John J. Collins, "The Mysteries of God: The Category 'Mystery' in Apocalyptic and Sapiential Writings," in *Wisdom and Apocalypticism in the Dead Sea Scrolls and in the Biblical Tradition* (ed. F. García Martínez; BETL 168; Leuven: Peeters-Leuven University Press, forthcoming). Note also that the latter portion of 4Q418 81 1 can be translated "Long ag]o, he separated you from every fleshly spirit." This is in reference to the addressee. See Tigchelaar, *To Increase Learning*, 231. This reading is plausible but the key phrase for the matter at hand, "Long ag]o" (מא[ז), is too fragmentary to regard as definitive.

[84] One can also understand the two contrasting types of humankind not as grounded in the creation of two separate Adams, but rather in two distinct stages in his life. In this reading the "spiritual people" correspond to Adam when he was in the garden and "fleshly spirit" with Adam once he had been removed from the garden. This option is a possibility but cannot be affirmed conclusively.

2.4.1 The Garden of Eden and the Acquisition of Wisdom

4QInstruction can be understood as revealing the vision of Hagu to both the "spiritual people" and Adam. This interpretation is supported by the fact that the addressee is presented in relation to Adam. His elect status is depicted as a restoration of the idyllic relationship God originally enjoyed with the first patriarch. This is expressed in the claim that the addressee has authority over the garden of Eden.[85] The key text in this regard is 4Q423 1.[86] This fragment begins: "every fruit that is produced and every delightful tree, pleasing to give knowledge (כל עץ נעים נחמד להשכיל). Is [it] not a ple[asant] (נ[עים]) garden [and pleasing] to gi[ve] g[re]at knowledge?"[87] Elgvin, the editor of this text, notes that it conflates material from Genesis 2:9 (כל־עץ נחמד) and 3:6 (נחמד העץ להשכיל).[88] Every tree in the garden has the ability to bestow knowledge. Their beauty is similar to the trees in orchards that Enoch visits on his travels.[89] 4QInstruction never mentions a prohibition against eating from any trees of the garden, an omission found in other sapiential texts.[90]

---

[85] Terje Stordalen, *Echoes of Eden: Genesis 2-3 and Symbolism of the Eden Garden in Biblical Hebrew Literature* (Leuven: Peeters, 2000); Eibert Tigchelaar, "Eden and Paradise: The Garden Motif in Some Early Jewish Texts," in *Paradise Interpreted: Representations of Biblical Paradise in Judaism and Christianity* (ed. G.P. Luttikhuizen; Leiden: Brill, 1999), 54-56.

[86] It is also possible that there is a connection between Adam and the revelation given to the addressee in a fragmentary text, 4Q423 13 4. This text is reconstructed in *DJD 34*, 528, as "נתן א[ל ביד האדם." This could be translated as "G]od [gave] through Adam."

[87] *DJD 34*, 505-33. Cf. 4Q418 251 1-2. It cryptically mentions "the inheri[tance] of Adam" (נ[חל]ת אדם]) and "your conduct," probably referring to the addressee's. See ibid., 456. See also Fletcher-Louis, *All the Glory of Adam*, 96; Bo Reicke, "The Knowledge Hidden in the Tree of Paradise," *Journal of Semitic Studies* 1 (1956): 193-201.

[88] *DJD 34*, 509. See also Esther Chazon, "The Creation and Fall of Adam in the Dead Sea Scrolls," in *The Book of Genesis in Jewish and Oriental Christian Interpretation: A Collection of Essays* (ed. J. Frishman and L. van Rompay; Leuven: Peeters, 1997), 18.

[89] See for example, *1 En.* 24:5, "Behold, this beautiful tree! Beautiful to look at and pleasant (are) its leaves, and its fruit very delightful in appearance"; 32:5, "This tree (is) beautiful! How beautiful and pleasing (is) its appearance!" See also 31:3; 32:2; *Jub.* 3:20. For further discussion of *1 Enoch* 24-32, see Tigchelaar, "Eden and Paradise," 38-49. Also note that *1 Enoch* mentions a "Garden of Righteousness" in 32:6; 60:23; and 77:3.

[90] This is the case in Ben Sira: "He filled them with knowledge and understanding, and showed them good and evil" (17:7). See also 4Q305 (4QMeditation on Creation C) 2 2: "He gave to Adam (אדם) knowled[ge." The next line of the text is fragmentary but may have mentioned the knowledge of good and evil: וידע לדעת[, "and evil(?) [ ]to know (?) ..." See *DJD 20*, 158. 4Q303 (4QMeditation on Creation A) 8-9, also fragmentary, suggests that Adam ate from the tree of knowledge without any sense of a prohibition: "... and insight of good and evil (שכל טוב ורע), to ... Adam (אדם) taking from it." The translation is from Tigchelaar, "Eden and Paradise," 51. See also *DJD 20*, 153. In the version of these texts presented in *DJD 20*, their editor, Timothy Lim, translates the word אדם as "man." Since they allude to creation and reformulate features of Genesis 1-3, the translation

It is reasonable to suppose that the knowledge available in the garden includes good and evil. A fragmentary passage of the manuscript mentions "[rejecting] the evil and knowing the good" (4Q423 2 i 7).[91] Since 4QInstruction relates the knowledge of good and evil to the mystery that is to be (4Q417 1 i 6-8; cf. 4Q418 221 5; 4Q423 5 6), the addressee's stewardship over Eden should be viewed in relation to the revelation given to him.[92] Referring to the garden, 4QInstruction declares to the addressee: "Over it he has given you authority (המשילכה) to serve it and till it (לעבדו ולשמרו)" (4Q423 1 2). The word המשיל is used elsewhere to refer to his elect status. 4Q418 81 3, for example, reads: "Over] his [in]heritance he has set you in authority" (cf. l. 9). This is also the case in 4Q416 2 iii 11-12: "and he has given you authority (המשילכה) over an inheritance of glory" (cf. 1QH 5:23-24). The addressee's elect status includes access to revelation.

The verb המשיל also alludes to the Adamic grant of dominion of Genesis 1. Reformulations of this grant regularly replace the verb רדה used in Genesis 1:28 with המשיל. The earliest example of this is Psalm 8:7: "You have given them dominion (תמשילהו) over the works of your hands; you have put all things under their feet."[93] This use of המשיל is also evident in 4QWords of the Luminaries. 4Q504 8 4-6 reads:

> [Adam] our [fat]her, you formed in the likeness of [your] glory ... [the breath of life] you [br]eathed into his nose, and understanding and knowledge ... [in the gard]en of Eden which you planted you made [him] ru[le (המשלת]ה אותו[).[94]

"Adam" is to be favored. Also note 4Q381 1 7-9. The prohibition against eating the fruit of the tree is mentioned in 4Q422 1 i 10; 4Q504 8 7; *Jub.* 3:18; and *1 En.* 25:4. See further Chazon, "Creation and Fall," 14, 20; James L. Kugel, "Some Instances of Biblical Interpretation in the Hymns and Wisdom Writings of Qumran," in *Studies in Ancient Midrash* (ed. J.L. Kugel; Cambridge: Harvard University Center for Jewish Studies, 2001), 164-65.

[91] The official edition of 4Q423 joins fragments 1 and 2 i. See *DJD 34*, 506. However, a distant join connects this material and, as Tigchelaar suggests, this should be treated with caution. In his edition of these fragments in *To Increase Learning*, 141, he does not combine them into a single text. See also his "Eden and Paradise," 55.

[92] Elgvin, "An Analysis of 4QInstruction," 279.

[93] Chazon, "The Creation and Fall of Adam," 15; *DJD 34*, 509. See also Tigchelaar, "Eden and Paradise," 53-56.

[94] This translation is from Davila, *Liturgical Works*, 244. See also Maurice Baillet, *Qumrân Grotte 4.III (4Q482-4Q520)* (DJD 7; Oxford: Clarendon, 1982), 162. Note the parallel in *2 En.* [A] 65:2: "He created man according to his image." See further Kugel, "Some Instances of Biblical Interpretation," 165.

4Q287 (4QBlessings^b) 4 2 also rephrases the grant of dominion: "You have made the man master (תמשל את האדם)."⁹⁵ 4Q422 (4QParaphrase of Genesis and Exodus) 1 i 9-10 portrays Adam as having the authority to eat the fruit of the garden, except for the tree of knowledge: "he set him in charge (המשילו) to eat the frui[t of the soil,] that he shoul[d n]ot eat from the tree that gives know[ledge of good and evil]."⁹⁶ 4Q381 (4QNon-Canonical Psalms^b) 1 7 uses the verb המשיל in a similar way: "And by his breath he made them stand, to rule (למשל) over all of these on earth …"⁹⁷ The Treatise on the Two Spirits also alludes to the Adamic grant of dominion: "He created Adam to rule (לממשלת) the world" (3:17-18; cf. 1Q34 3 ii 3).⁹⁸ The word המשיל has been reconstructed in Ben Sira 17 and *Jubilees* 2.⁹⁹ These texts allude to Genesis 1:28; in some this refers to rule over the world and in others that Adam has control over the garden of Eden. Like 4Q504 and 4Q422, 4Q423 1 2 uses the word המשיל to affirm that the addressee possesses stewardship over Eden, as Adam once did.¹⁰⁰

4QInstruction emphasizes that maintaining the garden of Eden requires work. The phrase "to serve it and till it" of 4Q423 1 2 incorporates language from Genesis 2:15, which reads: "The Lord God took the man and put him in the garden of Eden to till it and keep it (לעבדה ולשמרה)."¹⁰¹ In 4QInstruction the acquisition of wisdom is attained through the study of revealed mysteries. It also demands ethical conduct. The way of life advocated by 4QInstruction requires a great deal of ef-

---

⁹⁵ *DJD 11*, 55. B. Nitzan, the official editor of the text, acknowledges that it may refer to Adam in Genesis 1:28, but she prefers to interpret the phrase as an allusion "to the obligation of humanity to serve God ritually." See also Davila, *Liturgical Works*, 71.

⁹⁶ *DJD 13*, 421-22.

⁹⁷ *DJD 11*, 92-94.

⁹⁸ Note the parallel in Wis 9:2: "and by your wisdom (you) have formed humankind to have dominion (δεσπόζῃ) over the creatures you have made."

⁹⁹ J.C. VanderKam retroverts this verb in 4Q216 vii 2 (*Jub.* 2:14), a text that reworks the grant of dominion given to Adam. See *DJD 13*, 19. M.H. Segal uses המשיל in his reconstruction of Ben Sira 17:2: "He gave them a fixed number of days, but granted them authority over everything on the earth." See his *ספר בן סירא השלם* (Jerusalem: Bialik, 1958), 102. See also Chazon, "The Creation and Fall of Adam," 19; Jeremy Cohen, *"Be Fertile and Increase, Fill the Earth and Master It": The Ancient and Medieval Career of a Biblical Text* (Ithaca: Cornell University Press, 1989), 69.

¹⁰⁰ Tigchelaar, "Eden and Paradise," 56, questions whether 4QInstruction's use of this word can be compared to other Second Temple texts that allude to Genesis 1:28. He argues that it is used in 4QInstruction in a variety of ways. Nevertheless it occurs several times in reference to the addressee's elect status, which is associated with the garden of Eden.

¹⁰¹ *DJD 34*, 509; Chazon, "The Creation and Fall of Adam," 18. Notice that 4Q423 1 2 switches the gender of the suffix of the verbs it takes from this Genesis verse.

fort. The possession of Eden represents the successful acquisition of wisdom by the addressee.

4Q423 1 3 reformulates God's dictum that Adam will have to till difficult soil: "[the earth,] thorns and thistles it will sprout for you (קוץ ודרדר תצמיח לכה), and its strength will not yield to you." This is dependent on Genesis 3:18: "thorns and thistles it shall bring forth for you (קוץ ודרדר תצמיח לך); and you shall eat the plants of the field."[102] The phrase קוץ ודרדר is also used in 1QH 16:24-25: "But if I remove my hand it (the garden) will be like the acac[ia in the desert] ... thorns and reeds (קוץ ודרדר) shoot up." The phrase קוץ ודרדר is used in 1QH to describe a beautiful garden falling into disarray.[103] The phrase "thorns and thistles" in 4Q423 1 3 likewise represents an inversion of the idyllic setting of Eden. As the addressee's acquisition of wisdom is represented by possession of the garden of Eden, the garden can also depict the condition of not having this knowledge. This results in a life of wickedness, symbolized by Eden turning into thorns and thistles. Eden can be a metaphor for maintaining the lifestyle advocated by 4QInstruction and can also signify the addressee's failure to do so. Eden is used as a metaphor for the human condition.[104] Both the right path and the wrong path are represented by Eden.

2.4.2 The Addressee and the "Spiritual People"

4QInstruction offers a cryptic, enigmatic account of two contrasting kinds of people to the addressee (מבין; 4Q417 1 i 14) so that he may

---

[102] Elgvin points out that the second portion of 4Q423 1 3 alludes to Genesis 4:12: "When you till the ground, it will no longer yield to you its strength (לא־תסף תת־כחה לך); you will be a fugitive and a wanderer on the earth." See *DJD 34*, 510. 4QInstruction conflates material from both Genesis 3 and 4. Both Adam and Cain are forced to work land that can be difficult. Although not bearing on the immediate topic at hand, this combination is important for understanding 4QInstruction's use of Genesis. Its main concern is not exegesis *per se*. 4QInstruction is rather interested in how Genesis can be brought to bear on questions it brings to the text.

Note that 4Q423 3 2 connects the mystery that is to be with the statement that "Thus you will walk, and al[l your] c[rops will multiply." Line 1 of this fragment is "your st]rength will be s[pent] in vain." While cited from Leviticus 26:20, it seems also to allude to the tradition attested in Genesis 3:18 and 4:12 that occasionally the land will not yield to one's efforts. See *DJD 34*, 514; J. Dochhorn, "'Sie wird dir nicht ihre Kraft geben'—Adam, Kain und der Ackerbau in 4Q423 2₃ und Apc Mos 24," in *The Wisdom Texts from Qumran*, 351-64.

[103] The phrase is used to evoke an image of desolation in Hosea 10:8: "The high places of Aven, the sin of Israel, shall be destroyed. Thorn and thistle (קוץ ודרדר) shall grow up on their altars. They shall say to the mountains, Cover us, and to the hills, Fall on us." Cf. Heb 6:7-8.

[104] Chazon, "The Creation and Fall of Adam," 18.

study and contemplate it. An important lesson for the addressee, I believe, was to identify with the "spiritual people." They are given the
vision of Hagu, and the addressee has been given the mystery that is to
be. I have argued above that the content of the vision of Hagu includes
knowledge about the final judgment and of good and evil. The mystery
that is to be provides knowledge about the final judgment: "[Gaze upon
the mystery] that is to be, and grasp the birth-times of salvation (מולדי
ישׁע) and know who is inheriting glory and who ini[qu]ity" (4Q417 2 i
10-12). By means of the mystery that is to be the addressee can also
acquire the knowledge of good and evil (4Q417 1 i 6-8). He could have
also identified with the "spiritual people" because he is distinguished
from the "fleshly spirit" (4Q418 81 1-2; cf. 1QSb 5:1). By possessing
the garden of Eden, the addressee is linked to Adam. The *mebin* could
likewise associate the "spiritual people" with this patriarch.

2.4.3 The Addressee, his Holy Status, and the Angels

4QInstruction also teaches the addressee that he is like the angels. This
is another reason he could identify with the "spiritual people." For example, the angels enjoy eternal life (4Q418 69 ii 13), and the intended
audience is promised life after death (4Q417 2 i 10-12).[105]

The theme of the addressee's affinity with the angels is prominent in
4Q418 81. The first five lines of this text read as follows:

> He has opened up your lips as a fountain in order to bless the holy ones
> (לברך קדושׁים). And you, like an eternal fountain, praise [his name. Long
> ag]o, he separated you from every fleshly spirit. And you, keep yourself
> separate from all that he hates, and keep aloof from every abomination of
> [his] soul. [Fo]r he has made everyone and has given each man his own
> inheritance. He is your portion and your inheritance among the sons of
> Adam. [And over] his [in]heritance he has set you in authority. As for
> you, with this honor him: by consecrating yourself to him, as he has estab-
> lished you as (the) most holy one [of all] the world (לקדושׁ קורשׁים [לכול]
> תבל), and with all the [div]ine being[s] he has cast your lot. Your glory he
> has magnified greatly, and he has established you for himself as a first-
> born son among ...[106]

Lines 4-5 of this fragment present the addressee's affinity with the angels
as a feature of God's divine plan: "With all the [div]ine being[s] he has

---

[105] The fate of the elect is discussed in section 3 of Chapter 5.

[106] *DJD 34*, 300-01. Regarding the translation "Long ag]o," I tentatively follow Tigchelaar, *To Increase Learning*, 232. The word in question is in poor material condition
and cannot be reconstructed conclusively.

cast your lot (גורלכה)."[107] The Qumran community describes the relationship between group members and the angels in a similar way.[108] The Community Rule declares that God "has given them an inheritance in the lot of the holy ones (ינחילם בגורל קדושים)" (11:7-8; cf. 10:4).[109] The Hodayot affirms that people have the potential to join the elect and the angelic lot:

> You have purified man (אנוש) from offence, so that he can make himself holy (להתקדש) ... to become united wi[th] the sons of your truth and in the lot with your holy ones (בגורל עם קדושיכה) (19:10-12; cf. 14:13; 11Q13 2 8).[110]

The Songs of the Sage (4Q510-11) likewise describes the elect as being "in the lot of God with the ange[ls]" (4Q511 2 i 8).[111]

The addressee's similarity to the angels is clear in 4Q418 81 3-4. The relevant portion reads: "As for you, with this honor him: by consecrating yourself to him, as he has established you as (the) most holy one [of all] the world (תבל [לכול] לקדוש קודשים)."[112] The phrase לקדוש קודשים is a matter of debate.[113] It has been understood as a reference to the Holy of

---

107 See section 4.3 of Chapter 2.

108 For more on angels in the Qumran literature, see Devorah Dimant, "Men as Angels: The Self-Image of the Qumran Community," in *Religion and Politics in the Ancient Near East* (ed. A. Berlin; Bethesda: University Press of Maryland, 1996), 93-103; John J. Collins, *Apocalypticism in the Dead Sea Scrolls* (London/New York: Routledge, 1997), 130-49; Björn Frennesson, *"In a Common Rejoicing": Liturgical Communion with Angels in Qumran* (SSU 14; Uppsala: University of Uppsala Press, 1999); Fletcher-Louis, *All the Glory of Adam*, 88-135, 150-221; idem, "Some Reflections on Angelomorphic Humanity Texts among the Dead Sea Scrolls," *Dead Sea Discoveries* 7 (2000): 292-312; Mach, *Entwicklungsstadien*; Davidson, *Angels at Qumran: A Comparative Study of 1 Enoch 1-36, 72-108 and Sectarian Writings from Qumran* (JSPSup 11; Sheffield: Sheffield Academic Press, 1992); Elgvin, "An Analysis of 4QInstruction," 137, note 58. See also James H. Charlesworth, "The Portrayal of the Righteous as an Angel," in *Ideal Figures in Ancient Judaism: Profiles and Paradigms* (ed. J.J. Collins and G.W.E. Nickelsburg; SBLSCS 12; Chico: Scholars Press, 1980), 135-51.

109 This text also describes the special inheritance of group members as an "eternal possession" (אוחזת עולם). 4Q418 55 12 uses similar language to describe the elect status of the group to which it is addressed: "But they will inherit an eternal possession (והם אחזת עולם ינחלו)." See also *DJD 34*, 273.

110 Note that 4Q416 1 10 describes those who will be accepted with favor when God judges as "the sons of his truth" (בני אמתו).

111 Cf. Wis 5:5; Eph 1:18; Col 1:12.

112 My translation follows that of Tigchelaar, *To Increase Learning*, 231. Caquot, "Les textes de sagesse de Qoumrân," 23, translates "il a fait de toi un saint des saints." Also note that 4Q423 8 3 has the variant לק[דש] for the phrase לקדוש of 4Q418 81 4. 4Q418 81 4 has a *plene* spelling while 4Q423 8 3 is *defectiva*. Tigchelaar, *To Increase Learning*, 143, transcribes the word in question from 4Q423 8 3 as לק[דש], and joins the fragment with 4Q423 23.

113 The word קדוש in 4Q418 81 4 is probably an adjective in substantized form that functions as a noun. This is suggested by the fact that קודשים is a plural noun. Generally in

Holies.[114] Elgvin contends that if "Holy of Holies" were the proper translation it would have been spelled קודש קודשים rather than קדוש קודשים.[115] The phrase קודש קודשים is used to refer to the "Holy of Holies" in the Community Rule and the Rule of Benedictions (1QS 8:5-6; 1QSb 4:28). In the Hebrew Bible the phrase קדש קדשים can either refer to the Holy of Holies or have a superlative sense of "most holy."[116]

Aside from the variant spelling, there are other reasons that suggest the superlative reading. 4QInstruction contains no polemic against the Temple. The wisdom text never presents the holiness of the addressee as replacing the atoning and sacrificial functions of the Temple, in contrast to the Qumran rulebooks (1QS 8:5-10; 9:3-11; CD 6:11-7:6). This suggests that the addressee is not proclaimed to be the "Holy of Holies." If one does not read the phrase קדוש קודשים as an explicit reference to the Temple, the superlative reading is the best option available. The addressee is a "most holy one." 4Q418 81 4 adds to the superlative sense of לקדוש קודשים by making the bold claim that the addressee is the "most holy one [of all] the world (תבל [לכול])."[117] The phrase קדוש קודשים in 4QInstruction should be considered an allusion to the "Holy of Holies" rather than a direct reference to it. It is language that emphasizes the holiness of the addressee.

The theme of the holiness of the addressee is prominent in 4QInstruction. The holiness motif is highlighted by the priestly language of line 3 of 4Q418 81, which proclaims that the addressee has a special relationship with God: "He is your portion and your inheritance among the sons of Adam." The phrase "He is your portion and your inheritance" relies on Numbers 18:20, which attests a tradition that justified Aaronid jurisdiction over Temple sacrifices.[118] This allusion has been a focal point of interpretation of this text. Several commentators argue that the addressee is a priest. The editors of *DJD 34* argue that he has a "priestly or quasi-priestly authority."[119] Tigchelaar observes the diversity

---

the Hebrew Bible קדש is a noun, whereas קדוש is an adjective. See, for example, Exod 30:36 for the former and 29:31 for the latter.

[114] *DJD 34*, 302. This is also the translation used in García Martínez and Tigchelaar, *Dead Sea Scrolls Study Edition* (2 vols.; Leiden: Brill, 1997-98), 2.871, and by R. Eisenman and M.O. Wise, *The Dead Sea Scrolls Uncovered* (New York: Barnes and Noble, 1992), 249. The translation "most holy one" is offered in *DJD 34*, 15.

[115] Elgvin, "An Analysis of 4QInstruction," 136.

[116] For the former, see, for example, Exod 40:10; Lev 2:10. For the latter, see Exod 30:29. Cf. Lev 27:28 and 1 Chr 23:13.

[117] The supplement [לכול] is guaranteed by 4Q423 8 3.

[118] Baruch Levine, *Numbers 1-20* (AB 4A; New York: Doubleday, 1993), 436-37. Cf. Ezek 44:28.

[119] *DJD 34*, 20. This topic is also discussed in section 2 of Chapter 6.

of professions of the addressee throughout the composition and suggests that 4Q418 81 may have been written to priests, whereas other texts were not.[120] Fletcher-Louis makes a similar, but bolder, claim. He contends that 4Q418 81 was written to Aaronic priests who bless and glorify the rest of the community to which 4QInstruction is addressed.[121] Elgvin, by contrast, argues that the priestly motifs should not be taken literally but rather as a symbolic description of the elect status of the addressee.[122]

Elgvin's interpretation offers the best explanation of the priestly language of 4Q418 81 3. Cultic or halakhic issues are present in 4QInstruction (e.g., 4Q418 103 ii 1-9) but are by no means predominant concerns.[123] This suggests that the group to which the text is directed was not comprised of priests. This is also implied by the fact that some of its addressees are women (4Q415 2 ii 1-9). The addressee is not a priest. Rather, his elect status is described in priestly terms.

There are other ways that 4Q418 81 emphasizes the holiness of the addressee. It does so through use of the term "glory." Line 5 proclaims "Your glory (כבודכה) he has magnified greatly." While some texts of 4QInstruction emphasize that God has glory (4Q417 1 i 13; 4Q418 126 ii 9), even more claim that the addressee possesses this attribute.[124] He gives glory to God. After line 3 declares that God is the special inheritance of the addressee, it declares: "As for you, with this honor him (כבדהו)" (ll. 3-4). God has a special relationship with the addressee, and it follows naturally that he himself is holy.

4QInstruction elsewhere highlights the holiness of the addressee. It declares that he has a "holy spirit" that is more valuable than money (4Q416 2 ii 6-7).[125] The Qumran rulebooks likewise declare that the members of the Dead Sea sect have a "holy spirit" (1QS 3:7; 9:3; CD 7:3-4). 4QInstruction may teach the addressee that he has a "holy seed." If one grants the distant join of fragments of 1 ii and 2 i of 4Q415, lines 4-5 attest the phrase "your holy seed" (זרע // קודשכה). Combining these texts has no material basis but makes sense semantically. The join is

---

[120] *To Increase Learning*, 236. This is compatible with the view of Armin Lange that the composition was produced by circles based at the Jerusalem Temple. See his "In Diskussion mit dem Tempel: zur Auseinandersetzung zwischen Kohelet und weisheitlichen Kreisen am Jerusalemer Tempel," in *Qohelet in the Context of Wisdom* (ed. A. Schoors; BETL 136; Leuven: Leuven University Press/Peeters, 1998), 113-60.

[121] Fletcher-Louis, *All the Glory of Adam*, 178.

[122] Torleif Elgvin, "Priestly Sages? The Milieus of Origin of 4QMysteries and 4QInstruction," in *Sapiential Perspectives*.

[123] Lawrence H. Schiffman, "Halakhic Elements in the Sapiential Texts," in *Sapiential Perspectives*; Tigchelaar, *To Increase Learning*, 235.

[124] 4Q416 2 ii 18; 4Q416 2 iii 12, 18; 4Q416 2 iv 11; 4Q418 159 ii 6.

[125] This passage is examined in more detail in section 3.5.1 of Chapter 4.

used in *DJD 34* and endorsed by Tigchelaar.[126] The composite text attests the unfortunately fragmentary statement that "your seed will not
depart from the inheritance of ..." (ll. 5-6). Other incomplete texts mention an "inheritance of holi[ness]" (4Q418 234 1; cf. 4Q418 251 1) and
"your ho[ly] heart" (4Q418 236 3; cf. 4Q423 9 3).[127] These texts most
likely refer to the addressee. The theme of the holiness of the addressee
is well attested even if one does not consider 4Q415 1 ii-2 i. There is no
compelling reason, however, to dispute the combination of these fragments as a legitimate possibility.

Elgvin has argued that the phrase לקדוש קודשים of 4Q418 81 4 refers
to blessing the angels. He translates it as "to sanctify the holy ones."[128]
There is no reason to suggest that the angels need any act of sanctifica-
tion from the addressee to maintain their holiness. But Elgvin helpfully
suggests that the word קודשים should be taken as a reference to angels.
The Songs of the Sabbath Sacrifice uses this same term to refer to the
holiness of the angels. 4Q400 1 i 10 reads: "He es]tablished them [for]
himself as the ho[liest of the holy ones in the ho]ly of holies (קֹדֶֹ[י]
קודשים בק]וֹדש קודשים וְשִׂי לקד]וֹ [ל]ל)."[129] This describes God's ap-
pointment of the angels to minister in the heavenly temple. Notice the
reconstructed text's use of two different but similar phrases, קדושי
קודשים to refer to the 'most holy' angels, while קודש קודשים signifies the
heavenly temple. The phrase קדושי קודשים demonstrates that the angels
are 'most holy' beings in a sacred setting.

Along with the word קודשים in 4Q418 81 4, the fragment uses קדושים
to describe the relationship between the addressee and the angels. The
text begins: "He has opened up your lips as a fountain in order to bless
the holy ones (לברך קדושים). And you, like an eternal fountain, praise
..." (cf. 1QH 18:31). The relevant portion of lines 11-12 reads: "Before
you receive your inheritance from his hand, honor his holy ones (כבד
קדושיו) ... begin [with] a song (שִׂיר[ ] פתח) of all the holy ones."[130] There

---

[126] As Tigchelaar, *To Increase Learning*, 225-26, points out, the plausibility of this
join is suggested by that fact that the fragments in question have 4Q414 on the *verso*.
When the join is made 4Q414 produces a coherent text. Strugnell and Harrington suggest
in *DJD 34*, 46, that the term "seed" in this text refers to the children of the addressee. For
more on the term "holy seed" in Second Temple literature, see Christine Hayes, "Intermarriage and Impurity in Ancient Jewish Sources," *Harvard Theological Review* 92 (1999):
3-36.

[127] Tigchelaar, *To Increase Learning*, 226-29, combines these texts with fragments 14
and 235 of 4Q418.

[128] Elgvin, "An Analysis of 4QInstruction," 269.

[129] This translation is from Carol Newsom. See *DJD 11*, 178.

[130] Note that the phrase of line 12 translated above as "begin [with] a song of all the
holy ones" is given a much more conservative transcription by Tigchelaar. He leaves a

is a debate regarding the identity of the "holy ones" in 4Q418 81 1 and 11-12.   Fletcher-Louis, understanding this fragment as addressed to Aaronic priests, argues that the "holy ones" should be understood as "the laity of Israel" who are glorified by the priests.[131]   However the work nowhere else discusses priest and laity as two distinct groups.[132] This suggests that such a distinction should not be read into 4Q418 81. Stuckenbruck has taken issue with Fletcher-Louis's reading.[133] He points out that the phrase 'opening of lips' in biblical and late Second Temple literature generally refers to speech directed to God (e.g., Ps 51:15; 1QS 10:6).   Such an act, in his view, is therefore in 4QInstruction not "addressed to the righteous faithful so much as it is directed 'upwards', in this case towards angelic 'holy ones.'" The suggestion that the "holy ones" are angels is sound. It is a common term for angels in the Dead Sea Scrolls. Since the addressee is to open his lips to praise the "holy ones," this latter designation does not signify the elect group to which the composition is normally addressed. This suggests that the word refers to

lacuna between פחח and קד[ושים. The edition of this text in *DJD 34*, 301, however, makes sense on semantic grounds.

Following the material quoted above from line 12 is a fragmentary phrase which I tentatively translate as "All called by his name are holy o[nes]." While this phrase is vague, it seems to depict the intended audience of 4QInstruction as holy. After the phrase "by his name" (לשמו)—the *wāw* is a secondary addition—are the remnants of a word, קורש[. Strugnell and Harrington, *DJD 34*, 301, observe that there is one visible portion of a line-stroke after the *šîn*. They do not speculate on what letter it is used to form. Elgvin reads this stroke as a *yôd*, producing the reconstruction קורש[ים]. See "An Analysis of 4QInstruction," 136. The line stroke after the *šîn* from a material standpoint is not necessarily a trace of a *yôd*. However, coming after קורש[, it is likely that *yôd* as part of a plural ending would follow. Reading "holy ones" at the end of line 12 is also supported by the importance of this term in 4Q418 81 1-13. Elgvin understands כול הנקרא לשמו as referring to the elect. See his "The Mystery to Come," 125. Tigchelaar, *To Increase Learning*, 231, translates the phrase "And everyone who is called by His name, holy[."

131 *All the Glory of Adam*, 179.

132 Fletcher-Louis, ibid., 184, writes: "4Q418 81 13 is formally distinct from other parts of 4QInstruction because it is not addressed to a maven, a member of the laity, but to a priest." The author argues that 4Q423 5 1-4 is addressed to different priestly groups. "Levi the prie[st]" is mentioned in line 1 of this text in a fragmentary context. The "judgment of Korah" in line 2 occurs in the context of judgment. This is clear in line 4: "[He will judg]e all of them in truth and visit upon fathers and sons, [upon proselyte]s together with every native born." 4Q423 5 1-4 clearly discusses different groups of people. But there is no sense that they represent different cultic or priestly classes. Rather the stress of the passage is that all people will be judged.

133 Loren T. Stuckenbruck, "'Angels' and 'God': Exploring the Limits of Early Jewish Monotheism," in *Exploring Early Jewish and Christian Monotheism* (ed. L.T. Stuckenbruck and W. Sproston North; New York/London: Continuum, forthcoming).

angels. If the "holy ones" of line 1 are angels, the term should also be understood as referring to them in lines 11 and 12.[134]

In the literature of the Qumran sect the term "holy ones" is used ambiguously, and can often be reasonably interpreted as referring either to angels or the elect who have a close relationship with the angels.[135] A similar ambiguity is in 4QInstruction, even though it uses different spellings of "holy ones." In line 1 of 4Q418 81 the "holy ones" (קדושים) refers to angels, whereas in lines 4-5 the addressee is "most holy" (קדוש קודשים) and is in the angelic lot. Line 5 may elaborate this theme by proclaiming: "he has established you for himself as a first-born son (בכור) among ..." (cf. 1Q26 3 2). It is has been noted that this statement implies that the addressee is among the sons of God.[136]

4QInstruction stresses that the addressee's affinity with the angels is not automatic. It is something he must nurture and develop. The angels represent an ideal state to which he should aspire. They never tire of the acquisition of wisdom: "Indeed, would they say: 'We are tired of works of truth, [we] are weary of ...' Do [they] not wal[k] in eternal light? ... [gl]ory and an abundance of splendor are with them ..." (4Q418 69 ii 13-14). This perspective is echoed in 4Q418 55 8-11:

> Do] you [not k]now, or have you not heard, that the angels of holiness are h[is] (God's) in heaven ... They pursue after all the roots of understanding and are vigilant for ... [ac]cording to their knowledge they are glorified, each more than his neighbor, and according to one's intelligence his splendor is increased ... Are they like man because he is sluggish, or like a human because he dies?[137]

4QInstruction teaches the addressee that he has a natural predisposition that makes him similar to the angels. He is to comport himself in a way

---

[134] Contra Elgvin, "An Analysis of 4QInstruction," 136-37, who, while arguing that the phrase "holy ones" refers to the angels in lines 1 and 11, contends that in line 12 it refers to the elect.

[135] See, for example, 1QSb 4:23 and 1QM 12:7. Also note 4Q511 35 2-4: "Among the holy ones (בקדושים), God makes (some) hol[y] ([ש]יקד) for himself like an everlasting sanctuary ... And they shall be priests, his just people, his army and servants, the angels of his glory (מלאכי כבודו)" (cf. 4Q511 2 i 6). *1 Enoch* 100:5 describes the elect as "holy" when associating them with angels: "And he will set guards from the holy angels over all the righteous and holy." See John J. Collins, *Daniel* (Hermeneia; Minneapolis: Fortress, 1993), 313-17. See also Elgvin, "An Analysis of 4QInstruction," 136-37; Fletcher Louis, *All the Glory of Adam*, 167.

[136] Elgvin, "An Analysis of 4QInstruction," 140; Tigchelaar, *To Increase Learning*, 233. Elgvin's comprehensive review of the relevant material (e.g., *T. Jud.* 24:1-3; *Pss. Sol.* 13:9) concludes that 4QInstruction "seems to be the first source to call the *elect individual* a 'firstborn son' of God." Italics his.

[137] 4Q418 55 10 matches 1QH 18:27-28 very closely. This point is discussed in section 2 of Chapter 6. See also Harrington, *Wisdom Texts*, 76; Elgvin, "An Analysis of 4QInstruction," 160.

that accords with that inherent tendency. While the main writings of the Dead Sea sect describe the elect as in the angelic lot, they never hold up the angels as a model for conduct in the manner of 4QInstruction.

Regarding the "holy ones" of 4Q418 81 1, 11-12, Stuckenbruck contends that these lines attest the "veneration of angels."[138] He does not claim that 4QInstruction includes a cult of angel worship.[139] Rather he contends that this composition, like other late Second Temple texts, "suggest[s] that angelic beings could on occasion be regarded with an esteem analogous to that attributed to God" (e.g., 11Q14; Tob 11:14).[140] Praise of both God and the angels is part of the way of life that 4QInstruction advocates for the addressee. Line 1 of 4Q418 81, along with its call to "bless the holy ones," has been reconstructed as also encouraging the addressee to praise the name of God (cf. 4Q416 2 iii 11-12; 4Q417 1 ii 6, 9).[141] Line 4 of the fragment tells the addressee to "honor him (כבדהו)," referring to God. According to line 3, he glorifies him with his inheritance, 4QInstruction's term for his elect status. In 4Q418 81 1, 11-12 he is told, respectively, to "bless" (ברך), "honor" (כבד), and "begin [with] a song (פתח[ ]שׂיֹר) of" the holy ones.

The theme of praise helps clarify the relationship between the addressee and the angels. Depicting the angels as in heaven praising God is a common Second Temple trope (e.g., Dan 7; *1 En.* 14; *Apoc. Ms.* 22:3).[142] The literature of the Qumran sect describes angels as praising while emphasizing that praise is an important part of community life (e.g., 1QM 12:1-2; 1QS 1:21-22; 11:15; cf. 4Q504 1-2 vii 1-13).[143] 4Q418 126 ii 10 is fragmentary but may mention angels praising God: "Continually they praise his name."[144] Line 11 begins with ואתה, "But you ..." This suggests that the antecedent of line 10 is not the normal addressee of the text. The antecedent could be the "children of Eve" of line 9. This phrase may refer to the intended audience of 4QInstruction, since this expression is somehow associated with the "might of God and

---

[138] Stuckenbruck, "'Angels' and 'God.'"

[139] For more on the exaltation of angels in Second Temple Judaism, see Loren T. Stuckenbruck, *Angel Veneration and Christology: A Study in Early Judaism and in the Christology of the Apocalypse of John* (WUNT 2/70; Tübingen: J.C.B. Mohr [Paul Siebeck], 1995); Larry W. Hurtado, *One God, One Lord: Early Christian Devotion and Ancient Jewish Monotheism* (2nd ed.; Edinburgh: T. & T. Clark, 1998 [orig. pub., 1988]); Carey C. Newman et al., ed., *The Jewish Roots of Christology* (JSJSup 63; Leiden: Brill, 1999). See also Fletcher-Louis, *All the Glory of Adam*, 1-32.

[140] Stuckenbruck, "'Angels' and 'God.'"

[141] *DJD 34*, 302. This reading is endorsed in Tigchelaar, *To Increase Learning*, 231.

[142] Mach, *Entwicklungsstadien*, 219-28.

[143] Dimant, "Men as Angels," 101.

[144] See *DJD 34*, 350. Tigchelaar, *To Increase Learning*, 102-03, joins this fragment with 4Q418 122 ii. This possibility does not affect the interpretation of the text at hand.

the abundance of His glory" of line 8. In this case, those praising would be a third person reference to the group that includes the addressee. Even if one does not understand 4Q418 126 ii 10 as referring to angels, it is reasonable to understand the addressee's call to praise the angels in relation to the motif of angels praising God. In 4Q418 81 the addressee is urged to praise the angels and God in a way that underscores his special relationship with them. 4QInstruction encourages him to act in a way that is like the angels.

Understanding that the theme of praise highlights the affinity between the addressee and the angels may provide the key to interpreting the phrase "eternal planting" in 4Q418 81 13. This line is fragmentary and difficult to translate. I offer the translation " ... during all periods (is) his splendor, his grandeur (is) with the eter[nal] planting (עם כול קצים הדרו [פארתו מטעת עו]לם)."[145] It is well-known from other Second Temple sources that the term "eternal planting" is used to refer to a community with elect status.[146] *1 Enoch* 93:10, for example, describes how the elect will become "the et[ern]al p[lant] of righteousness (נ]צבת [קשֹׁט עֹ]למ[א)" and given sevenfold wisdom (4QEn^g 1 iv 12-13).[147] The phrase is presumably derived from Third Isaiah, where it refers to the glory of the restored Zion (60:21; 61:3; cf. 65:22).[148]

---

[145] Elgvin, transcribing הדרי פארתו, translates the phrase as "for all the eras the splendors of his sprout, an [ete]rnal plant ..." This reading understands פארתו not as the word for "beauty" or "splendor" but פארה, "bough" (cf. Isa 10:33). But since פארתו is clearly "his glory," הדרו is probably a parallel expression with a *wāw*, "his splendor." See Torleif Elgvin, "An Analysis of 4QInstruction, 325; idem, "Wisdom and Apocalypticism in the Early Second Century BCE—The Evidence of 4QInstruction" in *The Dead Sea Scrolls Fifty Years After Their Discovery: Proceedings of the Jerusalem Congress, July 20-25, 1997* (ed. L.H. Schiffman, E. Tov, and J.C. VanderKam; Jerusalem: Israel Exploration Society/Shrine of the Book, Israel Museum, 2000), 241.

Tigchelaar, *To Increase Learning*, 94, 231, offers a conservative transcription of 4Q418 81 13: [לם[פארתו למטעת עו]ִֹ   ]קֹ כול עם. He translates this as "with all [   ] his beauty for the eter[nal] plantation." The letters he leaves out are on one scrap that is part of 4Q418 81, according to plate XVIII of *DJD 34*. Apparently in Tigchelaar's view the fragment in question should not be considered part of 4Q418 81. The piece seems to fit well where it is placed and there is no reason to exclude it.

[146] P.A. Tiller, "The 'Eternal Planting' in the Dead Sea Scrolls," *Dead Sea Discoveries* 4 (1997): 312-35; Stuckenbruck, "4QInstruction and the Possible Influence of Early Enochic Traditions," 249-57; Nickelsburg, *1 Enoch*, 444-45; Elgvin, "An Analysis of 4QInstruction," 128-34. See also S. Fujita, "The Metaphor of Plant in Jewish Literature in the Intertestamental Period," *Journal for the Study of Judaism* 7 (1976): 30-45.

[147] This transcription is given in Michael Knibb, *The Ethiopic Book of Enoch* (2 vols.; Oxford: Clarendon, 1978), 2.225. See also *1 En.* 10:3, 16; 84:6; 93:5; CD 1:6-7; *Jub.* 1:16; 16:26; 21:24. Cf. 1 Cor 3:9.

[148] Tiller, "The 'Eternal Planting,'" 313. The phrase is similar to the botanical metaphor of the messianic title "Branch of David" (צמח דוד) (e.g., Isa 11:1-9; Jer 23:5-6).

The interpretation of the "eternal planting" in 4Q418 81 13 is diffi-cult. This is primarily because of the fragmentary condition of the line. Tiller, in an early study of this text, concludes "It is impossible to iden-tify either the meaning or the referent of the 'eternal planting.'"[149] Elgvin has argued that the phrase is a reference to the "remnant community."[150] 4QInstruction, however, never employs remnant language. He later re-vised his view, arguing that the phrase is a "metaphor for the righteous community" and that the term "indicates that the author of 4QInstruction viewed his circles as the nucleus of the community of the end-time, that will exist forever."[151] While 4QInstruction exhibits none of the eschato-logical urgency that is often evident in groups for which the end seems near, Elgvin is probably correct to understand the phrase as a reference to the elect community that includes the addressee. This interpretation is likely given the meaning of "eternal planting" elsewhere in Second Tem-ple sources.

Stuckenbruck interprets the phrase "eternal planting" in light of the comparison in 4Q418 81 1 of the addressee's praise to an "eternal foun-tain" (מקור עולם) (cf. 4Q418 127 1). He argues that "the watering from the fountain may thus signify the participation of the community in the activities that characterise God's holy ones in heaven."[152] If this is the case, the "eternal planting," he contends, refers to "the elect community *insofar as it participates in the angelic community* in anticipation of eternal life" (italics his). This interpretation of the "eternal planting" is supported, he proposes, by the fact that the composition describes the angels as having "eternal life" (חיים עולם) and an "eternal possession" (אחזת עולם) (4Q418 69 ii 13; 4Q418 55 12; cf. 1QS 11:7). This interpre-tation is attractive. The "fountain" of line 1 is explicitly associated with the praise of angels. Both the Community Rule and the Hodayot de-scribes the elect as an "eternal planting" in relation to angelic fellowship. Like 4Q418 81, both 1QS 11:7-9 and 1QH 14:12-16 depict the elect as being in the lot of the holy ones and as an "eternal planting" (cf. 1QS 8:5).[153] 4QInstruction, however, never depicts the addressee as worship-

---

[149] Tiller, "The 'Eternal Planting,'" 325.

[150] "The Mystery to Come," 125.

[151] Elgvin, "An Analysis of 4QInstruction," 130. See also idem, "Wisdom and Apoca-lypticism," 242-43.

[152] Stuckenbruck, "'Angels' and 'God.'" See also idem, "4QInstruction and the Possi-ble Influence of Early Enochic Traditions," 252; Michael Fishbane, "The Well of Living Water: A Biblical Motif and its Ancient Transformations," in *Sha'arei Talmon: Studies in the Bible, Qumran, and the Ancient Near East presented to Shemaryahu Talmon* (ed. M. Fishbane and E. Tov; Winona Lake: Eisenbrauns, 1992), 3-16.

[153] Stuckenbruck, "4QInstruction and the Possible Influence of Early Enochic Tradi-tions," 253.

ping in unison with the angels as in the Hodayot.[154] The psalms of the Dead Sea sect depict liturgical fellowship with the angels to an extent not found in 4QInstruction. Nevertheless, by praising the angels, its addressee behaves like them. By doing so he actualizes the elect status that God established for him when he was placed in the angelic lot. While the immediate context of 4Q418 81 13 is unclear, it seems that the term "eternal planting" is used to describe the flourishing of the addressee who acts in a way that nurtures the divine favor that has been bestowed upon him.[155] This suggests that the expression hints at the reward of eternal life that is offered to the addressee.[156]

Elgvin has also observed that there might be a connection between the "fountain" of line 1 and the "eternal planting" of line 13 of 4Q418 81.[157] Additionally, he points out that the word "planting" (מטע) occurs in a fragmentary context in 4Q423 1 7. If one accepts the distant join connecting fragments 1 and 2 i of 4Q423, this word is on the same line as a reference to the knowledge of good and evil. While such a connection remains tentative on text-critical grounds, 4Q423 1 clearly describes the elect status of the addressee as his charge to maintain the garden of Eden. The hymns of the Hodayot also use Eden as a metaphor to describe the elect. In 1QH 16:6 Eden is depicted not only as something that can either flourish or dry up like a desert, but also as an "eternal plantation" (cf. *Pss. Sol.* 14:3-5).[158] This suggests that the word "planting" of 4Q423 1 7 may be a remnant of a connection between the "eternal planting" and Eden originally asserted in the fragment, as in 1QH 16.[159] If so, this

---

[154] See, for example, 1QH 11:19-23. Collins, *Apocalypticism in the Dead Sea Scrolls*, 120; Frennesson, *"In a Common Rejoicing"*, 115-17.

[155] It is possible that the phrase "inheritors of the earth" (נוחלי ארץ), which occurs in 4Q418 81 14, may be another phrase that describes the elect. Stuckenbruck, "4QInstruction and the Possible Influence of Early Enochic Traditions," 249, has argued that the phrase relates to the "inheritance" of the addressee and signifies "a kind of participation in the privileges accorded to angels." Elgvin, "An Analysis of 4QInstruction," 273, also relates the "inheritors of the earth" to the "eternal planting." The views of Elgvin and Stuckenbruck are plausible, given the importance of the word "inheritance" for the elect status of the addressee. See section 4.3 of Chapter 2. Unfortunately the context of the phrase "inheritors of the land" is fragmentary, and assessments of this phrase remain tentative.

[156] See section 3 of Chapter 5.

[157] "An Analysis of 4QInstruction," 128.

[158] Ibid., 129.

[159] Elgvin uses the images of "planting" and Eden to argue that 4QInstruction depicts its intended audience as a "spiritual temple." See ibid., 133. However, the composition, while it alludes to the Temple to describe the holiness of the addressee (4Q418 81 4), never depicts his special status as replacing the atoning and sacrificial functions of the Temple.

would strengthen the link between the "eternal planting" and the elect status of the addressee.

2.4.4 The "Likeness of the Holy Ones" and 1 Enoch

Both 4QInstruction and *1 Enoch* portray recipients of revelation as similar to angels. The "spiritual people" receive the vision of Hagu because they are in the likeness of the angels. This is similar to the account of Noah in *1 Enoch*. He receives revelation (*1 En.* 89:1-4).[160] Noah is also depicted as angelic. Chapter 106, which R.H. Charles identified as part of a lost Book of Noah, describes his birth.[161] The angelic features of this child disturb his father Lamech, who says to his father Methuselah:

> I have begotten a strange son; he is not like a man, but is like the children of the angels of heaven, of a different type, and not like us. And his eyes (are) like the rays of the sun, and his face glorious (106:5; cf. 69:11).[162]

Methuselah goes to Enoch, who can explain the matter because "his dwelling is with the angels" (106:7; cf. 1QapGen ar 2:20; *Jub.* 4:21).

---

[160] Nickelsburg, *1 Enoch*, 375; Elgvin, "An Analysis of 4QInstruction," 68.

[161] R.H. Charles, *The Book of Enoch* (Oxford: Clarendon, 1912), 264. He based the existence of this book on *Jubilees* 10:13 and 21:10, which claim that Noah wrote a book. In 21:10 the "words of Noah" are on equal par with the "words of Enoch," suggesting that there might have actually been such a book. According to Milik, *The Books of Enoch*, 56, a Greek variant of the Aramaic *Testament of Levi* quotes from the Book of Noah. Genesis Apocryphon 5:29 also mentions this book. The existence of this book is doubted in Devorah Dimant, "Noah in Early Jewish Literature," in *Biblical Figures Outside the Bible* (ed. M.E. Stone and T.A. Bergen; Harrisburg: Trinity Press International, 1998), 144-46. See also R.C. Steiner, "The Heading of the 'Book of the Words of Noah' on a Fragment of the Genesis Apocryphon: New Light on a 'Lost' Work," *Dead Sea Discoveries* 2 (1995): 66-71. See also Fletcher-Louis, *All the Glory of Adam*, 33-41.

[162] A similar account is preserved in Genesis Apocryphon 5. 1QapGen ar 5:7 reads "Lamech your son is afraid of his appearance ..." Also note 5:12: "his eyes shine like [the] sun ..." (cf. 2:12). J.A. Fitzmyer recognizes a correspondence between the Genesis Apocryphon and *1 Enoch* 106. See his *The Genesis Apocryphon of Qumran Cave 1: A Commentary* (2nd ed.; BibOr 18a; Rome: Biblical Institute Press, 1971), 54-55, 97, 188-191. Fitzmyer, ibid., 187, points out that another account of Noah's miraculous birth may be preserved in 1Q19, which is for that reason titled 1QBook of Noah. 1Q19 3 3-4 reads: "[(not like the children of men) the fir]st-born is born, but the glorious ones ... his father, and when Lamech saw ..." See *DJD 1*, 84-86, 152; Milik, *The Books of Enoch*, 59-60; Dimant, "Noah in Early Jewish Literature," 130-31; James C. VanderKam, "The Birth of Noah," in *Intertestamental Essays in Honour of Jósef Tadeusz Milik* (ed. Z.J. Kapera; Krakow: Enigma, 1992), 213-31; idem, *The Book of Jubilees* (Sheffield: Sheffield Academic Press, 2001), 147; Mach, *Entwicklungsstadien*, 135.

Also note the parallel in *Joseph and Aseneth* 22:7, which describes Jacob as "a handsome (young) man, and his head was all white as snow ... and his eyes (were) flashing and darting (flashes of) lightning, and his sinews and his shoulders and his arms were like (those) of an angel." See Fletcher-Louis, *All the Glory of Adam*, 38.

Enoch discloses to him the coming flood and Noah's ordained role as a righteous remnant (cf. *Jub.* 7:38). For the word "type" of 106:5 the Greek text has τύπος, which is used by the LXX to translate תבנית in Exodus 25:40—the very word used in 4Q417 1 i 17 to express the likeness of the "spiritual people" to the angels.[163] תבנית, or its Aramaic equivalent, very well could have been in the original version of *1 Enoch* 106:5.

There are, however, important differences between the two texts. *1 Enoch* 106 describes the miraculous birth of a figure of biblical lore. He is depicted as physically resembling an angel, with his complexion "whiter than snow" and his eyes emitting light (*1 En.* 106:10). 4QInstruction's addressee is never described as physically resembling an angel. The "spiritual people" are also not described as resembling angels in terms of appearance. Nevertheless, 4QInstruction and *1 Enoch* both attest a tradition about people who receive revelation as having a "typos" similar to the holy ones. They may have both used the word תבנית to make this point.

2.5 4QInstruction's Use of Genesis 1-3 in its Second Temple Context

The author of 4QInstruction turned to Genesis 1-3 when reflecting on the nature of humankind. This is the case with other Second Temple sages.[164] 4QInstruction should be understood against this background. Second Temple Jews interested in this problem also based their thoughts on the Watchers myth, which attributes evil to fallen angels. The best example of this approach to the issue is the *Book of the Watchers* in *1*

---

[163] See Campbell Bonner, ed., *The Last Chapters of Enoch in Greek* (Darmstadt: Wissenschaftliche Buchgesellschaft, 1968), 79. For the word תבנית of Exodus 25:9 the LXX uses παράδειγμα. *1 Enoch* 106:10 also says that Noah's "form and type" are like that of a human, using τύπος and εἰκών, respectively. The Aramaic of *1 Enoch* 106:5, 10 is unfortunately not preserved. It would have appeared at the beginning portion of 4QEn^c 5 ii (*1 En.* 106:13-107:2), the first fifteen lines of which have not survived. See Milik, *The Books of Enoch*, 209.

[164] For the interpretation of Genesis 1-3 in the late Second Temple period, see John J. Collins, "Wisdom, Apocalypticism and the Dead Sea Scrolls," in *Seers, Sibyls and Sages*, 369-83. See also J.R. Levison, *Portraits of Adam*; Geza Vermes, "Genesis 1-3 in Post-Biblical Hebrew and Aramaic Literature before the Mishnah," *Journal of Jewish Studies* 43 (1992): 221-25; James L. Kugel, *The Bible As It Was* (Cambridge: Harvard University Press, 1997), 65-82; Fletcher-Louis, *All the Glory of Adam*, 92-103; Brooke, "Biblical Interpretation in the Wisdom Texts from Qumran," 212-14; Beyerle, "Und dann werden die Zeichen der Wahrheit erscheinen ...," 525-49; Moshe Bernstein, "Contours of Genesis Interpretation at Qumran: Contents, Context, and Nomenclature," in *Studies in Ancient Midrash*, 57-85. See also Dexter E. Callender, Jr., *Adam in Myth and History: Ancient Israelite Perspectives on the Primal Human* (HSS 48; Winona Lake: Eisenbrauns, 2000).

Enoch 1-36. The other main option was Genesis 1-3. Ben Sira, the Treatise on the Two Spirits, and Philo all relate conceptions of two different types of humankind to these chapters. To develop a fuller understanding of the use of Genesis 1-3 in 4QInstruction, these other texts will be examined in turn.

2.5.1 Ben Sira

Ben Sira uses Genesis 1-3 to explain the human condition. He declares that God gave Adam and Eve the knowledge of good and evil: "He filled them with knowledge and understanding, and showed them good and evil" (17:7).[165] Ben Sira, like 4Q423, discusses the Eden story without mention of the prohibition of Genesis 2:17. Also similar to 4QInstruction, Ben Sira utilizes the two contrasting portrayals of Adam in Genesis 1-3. He alludes to both Genesis 1:27 and 2:7. In 17:1 Ben Sira says "The Lord created human beings out of earth, and makes them return to it again" (cf. 41:4) yet asserts that "He endowed them with strength like his own, and made them in his own image" (17:3).[166] Ben Sira's description of the human condition relies on Genesis 1-3. He views humanity as similar to both the divine and creaturely realms. Every human being dies and is made of earth but nevertheless was fashioned in the divine image.[167] Yet Ben Sira emphasizes that there are two very different kinds of people. This is most clearly expressed in 33:10-13:

> All human beings come from the ground, and humankind was created out of the dust. In the fullness of his knowledge the Lord distinguished them and appointed their different ways. Some he blessed and exalted, and some he made holy and brought near to himself; but some he cursed and brought low, and turned them out of their place. Like clay in the hand of

---

[165] Collins, *Jewish Wisdom*, 83, 126; Chazon, "The Creation and Fall of Adam," 19; Di Lella and Skehan, *Wisdom of Ben Sira*, 282; Fletcher-Louis, *All the Glory of Adam*, 116.

[166] Levison, *Portraits of Adam*, 36-37. Elements of Genesis 1:27 and 2:7 are also combined in 4QWords of the Luminaries. 4Q504 8 4 declares that God made Adam "in the likeness of [your] glory" but in line 9 it describes Adam as "flesh." Line 5 of this fragment alludes to Genesis 2:7 by declaring "[the breath of life] you [br]eathed into his nose." See Davila, *Liturgical Works*, 244.

[167] R. Gordis has argued that a similar tension is expressed in Psalm 82:6-7: "I say, 'You are gods, children of the Most High, all of you; nevertheless, you shall die like mortals (כאדם), and fall like any prince.'" Cf. Hos 6:7; Job 31:33. See his "The Knowledge of Good and Evil,"127.

the potter, to be molded as he pleases, so all are in the hand of their Maker, to be given whatever he decides (cf. 11:14; 42:24).[168]

Ben Sira makes this dualism even more explicit: "Good is the opposite of evil, and life the opposite of death; so the sinner is the opposite of the godly. Look at all the works of the Most High; they come in pairs, one the opposite of the other" (33:14-15). This is a more pronounced dualism than that of 4QInstruction. While the Qumran text alludes to Genesis 2:7 in reference to the "fleshly spirit" rather than the "spiritual people," in 33:10-13 Ben Sira appeals to this verse from Genesis to underscore that God made both the blessed and cursed. Ben Sira also emphasizes death to a greater extent than 4QInstruction when characterizing the human condition. In a manner similar to Qoheleth, Ben Sira emphasizes that all humans die (e.g., Sir 14:17). In 4QInstruction the "fleshly spirit" will be destroyed (4Q416 1 12), while the addressee is promised life after his physical body expires.[169]

Ben Sira highlights the role of human choice, which is in tension with the determinism stressed in chapter 33.[170] Putting forth a Deuteronomic perspective, he claims: "It was he who created humankind in the beginning, and he left them in the power of their own free choice (ביד יצרו)" (15:14; cf. Deut 30:15). As discussed earlier, the addressee of 4QInstruction, while predisposed to ethical conduct, is free to make his own moral choices. The view is at odds with the composition's deterministic worldview. Both Ben Sira and 4QInstruction have an unresolved tension between the role of free will and divine determinism in their reflection on the problem of human sin.

Perhaps the biggest difference between Ben Sira and 4QInstruction regards how God made the knowledge of good and evil available. In both texts God situates this knowledge in the garden of Eden (Sir 17:7; 4Q423 1). Ben Sira's understanding of Genesis, like his reception of the wisdom tradition, is colored by Torah piety. The knowledge of good and evil is associated with the Torah: "He bestowed knowledge upon them, and allotted to them the law of life. He established with them an eternal covenant, and revealed to them his decrees" (17:11-12). Ben Sira 45:5 declares that the "law of life" was given to Moses at Sinai.[171] Ben Sira combines Sinai and Eden. This is compatible with his association of wisdom with the law in chapter 24. 4QInstruction relates the knowledge

---

[168] Cf. Isa 29:16; 45:9; Jer 18:6. See also Lange, *Weisheit und Prädestination*, 38-40; Collins, *Jewish Wisdom*, 83-86.

[169] See section 3 of Chapter 5.

[170] Collins, *Jewish Wisdom*, 83.

[171] Collins, "Wisdom, Apocalypticism and the Dead Sea Scrolls," in *Seers, Sibyls and Sages*, 375.

of good and evil to the mystery that is to be rather than the Torah (4Q417 1 i 6-8). This mystery is associated with creation (4Q417 1 i 8-9). Ben Sira, in similar fashion, roots the Torah in creation. It is understood as chronologically prior to its opening narrative about Adam and Eve. Unlike Ben Sira, in 4QInstruction the knowledge of good and evil is not publicly available in the Torah. Rather it is accessible through the revelation of divine mysteries.

2.5.2 The Treatise on the Two Spirits

The Treatise claims that God set within humankind two opposing spirits, one of truth and light, the other of darkness and deceit.[172] God "placed within him two spirits so that he would walk with them until the moment of his visitation" (1QS 3:18). Although these spirits are grounded in the creation of humanity, no exegetical basis is given for them.[173] These two spirits struggle against one another within every human; good and evil conduct is attributed to them. God has predetermined the portions of each spirit and their behavior: "From the God of Knowledge stems all there is and all there will be" (3:15). This highly deterministic and dualistic understanding of human conduct is compatible with that of Ben Sira 33 and 4QInstruction but is presented in a more absolute form. The Treatise's struggle between good and evil is cast in a mythological idiom of light and darkness (3:20-21) that is paralleled in neither 4QInstruction nor Ben Sira. Both of these texts posit the creation of two contrasting types of humanity, although they grant the exercise of human choice. All three compositions envision two opposing types of humanity, but do so in different ways.

Although the Treatise's two spirits have no explicit basis in Genesis 1-3, the composition turns to these chapters to explain the human condition. The Community Rule alludes to the grant of dominion of Genesis 1:28: "He created Adam (אנוש) to rule the world" (3:17-18). Humans in whom the spirit of light is more powerful than the spirit of darkness are construed as heirs to Adam in a way that is superior to the rest of humankind: "For those God has chosen for an everlasting covenant and to them will belong the glory of Adam (כבוד אדם)" (4:22-23). The Treatise describes the elect as being in continuity with Adam. While the Com-

---

[172] For fuller treatments of the Treatise, see Lange, *Weisheit und Prädestination*, 121-70; P. Wernberg-Møller, "A Reconsideration of the Two Spirits in the *Rule of the Community* (1QSerek III, 13 – IV, 26)," *Revue de Qumran* 3 (1961-62): 413-41.

[173] Collins, *Jewish Wisdom*, 129, suggests that they might be based upon the phrases נשמת חיים and נפש חיה from Genesis 2:7.

munity Rule describes the "glory of Adam" as something they will attain, 1QH 4:14-15 presents this glory as something they already possess.[174] The "glory of Adam" is also mentioned in CD, where the phrase occurs in the context of eternal life.[175] I argue in Chapter 5 that the addressee of 4QInstruction, who has affinity with Adam, is likewise promised eternal life.

The Treatise equates the deterministic divine framework that guides reality with the knowledge of good and evil: "He (God) knows the results of their deeds for all times [everlas]ting and has given them as a legacy to the sons of man so that they know good [and evil] ... [until the time of] the visitation" (4:25-26). As with Ben Sira and 4QInstruction, in the Treatise the knowledge of good and evil is attainable. It never, however, mentions this knowledge in relation to a tree or garden. As in 4QInstruction, in the Treatise the knowledge of good and evil requires an understanding of the divine framework of reality.[176]

2.5.3 Philo

4QInstruction's two types of humankind are similar to the "double creation of man" of Philo.[177] This is an exegetical attempt to explain why Genesis 1-3 has two different accounts of Adam. Philo contends that the book offers two separate creations of man, one heavenly and one earthly. After citing Genesis 2:7 he writes:

> By this (verse) also he shows very clearly that there is a vast difference between the man thus formed (i.e., with clay) and the man that came into existence earlier after the image of God: for the man so formed is an object of sense-perception ... by nature mortal; while he that was after the (Divine) image was an idea or type or seal, an object of thought (only), incorporeal, neither male nor female, by nature incorruptible (*Opif.* 134).[178]

---

[174] Fletcher-Louis, *All the Glory of Adam*, 96.

[175] CD 3:20: "Those who remained steadfast in it will acquire eternal life, and all the glory of Adam is for them."

[176] This is discussed in section 4.2 of Chapter 2.

[177] Collins, "In the Likeness of the Holy Ones," 617.

[178] In *Allegorical Interpretation* 1.31 Philo cites Genesis 2:7 and writes "There are two types of men; the one a heavenly man, the other an earthly man." For more information, see Thomas Tobin, *The Creation of Man: Philo and the History of Interpretation* (CBQMS 14; Washington, D.C.: The Catholic Biblical Association, 1983), 108-12. See also B.A. Pearson, *The Pneumatikos-Psychikos Terminology in 1 Corinthians: A Study in the Theology of the Corinthian Opponents of Paul and its Relation to Gnosticism* (SBLDS 12; Missoula: Society of Biblical Literature, 1973), 18-20; Levison, *Portraits of Adam*, 69-74, 81-82; Karina Martin Hogan, "The Exegetical Background of the 'Ambiguity of Death' in the Wisdom of Solomon," *Journal for the Study of Judaism* 30 (1999), 4-11.

Philo is more explicit than 4QInstruction that Genesis 1-3 attests two separate creation stories.

Both 4QInstruction and Philo base a dualistic understanding of humanity in Genesis 1-3.[179] They do so, however, in different ways. Philo is more exegetical than 4QInstruction. In *De Opificio Mundi* 134 and *Allegorical Interpretation* 1.31, Philo presents his views on the two types of humanity as a way of explaining Genesis 1:27 and 2:7, citing the latter. 4QInstruction, by contrast, has no direct citation of Genesis 1-3, although it alludes to these chapters. Philo posits two different kinds of people in light of a Platonic division between two realms, one corporeal and mortal, the other incorporeal and immortal. This is similar to 4QInstruction's distinction between the "fleshly" and "spiritual" kinds of humanity but is not equivalent to it. Philo casts his description of the two different types in a philosophical idiom that is foreign to 4QInstruction. Their similarities suggest that Philo reshapes Palestinian sapiential traditions that are attested in 4QInstruction in the light of Hellenistic philosophy.

3. CONCLUSION

4QInstruction, like Ben Sira, the Treatise on the Two Spirits, and Philo, uses Genesis 1-3 to assess the nature of humankind. Scholars such as Elgvin have emphasized the similarities between 4QInstruction and *1 Enoch*. 4QInstruction's use of Genesis 1-3 is closer to instructional texts such as Ben Sira and the Treatise than the Enochic corpus. 4QInstruction and *1 Enoch*, however, have traditions and perspectives in common with regard to Genesis 1-3. For example, given that 4QInstruction asserts that the "fleshly spirit" does not have knowledge of good and evil, it is of interest that *1 Enoch* 25:4, which describes a "beautiful fragrant tree," declares that "no (creature of) flesh (οὐδεμία σάρξ) has authority to touch it."[180] The next verse declares "from its fruit

---

[179] This counters the claim made by Levison, *Portraits of Adam*, 85, that Philo's double creation is because of his *"Tendenz* and not early Jewish speculation." Levison's argument was made before 4QInstruction was available. See ibid., 29. See also Fletcher-Louis, *All the Glory of Adam*, 115.

[180] Some Enochic texts present the Watchers myth in terms of a flesh/spirit dichotomy. For example, *1 En.* 106:17 reads: "They will beget on the earth giants, not of spirit, but of flesh." Also note that *Jubilees* 4:23-25 places Enoch in Eden. For discussion, see James C. VanderKam, *Enoch and the Growth of an Apocalyptic Tradition* (CBQMS 16; Washington, D.C.: Catholic Biblical Association, 1984), 184-88. See also Matthew Black, ed., *Apocalypsis Henochi Graeci in Pseudepigrapha Veteris Testamenti* (PVTG 3; Leiden: Brill, 1970), 35.

life will be given to the chosen."[181] Although both texts contrast the elect
with the "fleshly," 4QInstruction uses this distinction to put forward an
understanding of human wickedness grounded in creation, whereas *1
Enoch* attributes evil to fallen angels.[182]

When compared to the use of Genesis 1-3 in Ben Sira, the Treatise,
and Philo, 4QInstruction's utilization of this biblical material is distinguished by its appeal to revelation. This is also important in the Treatise.
But the theme is more pronounced in 4QInstruction. The vision of Hagu
is associated with a heavenly book in which is inscribed the judgment
against the wicked. The vision also seems to provide knowledge of good
and evil. As in the Treatise, in 4QInstruction the knowledge of good and
evil is not only an aptitude for moral conduct but also signifies awareness
of the divine framework of creation. The knowledge of good and evil
refers to heavenly wisdom. Since Adam also possessed this knowledge,
the revelation disclosed to the addressee can be seen as a restoration of
the relationship God once enjoyed with Adam. If the word אנוש of
4Q417 1 i 17 is interpreted as Adam, the addressee possesses the same
angelic wisdom once bestowed to this patriarch. This helps explain why
4QInstruction is so devoted to the addressee. It wants him to conduct
himself in a way that befits his elect status.

The addressee was given the vision of Hagu pericope as part of his instruction. The passage is dense and intentionally enigmatic. Its ambiguity makes it function well as an instructional text. The author of
4QInstruction wanted the addressee to think about the details of this
passage. To gain insights from it he had to decide how to interpret various aspects of it. The key realization, in my opinion, that the addressee
was to derive from the vision of Hagu pericope was that he is like the
"spiritual people." Like them he has been separated from the "fleshly
spirit" (4Q418 81 1-2). He is in the lot of the angels, as the "spiritual
people" are in the likeness of the angels. The addressee has access to
revelation, as do the "spiritual people." Like Adam before him, the addressee has authority over the garden of Eden (4Q423 1). The "spiritual
people" can also be associated with Adam, since אנוש is given the vision
of Hagu.

4QInstruction lays out two contrasting types of humankind. The
"spiritual people" and the "fleshly spirit" represent two different ways of
being human. 4QInstruction sets before the addressee a right path and a

---

[181] Note the parallel in *T. Levi* 18:9-11: "And he shall open the gates of paradise; he
shall remove the sword that has threatened since Adam, and he will grant to the saints to
eat of the tree of life." Cf. *Gen. Rab.* 65:25.

[182] John J. Collins, "The Origin of Evil in Apocalyptic Literature and the Dead Sea
Scrolls," in *Seers, Sibyls and Sages*, 287-99.

wrong path. The addressee should be devoted to righteous conduct and the acquisition of wisdom through the mystery that is to be. The author of 4QInstruction knew that the addressee might not act in this way. He is inclined towards righteousness, being in the lot of the angels. But this tendency by itself does not mean that this path will be taken. One must decide to live in this way. It demands work and daily effort (cf. 4Q418 55 3). 4QInstruction strives to make sure that the addressee will choose the right lifestyle. The addressee is to recognize aspects of the "spiritual people" in himself so that he would strive to be like them. The "spiritual people" comprise an ideal way of being human.

EXCURSUS: "SPIRITUAL" AND "FLESHLY" TYPES
OF HUMANKIND IN PAUL

Ben Sira, the Treatise on the Two Spirits, Philo, and 4QInstruction all ground the creation of two types of humanity in an interpretation of Genesis 1-3. This is also the case in Paul. He therefore merits some consideration. The flesh/spirit dichotomy is a central aspect of Pauline anthropology and has received an enormous amount of scholarly attention.[183] It is beyond the scope of this study to provide a full treatment of this subject. While a flesh/spirit dichotomy can be found throughout the Pauline corpus (e.g., Rom 8:5-11; Gal 5:16-26), this section will focus on 1 Corinthians. This is because this letter associates "fleshly" and "spiritual" kinds of humanity with Adam.

While Paul is clearly colored by his Hellenistic environment, 4QInstruction suggests that he is to some extent dependent upon Palestinian wisdom traditions for his flesh/spirit dichotomy.[184] Frey has argued that Paul's understanding of "flesh" is similar to that of

---

[183] Standard studies include Robert Jewett, *Paul's Anthropological Terms: A Study of their Use in Conflict Settings* (AGJU 10; Leiden: Brill, 1971) and Pearson, *The Pneumatikos-Psychikos Terminology in 1 Corinthians*. For more recent scholarship, see Dale Martin, *The Corinthian Body* (New Haven: Yale University Press, 1995); Jeffery R. Asher, *Polarity and Change in 1 Corinthians 15: A Study of Metaphysics, Rhetoric, and Resurrection* (HUT 42; Tübingen: Mohr-Siebeck, 2000); James D.G. Dunn, *The Theology of Paul the Apostle* (Grand Rapids: Eerdmans, 1998), 51-78; Daniel Boyarin, *A Radical Jew: Paul and the Politics of Identity* (Berkeley: University of California Press, 1994), 57-85; Jörg Frey, "The Notion of 'Flesh' in 4QInstruction," 197-226; idem, "Die paulinische Antithese von 'Fleisch' und 'Geist' und die palästinisch-jüdische Weisheitstradition," *Zeitschrift für die neutestamentliche Wissenschaft* 90 (1999): 45-77; idem, "Flesh and Spirit," 367-404.

[184] Troels Engberg-Pedersen, ed., *Paul Beyond the Judaism/Hellenism Divide* (Louisville: Westminster John Knox, 2001).

4QInstruction.[185] Frey considers the composition to be a pre-Essene text that was known in Pharisaic circles. He speculates that Paul was exposed to texts like 4QInstruction and the Book of Mysteries during his Pharisaic education in Jerusalem. Although 4QInstruction probably should not be linked to the Pharisees, Frey helpfully suggests that 4QInstruction and Paul have sapiential traditions in common.[186]

Paul's presentation of two different kinds of people is evident in 1 Corinthians: "And so, brothers and sisters, I could not speak to you as spiritual people (ὡς πνευματικοῖς), but rather as people of the flesh (ὡς σαρκίνοις), as infants in Christ" (3:1). 1 Corinthians 1-4 is well known as distinct within the Pauline corpus for its unusually large amount of sapiential terminology.[187] The "spiritual people" and "people of the flesh" of Paul are not as starkly opposed as the "spiritual people and "fleshly spirit" of 4QInstruction. Paul's "people of the flesh" are "infants in Christ" who are not fully mature in terms of their development as ethical followers of Christ. Paul presumes that one who is among the fleshly people can become a member of the spiritual people. Otherwise there would be no reason for him to continue his missionary work among them. The missionary aspect of Paul is at odds with 4QInstruction, which never addresses the "fleshly spirit" and has a hostile attitude towards it. In the wisdom text, however, the addressee is free to make moral decisions. In both Paul and 4QInstruction an individual can act either 'fleshly' or 'spiritually'.

Like 4QInstruction, Paul relates the difference between the spiritual and fleshly groups to Adam. 1 Corinthians 15:45-48 reads:

> Thus it is written, "The first man, Adam, became a living being (εἰς ψυχὴν ζῶσαν; cf. Gen 2:7)"; the last Adam became a life-giving spirit. But it is not the spiritual (πνευματικὸν) that is first, but the physical (ψυχικόν), and

---

[185] Frey, "The Notion of 'Flesh' in 4QInstruction," 225; idem, "Flesh and Spirit," 403.

[186] Certain terms of Paul suggest familiarity with Hebrew idioms that are attested in 4QInstruction. For example, the phrase כלי [ח]וֹקְכה of 4Q416 2 ii 21 has been compared to 1 Thessalonians 4:4. Elgvin has proposed that the word כלי of 4QInstruction is a reference to the phallus, whereas the editors of *DJD 34* suggest that it refers to one's wife. See *DJD 34*, 108-10; Torleif Elgvin, "'To Master His Own Vessel': 1 Thess 4:4 in Light of New Qumran Evidence," *New Testament Studies* 43 (1997): 604-19; J. Strugnell, "More on Wives and Marriage in the Dead Sea Scrolls (4Q416 2 ii 21 [Cf. 1 Thess 4:4] and 4QMMT, B)," *Revue de Qumran* 17 (1996): 537-47; Jay E. Smith, "Another Look at 4Q416 2 ii.21, a Critical Parallel to First Thessalonians 4:4," *Catholic Biblical Quarterly* 63 (2001): 499-504.

[187] For example, σοφία occurs sixteen times in this unit, but only three times elsewhere in Paul (Rom 11:23; 1 Cor 12:8; 2 Cor 1:12). For the sapiential flavor of 1 Corinthians 1-4, see Helmut Koester, *Ancient Christian Gospels* (Harrisburg: Trinity Press International, 1990), 55-62; Sigurd Grindheim, "Wisdom for the Perfect: Paul's Challenge to the Corinthian Church (1 Cor 2:6-16)," *Journal of Biblical Literature* 121 (2002), 692-97.

then the spiritual. The first man was from the earth, a man of dust; the second man is from heaven. As was the man of dust, so are those who are of the dust; and as is the man of heaven, so are those who are of heaven.[188]

Paul goes on to claim that followers of Christ will carry "the image of the man of heaven (τὴν εἰκόνα τοῦ ἐπουρανίου)" (v. 49). The word εἰκών is used to translate צלם in LXX Genesis 1:27. In Paul the elect are portrayed in relation to Adam, in that Christ is superior yet analogous to Adam. 4QInstruction posits a more direct relationship between the elect and Adam through the addressee's stewardship over the garden in 4Q423. The בצלם אלהים tradition of Genesis 1:27 is interpreted christologically in 1 Corinthians 15:49. 4QInstruction uses Genesis 1:27 to establish similarity between the "spiritual people" and the angels (4Q417 1 i 17). Paul in 1 Corinthians uses this verse to assert the believer's affinity with Christ.

Pearson has argued that in 1 Corinthians 15 Paul polemically adapts an interpretation of Genesis 1:27 and 2:7 that was current in Hellenistic Judaism, as attested by figures such as Philo, that was espoused by his Corinthian opponents.[189] This interpretation emphasizes "the divine, spiritual 'inbreathing' in man, by which earthly man participated in the spiritual εἰκὼν τοῦ θεοῦ (Gen 1.27)."[190] This exegetical tradition depends on a Platonic dichotomy of the heavenly and incorruptible vis-à-vis the earthly and corruptible. Paul reworks this perspective by placing this flesh/spirit dichotomy within an eschatological horizon, with the former associated with this world and the latter with the age to come. Paul describes this world as "fleshly," using terms such as σῶμα and σάρξ.[191] Pearson argues that Paul's use of these terms does not stem from the anthropology of his opponents but from Jewish exegetical traditions that are preserved in Qumran and rabbinic literature. For example, 1QS 11:20-22 alludes to Genesis 2:7 to emphasize the creaturely aspect of the human condition. 4QInstruction, with its opposition of the "spiritual people" and the "fleshly spirit," supports Pearson's contention that Paul is reliant on Palestinian traditions when distinguishing between "fleshly and "spiritual" types of humankind.[192]

---

[188] Cf. 1 Cor 15:22 and Rom 5:4. See further R. Scroggs, *The Last Adam: A Study in Pauline Anthropology* (Philadelphia: Fortress Press, 1966); Dunn, *The Theology of Paul*, 79-101.

[189] Pearson, *The Pneumatikos-Psychikos Terminology*, 24-26.

[190] Ibid., 24.

[191] Cf., for example, 1 Cor 15:44, 50. See Jewett, *Paul's Anthropological Terms*, 119-34, 254-87; Jeffrey R. Asher, "Σπείρεται: Paul's Anthropogenic Metaphor in 1 Corinthians 15:42-44," *Journal of Biblical Literature* 120 (2001), 106.

[192] See also Boyarin, *A Radical Jew*, 62-63.

4QInstruction and Paul also both associate the "spiritual people" with access to hidden wisdom. Paul portrays the elect as having access to mysteries.[193] The pious, who are described as "spiritual people" in 1 Corinthians 3:1, know the hidden wisdom of God: "Think of us in this way, as servants of Christ and stewards of God's mysteries (μυστηρίων θεοῦ)" (4:1).[194] Paul's claim of revealed mysteries to the elect is compatible with the disclosure of the mystery that is to be to the addressee in 4QInstruction.

Paul's flesh/spirit antithesis, like that of Philo, is undoubtedly colored by his exposure to the wider Hellenistic world. The missionary context of Paul makes the separation between "fleshly" and "spiritual" people less absolute than in 4QInstruction. Despite these differences, Paul and the author of 4QInstruction both relate the existence of "fleshly" and "spiritual" types of humanity to Genesis 1-3. This suggests that Paul attests a version of a Jewish sapiential-exegetical tradition regarding the dualistic creation of humankind. Variants of this tradition are also preserved in 4QInstruction, Ben Sira, Philo, and the Treatise on the Two Spirits.

---

[193] B. Rigaux, "Révélation des Mystères et Perfection à Qumran et dans le Nouveau Testament," *New Testament Studies* 4 (1958), 250-52; Raymond E. Brown, *The Semitic Background of the Term "Mystery" in the New Testament* (Biblical Series 21; Philadelphia: Fortress Press, 1968); Grindheim, "Wisdom for the Perfect," 697-701.

[194] See also 1 Cor 2:7: "But we speak God's wisdom, secret and hidden (θεοῦ σοφίαν ἐν μυστηρίῳ, τὴν ἀποκεκρυμμένην), which God decreed before the ages for our glory." Paul may be using esoteric wisdom traditions to distinguish his message from the wisdom of members of his Corinthian audience, some of whom were schooled in Greek rhetoric, a public form of wisdom (1:17-25). See Dale Martin, *The Corinthian Body*, 47.

CHAPTER FOUR

POVERTY, FINANCIAL INSTRUCTION,
AND THE ELECT STATUS OF THE ADDRESSEE

1. INTRODUCTION

4QInstruction teaches its addressee that he is among the elect. Chapter 2 examined the mystery that is to be and the revelation of God's divine plan. Chapter 3 argued that 4QInstruction encourages the addressee to be like the "spiritual people" and that his elect status represents a restoration of the blissful relationship God enjoyed with Adam in the garden of Eden. There is, however, an aspect of the addressee that at first seems to argue against the claim that God favors him highly—his poverty. While some Qumran texts identify the elect as "poor" (e.g., CD 19:9; 1QM 13:12-14), 4QInstruction's refrain of the phrase "you are poor" is without exact parallel in Second Temple literature (e.g., 4Q416 2 ii 20; 4Q416 2 iii 2). Often this "poverty" refers to material poverty. 4QInstruction offers advice to people enduring material hardship. For example, 4Q417 2 i 19 reads: "If you lack, borrow, being without m[on]ey for what you need, for he (God) does not lack treasure." Certain texts are addressed to farmers (4Q418 103 ii 2-9) and artisans who possess חכמת ידים, "manual skill" (4Q418 81 15, 19). Although 4QInstruction makes some extraordinary claims about its intended audience, its social setting seems quite ordinary. It is comprised of people in an agricultural society who are occasionally unable to meet their basic needs.

4QInstruction combines teachings about the addressee's elect status with financial advice. He is advised to pay off debts quickly because he should "exchange [his] holy spirit for no price, because there is no price equal [to it]" (4Q416 2 ii 6-7). The composition shows concern for the addressee's economic situation, giving him practical advice to ensure that he does not face destitute poverty. Utilizing realia of the addressee's life, 4QInstruction also uses his poverty as a way to teach him about his elect status.

The addressee's poverty is used in ethical teachings. For example, 4QInstruction tells him to honor his parents "in your poverty" (4Q416 2 iii 15). Concern for the poor and downtrodden is a common theme in

traditional wisdom. An interest in the addressee's elect status influences
4QInstruction's reception of older wisdom regarding poverty. In a society that has little class mobility, the financial struggles of the addressee
are an important point of reference in 4QInstruction's teachings on both
practical topics and his elect status.

The theme of poverty in 4QInstruction has not been fully examined.
Scholars such as Murphy and Collins have concluded that the author had
material poverty in mind and that it is a key theme of the work.[1] Other
commentators have dismissed its importance. The editors of *DJD 34*
claim that "there is little that is noteworthy" about 4QInstruction's poverty language, except for the odd infrequency of words such as עני and
ענוה.[2] Tigchelaar has doubted that the addressee can be considered poor.
His examination of 4QInstruction's use of the phrase "you are poor"
concludes: "The text does not, therefore, insist on the poverty of the
addressee, but envisages the possibility that the *Mebin* might be, or become, poor."[3] Elgvin gives little treatment to the theme of poverty. He
notes that some of the addressees were probably "rural farmers" and
observes that there is no discussion of suffering or persecution by the
wealthy or by foreign rulers. He concludes that this "indicates a distance
to the Maccabean/Hasmonean establishment."[4] While this may be the
case, Elgvin does little with the document's use of poverty in its own
right.

---

[1] Catherine M. Murphy, *Wealth in the Dead Sea Scrolls and the Qumran Community*
(STDJ 40; Leiden: Brill, 2002), 187; John J. Collins, *Jewish Wisdom in the Hellenistic
Age* (OTL; Louisville: Westminster John Knox, 1997), 118. See also Benjamin G. Wright
III, "The Categories of Rich and Poor in the Qumran Sapiential Literature," in *Sapiential
Perspectives: Wisdom Literature in Light of the Dead Sea Scrolls. Proceedings of the
Sixth International Symposium of the Orion Center, 20-22 May 2001* (ed. G. Sterling and
J.J. Collins; Leiden: Brill, forthcoming). Daniel J. Harrington, while writing that "it is
hard to say" if the addressee's poverty should be understood as material poverty, under-
stands his poverty as a real situation. He writes "poverty seems to be more of a reality of
the human condition than an ideal to strive for." See his *Wisdom Texts from Qumran*
(London: Routledge, 1996), 45.

[2] *DJD 34*, 25-26.

[3] Eibert J.C. Tigchelaar, "The Addressees of 4QInstruction," in *Sapiential, Liturgical
and Poetical Texts from Qumran: Proceedings of the Third Meeting of the International
Organization for Qumran Studies, Oslo 1998* (ed. D. Falk et al.; STDJ 35; Leiden: Brill,
2000), 71. He also observes, as does Harrington, that the attestations of the "you are
poor" formula are clustered in 4Q416 2 ii-iii. It does not follow, however, that the importance of this refrain is restricted to this section. See Harrington, *Wisdom Texts*, 45.

[4] Torleif Elgvin, "An Analysis of 4QInstruction" (diss.; Hebrew University of Jerusalem, 1997), 180; idem, "Wisdom, Revelation, and Eschatology in an Early Essene Writing," in *Society of Biblical Literature Seminar Papers 1995* (SBLSP 34; Atlanta: Scholars
Press, 1995), 444.

Catherine Murphy has offered a major contribution towards understanding the theme of poverty in 4QInstruction and its financial instruction. Her thorough examination of the presentation of wealth in the Dead
Sea Scrolls devotes a chapter to 4QInstruction.⁵ She argues that the composition was written to people in a range of occupations, and that many
of them were farmers. 4QInstruction also contends that the addressee
has a relatively open economic situation. This does not accord with the
assessment of the Qumran community as isolated socially and financially
from the rest of Israel. The audience of 4QInstruction, she claims, is
composed of people from different economic levels but that the group
"regularly finds itself in difficult circumstances."⁶ Murphy focuses more
on the financial teachings of 4QInstruction than its depiction of poverty.

In this chapter I will argue that the theme of poverty is important in
4QInstruction. I will first discuss poverty in traditional wisdom to provide a context for understanding the topic in 4QInstruction. Then I will
examine the financial teachings of 4QInstruction and the different ways
that the text presents the addressee's poverty. This analysis will clarify
the social world of the intended audience. I will also argue that
4QInstruction often focuses upon the material poverty of the addressee,
and that his economic situation is used as a basis for instruction about his
ethical comportment and his elect status.

2. POVERTY IN THE HEBREW BIBLE AND THE ANCIENT NEAR EAST

Concern for the poor is commonplace in the literature of the ancient Near
East. One of the virtues of a good king is charitable treatment of the
downtrodden of society.⁷ In the Hebrew Bible, God devotes special
attention to the poor.⁸ It routinely characterizes the wicked as exacerbat-

---

⁵ Murphy, *Wealth in the Dead Sea Scrolls*, 163-209. See also her "The Disposition of
Wealth in the *Damascus Document* Tradition," *Revue de Qumran* 19 (1999): 83-129.

⁶ Ibid., 209.

⁷ For the king as a herdsman ensuring the welfare of his people, see John Wilson,
"Egypt," in *The Intellectual Adventure of Ancient Man* (ed. H. Frankfort et al.; Chicago:
University of Chicago Press, 1977 [orig. pub., 1946]), 78-86. For idealized kingship in
Mesopotamia, see A. Leo Oppenheim, *Ancient Mesopotamia* (2nd ed.; Chicago: University
of Chicago Press, 1977 [orig. pub., 1964]), 102. See also F. Charles Fensham, "Widow,
Orphan, and the Poor in Ancient Near Eastern Legal and Wisdom Literature," *Journal of
Near Eastern Studies* 21 (1962): 129-39.

⁸ See, for example, Pss 72:2, 12; 74:21; 107:41; 113:7; 140:12; Prov 29:14; Jer 22:16;
and Isa 41:17.

ing the plight of the poor.[9] Anger about mistreatment of the poor is central to the message of prophets such as Isaiah and Amos (e.g., Isa 3:16-24 and Amos 2:8). In the Psalms the speaker often identifies himself as poor and/or lowly since God looks favorably upon such people.[10]

Scholarship has noted the prominence of the poor and poverty in the Hebrew Bible. Rainer Albertz has argued that the lower class was an important locus of devotion in the post-exilic period. He contends that the "piety of the poor" helped establish the theological view, particularly evident in the Psalms, that God would "restore dignity and hope" to the oppressed.[11] Pleins has observed that poverty is a fundamental theme in the Hebrew Bible, although it attests a diversity of viewpoints on the topic.[12] For example, while poverty is important in the prophetic and legal literature, it is markedly less so in the vast bulk of historiographic material, such as the books of Samuel or Kings.

The theme of poverty is prominent in sapiential literature. The plight of the poor is a frequent topic in the wisdom literature of the ancient Near East. For example, *Ahiqar* 105 reads "I have tasted even the bitter medlar, and have eaten endives, but there is nothing more bitter than poverty."[13] A Sumerian proverb declares "How lowly is the poor man! A mill house is (for him) the edge of the oven. His ripped garment will not be mended. What he has lost will not be sought for!" (2.29).[14]

---

[9] E.g., 2 Kgs 4:1-7; Neh 5:1-13; Jer 2:34.

[10] A representative example is Psalm 40:17: "As for me, I am poor and needy, but the Lord takes thought for me. You are my help and my deliverer; do not delay, O my God." See also Pss 34:7; 35:10; 37:11; 69:29; 70:5; 74:21; 82:3; 86:1; 109:22; and 140:12. Cf. *Pss. Sol.* 18:2. The most common language to designate poverty in this material is אביון and עני. See also J. David Pleins, *The Social Visions of the Hebrew Bible: A Theological Introduction* (Louisville: Westminster John Knox, 2001), 419-51.

[11] Rainer Albertz, *A History of Israelite Religion in the Old Testament Period* (OTL; 2 vols.; Louisville: Westminster/John Knox, 1994), 2.518-22. His views have been challenged by Johannes Un-Sok Ro, *Die sogennante "Armenfrömmingkeit" im nachexilischen Israel* (BZAW 322; Berlin: de Gruyter, 2002).

[12] Pleins, *Social Visions*, 517-35.

[13] See also *Ahiqar* 137: "[Do not amass] wealth, lest you pervert your heart" (cf. 207). See J.M. Lindenberger, *The Aramaic Proverbs of Ahiqar* (Baltimore/London: Johns Hopkins University Press, 1983).

[14] This is from the Sumerian *Proverb Collections* that are available in B. Alster, *Proverbs of Ancient Sumer: the World's Earliest Proverb Collections* (2 vols.; Bethesda: CDL Press, 1997). See also "Wealth is far away, poverty is near" (1.15); "Let the poor man die, let him not live. When he finds bread, he finds no salt. When he finds salt, he finds no bread. When he finds condiments, he finds no meat. When he finds meat, he finds no condiments" (1.55); "The poor man is not appreciated" (2.18); "The poor man chews what(ever) he receives" (2.19); "The poor are the silent ones of the country" (2.32). Cf. UET 6/2 260-63, which is from the *Sumerian Proverbs from Ur*. See further Claus Westermann, *The Roots of Wisdom* (Louisville: John Knox Press, 1995), 150-54; Stuart Weeks, *Early Israelite Wisdom* (Oxford: Clarendon, 1994), 179-82.

Proverbs regarding the poor appear in Babylonian and Egyptian wisdom material.[15] Poverty is also an important theme of biblical wisdom.[16] The Book of Proverbs displays a prominent interest in wealth and poverty. Some of the Hebrew Bible's poverty terms occur disproportionately in its wisdom texts.[17] While Proverbs attests a range of views on the poor, it frequently displays sympathy and concern for their plight.[18] For example, Proverbs 22:22 reads "Do not rob the poor because they are poor, or crush the afflicted at the gate." At times the poor are associated with humility and ethical behavior: "Better to be poor and walk in integrity than to be crooked in one's ways even though rich" (Prov 28:6; cf. 19:1). There are, however, instances when poverty is considered a consequence of sloth or even folly.[19]

---

[15] See, for example, *Babylonian Theodicy* 70-71, "Those who neglect the god go the way of prosperity, while those who pray to the goddess are impoverished and dispossessed"; *Instruction of Amenemope* 14:5, "Do not covet a poor man's goods, nor hunger for his bread; a poor man's goods are a block in the throat, it makes the gullet vomit." See W.G. Lambert, *Babylonian Wisdom Literature* (Winona Lake: Eisenbrauns, 1996 [orig. pub., 1963]), 75; Miriam Lichtheim, *Ancient Egyptian Literature* (3 vols.; Berkeley: University of California Press, 1973-80), 2.154; Weeks, *Early Israelite Wisdom*, 163-78, 182-88.

[16] R.N. Whybray, *Wealth and Poverty in the Book of Proverbs* (JSOTSup 99; Sheffield: Sheffield Academic Press, 1990); J. David Pleins, "Poverty in the Social World of the Wise," *Journal for the Study of the Old Testament* 37 (1987): 61-78; idem, *Social Visions*, 452-83; H.C. Washington, *Wealth and Poverty in the Instructions of Amenemope and the Hebrew Proverbs* (SBLDS 142; Atlanta: Scholars Press, 1994); Raymond C. Van Leeuwen, "Wealth and Poverty: System and Contradiction in Proverbs," *Hebrew Studies* 33 (1992): 25-36. See also Ronald L. Giese, Jr., "Compassion for the Lowly in Septuagint Proverbs," *Journal for the Study of the Pseudepigrapha* 11 (1993): 109-17.

[17] ראש/רוש occurs 22 times in the Hebrew Bible, 15 of which are found in Proverbs 10-29. See Whybray, *Wealth and Poverty*, 16. 8 of the 13 occurrences of מחסור are found in Proverbs. See Pleins, *Social Visions*, 481. The extent to which such terms should be distinguished is a matter of debate. Whybray holds that there is "no significant distinction between the words for 'poor' and 'poverty.'" See his *Wealth and Poverty*, 23. Pleins, however, argues that each word has important nuances and that they should not be considered synonymous. See his *Social Visions*, 465-74. There does not seem to be any significant difference in the poverty terms of 4QInstruction. See also Murphy, *Wealth in the Dead Sea Scrolls*, 178.

[18] Roland Murphy, *The Tree of Life: An Exploration of Biblical Wisdom Literature* (3rd ed.; Grand Rapids: Eerdmans, 2002 [orig. pub., 1990]), 20. Pleins, *Social Visions*, 474, while acknowledging that Proverbs exhibits "ambivalence in its attitude toward the poor," characterizes the book as unduly hostile to the poor when he writes "To the wise, the poor are insignificant elements in the social order from which nothing can be gained, except perhaps insight."

[19] Prov 6:10-11, "A little sleep, a little slumber, a little folding of the hands to rest, and poverty will come upon you like a robber, and want, like an armed warrior" (=24:33-34); 12:24, "The hand of the diligent will rule, while the lazy will be put to forced labor"; 13:18, "Poverty and disgrace are for the one who ignores instruction, but one who heeds

The poor themselves are not addressed in Proverbs.[20] The book focuses rather on how they should be treated. Proverbs 14:20-21, for example, teaches "The poor are disliked even by their neighbors, but the
rich have many friends. Those who despise their neighbors are sinners,
but happy are those who are kind to the poor."[21] It is also stressed that
one should not take advantage of them.[22] One should be aware of their
plight: "The wealth of the rich is their fortress; the poverty of the poor is
their ruin" (10:15; cf. 18:11). How one treats the poor is an expression
of honoring or dishonoring God: "Those who oppress the poor insult
their Maker, but those who are kind to the needy honor him" (14:31).[23]
Kindness towards the poor ensures one's own good standing with God.
Proverbs 19:17 teaches that God will pay back what has been given to
the poor: "Whoever is kind to the poor lends to the Lord, and will be
repaid in full" (cf. Sir 35:13).[24] Some proverbs recommend giving to the
poor to ensure that God will hear the pleas of one who is charitable when
he is in need: "If you close your ear to the cry of the poor, you will cry
out and not be heard" (21:13).[25]

The rich are singled out for their abuse of the poor: "The rich rule
over the poor, and the borrower is the slave of the lender" (Prov 22:7).
The book also includes criticism of ill-gotten gains and excessive dependence upon wealth: "Treasures gained by wickedness do not profit,
but righteousness delivers from death" (10:2).[26] Pleins observes that
Proverbs presents poverty as "an ugly situation, leaving one at the mercy

---

reproof is honored"; 28:19, "Anyone who tills the land will have plenty of bread, but one
who follows worthless pursuits will have plenty of poverty." Cf. 10:4; 12:11.

[20] Whybray, *Wealth and Poverty*, 113.

[21] See also Prov 19:1, "Better the poor walking in integrity than one perverse of speech
who is a fool"; 28:27, "Whoever gives to the poor will lack nothing, but one who turns a
blind eye will get many a curse"; 29:7, "The righteous know the rights of the poor; the
wicked have no such understanding"; 29:14, "If a king judges the poor with equity, his
throne will be established forever"; 31:9, "Speak out, judge righteously, defend the rights
of the poor and needy"; 31:20, "She opens her hand to the poor, and reaches out her hands
to the needy." Cf. 13:7; 28:3.

[22] Prov 22:16: "Oppressing the poor in order to enrich oneself, and giving to the rich,
will lead only to loss."

[23] Prov 17:5: "Those who mock the poor insult their Maker; those who are glad at calamity will not go unpunished." Proverbs 22:2 and 29:13 proclaim that God has created
the rich and poor alike (cf. Sir 10:22; *Papyrus Insinger* 31:16-17). See Whybray, *Wealth
and Poverty*, 41-42.

[24] Richard Clifford, *Proverbs* (OTL; Louisville: Westminster John Knox, 1999), 178.
See also *Pirke Avot* 3:14: "Tithes are a fence around riches."

[25] Prov 22:9: "Those who are generous are blessed, for they share their bread with the
poor." The righteous may be understood to be poor in 18:10-11.

[26] Prov 13:11, "Wealth hastily gotten will dwindle, but those who gather little by little
will increase it"; 28:22, "The miser is in a hurry to get rich and does not know that loss is
sure to come."

of the often unsympathetic whims of the rich."[27]   The text displays an awareness of the difficulties of being poor, and does not want people to join their ranks. Yet at times Proverbs depicts poverty in a surprisingly positive light. It occasionally associates conduct it advocates with the poor and the rich with behavior it discourages: "Better is a little with righteousness than large income with injustice ... It is better to be of a lowly spirit among the poor than to divide the spoil with the proud" (16:8, 19).[28]

Proverbs's concern for the poor is evident in its advice on debts and surety.[29] Instruction on this topic is not oriented to the poor specifically. Its financial proverbs are valid for people at all levels of society. The book's basic advice is to shun unsound financial entanglements. Surety is to be avoided: "It is senseless to give a pledge, to become surety for a neighbor" (17:18).[30] Proverbs 6:1-5 offers a well-known vignette of a guarantor (one who has gone surety) who pleads and pesters the neighbor to annul the obligation:

> My child, if you have given your pledge to your neighbor, if you have bound yourself to another ... save yourself, for you have come into your neighbor's power: go, hurry, and plead with your neighbor. Give your eyes no sleep and your eyelids no slumber; save yourself like a gazelle from the hunter, like a bird from the hand of the fowler.

Borrowing is also considered suspect (Prov 22:7). One is, however, encouraged to take surety from those who go surety for strangers: "Take the garment of one who has given surety for a stranger (זר); seize the pledge given as surety for foreigners (נכרים)" (20:16 = 27:13). This could be an ironic proposal that underscores that surety is to be avoided.[31] It may teach that one who guarantees a loan for a stranger is a

---

[27] Pleins, *Social Visions*, 467.

[28] Prov 15:16-17, "Better is a little with the fear of the Lord than great treasure and trouble with it. Better is a dinner of vegetables where love is than a fatted ox and hatred with it" (cf. Sir 29:22); 17:1, "Better is a dry morsel with quiet than a house full of feasting with strife"; 18:23, "The poor use entreaties, but the rich answer roughly"; 28:11, "The rich man is wise in self-esteem, but an intelligent poor person sees through the pose." See also 22:1 and 28:6.

[29] "Surety" refers to securing a loan by pledging an item of great value as collateral. It was a way of acquiring credit. One could go surety for another, putting himself at risk. The terms that refer to this practice are ערב and חבל. The verb חבל may refer not to pledging something to secure a loan, but rather to the seizing of property to compensate for a loan that has fallen in arrears, as suggested by texts such as Job 24:3. See Shalom Paul, *Amos* (Hermeneia; Minneapolis: Fortress, 1991), 85.

[30] Prov 11:15, "To guarantee loans for a stranger brings trouble, but there is safety in refusing to do so"; 22:26, "Do not be one of those who give pledges, who become surety for debts." See also 28:8.

[31] Clifford, *Proverbs*, 184.

fool.[32]   As such, he can be treated harshly.   In either case the proverb underscores that going surety entails risk.   The "strangers" could be Gentiles, but this is not necessarily the case.   The term could easily refer to anyone with whom one is unacquainted.

Proverbs's position on debts and surety is compatible with that of covenantal law.   The legal tradition stipulates protection from abusive practices by creditors.   For example, Deuteronomy 24:6 protects the debtor: "No one shall take a mill or an upper millstone in pledge, for that would be taking a life in pledge."[33]   This concern is widespread in the Hebrew Bible, in which debts are often portrayed as the means by which the rich abuse the poor.[34]   As in Proverbs, moral standards in financial dealings with strangers are lowered in covenantal law.   Deuteronomy forbids charging interest on loans, except in the case of foreigners.[35]   Concern for the debtor is also attested in other literature of the ancient Near East.[36]

Regarding poverty and the poor, there is some distinction to be made between Proverbs 1-9 and 10-31.   While sayings such as 15:16-17 and 16:8-9 show a mistrust of riches, chapters 1-9 depict wisdom as great wealth.   Proverbs 3:15-16 is representative of this viewpoint: "She is more precious than jewels, and nothing you desire can compare with her. Long life is in her right hand; in her left hand are riches and honor" (cf. 1:9; 4:9; 8:11, 18).   An association of wisdom with riches is also evident in figures such as Solomon and Qoheleth, who were both wealthy.[37] While some proverbs of chapters 10-31 mistrust wealth, others understand riches as a reward of wisdom.   In a manner similar to Proverbs 3:15-16, 22:4 affirms "The reward for humility and fear of the Lord is

---

[32] The person who goes surety for a stranger could also be unscrupulous. The incentive to do so would not be loyalty to a friend in need but the opportunity to make money. According to this view, the normal money ethics the book lays out do not apply to this type, and one can take surety from him. See Fox, *Proverbs 1-9*, 215.

[33] See Exod 22:25-27; Lev 25:23-55; Deut 15:1-2; 24:10-15, 17.   See also Clifford, *Proverbs*, 207-08.

[34] E.g., Amos 2:8; Jer 15:10; 2 Kgs 4:1-7; Ps 109:11; Isa 50:1; Neh 5:1-13; and 10:32.

[35] See Deut 23:20: "On loans to a foreigner you may charge interest, but on loans to another Israelite you may not charge interest." See also 15:6.

[36] See, for example, *Ahiqar* 111, "I have carried sand and hauled salt, but there is nothing more burdensome than [de]b[t]; 130-31, "Do not take a heavy loan from an evil man. And if you take a loan (at all), give yourself no peace until [you have re]pa[id] it. A loan is pleasant as ... but paying it back is a houseful" (cf. 171-72); *Instruction of Shuruppak* 12-13 (obverse), "Do not be a security ... Then you [will be] a security ..."; *Instruction of Amenemope* 16:5-8, "If you find a large debt against a poor man, make it into three parts; forgive two, let one stand, you will find it a path of life." See Lambert, *Babylonian Wisdom Literature*, 95; Lichtheim, *Ancient Egyptian Literature*, 2.155-56.

[37] Cf. Sir 1:16; Wis 7:11.   Also compare *Pirke Avot* 6:7, which cites several verses from Proverbs that describe wisdom as a type of wealth.

riches and honor and life" (cf. 24:3-4). The poetic description of wisdom
as a jewel or a crown is characteristic of chapters 1-9. This viewpoint is
compatible with most of chapters 10-31. Proverbs in general promotes
worldly success and is not against wealth in principle, although it grants
that it can be abused. A more significant difference between the two
sections is that chapters 1-9 have minimal interest in the poor, while this
is an important theme throughout chapters 10-31.[38] This may be because
chapters 1-9 reflect an aristocratic pedagogical setting while most of
chapters 10-31 have a folk provenance.[39] Regardless of the book's origins, however, Proverbs 1-9 and 10-31 have different presentations of
poverty.

The importance accorded to the poor and their ethical treatment in traditional wisdom is evident in its reception by Job and Qoheleth. Both
echo views on the poor preserved in Proverbs and modify them in light
of their own idiosyncrasies and concerns. Job, for example, reiterates the

---

[38] Whybray, *Wealth and Poverty*, 102-05, makes an important point but overstates his
case when he claims that "there is no mention" of the poor in the wisdom poems and
discourses of Proverbs 1-9. Poverty is mentioned in 6:10-11 as a consequence of sloth.
The exhortation to avoid surety in 6:1-5 has no connotation of dire circumstances, but is
compatible with a concern for the poor. See also Gerlinde Baumann, *Die Weisheitsgestalt
in Proverbien 1-9* (FAT 16; Tübingen: J.C.B. Mohr [Paul Siebeck], 1996), 102-07.

[39] Whybray, *Wealth and Poverty*, 102-106, 113-14, argues that because of their no-
ticeably different presentations of poverty, chapters 1-9 should be attributed to upper-class
scribal circles, whereas chapters 10-29 for the most part stem from rural farming culture.
This, however, is not a necessary conclusion. H.C. Washington notices the concern for
poverty in *Amenemope* and concludes that Proverbs combines Judean village wisdom with
ancient near Eastern sapiential traditions that stress concern for the poor. Scribal influence is thus seen in the book as a whole, not just chapters 1-9. This produces tension in
the portrayal of rich and poor throughout the book, but Proverbs in general has "an af-
firmative ethic of social equity." See his *Wealth and Poverty*, 204. Pleins, *Social Visions*, 457, understands Proverbs as a "product of the ruling elite," and follows the view of
von Rad that the book was composed by a patrician class that had little contact with the
poor. However, while some proverbs clearly presuppose an upper-class setting (e.g.,
23:1-2), some reflect a rural, agricultural context, such as Proverbs 14:4: "Where there are
no oxen, there is no grain; abundant crops come by the strength of the ox" (cf. 10:5). Leo
G. Perdue has argued that the authors of Proverbs 1-9 should be associated with Zadokite
priests. See his "The Vitality of Wisdom in Second Temple Judaism during the Persian
Period," in *Passion, Vitality, and Foment: The Dynamics of Second Temple Judaism* (ed.
L.M. Luker; Harrisburg: Trinity Press International, 2001), 119-54. For more on the
debate regarding the provenance of Proverbs, see R.N. Whybray, *The Book of Proverbs: A
Survey of Modern Study* (Leiden: Brill, 1995), 35-42, 62-71; Murphy, *The Tree of Life*,
19; Claus Westermann, *The Roots of Wisdom* (Louisville: John Knox Press, 1995), 3-5;
Gerhard von Rad, *Wisdom in Israel* (London/Valley Forge: SCM Press Ltd./Trinity Press
International, 1972), 15-24; John J. Gammie, "From Prudentialism to Apocalypticism:
The Houses of the Sages amid the Varying Forms of Wisdom," in *The Sage in Israel and
the Ancient Near East* (ed. J.G. Gammie and L.G. Perdue; Winona Lake: Eisenbrauns,
1990), 483.

position of Proverbs 19:17 and 21:13 that God rewards those who have
been kind to the poor. This idea helps form the basis of his complaint as
to why God has punished him. His situation, he laments, would make
sense if he had not helped the poor and needy:

> If I have withheld anything that the poor desired, or have caused the eyes
> of the widow to fail ... if I have seen anyone perish for lack of clothing, or
> a poor person without covering ... then let my shoulder blade fall from my
> shoulder, and let my arm be broken from its socket (31:16-22; cf. 30:25).[40]

Qoheleth, like Proverbs, shows an awareness of the plight of the downtrodden. But rather than give advice about the proper treatment of the
poor, he takes a defeatist attitude towards their misery: "If you see in a
province the oppression of the poor and the violation of justice and right,
do not be amazed at the matter; for the high official is watched by a
higher, and there are yet higher ones over them" (5:8). He also teaches
that a poor man who is wise will be ignored (9:15-16; cf. 4:13-14; 6:8).

Ben Sira also displays concern for the poor that reflects older wisdom.
He writes, for example:

> My child, do not cheat the poor of their living, and do not keep needy eyes
> waiting. Do not grieve the hungry, or anger one in need. Do not add to the
> troubles of the desperate, or delay giving to the needy. Do not reject a sup-
> pliant in distress, or turn your face away from the poor (4:1-4).

Ben Sira's attitude to the poor is similar to that of Tobit.[41] This is presumably because both are influenced by traditional wisdom.

Ben Sira emphasizes the vulnerability of the poor and that one should
not take advantage of them: "The bread of the needy is the life of the
poor; whoever deprives them of it is a murderer" (34:25).[42] He also

---

[40] See also 20:10, 19; 24:4, 9, 14; 29:12; 34:19, 28.

[41] Tob 4:16, "Give some of your food to the hungry, and some of your clothing to the
naked. Give all your surplus as alms, and do not let your eye begrudge your giving of
alms"; 12:8-9, "Prayer with fasting is good, but better than both is almsgiving with righteousness. A little with righteousness is better than wealth with wrongdoing. It is better to
give alms than to lay up gold. For almsgiving saves from death and purges away every
sin. Those who give alms will enjoy a full life." Cf. 1:3; 4:7-11. See G.W.E. Nickelsburg, "Riches, the Rich, and God's Judgment in 1 Enoch 92-105 and the Gospel according
to Luke," *New Testament Studies* 25 (1979), 342; Benedikt Otzen, *Tobit and Judith*
(Sheffield: Sheffield Academic Press, 2002), 35-37.

[42] See also Sir 4:8, "Give a hearing to the poor, and return their greeting politely";
7:32, "Stretch out your hand to the poor, so that your blessing may be complete"; 10:14,
"The Lord overthrows the thrones of rulers, and enthrones the lowly in their place"; 10:23,
"It is not right to despise one who is intelligent but poor, and it is not proper to honor one
who is sinful"; 21:5, "The prayer of the poor goes from their lips to the ears of God, and
his judgment comes speedily"; 31:4, "The poor person toils to make a meager living, and
if ever he rests he becomes needy"; 34:24, "Like one who kills a son before his father's
eyes is the person who offers a sacrifice from the property of the poor." Cf. 10:30; 35:16;

draws support from the covenantal tradition: "Help the poor for the commandment's sake, and in their need do not send them away empty-handed" (29:19; cf. Deut 15:7-11).[43]

The sage demonstrates an acute awareness of the difference between the rich and poor, although he is never critical of the wealthy to the extent of texts such as Proverbs 18:23 and 22:7. Reflecting a dualistic mode of thought, Ben Sira describes the conflict between rich and poor in sharper language than Proverbs:

> What does a wolf have in common with a lamb? No more has a sinner with the devout. What peace is there between a hyena and a dog? And what peace between the rich and the poor? Wild asses in the wilderness are the prey of lions; likewise the poor are feeding grounds for the rich. Humility is an abomination to the proud; likewise the poor are an abomination to the rich (13:17-20; cf. 33:10-15).[44]

This chapter also describes the advantages the wealthy have over the poor:

> When the rich person totters, he is supported by friends, but when the humble falls, he is pushed away even by friends. If the rich person slips, many come to the rescue; he speaks unseemly words, but they justify him. If the humble person slips, they even criticize him; he talks sense, but is not given a hearing. The rich person speaks and all are silent; they extol to the clouds what he says. The poor person speaks and they say, "Who is this fellow?" And should he stumble, they even push him down (vv. 21-23).

Although aware of the difficulties that the poor face, occasionally Ben Sira does not seem particularly sympathetic to their plight. For example, in 35:15-16, in complete contrast to the common view in Proverbs and Psalms, he claims that God "will not show partiality to the poor (דל)."[45] This is not an attack upon the downtrodden. The teaching affirms that God will "not ignore" the widow or the orphan (35:17). The point is that God will show no partiality.[46] He will only show favor towards those who have been unjustly treated. By using the poor as an example of

---

38:19. See also Maurice Gilbert, "Wisdom of the Poor: Ben Sira 10,19-11,6," in *The Book of Ben Sira in Modern Research: Proceedings of the First International Ben Sira Conference, 28-31 July 1996, Soesterberg, Netherlands* (ed. P.C. Beentjes; BZAW 255; Berlin/New York: Walter de Gruyter, 1997), 153-69.

[43] Alexander Di Lella and Patrick W. Skehan, *The Wisdom of Ben Sira* (AB 39; New York: Doubleday, 1987), 370.

[44] Victor Tcherikover, *Hellenistic Civilization and the Jews* (trans. S. Applebaum; Philadelphia/Jerusalem: Jewish Publication Society of America/The Magnes Press, 1961), 147; Collins, *Jewish Wisdom*, 29.

[45] See also 10:31: "One who is honored in poverty, how much more in wealth! And one dishonored in wealth, how much more in poverty!"

[46] Di Lella and Skehan, *The Wisdom of Ben Sira*, 419.

those who are not in this category, he shows a lack of sensitivity to their situation. This is not in keeping with texts such as 4:1-4 or 34:25.

Aware of the power they possess, Ben Sira is critical of the wealthy who abuse their advantages. He warns his students to be wary of others who are wealthier than they are: "Do not quarrel with a rich man, lest his resources outweigh yours; for gold has ruined many, and has perverted the minds of kings" (8:2; cf. 13:2).[47] He is also critical of the wealthy who are overly consumed with greed for additional riches: "A merchant can hardly keep from wrongdoing, nor is a tradesman innocent of sin. Many have committed sin for gain, and those who seek to get rich will avert their eyes" (26:29-27:1; cf. 5:8; 13:4-7; 31:5-7).

Yet Ben Sira stops short of condemning the wealthy. There is none of the disdain for the wealthy that is characteristic of the *Epistle of Enoch* or the gospel of Luke.[48] While Ben Sira shows disdain for greed, there is nothing comparable in his instruction to the sentiment of texts such as Proverbs 28:22, which teaches that the miser will inevitably come to ruin. Rather, in a Qoheleth-like manner, Ben Sira complains that the person who becomes wealthy through a lifetime of hard work will be able to enjoy his money only when he has a few years left (11:18-19).

Comparing Proverbs 15:16-17 with Ben Sira 29:22 can illustrate aptly the difference between these two books with regard to the rich and the poor. The former (cited above) teaches that it is better to have a dinner of vegetables in a stable home than to eat a "fatted ox" in a house filled with hatred. Ben Sira 29:22 reads: "Better is the life of the poor under their own crude roof than sumptuous food in the house of others." Ben Sira's proverb, like the saying from Proverbs, teaches that it is better for a poor person to be at home.[49] But he plays down the contrast between poor and rich. Rather, he emphasizes that it is better for the poor person to be at home than at a stranger's house. Whereas the saying from Proverbs 15 associates the home serving an ox with "hatred," Ben Sira does not associate the house with "sumptuous food" with any negative trait. Both proverbs teach that one should be content with what one has. Prov-

---

[47] Tcherikover, *Hellenistic Civilization*, 147; Collins, *Jewish Wisdom*, 30.

[48] See, for example, *1 En.* 94:8, "Woe to you, you rich, for you have trusted in your riches, but from your riches you will depart, for you did not remember the Most High in the days of your riches" (cf. 97:8-10); Luke 6:24-25, "But woe to you who are rich, for you have received your consolation. Woe to you who are full now, for you will be hungry. Woe to you who are laughing now, for you will mourn and weep." Cf. 12:13-34; 16:1-13. See further Nickelsburg, "Riches, the Rich, and God's Judgment," 324-44; idem, "Revisiting the Rich and Poor in 1 Enoch 92-105 and the Gospel according to Luke," in *Society of Biblical Literature Seminar Papers* 1998 (SBLSP 37; Atlanta: Scholars Press, 1998), 579-605.

[49] Di Lella and Skehan, *The Wisdom of Ben Sira*, 375.

erbs does this in a way that expresses more criticism of the rich than Ben Sira.

Ben Sira's financial instruction is often at odds with that of Proverbs. In a complete inversion of Proverbs 17:18 and 22:26, he instructs one to lend and go surety for his neighbor, even though such measures would put him at risk. It is one's ethical duty to help his neighbor financially: "Lend to your neighbor in his time of need; repay your neighbor when a loan falls due" (29:2; cf. v. 20). Ben Sira 29 is a key text for his financial teaching.[50] It describes how one should lend even though debtors are often not willing to fulfill their obligations (vv. 1-7). Ben Sira advocates the ethical use of wealth: "Lose your silver for the sake of a brother or a friend, and do not let it rust under a stone and be lost" (29:10). One should be willing to spend money to help the poor and those in need. The sage exhorts his students to "not forget the kindness of your guarantor," the person who helps one secure a loan (29:15). Promoting an ethic of charity, Ben Sira reminds his students that they are obliged to give to the poor (29:9; cf. 18:25; 31:9-11). He also encourages his students to be well stocked in order to be able to help themselves or their neighbors in time of need: "Store up almsgiving in your treasury, and it will rescue you from every disaster" (29:12; cf. v. 14).[51] Ben Sira assumes that his students have the wherewithal to follow this advice.[52] One should go surety even though this practice has ruined people because debtors sometimes do not pay back loans (29:16-18). Ben Sira also gives advice on how to lend and give surety in 8:12-13: "Do not lend to one who is stronger than you; but if you do lend anything, count it as a loss. Do not give surety beyond your means; but if you give surety, be prepared to pay" (cf. 18:33). In 20:15 the fool is depicted as not knowing how to lend properly: "Today he lends and tomorrow he asks it back; such a one is hateful to God and humans." Ben Sira teaches his students to be ethical creditors and that one has a moral obligation to lend money. He may be drawing on wisdom traditions poorly represented by Proverbs. For example, his instruction regarding the difficulty of collecting loans is similar to the Babylonian *Dialogue of Pessimism*: "Making loans is like loving [a woman;] getting them back is like having children" (67).[53]

---

[50] Ibid., 368-72.

[51] One is also encouraged to lend in the Sermon on the Mount: "Give to everyone who begs from you, and do not refuse anyone who wants to borrow from you" (Matt 5:42).

[52] Note also 40:28-29: "My child, do not lead the life of a beggar; it is better to die than to beg. When one looks to the table of another, one's way of life cannot be considered a life. One loses self-respect with another person's food, but one who is intelligent and well instructed guards against that."

[53] Lambert, *Babylonian Wisdom Literature*, 149. Note the parallel in the Egyptian *Instruction of Ankhsheshonq*: "Do not lend money at interest without obtaining a security.

Ben Sira shows sympathy for the poor, as does traditional wisdom. But his views on the poor and his financial advice are clearly colored by his upper-class background.[54] While Proverbs shows disdain for creditors who abuse the poor, Ben Sira warns the lender about the debtor who won't pay up.

3. POVERTY AND FINANCIAL ADVICE IN 4QINSTRUCTION

As in biblical wisdom, poverty and financial advice are prominent themes of 4QInstruction. There is a significant degree of common ground between 4QInstruction and Proverbs. At times, however, 4QInstruction's financial advice includes elements not found in older wisdom. First I will examine the similarities between Proverbs and 4QInstruction regarding these topics. Then aspects of the theme of poverty in 4QInstruction and its financial instruction that are without analogue in traditional wisdom will be treated.

3.1 Common Ground on Borrowing and Surety

Like Proverbs and *Ahiqar*, 4QInstruction encourages its addressee to avoid risky financial entanglements.[55] Echoing traditional wisdom, surety is discouraged in 4QInstruction. This is expressed in 4Q416 2 ii 4-6:

> As much as [the one lending to him, if in money (כמה [אם בהון הנושה בו) ... quickly] repay, and you will be on equal footing with him. For the money-bag of your treasures (צפונ֗כֿה // כֿיֿס) you have re[ckoned to the one lending to you on account of your neighbors (בעד רעיכה);] you [have giv]en all your life (כל חייכה) to him. Quickly give what belongs to him, take back [your] money-bag, [and do not] be feeble-[spirited with your words].[56]

Do not be too trusting lest you become poor" (16:21-22). See Lichtheim, *Ancient Egyptian Literature*, 3.172.

[54] His retainer class background is evident, for example, in chapter 38, in which the life of a sage is praised as superior to a variety of menial trades. See Oda Wischmeyer, *Die Kultur des Buches Jesus Sirach* (BZNW 77; Berlin: Walter de Gruyter, 1995), 49-69.

[55] H. Niehr, "Die Weisheit des Achikar und der *musar lammebin* im Vergleich," in *The Wisdom Texts from Qumran and the Development of Sapiential Thought* (ed. C. Hempel, A. Lange, and H. Lichtenberger; BETL 159; Leuven: Leuven University Press/Peeters, 2002), 173-86.

[56] *DJD 34*, 90, and Tigchelaar, *To Increase Learning*, 46, provide versions of the opening of this passage that are different from one another. The reconstruction given above follows that of Tigchelaar. The first portion of this passage, according to *DJD 34*, 90, is

The fragmentary nature of this text makes interpretation difficult. The topic seems to be surety.[57] This is suggested by the fact that the addressee risks his "life" on behalf of acquaintances ("neighbors"). Deuteronomy 24:6 and Ben Sira 29:15, as discussed above, acknowledge that one risks his "life" for another by going surety. In 4QInstruction this practice is not prohibited categorically, as in 4QD^b 4 8-11 (cf. 4Q417 2 i 21).[58] Proverbs 17:18 forbids one "to become surety for a neighbor (רעהו)." 4Q416 2 ii 5 warns the addressee about going surety for "neighbors" (רעיכה) but assumes that he has already done so.[59] 4Q416 2 ii 4-6 begins by discussing a loan, in "money" (הון), from a creditor to a third party. It likely refers to a cash loan but it could also be some other valuable item. Presumably the person who received the loan is one of the "neighbors" of line 5. This would explain why the addressee is to pay back a loan given to someone else. 4QInstruction is advising the addressee to extract himself from a risky financial situation. By buying out the loan he will be able to get his "money-bag of treasures" back from the creditor. This is an item of value or an amount of money that was used as collateral to guarantee the loan for the third party. The addressee is also told to not "be feeble-[spirited with your words]" when he approaches the creditor. This suggests that he might be unwilling to part with the item.

That the addressee risks his life on behalf of his "neighbors" suggests that he is willing to use his wealth to help someone who is in need. Ben Sira, most notably in chapter 29, heartily endorses such practices. 4QInstruction has a much more cautious approach. Rather than applaud the addressee for being an ethical lender, the composition advises him to get out of the deal quickly. 4QInstruction never tells him to give his "money-bag" to a creditor for the sake of a neighbor. The stress is on getting it back. The mindset of 4Q416 2 ii 4-6 is compatible with that of Proverbs 6:1-5. Both texts portray going surety as a dangerous predicament that one should resolve as soon as possible. This is never the case in Ben Sira, although he acknowledges that the practice entails risk (cf.

כמה[בהון ישכה הנושה בו. Line 17/3 of a composite text of 4Q418 fragments (64 + 199 + 66, 7b, 26 + 27, 8 + 8a + 8b) reconstructed by Tigchelaar, ibid., 76, attests the word אם before the expression בהון as visible in 4Q418 8 3. For this reason I go by Tigchelaar's version, but the text is too fragmentary to resolve the matter with confidence. His version also has no room for the word ישכה given in *DJD 34.*

[57] Murphy, *Wealth in the Dead Sea Scrolls,* 181.

[58] Ibid., 45-47.

[59] Note the parallel in 4Q424 2 3: "do not give surety for him (the hypocrite) among the poo[r (י)] עניך בתוך תערבהו (אל)." See Stephen J. Pfann et al., *Qumran Cave 4.XXVI: Cryptic Texts and Miscellanea, Part 1* (DJD 36; Oxford: Clarendon, 2000), 341. See also G. Brin, "Studies in 4Q424, fragments 1-2," *Revue de Qumran* 18 (1997), 41-42.

Sir 29:18-20). This suggests that, when a loan defaults, the addressee of
4QInstruction is more vulnerable to harm or financial ruin at the hands of
creditors than the students of Ben Sira.

Surety is addressed elsewhere in 4QInstruction. 4Q415 8 2 matches
the general sentiment of Proverbs: "Do not go surety" (אל תערב). This
text is fragmentary and it is likely that this vetitive was accompanied by
qualifications that have not survived. Surety is also the subject of 4Q418
88 3: "Take care for yourself lest you go surety (השמר לכה למה תערב)."
4Q418 87 7 is fragmentary but preserves remnants of a teaching on
surety with regard to strangers. Its visible portion reads: "Go surety for a
stranger in … (]ב זר ערוֹב[)." Given 4QInstruction's mistrust of borrowing and surety, this text probably did not originally recommend going
surety for a stranger. Proverbs treats people who do so harshly by affirming that pledges may be seized from them (20:16; 27:13). There is
no reason that 4QInstruction would promote going surety for strangers.
The visible text of 4Q418 87 7 was probably preceded by a negation
such as אל—"[Do not] go surety for a stranger."

Surety may also be the topic of 4Q416 2 iii 3-5:

> [and if asset]s (חפצ[י]ם) are entrusted (פּוֹקד) to you, do not set your hand
> upon them, lest you be scorched [and] your body will burn with his fire; a[s
> you have tak]en it so return it, and you will have joy if you are freed of it.[60]

The item or items that the addressee has in his care are monetary.
Strugnell and Harrington suggest that it could be a deposit or loan that
has been put in the addressee's charge.[61] Given the seriousness of the
punishment described for touching it, they are probably right. The text
seems to refer to taking surety since the passage describes accepting an
item of value that guarantees a loan. The intended audience of
4QInstruction was aware of the abuse creditors could inflict. 4Q416 2 iii
3-5 teaches that if the addressee is ever in a similar position he should
not behave unscrupulously. If he does take surety, he is to do nothing

---

[60] Neither Strugnell and Harrington, *DJD 34*, 110, nor Tigchelaar, *To Increase Learning*, 47, reconstruct the word חפצים from ם[י. The reading of Elgvin, "An Analysis of
4QInstruction," 221, is adopted here. Context demands that the word, for which only the
plural ending is visible, is a financial term. חפץ is a common financial term in
4QInstruction. The word חפץ often refers to "delight" or "pleasure" in the Hebrew Bible
(e.g., Ps 111:2), but it can also take the meaning of "business." For example, the word has
a business sense in 4Q418 126 ii 12: חפצו ידרוש מטנאכה, "from your basket he will seek
what he wants." Cf. 4Q418 81 18; 4Q418 102 4; 4Q418 127 4 (?); and 4Q418 158 3.
See also Tigchelaar, *To Increase Learning*, 237-38. Note that reading חפצ[ים in 4Q416 2
iii 3 demands that one read the word בו of line 4 as referring to a plural noun. This may be
because of the nature of the term חפצ[ים. It signifies assets that are referred to as a lump
sum that is entrusted to the addressee.

[61] *DJD 34*, 112.

with the pledge except hold onto it. Returning the pledge will provide relief to the addressee who will no longer have to worry about keeping it.

4Q416 2 iii continues by expressing additional caution regarding financial transactions: "Also, from anyone whom you do not know do not take money lest it will increase your poverty. And if they hold you responsible for it, till death account for it" (ll. 5-7). This text declares that the addressee should not have a financial relationship with people whom he does not know, while acknowledging that transactions with such people can take place. This implies that the intended audience of 4QInstruction is not cut off from the outside world but is rather immersed in ordinary economic activity. Whether the creditor is known or not, the addressee should repay what he has borrowed.

4QInstruction's attitude towards borrowing is compatible with that of biblical wisdom. 4Q417 2 i 21-22 teaches that the addressee should treat his debt seriously:

> if you borrow the wealth of m[e]n for your need (למחסורכה), there will be no [sleep for y]ou day or night, and there will be no rest for your soul [until] you pay back [your] credit[or his loan] (cf. 4Q416 2 ii 9-10).[62]

Proverbs 6:1-5 also uses the image of a person going without sleep to depict having gone surety as a crisis. Sleep in Qoheleth and Ben Sira is associated with having no financial worries.[63] The importance of repaying debts is stressed in 4Q416 2 iii 5-7.[64]

A proper understanding of borrowing is an important goal of 4QInstruction. 4QInstruction supplements the exhortation on paying debts in 4Q417 2 i 21-22 with lines 22-24: "Do not lie to him lest you bear guilt. And also because of reproach to [your] cr[editor ... And you will no long]er [trust] his neighbor, and when you are in need he will be

---

[62] Tigchelaar, *To Increase Learning*, 55, offers a more conservative reconstruction of this text than *DJD 34*. The latter is adopted here. Two supplements supplied by the editors of *DJD 34*, "[sleep for y]ou" (דומי ל[ך]) and "his loan" (משיו), are not included in Tigchelaar's transcription. For a discussion of the word מחסור, see section 3.3 of this chapter. See also Murphy, *Wealth in the Dead Sea Scrolls*, 180.

[63] For Qoheleth see 5:12: "Sweet is the sleep of laborers, whether they eat little or much; but the surfeit of the rich will not let them sleep." For Ben Sira see 31:1-2: "Wakefulness over wealth wastes away one's flesh, and anxiety about it drives away sleep. Wakeful anxiety prevents slumber, and a severe illness carries off sleep." Cf. 31:4, 20; 40:5-6; 42:9. In Proverbs sleep can also be a sign of laziness (e.g., 19:15).

[64] Rabbinic literature also espouses the timely repayment of debts. For example, *Deuteronomy Rabbah* 4:10 preserves a story of man asking to be tested by his creditor by asking for a loan that he repays promptly. *Numbers Rabbah* 9:6 underscores the right of a creditor to collect a debt.

tight-fisted (במחסורכה יקפיץ ידו)."[65] The idiom יקפיץ ידו denotes stingi-
ness.[66] If the addressee treats his creditor with deceit, or reproaches him,
he will earn a bad reputation among the lender's colleagues. It will then
be difficult to obtain credit the next time he is in need. It is important for
the addressee to maintain good standing with creditors, although dealings
with them can be risky.[67] 4QInstruction is concerned that he might be
beaten (4Q417 2 i 25). 4Q417 2 i 21-25 assumes that the addressee is
occasionally in need of credit, suggesting that he struggled financially.[68]

The low-income economic position of the intended audience of
4QInstruction is highlighted when the text is compared to Ben Sira. He
also discusses unethical behavior by borrowers. Ben Sira 29:5 reads:

> One kisses another's hands until he gets a loan, and is deferential in speak-
> ing of his neighbor's money; but at the time for repayment he delays, and
> pays back with empty promises, and finds fault with the time (cf. 29:17).

4Q417 2 i 22-23 affirms that borrowers might lie to those who lend them
money. It does so from the standpoint of the borrower, the addressee
who should be courteous to creditors. Ben Sira mentions the problem of
lying to creditors in a way that emphasizes the perspective of the lender:
"Many refuse to lend, not because of meanness, but from fear of being

---

[65] Tigchelaar's transcription of this text does not include the supplement "[your]
cr[editor" ([לנ]ושה בכה)," that is offered in *DJD 34*, 173. See *To Increase Learning*, 55.
Since the passage discusses borrowing, the version in *DJD 34* is entirely plausible.

[66] See Deut 15:7: "If there is among you anyone in need ... do not be hard-hearted or
tight-fisted toward your needy neighbor (ולא תקפץ את־ידך מאחיך האביון)." Cf. Sir 4:31: "Do
not let your hand (ידך) be stretched out to receive and closed (קפוצה) when it is time to
give." The idiom is also used in 4Q418 88 5 (יקפץ ידו ממחסורכה). The word יקפץ has a
partially erased *wāw* with a cancellation dot. Cf. 4Q416 2 ii 2-3. See *DJD 34*, 173;
Tigchelaar, *To Increase Learning*, 97.

[67] Compare *Ahiqar* 171-72: "If a wicked man grasps the fringe of your garment, leave
it in his hand. Then appeal to Shamash; he [will] take what is his and will give it to you."
This text advocates the tolerance of creditor abuse. One is told not to confront the lender
about his deceitful practices because Shamash will eventually correct this wrong.

[68] 4QInstruction's recognition of the addressee's need for credit is analogous to Hillel's
enactment of the *Prosbul*. He made credit easier to obtain for the small landowner by a *de
facto* annulment of the cancellation of debts in the sabbatical year, which discouraged
creditors from making loans. Cf. *m. Sheb.* 9:3; *b. Git.* 36b; Mur 18 (papAcknowledge-
ment of Debt ar). See also Ephraim Urbach, *The Sages* (Cambridge/London: Harvard
University Press, 1975), 373, 580; Murphy, *Wealth in the Dead Sea Scrolls*, 187. Martin
Goodman argues that the wealthy gained from the *Prosbul* because they acquired property
through the foreclosure of holdings of borrowers. See his *The Ruling Class of Judaea:
The Origins of the Jewish Revolt, A.D. 66-70* (Cambridge: Cambridge University Press,
1987), 57-58.

defrauded needlessly" (29:7). Ben Sira and 4QInstruction promulgate similar debt-ethics but address them to different segments of society.[69]

3.2 The Economic Sitz im Leben of 4QInstruction

By advocating timely repayment of debts and good relations with creditors, 4QInstruction stresses not only that borrowing entails risk but that the addressee at times needs to obtain credit. This financial advice accords with what is known, which is admittedly limited, about the economic conditions of Palestine in the latter centuries of the Second Temple period.[70] In this period commoners were often forced to borrow and indebtedness was a widespread problem. According to 1 Maccabees, people took refuge in the Temple because they could not pay their debts (10:43; cf. 15:8).[71] In the uprising of 68-74 CE long standing class conflicts were exacerbated and came to a head. According to Josephus, when the *Sicarii* burned the houses of the Ananias the high priest and other elites, they made sure to burn the Record Office "to prevent the recovery of debts" (*J.W.*, 2.427).[72] The problem of indebtedness is also clear in Simeon bar Giora's declaration that freed all the slaves, many of whom were enslaved through their inability to repay loans (*J.W.*, 4.508).[73] This social reality is also behind New Testament texts such as Matthew 18:23-35, the parable of the unforgiving debtor.

---

[69] Daniel J. Harrington, "Two Early Jewish Approaches to Wisdom: Sirach and Qumran Sapiential Work A," *Journal for the Study of the Pseudepigrapha* 16 (1997): 25-38; Wright, "The Categories of Rich and Poor."

[70] Jack Pastor, *Land and Economy in Ancient Palestine* (London/New York: Routledge, 1997); Z. Safrai, *The Economy of Roman Palestine* (London/New York: Routledge, 1994); D.A. Fiensy, T*he Social History of Palestine in the Herodian Period: The Land is Mine* (Lewiston/Queenston/Lampeter: The Edwin Mellen Press, 1991); S. Applebaum, "Judaea as a Roman Province: The Countryside as a Political and Economic Factor," *Aufstieg und Niedergang der romischen Welt* II.8 (Berlin/New York: de Gruyter, 1977): 355-96; J. Klausner, "The Economy of Judea in the Period of the Second Temple," in *The Herodian Period* (ed. M. Avi-Yonah; New Brunswick: Rutgers University Press, 1975), 179-205; H. Kreissig, "Die landwirtschaftliche Situation in Palästina vor dem judäischen Krieg," *Acta Antiqua* 17 (1969): 223-54.

[71] Jonathan A. Goldstein, *1 Maccabees* (AB 41; Garden City: Doubleday, 1976), 413. See also Josephus' account of this situation (*J.A.*, 12.142-44).

[72] Fiensy, *The Social History of Palestine*, 13; Pastor, *Land and Economy*, 157; Goodman, *The Ruling Class of Judaea*, 18. The Zealots retaliated against "those with whom any had ancient quarrels ... and none escaped save those whose humble birth put them utterly beneath notice" (*J.W.*, 4.364-65). This suggests that the "ancient quarrels" refers, at least in part, to long-standing class conflict. See also Richard Horsely, *Bandits, Prophets, and Messiahs: Popular Movements in the Time of Jesus* (2nd ed.; Harrisburg: Trinity Press International, 1999 [orig. pub., 1985]), 225.

[73] Klausner, "The Economy of Judea," 193.

The nature of landownership in Palestine's agrarian economy in the latter half of the Second Temple period made life difficult for most of the population. The elite class, perhaps best represented by the Tobiad family, produced its wealth in part through large land holdings that the lower segments of the population worked.[74] The Zeno papyri, a crucial source for Palestine in the 3rd century BCE, records Zeno's business travels. This work was conducted for someone who was a large importer of grain and owned a large estate in Bet-Anath in Galilee that produced wine.[75] These documents indicate that indebtedness was a problem. Zeno sent a collector to a man named Jeddous, because he owed a debt. The collector was chased out of Jeddous's village.[76] The Dead Sea Scrolls, though preserving relatively few documentary texts, include formal debt acknowledgements.[77] Many commoners at the time were tenant farmers and day laborers who worked plots of land for an absentee landlord. There were also small freeholders who were mainly subsistence farm-

---

[74] Fiensy, *The Social History of Palestine*, 21-60; Pastor, *Land and Economy*, 26. The Tobiads became incredibly wealthy in the third century BCE when Joseph ben Tobiah was given wide-ranging powers by the Ptolemaic rulers to collect taxes in Palestine. See Tcherikover, *Hellenistic Civilization*, 126-42. Josephus' biography of Joseph and his son Hycranus (*J.A.*, 12.154-236) is a useful source of information but has some fabulous elements.

[75] Martin Hengel, *Judaism and Hellenism* (2 vols.; Philadelphia: Fortress, 1973), 1.39. The Hefzibah inscription, which contains correspondence between King Antiochus III and Ptolemy son of Thraseas, *strategos* of Syria and Phoenicia, also sheds light on land ownership in the region. It records the granting of numerous land holdings to Ptolemy from the Seleucid crown as a reward for his services. See Pastor, *Land and Economy*, 28-29. It is implied in Hecataeus that landownership was disproportionately controlled by the wealthy when he claims that in the early Hellenistic period there was a law in "Judea prohibiting private individuals from selling their estates in order to prevent the wealthy from concentrating land in their hands" (*Diodorus Siculus* 40.3, 7). See ibid., 20; Tcherikover, *Hellenistic Civilization*, 122.

[76] Pastor, *Land and Economy*, 33.

[77] See 4Q344 (4QDebt Acknowledgement ar), which is available in H.M. Cotton and A. Yardeni, *Aramaic, Hebrew, and Greek Documentary Texts from Naḥal Ḥever and Other Sites* (DJD 27; Oxford: Clarendon, 1997), 289-91. This text is fragmentary but preserves a promise, presumably by one Eleazar ben Joseph, to repay a debt. If he does not repay he acknowledges in line 5 to the creditor that "what I shall acquire you shall receive (די אקנה לקבלך)." The context of this statement can be reconstructed with the help of Murabbaʿat 18, which is available in P. Benoit, J.T. Milik, and R. de Vaux, *Les Grottes de Murabba'at* (DJD 2; Oxford: Clarendon, 1961), 100-04. This text is dated to 55/56 CE since it claims to have been composed in the second year of Nero. This papyrus preserves a formal declaration of a man named Absalom bar Hanin that he has borrowed from Zachariah bar Yohanan bar H---. If he does not pay back the loan, with interest, he acknowledges to the lender that "what I shall acquire you shall receive (די אקנה לקובליך)" (l. 8). The editors of *DJD 2* translate lines 7-8 as "Et si je ne le faisais pas, dédomage[ment] t'en sera (fait) sur mes biens, et sur tout ce que j'acquerrerai tu auras droit de saisie."

ers.[78] In times of poor productivity farmers easily became indebted and were susceptible to losing their land, if they had any.[79] They also suffered from high taxation, although no exact figures are available.[80] Some creditors used loans as a type of capital investment by granting loans that cannot be repaid, in order to seize the land of the borrowers, who then must work their plot as tenants.[81] The plight of the farmers is expressed aptly by Proverbs 13:23: "The field of the poor may yield much food, but it is swept away through injustice."

The intended audience of 4QInstruction includes farmers. 4Q418 103 ii is designed explicitly for farmers, who, in keeping with Deuteronomy 22 and Leviticus 19, are warned to obey the ban against mixing crops of diverse kinds.[82] Lines 7-8 of this fragment warn the addressee not to mix crops together "(lest) your toil be like one who plo[ws] with ox and a[s]s [to]geth[er]. And moreover, (lest) your crops b[e for you like] (those of) one who sows diverse kinds." The addressee is also understood to be a farmer in 4Q423 5 5-6: "[If you are a f]armer (lit. "man of the soil"), observe the appointed times of the summer, gather your crops in their time, and the season [of harvest in its appointed time]" (cf. 4Q423 3 2; 4Q423 4 2).[83]

---

[78] Fiensy, *The Social History of Palestine*, 76-105.

[79] Klausner, "The Economy of Judea," 189.

[80] Fiensy, *The Social History of Palestine*, 99-105. There is a great deal of rabbinic discussion about tenant farmers, the relevance of which to the Second Temple period is not clear. They describe several types of tenants, none of which are found in Second Temple texts. According to this literature, the tenant pays the owner anywhere from a fourth to two-thirds of his crops. See ibid., 81. Also note that in 1 Maccabees, King Demetrius I, in an effort to consolidate Jewish support for his rule, promises that he will refrain from "collecting the third of the grain and the half of the fruit trees that I should receive" (10:30; cf. 15:5).

[81] Goodman, *The Ruling Class of Judaea*, 57; idem, "The First Jewish Revolt: Social Conflict and the Problem of Debt," *Journal of Jewish Studies* 33 (1982): 419-28; Pastor, *Land and Economy*, 149.

[82] Strugnell and Harrington, *DJD 34*, 330, argue that the agricultural language of this fragment should be taken literally. 4QMMT B 72-82 (4Q396 1-2 iv 1-11) interprets the law of diverse kinds metaphorically, using it to argue for the separation of the seed of Aaron. Strugnell has changed his view regarding 4Q418 103 ii and argues that it should be interpreted in a way that is similar to 4QMMT, since this would emphasize the priestly nature of the addressee (personal communication). However, 4QInstruction shows a real interest in the addressee's crops. This suggests that 4Q418 103 ii should be interpreted literally. It wants the addressee to maintain a state of purity that is reflected in his agricultural practices. Either option underscores a priestly attitude. For the text of 4QMMT B 72-82, see Elisha Qimron and John Strugnell, *Qumran Cave 4.V (Miqsat Ma'aśe Ha-Torah)* (DJD 10; Oxford: Clarendon, 1994), 20, 54-56.

[83] The transcription of Tigchelaar, *To Increase Learning*, 142, differs slightly from that of *DJD 34*, 518, which is used above. He does not include the supplements "[If you]" ([אם אתה]) and "of harvest in its appointed time" (הקציר למועדו). The additions are plausible and fit well with the passage semantically.

Fiensy observes that because of a farmer's constant need for financial assistance, a common way for him to supplement his income was secondary work as an artisan.[84] 4QInstruction's intended audience includes artisans and people who supplement their income with a trade. The composition emphasizes that the addressee has חכמת ידים, "manual skill."[85] 4Q418 81 19 presents this ability as means to achieve material satisfaction: "You shall be satisfied with an abundance of good things and from your manual skill [your treasuries shall be filled]."[86] Line 15 attributes this ability to God: "if he has given you authority over manual skill." The difficulty of ordinary life for the addressee helps explain why his ability to earn a living is presented as a divine gift.

Like Proverbs, 4QInstruction emphasizes paying debts quickly. Both texts teach that borrowing is risky and that indebtedness should be avoided. Yet 4QInstruction goes beyond Proverbs by stressing the need to obtain credit by maintaining good relations with lenders, even though they could be unscrupulous. The Qumran wisdom text mistrusts borrowing but acknowledges that at times its addressee will have to do so. Some of its texts are addressed to farmers and craftspeople. This suggests that the intended audience of 4QInstruction included a substantial number of commoners, living in an agricultural society in which indebtedness was a wide-scale problem.

3.3 The Addressee's Poverty

Like Proverbs and other wisdom texts, 4QInstruction shows sincere concern for the poor. For example, 4Q418 137 3, though badly preserved, calls for just compensation for the labor of the addressee: "righteousness in your wage, for in your labor (צֹדק במשׂכרתכה כֹי לעבודתכה[) ..." Similarly, if reconstructed correctly, 4Q418 146 2 reads: "You shall n[ot] defraud the w[age of a laborer] (לֹו[א] תעשׂוֹק שׂ[כר שכיר])."[87] In complete contrast to Proverbs, however, 4QInstruction addresses the poor directly. The composition in general does not show an interest in the

---

[84] Fiensy, *The Social History of Palestine*, 95.

[85] Note the contrast with Ben Sira 38:24-34, which touts the superiority of scribes over menial laborers. This suggests that 4QInstruction and Ben Sira were addressing different segments of society. See *DJD 34*, 311. The phrase "manual skill" (literally "wisdom of the hands") is also found in 4Q418 102 3; 4Q418 137 2; 4Q418 139 2; and 4Q424 3 7. In Ben Sira 9:17 the phrase בחכמי ידים is translated as ἐν χειρὶ τεχνιτῶν.

[86] The last portion of this text follows the supplement in *DJD 34*, 303. It is not included in Tigchelaar, *To Increase Learning*, 94.

[87] *DJD 34*, 371-72. 4Q424 also displays sympathy for the poor: "A man of generosit[y perfo]rms charity for the poor ... he takes care of all who lack property" (3 9-10; cf. 1Q27 1 ii 5-7). See *DJD 36*, 346.

poor as a broad segment of society. Rather, its concern for the poor is concentrated on its addressee. It emphasizes that he is "poor." This is one of the hallmarks of the composition. Its repetition of the phrase "you are poor," using ראש/רש or אביון, is a Leitmotif that is unique in Second Temple literature (4Q415 6 2; 4Q416 2 ii 20; 4Q416 iii 2, 8, 12, 19; and 4Q418 177 5).[88] The interpretation of the phrase has been disputed. Tigchelaar has argued that the "you are poor" refrain should be considered conditional, on the basis of 4Q416 2 iii 19, where the phrase is part of an "if" clause.[89] He bases this view in part on the fact that in Late Biblical Hebrew a clause can be conditional even when the word אם is not present. While philologically plausible, this interpretation does not explain why poverty is a major theme in 4QInstruction. Harrington understands 4QInstruction's focus on the addressee's poverty as reflecting "a reality of the human condition."[90] Murphy and others have likewise understood 4QInstruction as describing material poverty.[91]

4QInstruction uses the "you are poor" refrain in different ways. It refers to the material poverty of the addressee but also is related to his elect status. Several attestations of the refrain are by themselves difficult to interpret because their immediate context has not survived. This is the case for lines 2 and 19 of 4Q416 2 iii, the relevant portions of which are, respectively, "And remember that you are poor ... (וזכור כי ראש אתה)," and "If you are poor, as ... (ואם רש אתה כשה°)."[92] The latter is the only instance in which the refrain is conditional. Likewise, no immediate context is available for 4Q418 177 5 or 4Q415 6 2, which associate the "poor" addressee with nobles and kings, respectively.[93]

---

[88] Strugnell and Harrington reconstruct 4Q418 148 ii 4 to read איש °ל̇ו̇ אתה. See *DJD 34*, 375. The letters ל̇ו̇° could be a remnant of רוש or ריש. I agree with Tigchelaar's reading of the fragment. He argues that the two descenders following איש are too close together to be read as *rēš* and *wāw*. See his "The Addressees of 4QInstruction," 70. Cf. also 4Q418 249 3, רש הוא ואן[ביון] ("poor is he and ne[edy]"). Also note that Elgvin, "An Analysis of 4QInstruction," 210, has reconstructed the phrase "remember that you are poor" in 4Q416 2 ii 14, transcribing זכור כי אתה ענ[י]. This proposal is discussed in the following section.

[89] Tigchelaar, "The Addressees of 4QInstruction," 71.

[90] Harrington, *Wisdom Texts*, 45; idem, "Wisdom at Qumran," 145.

[91] Murphy, *Wealth in the Dead Sea Scrolls*, 187; Collins, *Jewish Wisdom*, 118; Wright, "The Categories of Rich and Poor."

[92] The last word of the phrase in line 19 could be a noun with a *kāp* preposition. Strugnell and Harrington speculate that כשה could be a portion of a relative form. See *DJD 34*, 122. If a noun with a preposition, the question would not be whether the addressee is poor or not, but rather if he is as poor as something else (the word that did not fully survive). The matter cannot be resolved conclusively.

[93] 4Q418 177 5, "you are poor, and nobles ... (אתה רש ונדיבים)" (cf. 4Q418 149 2; 4Q418 158 5); 4Q415 6 2, "y[o]u are poor, and king[s ·... (אביון א[ת]ה̇ ומֹ̇לֹכֹ]י̇ם)" (cf. 4Q418a 7 3).

The different ways that 4QInstruction uses poverty are combined in
4Q416 2 iii. Line 8 of this fragment reads: "You are poor, do not desire
anything except your inheritance (אביון אתה אל תתאו זולת נחלתכה)."
The addressee's poverty is presented as a rationale for focusing on his
"inheritance," a term that signifies his elect status.[94] Material wealth
should be kept in its place lest he lose sight of this status. The fleeting
nature of money is highlighted in 4Q418 103 ii 9: "[More]over your
wealth is together with your flesh (הונכה עם בשרכה). [When the days
of] your life [come to an end], they (also) will come to an end together
(יתמו יחד)."[95] His "inheritance" is a type of wealth more valuable than
material riches. In 4Q416 2 iii 11-12 this is made more explicit:

> He (God) has raised your head out of poverty (מראש הרים רא'שכה). With
> the nobles (נדיבים) (cf. 4Q418 177 5) he has placed you, and he has given
> you authority over an inheritance of glory (בנחלת // כבוד המשילכה).

In Chapter 5 I argue that the term "nobles" in this text should be understood as a reference to angels. The addressee's elect status is depicted as
a heavenly form of wealth. 4Q416 2 iii 11-12 asserts that he enjoys a
form of wealth and emphasizes this by declaring that he is no longer
poor. Yet 4QInstruction continues by reminding the addressee of his
poverty:

> You are poor (אביון אתה); do not say "I am poor but I do n[ot] seek knowl-
> edge." Bring your shoulder under all instruction. And in all [knowled]ge
> purify your heart and with a multitude of understanding your thoughts (ll.
> 12-14).[96]

The addressee's poverty should not be used as an excuse not to acquire
wisdom.[97] This would not make sense if poverty were understood in an

---

[94] See section 4.3 of Chapter 2.

[95] Strugnell and Harrington, *DJD 34*, 331, translate בשרכה as "your cattle/property."
The rationale for this translation is that it is in parallelism with "wealth." However, given
that 4QInstruction proclaims the destruction of the "fleshly spirit" in 4Q416 1 12 and that
בשרכה is used in 4Q418 103 ii in reference to death, it is fitting to translate it as "your
flesh." See also Murphy, *Wealth in the Dead Sea Scrolls*, 205; Tigchelaar, *To Increase
Learning*, 99. The poorly preserved fragment 4Q418 122 i may be a remnant of instruction on the proper understanding of wealth. Line 5 reads "understand your merchandise
(הבן במסחורכה) and do not ..."

[96] The word "[knowled]ge" is from the reconstruction of Elgvin, "An Analysis of
4QInstruction," 222. It does not have a strong material basis. He transcribes ה[דע]. It is
favored on semantic grounds because the passage stresses the importance of acquiring
knowledge. Strugnell and Harrington, *DJD 34*, 112, grant that this reconstruction is a
possibility but do not use it in their transcription of the fragment. The word is not reconstructed in Tigchelaar, *To Increase Learning*, 48.

[97] Note the parallel in *Avot de Rabbi Nathan* 6: "In the future, at Judgment, Rabbi
'Akiba will put all the poor in a guilty light. For if they are asked, 'Why did you not study
Torah?' and they say, 'Because we were poor,' they shall be told: 'Indeed, was not Rabbi

idealized or spiritual sense. The declaration that the addressee has been lifted out of poverty is sandwiched between reminders of his poverty (ll. 8, 12). This indicates that poverty is used in different ways. It often refers to the material poverty of the addressee. The declaration that he has been lifted out of poverty is a metaphor for his elect status. The addressee is poor but his elect status is portrayed as a form of wealth.

The depiction of the addressee's elect status as a type of wealth explains why 4QInstruction exhibits none of the hatred for the rich that is characteristic of the *Epistle of Enoch*:

> Woe to you who acquire silver and gold, but not in righteousness, and say: "We have become very rich and have possessions and have acquired everything that we desired" ... And like water your lie will flow away, for your riches will not stay with you but will quickly go up from you (*1 En.* 97:8-10).

In 4QInstruction wealth is not one of the nets of Belial, as in the Damascus Document: "They are Belial's three nets ... by which he catches Israel ... the first is fornication, the second, wealth, the third, defilement of the temple" (4:15-18).[98]   By contrast, 4QInstruction declares to its addressee that he has access to a unique form of wealth—an "inheritance of glory." His elect status does not heighten class tension but mitigates it.[99]

The "you are poor" refrain is also employed to discourage boasting: "Do not glorify yourself with what you lack, for you are poor (אל תתכבד במחסורכה ואתה רֹוֹשׁ)" (4Q416 2 ii 20). This sentiment is also expressed in 4Q417 2 i 9: "And do not for yourself alone boast (תרהב) [in your poverty]."[100]   4QInstruction reminds the addressee of his poverty while

---

'Akiba even poorer and in more wretched circumstances!'" See Judah Goldin, *The Fathers According to Rabbi Nathan* (YJS 10; New York/London: Yale University Press, 1983 [orig. pub., 1955]), 42.

[98] Murphy, *Wealth in the Dead Sea Scrolls*, 37-40.

[99] 4Q417 2 i 2 may teach the addressee to forgive the rich: "without reproaching the noble (הכשר), forgive him." Murphy, *Wealth in the Dead Sea Scrolls*, 175, argues that 4Q417 2 i 1-6 contains instruction on social relations with nobles. It is not clear, however, that this is the case. The key word הכשר in line 2 is ambiguous and not enough of the context of this phrase has survived to interpret it fully. Nowhere else does 4QInstruction provide advice regarding interactions with the upper class. See also *DJD 34*, 174.

[100] Portions of this passage are taken from the variant text 4Q416 2 i 4. The transcription of the word listed above as תרהב is disputed. Strugnell and Harrington, *DJD 34*, 173, and Tigchelaar, *To Increase Learning*, 55, transcribe this word with a *ḥet*, producing the word "to enlarge" or "to widen." The translation in *DJD 34* of this stich reads: "And not for thyself alone shalt thou increase [thy appetite when thou art in poverty]." This rendering produces a line that discusses moderation with food, a topic that is discussed in 4Q416 2 ii 18-20. The editors grant, however, that a *hē* is possible. See *DJD 34*, 175. This is how Elgvin, "An Analysis of 4QInstruction," 196, transcribes the word. Examination of

admonishing him not to be overly boastful about it.[101]   That material
poverty is intended is clear from its use of the word מחסור.

Frequent use of the term מחסור is a distinctive trait of 4QInstruction.
It refers to lacking material needs. 4Q417 2 i 21 acknowledges that the
addressee may be forced to borrow: "But if you borrow the wealth of
m[e]n for your need (למחסורכה) ..." (cf. 4Q416 2 iii 2-3).[102] Line 24 of
this fragment also discusses the addressee's material concerns: "and
when you are in need he will be tight-fisted" (cf. 1. 17; 4Q416 2 ii 1).[103]
The word מחסור is also used in 4Q418 126 ii 13: "if he is unable to meet
your need and the need of his resources (למחסורכה ומחסור אוטו) ..."[104]

PAM 43.516 suggests that traces of the characteristic long top stroke of a *hé* are visible.
Both options are possible semantically but on material grounds Elgvin's is to be favored.

[101] Contrast Sir 10:28: "My son, honor yourself with humility (בני בענוה כבד נפשך)."

[102] Cf. 4Q418 127 1. There are other attestations of מחסור in fragmentary texts that
cannot be properly interpreted: 4Q415 9 9; 4Q416 1 6; 4Q418 14 1 (?); 4Q418 16 3;
4Q418 87 6; 4Q418 88 5; 4Q418 97 2; 4Q418 107 3; 4Q418 122 i 7; 4Q418 159 ii 5;
4Q418 240 3; and 4Q423 12 1. Almost all of these attestations have a second person
singular pronoun.

[103] See also 4Q424 1 7-8: "do not exp[ect from him] (a dullard) to receive money when
you are in need (לקחת הון למחסורך)." Cf. 1QH 7:19. See Brin, "Studies in 4Q424, fragments 1-2," 36; *DJD 36*, 336-37.

[104] The word אוט, also spelled אט, has troubled commentators. It is a common word in
4QInstruction although its meaning is elusive. Outside of 4QInstruction the word occurs
nowhere in late Second Temple literature except 4Q424 1 6. It is attested sixteen times in
4QInstruction: 4Q415 18 2; 4Q416 2 ii 1 (par 4Q417 2 ii 3), 12 (par 4Q418 8 13); 4Q418
79 2; 4Q418 81 16; 4Q418 101 i 3; 4Q418 103 ii 6; 4Q418 107 4; 4Q418 126 ii 2, 12,
13; 4Q418 127 5; 4Q418 177 8; and 4Q423 2 i 5. The majority of these attestations are in small fragments that do
not preserve the immediate context of the word. Making matters more difficult, the אט of
biblical Hebrew seems to be of no assistance. There it is an adverb that can be understood
as "gently," "softly," or "dejectedly." (See 1 Kgs 21:27; 2 Sam 18:5; Isa 8:6; Gen 33:14.
Also note the word האטים of Isa 19:3, which means "spirits of the dead.") אט in
4QInstruction does not seem to have this sense of "gentleness." (Contra Harrington,
"Wisdom at Qumran," 145.) Strugnell and Harrington, *DJD 34*, 31, consider its meaning
"uncertain" and throughout the volume it is translated as "secret" or left untranslated.
Murphy, *Wealth in the Dead Sea Scrolls*, 170, is inclined toward the meaning "secret"
while granting that it might refer to business affairs. With Elgvin, I do not use the translation "secret" but prefer "assets" or "resources." See "An Analysis of 4QInstruction," 154,
213. אט is not a term signifying revelation in the manner of רז. It is never used to refer to
divine mysteries and is not combined with imperatives in the manner of the mystery that is
to be. It is used several times in connection with all of humanity: 4Q418 81 16, אוט לכול
הולכי אדם, "resources for all humanity"; 4Q418 126 ii 2, באמת מיד כול אוט אנשים, "in truth
from the hand of every asset of men." There are several instances of the word that suggest
that it has some sort of business sense, or at least refers to basic sustenance needs that can
be met through trade. In 4Q416 2 ii 1 and 4Q418 81 16 אט is used in connection with טרף,
"food." 4Q416 2 ii 1 affirms that God provides for the material needs of humankind. As
in 4Q418 126 ii 13, in 4Q416 2 ii 1 אט is used in conjunction with מחסור. In 4Q418 103 ii
6 and 4Q418 107 4 אט is found with מסחור, "merchandise." In 4Q418 126 ii 12 the word
comes before the phrase "from your basket he will seek what he wants (מטנאכה ידרוש

The subject of the sentence is probably one with whom the addressee is to have business relations. מחסור also refers to meeting material needs in biblical wisdom. Proverbs 21:17 reads: "Whoever loves pleasure will suffer want (מחסור); whoever loves wine and oil will not be rich."[105] The use of the word מחסור in 4QInstruction reflects an abiding interest in the addressee's ability to provide for his basic necessities. It also suggests that he could have difficulty in meeting them.

While the undisputed texts of the Dead Sea community occasionally refer to the elect as poor, this characterization is not as prominent as in 4QInstruction.[106] The Community Rule never describes group members as poor. The Damascus Document in general never identifies the sectarian community as the poor. One exception is CD 19:9, which cites Zechariah 11:11 to describe the ones who revere God. They are to be spared in the judgment as "the poor ones of the flock" (עניי הצאן).[107] In 1QM 13:12-14 the elect are associated with the poor: "We, instead, in the

_____

חפצו)"; this refers to someone else having their material needs met through trade with the addressee. The use of the word in 4Q424 1 6 is ambiguous but may refer to business affairs: "Into the hand of one who is stupid do not entrust resources (אט), for he will not keep private your affairs." (Cf. Prov 10:26.) This translation is that of Sarah Tanzer, *DJD 36*, 337, except for her rendering of אט. She translates it as "secret," although she grants it could be translated as "humble resources." G. Brin translates the word as "affair." See his "Studies in 4Q424, fragments 1-2," 31-32. It is reasonable to conclude with Elgvin that אט should be situated within the same semantic field as מחסור and חפץ, not רז. אט is a monetary term, the precise meaning of which is not clear. See also A. Schoors, "The Language of the Qumran Sapiential Works," in *The Wisdom Texts from Qumran*, 77-78.

The phrase מחסור אוטו of 4Q418 126 ii 13, translated here as "the need for his resources," is difficult to interpret. It seems to refer to resources of the addressee's trading partner that themselves have material needs to be met. It is possible that the resources in question are livestock, but one cannot resolve the matter conclusively.

[105] The majority of the attestations of this word in the Hebrew Bible occur in Proverbs. See 6:11 = 24:34; 11:24; 14:23; 21:5; 22:16; 28:27. Cf. Sir 40:26: "there is no want [with] the fear of the Lord (אין [ב]יראת יי מחסור)."

[106] Murphy, *Wealth in the Dead Sea Scrolls*, 447-55; Leander Keck, "The Poor among the Saints in Jewish Christianity and Qumran," *Zeitschrift für die Neutestamentliche Wissenschaft* 57 (1966): 54-78; Hans-Joachim Kandler, "Die Bedeutung der Armut im Schriftum von Chirbet Qumran," *Judaica* 13 (1957): 193-209; I. Hahn, "Die Eigentumsverhältnisse der Qumransekte," *Wissenschaftliche Zeitschrift* 12 (1963): 263-72; Norbert Lohfink, *Lobgesänge der Armen* (Stuttgart: Verlag Katholisches Bibelwerk, 1990); William R. Farmer, "The Economic Basis of the Qumran Community," *Theologische Zeitschrift* 11 (1955): 295-308; Martin Hengel, *The Zealots* (Edinburgh: T. & T. Clark, 1989 [orig. pub., 1961]), 335, note 121; Un-Sok Ro, *Die sogenannte "Armenfrömmigkeit"*, 9-34. Lohfink, *Lobgesänge der Armen*, 134, mentions a work which I was unable to consult: H.-G. Schmalenberg, "Der Begriff 'Arm' als Selbstbezeichnung des Beters in den Qumrantexten (Lizentiatarbeit; Münster, 1970-71).

[107] This text is not found among the Qumran Damascus Document texts and may be a product of a later recension. In the parallel text of CD 7, Isaiah 7:17 and Amos 5:26-27 are cited instead. These citations do not discuss poverty.

lot of your truth, rejoice in your mighty hand … Who is like you in strength, God of Israel, whose mighty hand is with the poor?" (cf. 11:7-9).[108] The hymns of the Hodayot generally do not use poverty language in terms of characterizing the sect. The elect may be understood as poor in 1QH 23:14. In this line the speaker describes himself as "a herald … to proclaim to the poor (ענוים) the abundance of your compassion" (cf. 11:25).[109] The text is ambiguous and can be interpreted in different ways. Murphy argues that it affirms that group members are to help the poor (cf. 9:36).[110] At times in the Hodayot the speaker identifies himself as a poor man. He declares that God has "freed" him from the "mediators of deceit" and then that God has "freed the life of the poor person (אביון) which they thought to finish off" (10:31-32; cf. 13:13-14). The Hodayot gives no financial instruction to people in poverty. 1QH probably continues the conceit found in the Psalms in which the speaker emphasizes his lowly status during his entreaty to God.

The most explicit identification of the elect as poor in the main writings of the Dead Sea sect is found in the Psalm 37 Pesher.[111] It interprets Psalm 37:11, the basis of the famous μακάριοι οἱ πραεῖς of Matthew 5:5, as referring to "the congregation of the poor (עדת האביונים) who will tough out the period of distress and will be rescued from all the snares of Belial" (2 9-11). In column 3 of this pesher, Psalm 37:21-22 is understood as referring to "the congregation of the poor [to whom is] the inheritance of the whole … They will inherit the high mountain of Isra[el and] delight [in his] holy [mou]ntain" (ll. 10-11). The Habakkuk Pesher condemns the Wicked Priest for attempting "to destroy the poor" (לכלות אביונים), which may be a reference to his efforts to oppose the sectarian community (12:6; cf. l. 3; 9:4-8). Poverty as a defining characteristic of the sect is an established theme in the uncontested literature of the Qumran sect. But it is not as prominent as in 4QInstruction.

The writings of the Dead Sea sect exhibit a genuine concern for the poor as a general economic class. For example, the Damascus Document stipulates the provision of a common fund that is slated for the needs of the poor and misfortunate (14:12-17). 1QH also displays sympathy for

---

[108] 1QM 14:7 includes the expression "poor in spirit" (עני רוח), which occurs in a fragmentary context. This phrase is similar to the πτωχοὶ τῷ πνεύματι of Matthew 5:3. Cf. 1QH 6:3.

[109] Keck observes that this line is similar to Isaiah 61:1. See his "The Poor among the Saints," 71, 76. See also Kandler, "Die Bedeutung der Armut," 200.

[110] *Wealth in the Dead Sea Scrolls*, 247.

[111] Maurya P. Horgan, *Pesharim: Qumran Interpretations of Biblical Books* (CBQMS 8; Washington, D.C.: Catholic Biblical Association, 1979), 192-226; Murphy, *Wealth in the Dead Sea Scrolls*, 240-41. See also Timothy H. Lim, *Pesharim* (Sheffield: Sheffield Academic Press, 2002).

the poor: "All of you, of perfect way, strengthen ... the poor!" (9:36). 4QInstruction, by contrast, shows minimal interest in poor people in general. There is no call for almsgiving as in Ben Sira and Tobit.[112] Unlike the texts written by the Dead Sea sect, 4QInstruction is focused on poverty almost exclusively in relation to the addressee and his financial decisions.

The financial advice of 4QInstruction is different in other ways from that of the undisputed literature of the Qumran community. The monetary instruction of 1QS and CD is generally communal in nature, coming in the form of dictates that members are required to follow. Financial transactions by sectarians are monitored and controlled by the "Inspector of the camp" (e.g., CD 13:16).[113] The rulebooks, particularly the Damascus Document, stipulate numerous rules regarding wealth.[114] There is nothing like this in 4QInstruction. Its financial teachings are never presented as rules in a legal or halakhic format. No penal code mandates punitive action if the addressee does not heed its advice. The composition simply gives recommendations that will help the addressee financially. In this sense the text is closer to biblical wisdom than the Qumran rulebooks. The nature of the community that 4QInstruction addresses appears quite different from the Qumran sect.[115]

3.4 Differing Levels of Poverty in 4QInstruction

It has already been suggested that the addressee of 4QInstruction is often considered materially poor. The composition, however, offers advice for a range of poverty levels. This suggests that it is addressed to more than one person, and that their economic situations can fluctuate. Some teachings are designed for someone who faces financial hardship but can make ends meet. 4Q417 2 i 17-18 reads:

> And as for you, if you have need for food, [br]ing your surpluses [together (ביחד), i]f you have surplus, (and) carry (them) to the place of his business (מחוֹז חפצו), and receive your inheritance (נחלתכה) from him, but do not (take) any mo[re] (cf. 4Q418 126 ii 15).[116]

---

[112] Sir 3:30; 17:22; 29:12; 40:17, 24; Tob 4:10-11; 12:8-9; 14:11.

[113] Note also the injunctions of 1QS 6:17, 22, 8:23, and 9:8, which require that one does not "mingle" (ערב) his wealth with that of the impure.

[114] One is also forbidden from lending on the Sabbath (10:18; 11:15). One is also stipulated to avoid the wealth of sinners (20:7). For these and other regulations regarding wealth in the Damascus Document, see Murphy, *Wealth in the Dead Sea Scrolls*, 25-162.

[115] See section 2 of Chapter 6.

[116] This translation adopts a proposed join by Tigchelaar. See his "הבא ביחד" in *4QInstruction (4Q418 64 + 199 + 66 par 4Q417 1 i 17-19) and the Height of the Columns*

Murphy interprets this passage as referring to the "sectarian pooling of resources."[117]   However, the addressee is never told to coordinate his financial decisions with other group members or in deference to the authority of a group leader.   The financial teachings of 4QInstruction assume that the addressee is free to make his own decisions in a relatively unrestricted economic context.   There is no reason to interpret the word יחד in this passage in the sectarian sense that it is used in the Qumran rulebooks.[118]

Strugnell and Harrington understand 4Q417 2 i 17-18 as referring to the "moderate use of resources."[119]   This is certainly the case, since the addressee is to "not (take) any mo[re]" than what is required.   The addressee does not have to show restraint with regard to sumptuous excess. The resources in question seem rather modest.   In this passage the addressee is advised to prepare items for trade when he lacks food.   While he is poor enough to be short on food, he has some means of economic viability.   The text grants, however, that this might not be the case ("if you have a surplus …").   The phrase מחוז חפצו is dependent upon Psalm 107:30, where the equivalent phrase is translated "their desired haven" (מחוז חפצם).   But since this phrase in 4QInstruction occurs in the context of trade and commerce, it is better understood as the "place of his business."[120]   It refers to the location where one's trading partner does business.   The psalm depicts God controlling the seas to underscore his power and the utter dependence of humanity on him for life.[121]   This

---

of 4Q418," *Revue de Qumran* 18 (1998): 589-93. See also idem, *To Increase Learning*, 55, 77. The phrase ביחד is from 4Q418 199. Strugnell and Harrington, *DJD 34*, 420, are critical of Tigchelaar's join because 4Q417 2 i has a different surface than fragments 64 and 66. But their transcription of this column of 4Q417 includes the expression ביחד. See *DJD 34*, 173. Tigchelaar, "הבא ביחד in *4QInstruction*," 590-91, suggests that the material differences between these fragments can be attributed to different conditions of preservation. The fragments fit well together and I see no reason to refute Tigchelaar's join.

[117] Murphy, *Wealth in the Dead Sea Scrolls*, 179.

[118] Tigchelaar, "הבא ביחד in *4QInstruction*," 592.

[119] *DJD 34*, 186.

[120] That the phrase מחוז חפצו should be understood in terms of commerce is also suggested by the semantic field of the word חפץ (see section 3.1 of this chapter). The word מחוז comes to mean "trading post" in rabbinic Hebrew; 4Q417 2 i 17-18 is apparently an early attestation of this usage.

[121] Ps 107:30 reads: "Then they were glad because they had quiet, and he brought them to their desired haven." In the psalm sailors almost die in a storm raised up by God. (There might have been a similar image in 4Q418 148 i 7, which reads "the sailors of the sea [חבלי ים]." See Elgvin, "An Analysis of 4QInstruction," 156.) They cry out to God for help and are delivered, in verse 30, safely to port. They are then enjoined to praise God and live in a land made fertile by God. They grow crops and sustain themselves (vv. 37-38). The psalm ends by declaring that one who knows that God helps the poor and needy is "wise" (חכם; v. 43). Psalm 107 is quoted in 4Q418b and alluded to in *1 Enoch* 101 and

theme of dominion may suggest why 4QInstruction alludes to this psalm. 4Q417 2 i 15-17 affirms the power of God in judgment: "F[or] before [his anger] none will stand. Who is righteous in his judgment? Without forgiveness (בלי סליחה) [h]ow [can any] poor man (אביון) [stand before him?]"[122] Psalm 107 might have also been attractive to the author of 4QInstruction because it affirms that God raises up the poor (v. 41).

The term "inheritance" in 4Q417 2 i 18 refers to acquiring items or money in trade that allow the addressee to meet his basic needs. Normally it describes his elect status.[123] Elgvin translates the word as "your portion."[124] He understands 4Q417 2 i 17-18 as referring to tithing produce to God.[125] But the business context of this passage suggests that it simply provides advice to help the addressee make ends meet.

4QInstruction advocates business dealings in ways that do not emphasize poverty. 4Q418 107 4 reads: "the resources, your merchandise, and the recompense in the business dealings of (אוטים מסחורכה ופעולתכה בחפצי) ..."[126] Though fragmentary, this text wants to ensure that the addressee is compensated appropriately when trading. He seems encouraged to defend his financial interests in 4Q417 2 i 12: "Be an advocate for your business deals (היה בעל ריב לחפצכה)."[127] 4Q418 81 18 tells the addressee to "Bring forth what you need to all those who seek business (הוצא מחסורכה לכול דורשי חפץ)." This line, coming after the assertion in lines 15-16 that the addressee can support himself by means of his "manual skill," encourages him to trade with people who can help him meet his basic needs. It assumes that he has the wherewithal to engage in trade. There is also business instruction in 4Q418 126 ii 12: "from your basket he will seek what he wants (מטנאכה ידרוש חפצו)." By mentioning the addressee's "basket," 4QInstruction apparently teaches him that he is to sell agricultural produce (cf. 4Q418 103 ii 3). 4Q418 126 ii grants in line 13 that this trade might not be successful: "But if he is unable to meet your need (למחסורכה) and the need of his resources ..." The subject of line 13 is probably that of the word ידרוש of the previous line, the

---

Ben Sira 43. Cf. also 1QH 11. See *DJD 34*, 186; R.A. Argall, *1 Enoch and Sirach* (SBLEJL 8; Atlanta: Scholars Press, 1995), 110-11, 151.

[122] This follows the reconstruction in *DJD 34*, 173. It relies on attestations of this text in 4Q418 7a 2 and 4Q418a 22 4-5. See also Tigchelaar, *To Increase Learning*, 55.

[123] See section 4.3 of Chapter 2.

[124] Elgvin, "An Analysis of 4QInstruction," 198.

[125] Ibid., 206.

[126] *DJD 34*, 336-37.

[127] It is not clear how exactly בעל ריב is to be understood. Strugnell and Harrington, *DJD 34*, 183, understand the phrase as similar in meaning to the phrase איש ריב in biblical Hebrew (e.g., Judg 12:2) or יריב, which can mean "adversary" or "advocate" (e.g., Jer 18:19). See also 1QH 15:22-23.

person with whom the addressee is trading. That the transaction might not earn enough for the addressee suggests that neither he nor the person with whom he is trading has a great deal of material wealth. The last few lines of 4Q418 126 ii are not well preserved but apparently contained instruction on how to meet one's needs through trade. Line 15 reads "… [in] your hand as a surplus, and yo[ur] property will increase … ([ה]כניק מ פרץ ו למות ה כ ד[ב])."[128] Although the addressee might not be successful, he is ultimately responsible for his own financial affairs.[129]

4QInstruction includes a substantial amount of advice regarding the addressee's business dealings. This qualifies his material poverty. 4QInstruction's business teachings presuppose that the addressee has something to trade, implying that he has stable means of support. None of its trade instruction, however, seems designed for someone who is wealthy. It emphasizes trade as a means to meet basic needs, not as a way to make profit. This suggests that the intended addressees of the composition were primarily commoners.

4QInstruction gives advice to people whose financial outlook is bleak. 4Q417 2 i 17-18 gives instruction for an addressee with a surplus to trade. The advice immediately following is for when he has no such surplus: "If you lack, borrow (לוא), being without m[on]ey for what you need (מחסורכה ה[ו]ן מבלי), for he (God) does not lack treasure" (l. 19).[130] Without items of value to trade, the addressee is encouraged to "borrow" from God. Similar to Proverbs 19:17, 4Q417 2 i 19-20 proclaims that God cares for one's needs: "[By] his mouth everything comes into being. And that which he provides for you, eat, and take no more."[131] Addressing someone without sufficient ability to earn, 4QInstruction recommends, in a manner similar to the Sermon on the

---

[128] The letter *bêt* is not in the transcription in *DJD 34*, 350, or Tigchelaar, *To Increase Learning*, 103.

[129] Murphy, *Wealth in the Dead Sea Scrolls*, 172.

[130] The word לוא should not be read as "no" but as an alternative spelling of the verb לוה. See *DJD 34*, 187; Elgvin, "An Analysis of 4QInstruction," 207. This word means "borrow" in the Qal and "lend" in the Piel. Context demands that this word be read as a Qal imperative of לוה. Regarding the word ה[ו]ן, Strugnell and Harrington, *DJD 34*, 173, transcribe הון. But as pointed out by Tigchelaar, *To Increase Learning*, 56, the *wāw* is not visible in the fragment. See also Murphy, *Wealth in the Dead Sea Scrolls*, 179.

[131] 4Q416 2 i 22-ii 1 is fragmentary but also suggests that one should rely on God for food: "Ask for your food for he has let loose his compas[sion]." 4Q417 2 i 24 may make a similar point: "Borrow like him and know the one who lend[s] (to you) (כמוהו לוה ודע [ר]מאנ[)." This follows the edition in *DJD 34*, 173. The transcription of this line is in dispute. According to Tigchelaar, *To Increase Learning*, 55, the final phrase of this stich is ודע מאור. This line may ask one to "borrow" from God in the manner of line 17 of 4Q417 2 i but is too fragmentary to interpret with confidence.

Mount, that he rely on the natural bounty of God rather than trade or money.[132]

4QInstruction also advises its addressee to tolerate harsh treatment from superiors. Some teachings depict the *mebin* as a laborer in a difficult situation. 4Q416 2 ii 9-10 reads: "If he accounts his service to you, [there will be no rest in your soul, and n]o sleep for your eyes until you do [his] command[ments] ... if it is possible to be hu[mble ...]." Though fragmentary, this stresses obedience to an extreme degree. Lines 12-15 of this fragment predict that if the addressee does good work his superior will be gracious towards him, while granting that this employer can be difficult:

> If in his favor you hold fast to his service (עבודתו) and his ability to earn assets (חכמת אוטו) ... you will advise him [so that you may become] for him an eldest son (בן בכור), and he will be merciful to you as a man is to his only child ... [because you are his servant and] his [chose]n one. And as for you, do n[ot] be (overly) trustful lest you hate him (א[ל] תבטח למה and do not be (overly) anxious about your oppressor (אל תשקוד ממרדהבכה). [And you shall become a wis]e [servant to him].[133]

<hr />

[132] Compare, for example, Matt 6:26: "Look at the birds of the air; they neither sow nor reap nor gather into barns, and yet your heavenly Father feeds them." John the Baptist and Bannus (*Life*, 11) are examples of people who lived solely on that which the Lord provides; they refused to eat cultivated foods. See Joan E. Taylor, *The Immerser: John the Baptist within Second Temple Judaism* (Grand Rapids: Eerdmans, 1997), 32-42.

[133] This text is reconstructed in part with material from 4Q417 2 ii 16-19, 4Q418 8 13-14, and 4Q418a 19 1-2. Several text-critical issues in this passage merit discussion. One is the phrase "his servant" (עבדו). This is the reconstruction proposed in *DJD 34*, 90. It is supported in Tigchelaar, *To Increase Learning*, 46. Only the first and part of the second letters of the word are visible. They are from 4Q417 2 ii 18. Elgvin, "An Analysis of 4QInstruction," 210, transcribes ענ]י. Regarding the second letter, both *bêt* and *nûn* are possible materially. This forces the interpreter to decide between the two on semantic grounds. Elgvin reconstructs the entire phrase as ען]י כי אתה [זכור, which produces the phrase "remember that you are poor." This transcription is attractive given the refrain "you are poor" in 4QInstruction. However, the reconstruction "his servant" of *DJD 34* is to be preferred. The "you are poor" refrain uses אביון and ראש/רוש, never עני. Also the immediate context of this term suggests that "servant" is more appropriate. 4Q416 2 ii 9-15 gives instruction regarding a superior in the context of employment. Line 15 encourages the addressee to become a "wis]e [servant."

The word transcribed here as תשׂנו ("lest you hate him") is hard to read materially. Strugnell and Harrington, *DJD 34*, 90, transcribe תשׂנא, producing a phrase that they translate as "(Lest) thou become hated." This reading is supported by Tigchelaar, *To Increase Learning*, 46. Elgvin, "An Analysis of 4QInstruction," 210, transcribes תשׂנו. This would be the product of the verb שנא with a נו- suffix, with this merger causing the *'ālep* to drop out. The phrase in question is ואתה א[ל] תבטח למה תשׂנו. The first issue to decide is whether the disputed last word of this phrase should be rendered as an active or passive verb. On this point parallelism can assist the interpreter. The phrase immediately following the one in question is active: ואל תשקוד ממרדהבכה. This suggests that the passive rendering offered in *DJD 34* ("thou become hated") is not likely. This would leave two other options. One

This passage is about work relations with a superior.[134] This is explicit in line 12: "If in his favor you hold fast to his service." The addressee is to do good work so that his superior will treat him with mercy. He is to become close enough to him to be thought of as his eldest son. As explained in the previous section, the intriguing phrase of line 12, חכמת אוטו, seems to signify the superior's "ability to earn assets." The addressee is to do good work in part because his superior has the financial ability to help provide for the addressee's material needs.

The addressee is encouraged to be congenial and professional even though his superior may treat him harshly. The addressee can "hate" his superior if he is trusted too much. The phrases תבטח א[ל] [al] and אל תשקוד, translated here as "do n[ot] be (overly) trustful" and "do not be (overly) anxious," respectively, should be read as a pair. One should not be too trustful or anxious when dealing with one's oppressor. The former teaches that he is capable of unscrupulous behavior and the latter that the addressee would do poor work if he became too stressed or frustrated. If he does not have a proper and balanced attitude with regard to this figure he will hate him and make relations even more difficult.[135] 4QInstruction advocates moderation, a theme common in the wisdom tradition, amidst oppressive conditions. The laborer who achieves the moderation advocated by 4QInstruction is called a "wis]e [servant" ([עבד משכי]ל) (4Q416 2 ii 15).[136] This expression seems to draw from the sapiential tradition. In Proverbs 17:2 a "wise servant" endures difficult circumstances in order to be rewarded by his superior: "A wise servant (עבד משכיל) who deals wisely will rule over a child who acts shamefully, and will share the inheritance as one of the family" (cf. Sir 10:25).

---

would be to transcribe תשנא and translate למה as מה + ל. This would yield the translation "Do not trust in that which you hate." The other would be to understand the word למה as "lest." This would require a suffix for the verb, as Elgvin's תשנו does, producing the translation: "Do not be trustful lest you hate him." I argue for the latter. למה is generally used in 4QInstruction as "lest." Also the parallelism of the phrase indicates that that which is hated is a person rather than an object. For the latter one would expect לאשר rather than למה. The addressee is warned about his oppressor (מרהבכה) and it is reasonable to understand the verb שנא in relation to this figure. For this reason Elgvin's interpretation is favored here. See also Murphy, *Wealth in the Dead Sea Scrolls*, 182-84.

[134] Elgvin, "An Analysis of 4QInstruction," 216. Strugnell and Harrington speculate that the superior in question could be God. See *DJD 34*, 11. This proposal is unlikely. Such a reading of 4Q416 2 ii 13-15 would imply that the addressee could hate God and give him counsel.

[135] It is stressed that the addressee should maintain his dignity in this difficult context: "And also do not debase (תשפל) yourself to one who is not your equal (לא ישוה בכה)" (4Q416 2 ii 15).

[136] Tigchelaar, *To Increase Learning*, 46; *DJD 34*, 90.

4Q416 2 ii 9-15 lays out guidelines of conduct for a servant who must work for a person who at times can be difficult. Finding other work is not presented as an option. The instruction is designed for someone who has no alternative but to tolerate the situation. This suggests that the addressee has little social mobility. This is another indication that that the intended audience is composed mainly of commoners.

The supervisor of the addressee is called "your oppressor" (מדהבכה) (4Q416 2 ii 14). The emphasis of the passage on paying debts (ll. 4-6) suggests that the oppression in question has an economic aspect.[137] Elgvin translates מדהבה as "creditor."[138] The editors of *DJD 34* translate this word as "oppressive tax-gatherer."[139] Harrington and Murphy have speculated that 4Q416 2 ii 9-15 describes a labor situation caused by debt-slavery.[140] This interpretation is not certain but is attractive for several reasons. Given that indebtedness was a wide-scale problem in Second Temple Palestine, indentured servitude was also common.[141] 4Q416 2 ii 9-15 precedes instruction on paying debts. Line 17 also suggests some type of indentured servitude since the addressee is to work without payment: "and for free you will serve your persecutors (וחנם תעבוד נוגשיכה)."[142]

---

[137] The word מדהבה is a biblical hapax that is in parallelism with נגש, "to persecute," in Isaiah 14:4 (cf. 4Q416 2 ii 17). See *DJD 34*, 93, 104. Murphy translates the word in question in 4Q416 2 ii 14 as "oppression/distress," based on the use of מדהובם in CD 13:9. See her *Wealth in the Dead Sea Scrolls*, 183. CD 13 alludes to Isaiah 58:6-7, which is a call to release the poor from their financial burdens, and stipulates similar measures for the Many: "He (the Examiner) will undo all the chains which bind them, so that there will be neither harassed nor oppressed in his congregation" (l. 10). This suggests that CD 13 refers to the elimination of oppressive debts. As in 4Q416 2 ii 14, the word refers to economic distress. CD and 4QInstruction both discuss financial oppression but presuppose different institutions. In CD 13 the superior is committed to those under him; 4Q416 2 ii 9-15 places the addressee at the mercy of his superior. In CD 13:9-10 the Examiner is described as being compassionate towards the Many. In 4Q416 2 ii 13 the addressee struggles to ensure that his superior will be merciful towards him. The Examiner is told to be like "a father for his sons" in CD 13:9; the addressee is told to become like the first-born son of his superior in 4Q416 2 ii 13, although he could treat him cruelly. 1QH 11:25 has the phrase הוות מרהבה, translated as "the calamities of hardship." The distress the phrase refers to is endured by the poor: "The soul of a poor person (נפש אביון) lives amongst great turmoil and the calamities of hardship are with my footsteps" (cf. 20:18). The phrase בהוות מרהבה also occurs in 4Q418 176 3 (cf. 4Q418a 16 3). See also Joseph M. Baumgarten, *Qumran Cave 4.XIII: The Damascus Document (4Q266-273)* (DJD 18; Oxford: Clarendon, 1996), 108.

[138] Elgvin, "An Analysis of 4QInstruction," 218.

[139] *DJD 34*, 93.

[140] Harrington, *Wisdom Texts*, 46; Murphy, *Wealth in the Dead Sea Scrolls*, 182.

[141] Fiensy, *The Social History of Palestine*, 90. See also Goodman, *The Ruling Class of Judaea*, 58.

[142] The economic nature of the servitude of the "oppressor" is also suggested by the obscure phrase in 4Q416 2 ii 10, הון בלוֹ, which can be translated as "tribute money."

4QInstruction's financial teachings take into consideration a range of poverty levels. The sequence of instruction in 4Q417 2 i presupposes that the addressee has the means to earn a living through trade, that he does not and must borrow, and that he must rely entirely on God, utterly destitute. This range of different economic positions suggests that the composition is directed to multiple addressees and that they were at a variety of different poverty levels. It also implies that some of them had means of support that are not reliable. This is additional evidence that 4QInstruction was addressed to commoners.

3.5 Poverty as a Basis for Ethical Instruction

At times 4QInstruction discusses the poverty of the addressee in ways that do not bear only on his economic situation. The text also gives financial instruction that is related to topics such as ethics and the addressee's elect status. First I will examine poverty in relation to ethics.

The addressee's poverty is mentioned when giving him ethical guidelines regarding family relations. 4Q416 2 iii 15-16 reads: "Honor your father with your poverty and your mother with your lowly status (במצערׄיכה)."[143] Shortly thereafter the addressee is told: "you have married a woman in your poverty (אשה לקחתה ברישכה)" (l. 20). Traditional wisdom stresses filial piety and the importance of marriage.[144] Proverbs, however, does not emphasize poverty in its instruction on these subjects.[145] The expression במצערׄיכה is in parallelism with ברישכה. The word מצער can refer to something small, insignificant, or brief.[146] In 4Q416 2 iii 15-16 poverty does not refer to lowliness in a financial sense but rather in an ethical one. 4QInstruction does not teach that the key to filial piety and success in marriage is to have no money. One honors one's parents and has a good marriage by having a humble, reverent

---

Much of its immediate context has not survived, making interpretation difficult. בלו is an administrative Aramaic term that occurs in Ezra (4:13, 20; 7:24) where it is translated as "tribute." It could be an Akkadian loan word. Its exact meaning is not clear, although it is an economic term. See Joseph Blenkinsopp, *Ezra-Nehemiah* (OTL; Philadelphia: Westminster, 1988), 110; *DJD 34*, 101.

[143] For the transcription of במצערׄיכה, see section 4.5 of Chapter 2.

[144] For Proverbs on marriage see 12:4: "A good wife is the crown of her husband, but she who brings shame is like rottenness in his bones" (cf. 18:22; 19:14; Sir 25:1, 8; 26:1-3, 15-16; 36:29-30; 40:19, 23).

[145] Collins, *Jewish Wisdom*, 118.

[146] See, for example, Job 8:7: "Though your beginning was small (מצער), your latter days will be very great." Cf. Gen 19:20; Mic 5:1; Ps 119:141; Isa 60:22; Sir 30:32; 33:10.

attitude when interacting with family members and one's spouse. This comportment is associated with poverty.[147]

4QInstruction combines ethics with poverty in an eschatological context in 4Q417 2 i 15-17.[148] After underscoring the might of God's anger, 4QInstruction asks "Who is righteous in his judgment? Without forgiveness [h]ow [can any] poor man (אביון) [stand before him?]" Before this statement the addressee is encouraged to avoid sin in order to be spared: "Do not overlook your [transgress]ions. Be like a humble man (עֵנִי) when you strive for his judgment ... Then God will appear, his anger will turn aside, and he will take away your sins" (ll. 14-15). The addressee is not presented as sinless, hence the need for ethical instruction. The poor man needs God's mercy in order to be spared in the final judgment. He will receive divine compassion if he admits his sins and acts with humility during his lifetime. This is presumably the case with all humanity, not just the poor. But the humility that 4QInstruction recommends is associated with poverty. This is also emphasized by the word עֵנִי itself, which can refer to both poverty and humility.

Ethical conduct and material poverty are frequently presented as two aspects of the daily life of the addressee of 4QInstruction. The two are emphasized throughout the composition. In 4Q416 2 iii and 4Q417 2 i these themes come together. While the difficulties of material poverty are acknowledged, it is also connected to an ethical comportment that will spare one from eschatological judgment.

3.5.1 Poverty and the Addressee's Spirit

4QInstruction's financial advice is often reminiscent of biblical wisdom. But the justification this Qumran text provides for its instruction on this topic often has no analogue in Proverbs. 4QInstruction's concern for the addressee's poverty reflects an abiding interest in his elect status. This is evident in its teaching on debts. 4QInstruction recommends that the addressee should not maintain indebtedness (4Q416 2 ii 4-6). To underscore this advice, 4QInstruction affirms that one should "exchange your holy spirit for no price (הון), because there is no price equal (מחיר) [to

---

147 James L. Kugel has argued that honoring one's parents "in your poverty" also means that one should support his parents in old age even if he is not in a good financial condition. See his "Some Instances of Biblical Interpretation in the Hymns and Wisdom Writings of Qumran," in *Studies in Ancient Midrash* (ed. J.L. Kugel; Cambridge: Harvard University Center for Jewish Studies, 2001), 168.

148 Murphy, *Wealth in the Dead Sea Scrolls*, 166-74.

it]" (ll. 6-7; cf. 4Q418 76 3).[149] Indebtedness is portrayed as a loss of one's spirit, which has more value than something that can be bought with money. The term "holy spirit" generally refers to God in the Hebrew Bible (e.g., Isa 63:10; Ps 51:11) and the Hodayot.[150] This is also the case in the New Testament (e.g., Matt 12:32; Acts 2:4). The Qumran rulebooks describe the Dead Sea sect as having a "holy spirit" (1QS 3:7; 9:3; CD 7:3-4). The contrast between the better-attested meaning of the phrase as referring to God and its usage in 4QInstruction demonstrates how much the wisdom text values its addressee.

The addressee's "spirit" is emphasized in a financial context elsewhere in 4QInstruction. 4Q416 2 ii 17-18 reads:

> [Do not se]ll your soul for wealth. It is good that you are a servant in spirit (עבד ברוח) and without wages you will serve your persecutors. And for a price do not sell your glory. And do not pledge money (אל תערב הון) for your inheritance lest it dispossess your body.[151]

The use of "glory" is similar to the declaration earlier in this column that one should "exchange your holy spirit for no price." "Glory" signifies his elect status, as does the term "inheritance."[152] The exhortations not to pledge one's inheritance for money or sell one's glory for a price are intended to discourage the addressee from involvement in unwise financial entanglements.

As going surety is construed as a loss of one's inheritance in 4Q416 2 ii 18, it is likewise considered a loss of one's spirit in 4Q416 2 iii 6-7. After the fragment advises the addressee to pay back debts, it adds: "And do not pledge your spirit (רוחכה אל תחבל) with it." Surety is an option that should be avoided. Going surety is presented as putting one's

---

[149] The speaker of 1QH 6:20 similarly claims that he will not "exchange your truth for wealth (בהון אמתך)." See also Murphy, *Wealth in the Dead Sea Scrolls*, 182.

[150] Cf. 1QH 4:26; 6:13; 8:9, 11; 15:7; 17:32; 20:12. See Elgvin, "An Analysis of 4QInstruction," 215.

[151] There is no dispute about the phrase תערב הון but some clarification is in order. 4Q416 2 ii 18 reads תערבהו. תערב הון is attested in the variant of this text in 4Q417 2 ii 23. Strugnell and Harrington, *DJD 34*, 106, and Elgvin, "An Analysis of 4QInstruction," 210, agree that the variant reading produces a better text. If one reads תערבהו with 4Q416, the most immediate antecedent would be the word "glory" from the preceding phrase. In this case the phrase in question would recommend not pledging your glory for your inheritance, a *non sequitur*. See also Tigchelaar, *To Increase Learning*, 152.

[152] Murphy, *Wealth in the Dead Sea Scrolls*, 186, has argued that the term "inheritance" refers in 4Q416 2 ii 17-18 to "land or its value in cash." The word certainly refers to items that have a monetary trade value in 4Q417 2 i 18. But it is more likely that in the text at hand the term refers to the elect status of the addressee. Since the fragment contrasts the addressee's "glory" and "spirit" to monetary wealth, the term "inheritance" probably functions in a way that is similar to these terms.

"spirit" in the hands of the creditor.[153] Indebtedness jeopardizes the addressee's elect status.

The elect status of the addressee is more valuable than monetary wealth. The composition uses terms such as "holy spirit," "glory," and "inheritance" to describe this status. Specific features of his "inheritance," such as the access to revelation and affinity with the angels, were examined in Chapters 2 and 3. In the texts discussed in this chapter the addressee's special allotment is mentioned without discussion of its particular features. His elect status in general is introduced into specific contexts that deal with money matters. The financial instruction of the composition often considers the addressee to be materially poor. 4QInstruction has an interest in its intended audience's precarious economic position because of the elect status of its members.

3.5.2 Poverty, Joy, and Salvation

The addressee is promised that he will inherit joy if he avoids surety and pays off his debts. After warning the addressee about types of financial entanglements to be avoided in 4Q416 2 iii 3-6, lines 7-8 describe the rewards of heeding this advice: "Then you shall sleep (i.e., die) with the truth and when you die your memory shall blos[som fore]ver. And in the end you will inherit joy." It is clear from other texts that "joy" has an eschatological sense. In 4Q417 2 i 10-12 the addressee is told not to

> rejoice in your mourning lest you toil in your life. [Gaze upon the mystery] that is to be, and grasp the birth-times of salvation and know who is inheriting glory and who ini[qu]ity. Is not [joy established for those contrite of spirit?] Or eternal joy for those who mourn?[154]

The addressee is in a state of "mourning" in which he should not rejoice. The phrase "eternal joy" suggests life after death (cf. 4Q416 4 3; 4Q418 102 5).[155] The expression may be derived from Isaiah.[156] In 4Q417 2 i

---

[153] This context establishes that אל תחבל should be translated as "do not pledge." It is granted in *DJD 34*, 116, that this is a possibility, but the editors opt in their translation for "but let not thy spirit be corrupted by him/it." See also Elgvin, "An Analysis of 4QInstruction," 223.

[154] The supplement "joy established for those stricken of spirit?" is not found in Tigchelaar, *To Increase Learning*, 55. 4Q417 2 i 10-12 is also discussed in section 3 of Chapter 5. Cf. Luke 6:25; Jas 4:9; Heb 12:2.

[155] This claim is discussed in section 3 of Chapter 5.

[156] Elgvin has argued that 4Q417 2 i 10-12 rephrases Isaiah 61:3 and adopts the phrase שמחת עולם from Isaiah 61:7. See his "An Analysis of 4QInstruction," 203; idem, "Wisdom, Revelation, and Eschatology," 446. The phrase is used in 61:7 (cf. 66:10) in relation to a transformation of mourning to joy. This verse, as in 51:11 and 35:10, describes the restoration of Zion.

10-12 this joy is contrasted with "mourning," which is associated with the addressee's present condition. Experiencing "eternal joy" after death entails not only being pious and humble but also requires avoiding risky financial ventures.

Several other late Second Temple sources associate joy with salvation and eternal life. The *Epistle of Enoch* exhorts: "Be hopeful, and do not abandon your hope, for you will have great joy like the angels of heaven" (*1 En.* 104:4; cf. v. 13). Eternal life and glory are described as joy in the Treatise on the Two Spirits: "The reward of all those [who walk in the spirit of truth] will be ... eternal joy with endless life, and a crown of glory with majestic raiment in eternal light" (1QS 4:6-8).[157] The War Scroll proclaims that once judgment has been implemented "Justice will rejoice in the heights and all the sons of his truth will have enjoyment in everlasting knowledge" (1QM 17:8). The righteous are depicted as rejoicing forever in *Jubilees*: "The righteous ones will see (the destruction of their enemies) and give praise, and rejoice forever and ever with joy ... their bones will rest in the earth, and their spirits will increase joy" (23:30-31).[158] The *Testaments of the Twelve Patriarchs* also presents joy in an eschatological sense. For example, *Testament of Judah* 25:4 reads: "And those who died in sorrow shall be raised in joy; and those who died in poverty for the Lord's sake shall be made rich" (cf. *T. Ash.* 6:5). Similar sentiments are found in *Testament of Levi*:

> And the Lord will rejoice in his children; he will be well pleased by his beloved ones forever. Then Abraham, Isaac, and Jacob will rejoice, and I shall be glad, and all the saints shall be clothed in righteousness (18:13-14).[159]

4Q416 2 iii 7-8 offers two rewards for shunning risky financial predicaments: leaving a good reputation after death and inheriting joy. The first echoes traditional wisdom and the second is a Second Temple trope that describes joy as an eschatological reward of the righteous.

---

[157] Note that Ben Sira uses the phrase "eternal joy" in a non-eschatological sense: "When you stumble, there is eternal joy (שמחת עולם); and when you die, a curse is your lot" (41:9).

[158] George W.E. Nickelsburg, *Resurrection, Immortality, and Eternal Life in Intertestamental Judaism* (HTS 26; Cambridge: Harvard University Press, 1972), 32. See also Bar 4:29: "For the one who brought these calamities upon you will bring you everlasting joy (αἰώνιον εὐφροσύνην) with your salvation."

[159] The Hodayot depicts the elect as "in the community of jubilation (יחד רנה)" (11:23; cf. 5:12; 21:14). *2 Enoch* 20:4 presents the angels as taking part in the heavenly liturgy "in joy and merriment."

4. CONCLUSION

The theme of poverty is a significant feature of 4QInstruction. The composition, like Proverbs and other biblical books, advocates sympathy for the poor. This is also the case in writings of the Dead Sea sect such as the Damascus Document and the Hodayot. But unlike these texts from the Hebrew Bible and Qumran, 4QInstruction shows scant interest in the poor as an economic class. It is preoccupied with the poverty of the addressee and shows a pronounced interest in his economic situation. Sapiential traditions about the poor and the handling of money are adapted to suit 4QInstruction's dedication to its intended audience. By consistently reminding the addressee that he is poor, poverty is established as important for the self-understanding of the group to which the composition is addressed. The undisputed literature of the Dead Sea group occasionally associates the elect status of its members with poverty. Most notable in this regard is the Psalm 37 Pesher. But the claim is much more prominent in 4QInstruction. Its thematization of poverty is different from that of main texts of the Qumran community. The financial advice of 4QInstruction also presumes the addressee operates in a free and open economic context. This contrasts the tight control over financial transactions exhibited in the Qumran rulebooks.

4QInstruction often refers to the addressee's poverty and gives him financial advice designed to help him meet his daily needs. He was susceptible to economic hardship. His poverty is clearly material. The range of monetary teachings in 4QInstruction suggests it was addressed to a group of people who were at various economic levels. None of them appears to be rich. A substantial segment of them had means of support that were not always reliable. They were commoners at a time when people could lose everything with relative ease. Some texts clearly present the addressee as a farmer or an artisan. The ability of a person in these professions to support himself in Second Temple Palestine was susceptible to numerous factors outside of his control. Comparison with Ben Sira illustrates that the audience of 4QInstruction has a lower social status than that of the aristocratic sage.

As Murphy has stressed, 4QInstruction places the addressee's difficult economic situation in a larger framework. Its advice that relates to his financial situation is coordinated with some of the main pedagogical goals of the work. It reminds the addressee of his elect status while giving financial advice. He is encouraged to develop an attitude of reverence and respect that colors his daily life, including his financial affairs.

CHAPTER FIVE

THEOPHANIC JUDGMENT AND ETERNAL LIFE:
THE ESCHATOLOGY OF 4QINSTRUCTION

1. INTRODUCTION

4QInstruction is distinguished from traditional wisdom by its eschato-logical perspective. In Proverbs the best one can hope for after death is a good reputation, earned by living an ethical life: "The memory of the righteous is a blessing, but the name of the wicked will rot" (Prov 10:7; cf. 22:1).¹ This sentiment is also found in 4QInstruction: "your name will flourish forev[er]" (4Q417 4 ii 3; cf. 4Q416 2 iii 7). The composi-tion, however, goes further. It promises rewards after death.² The text offers advice designed to improve the addressee's social relations and financial stability while assuring him that he can obtain "eternal joy" (4Q417 2 i 10-12), a designation for eternal life.

4QInstruction also differs from biblical wisdom in its depiction of ret-ribution. In traditional wisdom the wicked bring on their own demise. In Proverbs 1:18, for example, those who lie in ambush are portrayed as taking their own lives rather than those of the innocent.³ In 4QInstruction the punishment of the wicked is meted out by God when he judges humanity in the eschatological future. The composition al-ludes to the final judgment, with its fullest accounts occurring in 4Q416 1 and 4Q418 69 ii. 4Q416 1, which is probably the opening passage of the composition, grounds the instruction that follows in the declaration that from "heaven he will judge over the work of wickedness" and that "all iniquity will come to an end" (ll. 10, 13). Demonstrating the text's dualism, 4QInstruction emphasizes the contrasting fates in store for the righteous and wicked. This eschatological horizon provides a theological rationale for heeding its ethical advice.

---

¹ See also Qoh 7:1; Sir 6:1; 15:6; and 41:11.
² Although it does not discuss 4QInstruction, note Roland E. Murphy, "Death and Af-terlife in the Wisdom Literature," in *Judaism in Late Antiquity. Part 4: Death, Life-After-Death, Resurrection and the World-to-Come in the Judaisms of Late Antiquity* (ed. J. Neusner and A.J. Avery-Peck; Leiden: Brill, 2000), 101-16.
³ For the Tat-Ergehen-Zusammenhang of biblical wisdom, see section 2 of Chapter 2.

While 4QInstruction's eschatology distinguishes it from traditional wisdom, this perspective is compatible with other sapiential texts of the late Second Temple period. In the Treatise on the Two Spirits, which is explicitly an instructional text (1QS 3:13), those who are upright will receive "eternal enjoyment with endless life, and a crown of glory with majestic raiment in eternal light" (4:7-8), while those who succumb to the "spirit of deceit" will endure "the scorching wrath of the God of revenge" (4:9, 12). The pivotal event of the Book of Mysteries is a judgment scene that depicts the obliteration of the wicked: "(Then,) just as smoke wholly ceases and is no more, so shall wickedness cease forever (1Q27 1 i 6).[4] Other sapiential texts also give practical advice while incorporating an eschatological perspective. For example, 4Q185, a wisdom text characterized by traditional commands and prohibitions, reminds its addressee of judgment: "Who can endure to stand before his angels? For with a flaming fire they will judge" (1-2 i 8-9).[5]

---

[4] This translation is from Lawrence H. Schiffman. See Torleif Elgvin et al., *Qumran Cave 4.XV: Sapiential Texts, Part 1* (DJD 20; Oxford: Clarendon, 1997), 38. See also D. Barthélemy and J.T. Milik, *Qumran Cave 1* (DJD 1; Oxford: Clarendon, 1955), 103. There is some debate as to whether or not the Book of Mysteries should be considered a sapiential text. D. Harrington includes Mysteries in his survey of Qumran wisdom. See his *Wisdom Texts from Qumran* (London: Routledge, 1996), 70-73. G. Vermes, however, puts the work in a section entitled "Apocalyptic Works." See his *The Complete Dead Sea Scrolls in English* (New York: Penguin, 1997), 389-91. F. García Martínez has placed the text in a section called "Other Compositions." See his *The Dead Sea Scrolls Translated* (2nd ed.; Leiden/Grand Rapids: Brill/Eerdmans, 1996), 399-401. It has been argued that Mysteries should be considered an eschatological text rather than a sapiential one. See Giovanni Ibba, "Il 'Libro dei Misteri' (1Q27, f.1): testo escatologico," *Henoch* 21 (1999): 73-84. These two aspects should not be considered incompatible. Mysteries should be considered a wisdom text because of its prominent sapiential terminology and its pedagogical ethos. See Harrington, *Wisdom Texts*, 73. The judgment scene in 1Q27 places a sapiential dichotomy between "knowledge" and "folly" in an eschatological context (1 i 7). The text purports to contain revealed knowledge that is understood as a higher form of wisdom: "With great intelligence he opened our ear, so that we would h[ear] the inclination of understanding for all who pursue knowledge" (4Q299 8 6-7). The Book of Mysteries is a sapiential work that contains eschatological instruction.

[5] This translation is based on John Strugnell, "Notes en marge du volume V des 'Discoveries in the Judaean Desert of Jordan,'" *Revue de Qumran* 7 (1970), 272. See also John M. Allegro, *Qumrân Cave 4.1 (4Q158-4Q186)* (DJDJ 5; Oxford: Clarendon, 1968), 86. There is a revised edition of this volume (DJD 5a) that is forthcoming from Moshe J. Bernstein and George J. Brooke. For more on 4Q185, see Harrington, *Wisdom Texts*, 35-39; H. Lichtenberger, "Eine weisheitliche Mahnrede in den Qumranfunden (4Q185)," in *Qumrân: sa piété, sa théologie et son milieu* (ed. M. Delcor; BETL 46; Paris: Duculot, 1978), 151-62; idem, "Der Weisheitstext 4Q185—Eine neue Edition," in *The Wisdom Texts from Qumran and the Development of Sapiential Thought* (ed. C. Hempel, A. Lange, and H. Lichtenberger; BETL 159; Leuven: Leuven University Press/Peeters, 2002), 127-50; Thomas H. Tobin, "4Q185 and Jewish Wisdom Literature," in *Of Scribes and Scrolls: Studies on the Hebrew Bible, Intertestamental Judaism and Christian Origins* (ed. H.W. Attridge et al.; Lanham: University Press of America, 1990), 145-52;

4QInstruction's eschatology is a topic of scholarly debate. Armin Lange has proposed that the text's emphasis on judgment represents the 'eschatologizing' of the traditional Tat-Ergehen-Zusammenhang of biblical wisdom.[6] The final punishment of the wicked in 4QInstruction is compatible with the assertion of biblical wisdom that the wicked will be destroyed. It is also important to emphasize 4QInstruction's indebtedness to the apocalyptic tradition regarding the theme of judgment. As Lange observes, 4QInstruction can be understood as 'eschatologizing' biblical wisdom since it grounds teachings that are reliant on traditional wisdom in an eschatological context.

An important topic of debate has been 4QInstruction's relation to *1 Enoch*. Elgvin has claimed that the latter is a source for the former.[7] He interprets the similarities between the eschatological perspectives of these works in light of this conclusion. For example, the phrase of 4Q418 69 ii 14, "do [they] not wal[k] in eternal light?" according to Elgvin "seems to be quoted from *1 Enoch* 92:4," which also has the image of walking in eternal light.[8] His claims have drawn criticism.[9] While 4QInstruction may have utilized Enochic traditions in some form, a direct literary link between the two texts is difficult to prove.

The eschatology of 4QInstruction also merits comparison with that of the undisputed writings of the Dead Sea sect. Elgvin understands 4QInstruction to have a "realized eschatology," reflecting his view that "salvation is a present reality" for the addressee.[10] This characterization of his eschatological rewards emphasizes the composition's similarity to texts such as the Hodayot. Elgvin contends that 4QInstruction is addressed to a "pre-Essene" community. Like the Hodayot, the wisdom text promises its addressee eternal salvation. The claim that this means salvation is a "present reality," however, needs to be qualified by the

---

Donald J. Verseput, "Wisdom, 4Q185, and the Epistle of James," *Journal of Biblical Literature* 117 (1998): 691-707.

   6 Armin Lange, *Weisheit und Prädestination: Weisheitliche Urordnung und Prädestination in den Textfunden von Qumran* (STDJ 18; Leiden: Brill, 1995), 305.

   7 Torleif Elgvin, "Early Essene Eschatology: Judgment and Salvation According to Sapiential Work A," in *Current Research and Technological Development on the Dead Sea Scrolls: Conference on the Texts from the Judean Desert, Jerusalem, 30 April 1995* (ed. D.W. Parry and S.D. Ricks; STDJ 20; Leiden: Brill, 1996), 126-65.

   8 Ibid., 163.

   9 Loren T. Stuckenbruck, "4QInstruction and the Possible Influence of Early Enochic Traditions: An Evaluation," in *The Wisdom Texts from Qumran*, 245-61; Eibert J.C. Tigchelaar, *To Increase Learning for the Understanding Ones: Reading and Reconstructing the Fragmentary Early Jewish Sapiential Text 4QInstruction* (STDJ 44; Leiden: Brill, 2001), 214-17.

   10 Elgvin, "Early Essene Eschatology," 144; idem, "An Analysis of 4QInstruction" (diss.; Hebrew University of Jerusalem, 1997), 117-18.

recognition that his eschatological fate is determined by his ethical conduct. Salvation is not automatically guaranteed: "Who is righteous in his judgment? Without forgiveness [h]ow [can any] poor man [stand before him?]" (4Q417 2 i 16-17).

The fact that a relatively large number of manuscripts of 4QInstruction was found at Qumran establishes that the text was important for the Dead Sea sect. But if there is a connection between this group and the intended audience of 4QInstruction, it is one that is quite loose.[11] The community to which the wisdom text is addressed is different in many ways from the Dead Sea sect. The *mebin*, the text's typical designation for the addressee, is not under the tight control of a leader, and there is no list of halakhic stipulations that he must follow. Also there are eschatological motifs that are prominent in the main writings of the Qumran community that are nowhere in 4QInstruction—such as messianism, Belial, or a heightened sense of imminent judgment.

The eschatology of 4QInstruction warrants investigation. This chapter will examine the composition's theme of judgment. I will argue that the text envisions the elimination of the wicked while promising eternal life with the angels to the righteous. I will also discuss 4QInstruction's conception of history as a sequence of periods that culminates in judgment. In this chapter I will also situate the composition's eschatology in its late Second Temple setting, particularly in relation to *1 Enoch* and the main texts of the Qumran community.

2. JUDGMENT AND ESCHATOLOGY IN 4QINSTRUCTION

4QInstruction contains no description of eschatological events as lengthy as those of the War Scroll or the Book of Revelation. Judgment, however, is frequently mentioned. 4Q417 1 i 24 is typical of its brief allusions to judgment. After urging the addressee to avoid wickedness, this line declares that the wicked "will not be treated as guiltless. According to his inheritance in it he will be tr[eated as wicked]."[12] In 4QInstruction the final judgment is not presented as a condemnation of national or religious events in the present age writ large. Rather it is oriented towards the ethics of the individual. The text's allusions to judgment suggest that the addressee is understood to have already had some eschato-

---

[11] See section 2 of Chapter 6.

[12] Other examples of 4QInstruction's reminders of judgment include 4Q417 1 ii 11; 4Q417 4 ii 4; 4Q418 68 2-3; 4Q418 77 3; 4Q418 113 1-2; 4Q418 121 1; 4Q418c 5; 4Q423 4 3a; and 4Q423 6 4.

logical instruction. 4QInstruction makes sure that he keeps judgment in mind. Its most frequent terms for judgment are פקודה[13] and משפט.[14]

One of the most extensive judgment scenes of 4QInstruction is in 4Q416 1. Lines 10-13 of this fragment read:

> From heaven he will judge over the work of wickedness. But all the sons of his truth will be accepted with favor ... They (the wicked) will be in terror (יפחדו). And all those who defiled themselves in it (wickedness) will cry out (יריעו). For the heavens will be afraid ... The [s]eas and the depths will be in terror ([י]מים ותהמות פחדו), and every fleshly spirit will be laid bare (יתערערו כל רוח בשר). But the sons of heave[n will rejoice on the day of] its [judg]ment and all iniquity will come to an end, and the period of tru[th] will be completed.[15]

---

[13] See 4Q416 1 9; 4Q416 7 2; 4Q417 1 i 7 [2x] (par 4Q418 43 5), 14; 4Q417 2 i 8; 4Q418 68 2-3; and 4Q418a 21 1. The word has been reconstructed in 4Q416 3 2 and 4Q418 169 + 170 2. For the use of this root as a verb, see 4Q417 1 i 19; 4Q417 ii 11; 4Q418 81 9; 4Q418 123 ii 7; 4Q418 209 2 (reconstructed); 4Q423 4 3a; and 4Q423 5 4. 4Q418 113 2 and 4Q418 126 ii 6 have the phrase פקודת ש[, which could be reconstructed as פקודת ש]לום (cf. 1QH 9:17; 11Q13 2 15). See also Tigchelaar, *To Increase Learning*, 240-42; A. Schoors, "The Language of the Qumran Sapiential Works," in *The Wisdom Texts from Qumran*, 90.

[14] See, for example, 4Q416 6 1; 4Q417 1 i 18; 4Q417 2 i 16; 4Q417 3 2; 4Q417 4 ii 5; 4Q418 69 ii 5, 7, 9; 4Q418 121 1; 4Q418 126 ii 6; and 4Q418 228 3. The word has also been reconstructed in 4Q415 19 2; 4Q416 1 15; 4Q418 34 1; 4Q418 214 2; and 4Q423 6 4. The version of 4Q416 1 13 in Tigchelaar, *To Increase Learning*, 175, reconstructs this word. See also ibid., 239.

[15] There are several text-critical issues regarding this text. While Strugnell and Harrington, *DJD 34*, 81, transcribe the first expression of this passage as מֹשׁמים, Tigchelaar, *To Increase Learning*, 174, lists it as בֹשׁמים. There is no major difference between the two options.

Tigchelaar's edition of this passage supplements 4Q416 1 11 with material from 4Q418 212. His version of the second sentence of this line thus includes some material not found in the edition in *DJD 34*: "For the heavens shall fear, and the earth shall be shaken from [its place]." The additional second phrase is attractive on thematic grounds and fits well with the sense of the passage. It is a hypothetical supplement that demands consideration. See ibid., 174, 180.

There have been several suggestions regarding how the difficult verb יתערערו in 4Q416 1 12 should be understood. Elgvin, "An Analysis of 4QInstruction," 245, proposes reading the verb as a Hithpael of ערה, "to be uncovered." Tigchelaar, *To Increase Learning*, 180, hypothesizes that יתערערו may be a mistake for יתרועעו, a Hithpolel of the verb רוע ("to shout"). See also his "Towards a Reconstruction of the Beginning of 4QInstruction (4Q416 Fragment 1 and Parallels)," in *The Wisdom Texts from Qumran*, 114. Strugnell and Harrington, *DJD 34*, 86, consider the verb "obscure" and do not offer a definitive interpretation. The word can be understood, on the basis of Jeremiah 51:58, as a Hithpalpel of the root ערר, "to make bare." If the root were עור, "to rouse" or "to be exposed," one would expect יתעוררו, although there is often confusion between geminate and hollow roots. While there is disagreement regarding this verb, all the suggested options understand it as describing the suffering of the "fleshly spirit" at the moment of judgment. See also Lange, *Weisheit und Prädestination*, 111.

4Q416 1 is generally considered to be the beginning of 4QInstruction due to its wide right margin (3.3 cm).[16] This length would be hard to explain if the text were from the middle of the work. By beginning with a judgment scene, the composition situates its teachings in an eschatological horizon.

Before 4Q416 1 describes the final judgment in lines 10-13, its fragmentary beginning recounts the orderly structure of creation: "season upon season ... according to their host to r[ule by dominion ... for kingdom] and kingdom, for pr[ovince and province, for each and every man ... the judgment of all of them belongs to him]" (ll. 3-6).[17] Tigchelaar has stressed that 4Q416 1 1-10 emphasizes the "orderly course of creation."[18] Though fragmentary, 4Q416 1 emphasizes both judgment and the regulated nature of the cosmos. The combination of these themes underscores the inevitability of judgment. Like the regular course of the seasons, judgment is a feature of the divine plan that structures the natural order. The themes of judgment and the ordered nature of creation are also combined in *1 Enoch* 1-5. These chapters describe the cosmos as structured and under divine control (2:1-5:4), while framing this account with affirmations of judgment (1:1-9; 5:5-9).[19]

The other major judgment scene of 4QInstruction is found in 4Q418 69 ii. Lines 6-9 of this fragment read:

> You were created ... and your return will be to the eternal pit (שחת עולם), for it will awaken [to condemn] you[r] sin ... its dark regions will roar against your case (יצרחו על ריבכם), and all who exist forever, those who seek truth, will rouse themselves for yo[ur] judgment. [And then] all the foolish of heart will be destroyed (ישמדו כול אוילי לב), and the sons of iniquity will be found no more (cf. 1QH 12:20), [and a]ll who seize wickedness will wither [away. And then] at your judgment the foundations of the

---

[16] This is discussed in section 2 of Chapter 1.

[17] *DJD 34*, 82. Tigchelaar's reconstruction of 4Q416 1 differs from that of *DJD 34*. He provides a composite text of 4Q416 1 that incorporates additional 4Q418 fragments. His beginning of 4Q416 1 emphasizes the rational structure of creation to a greater extent than the version of *DJD 34*. Tigchelaar's version of 4Q416 1 2-6 is "[they run from eternal time,] season upon season, and [without standing still. Properly they go,] according to their host, to ke[ep station (?), and to for kingdom] and kingdom, for pr[ovince and province, for each and every man ... And the regulation of them all belongs to him]." See *To Increase Learning*, 176. See also his "Towards a Reconstruction," 99-126.

[18] *To Increase Learning*, 177.

[19] Tigchelaar, *To Increase Learning*, 182; R.A. Argall, *1 Enoch and Sirach* (SBLEJL 8; Atlanta: Scholars Press, 1995), 101-07; George W.E. Nickelsburg, *1 Enoch: A Commentary on the Book of 1 Enoch, Chapters 1-36, 81-108* (Hermeneia; Minneapolis: Fortress, 2001), 135-64.

firmament will shout (ירׄיׄעוׄ מׄוׄסׄדׄי {ה}רקיע), and all ... will thunder (ירעמו)
    ...[20]

Like 4Q416 1, 4Q418 69 ii places judgment in a cosmological context.[21] The fragment has an auditory element not found in 4Q416 1, with the "dark regions" (מחשכיה) roaring and the firmament shouting (cf. 1QH 11:13). The first section of 4Q418 69 ii 7 declares: "its dark regions will roar against your case."[22] The "dark regions" probably refer to Sheol. The term is used this way in the Hebrew Bible (e.g., Pss 88:6; 143:3). The "dark regions" will roar and open wide to receive the wicked.[23]

There has been some question as to how 4Q418 69 ii should be understood in relation to 4QInstruction as a whole. There are several differences between 4Q418 69 ii and the rest of the work. As is the case with 4Q416 1, the mystery that is to be does not occur in 4Q418 69 ii. Neither text contains the word *mebin*, which is widespread in the rest of the work.[24] 4Q418 69 ii prefers the first and second person plural, whereas the composition in general employs the second person singular. The description of judgment in lines 4-9 is addressed to the "foolish of heart" (אוילי לב) who will be destroyed, whereas lines 10-15 are directed to the "truly chosen ones" (בחׄירׄי אמת).[25] 4QInstruction nowhere else opposes the "foolish of heart" and the "truly chosen ones." This latter group is encouraged to pursue truth as the angels do in order to be spared from the final judgment:

---

[20] The supplement "to condemn" in 4Q418 69 ii 6 is found in the version of this text in *DJD 34*, 283, but not in that of Tigchelaar, *To Increase Learning*, 210. The edition in *DJD 34* also supplements "You were created" with the phrase "[by the power of Go]d." Also note that there are traces of an erased letter *he* before the word רקיע in line 9. The verb translated above as "will wither [away" (יבשו) can be understood as "will be ashamed." Tigchelaar prefers this reading. See also Kasper Bro Larsen, "Visdom og apokalyptik i Musar leMevin (1Q/4QInstruction) [Wisdom and Apocalyptic in Musar leMevin (1Q/4QInstruction)]," *Dansk Teologisk Tidsskrift* 65 (2002), 7.

[21] É. Puech has written that this passage has a "resonance cosmologique." See his "Apports des textes apocalyptiques et sapientiels de Qumrân à l'eschatologie du judaïsme ancien," in *Wisdom and Apocalypticism in the Dead Sea Scrolls and in the Biblical Tradition* (ed. F. García Martínez; BETL 168; Leuven: Peeters-Leuven University Press, forthcoming). See also A. Caquot, "Les textes de sagesse de Qoumrân (Aperçu préliminaire)," *Revue d'histoire et de philosophie religieuses* 76 (1996), 22.

[22] Also note that 1Q26 1 7 (cf. 4Q423 4 3a) contains a fragmentary text that may have "your case" in parallelism with judgment: "... your case (ריבכה). And by his power he requites [your] ju[dgment]." This text apparently understands the moment of judgment as one's "case," as in 4Q418 69 ii 7, but the text is too fragmentary to state this conclusively. See *DJD 34*, 536.

[23] This topic is discussed in section 2.5 of this chapter.

[24] Tigchelaar, *To Increase Learning*, 217.

[25] While the word אויל occurs throughout traditional wisdom (e.g., Prov 10:14; 12:15), the phrase אוילי לב is found only in late Second Temple texts. See 4Q418 58 1; 4Q418 205 2; 4Q425 1 + 3 8; and 1QH 9:37. See *DJD 34*, 274.

> Indeed, would they (the angels) say: "We are tired of works of truth, [we]
> are weary of ..." Do [they] not wal[k] in eternal light? ... [gl]ory and an
> abundance of splendor are with them ... (4Q418 69 ii 13-14).

Strugnell and Harrington speculate that lines 4-15 contain two teachings
that "might have been originally composed (or functioned) as twin set-
pieces now integrated into the instruction for the maven."[26]

Tigchelaar has suggested that both 4Q418 69 ii and 4Q418 55 may
have a provenance that is separate from the rest of 4QInstruction.[27] Both
fragments favor the second person plural rather than the singular. 4Q418
55 8-11, like 4Q418 69 ii 13-14, urges its addressees to act like the angels:

> Do] you [not k]now, or have you not heard, that the angels of holiness are
> h[is] (God's) in heaven ... They pursue after all the roots of understanding
> and are vigilant for ... Are they like man because he is sluggish, or like a
> human because he dies?

The two texts have other affinities. Both use rhetorical questions, a rarity
in 4QInstruction in general. Neither 4Q418 55 nor 4Q418 69 ii attest the
word *mebin*.

The aspects of fragments 55 and 69 ii of 4Q418 that distinguish them
from the rest of 4QInstruction do not warrant positing that they have a
separate compositional history. There are no themes of 4Q418 55 and
4Q418 69 ii that are at odds with the rest of the composition. The pairing
of the "foolish of heart" and the "truly chosen ones" in 4Q418 69 ii is
compatible with the "fleshly spirit" and the "spiritual people" of 4Q417 1
i. Both the "spiritual people" and the "truly chosen ones" are related to
angels, and both the "foolish of heart" and the "fleshly spirit" will be
destroyed (4Q416 1 12). The "truly chosen ones" can be read easily as a
reference to the intended audience of 4QInstruction. The reliance on the
second person plural in fragments 55 and 69 ii of 4Q418 is not necessarily proof of a separate origin since 4QInstruction is designed for more
than one addressee.[28] Moreover, as Tigchelaar himself observes, these
texts include vocabulary that can be found throughout the composition,
such as נחל (4Q418 55 6; 4Q418 69 ii 13).[29] There is no reason to doubt
that 4Q418 69 ii, like 4Q416 1, is a key text for assessing
4QInstruction's eschatology.

---

[26] *DJD 34*, 14. See also Elgvin, "Early Essene Eschatology," 158.
[27] Tigchelaar, *To Increase Learning*, 217-21.
[28] See section 2 of Chapter 6.
[29] Tigchelaar, *To Increase Learning*, 222.

2.1 Resurrection in 4QInstruction?

Discussion of 4Q418 69 ii has focused on line 7. Elgvin has claimed that this line records a promise of resurrection to the righteous.[30] He translates the relevant text as "the seekers of truth will wake up to the judgments [of God]."[31] He grants that this line contains no explicit reference to resurrection. It is nevertheless present, he contends, because of the text's reliance on *1 Enoch*. Elgvin contends that 4Q418 69 ii 7 rephrases *1 Enoch* 91:10, which states that "the righteous will rise from sleep" (cf. 92:3).[32]

Puech has supported Elgvin's general view. He writes that 4QInstruction is one of the "texts clefs dans l'histoire de la croyance à la resurrection des seuls justes lors du jugement."[33] But he does not relate 4Q418 69 ii to *1 Enoch* in the manner of Elgvin. Rather Puech stresses the composition's similarity to other Qumran texts. He has argued that resurrection is an important aspect of Essene eschatology.[34] The extent to which members of the Qumran community believed that they would be resurrected has been questioned.[35] In any case, affirming that the

---

[30] Elgvin, "Early Essene Eschatology," 143-44. For more on resurrection in Second Temple literature, see John J. Collins, *Apocalypticism in the Dead Sea Scrolls* (London/New York: Routledge, 1997), 110-29; idem, "The Afterlife in Apocalyptic Literature," in *Judaism in Late Antiquity*, 119-38.

[31] He transcribes the final visible word of this phrase as למשפטיﬤ. See his "An Analysis of 4QInstruction," 248. Only a small trace remains after the *ṭet*. Strugnell and Harrington, *DJD 34*, 281, transcribe [כ]למשפטי ("you[r] judgment") but grant that a *yôd* could also follow the *ṭet* on material grounds, as proposed by Elgvin. Tigchelaar, *To Increase Learning*, 210, endorses the transcription of *DJD 34*. Since this text occurs in a section that addresses the "foolish of heart" who are to be judged, the version of *DJD 34* is to be preferred.

[32] Elgvin writes: "Although the texts do not speak clearly on this point, the connections with Danielic and Enochic traditions (cf. Dan 12:2, *1 En.* 91:10) indicate that this hope included a resurrection of the righteous." See "Early Essene Eschatology," 143-44. He also claims that 4Q416 1 and 4Q418 69 ii "fit Hippolytus's description of the eschatological teachings of the Essenes." Hippolytus in *Refutation of All Heresies* 27 contends that the Essenes believed in bodily resurrection.

[33] Puech, "Apports des textes apocalyptiques et sapientiels."

[34] Émile Puech, *La Croyance des Esséniens en la Vie Future: Immortalité, Resurrection, Vie Éternelle?* (2 vols.; Paris: Gabalda, 1993).

[35] Collins, *Apocalypticism in the Dead Sea Scrolls*, 115-24. Puech emphasizes 4Q385 and 4Q521, which contain the most explicit references to resurrection in the Qumran corpus. They are not, however, among the undisputed writings of the Dead Sea sect. Collins argues that the clearly sectarian texts include no unambiguous reference to the resurrection of the elect. See also George W.E. Nickelsburg, *Resurrection, Immortality, and Eternal Life in Intertestamental Judaism* (HTS 26; Cambridge: Harvard University Press, 1972), 166-67; Jan N. Bremmer, *The Rise and Fall of the Afterlife: The 1995 Read-Tuckwell Lectures at the University of Bristol* (London/New York: Routledge, 2002), 41-55.

wisdom text attests a belief in resurrection strengthens Puech's conclusion that "l'*Instruction* semble dépendre du même milieu culturel que les
compositions esséniennes."[36]

The claim that 4QInstruction attests a belief in resurrection has been
challenged. Tigchelaar has argued that 4Q418 69 ii 7 should be compared to *1 Enoch* 100:4, which promises divine judgment, rather than
91:10, which discusses resurrection (cf. Ps 35:23).[37] Collins has argued
that 4QInstruction, like the Treatise on the Two Spirits, envisions eternal
life for the righteous without promising any form of resurrection (cf. 1QS
4:6-8).[38]

Puech and Elgvin both rely on descriptions of resurrection elsewhere
to strengthen the claim that it is attested in 4QInstruction. The evidence
within the wisdom text itself supports the view of Tigchelaar and Collins.
Above I translated the key portion of 4Q418 69 ii 7 as follows: "All who
exist forever, those who seek truth, will rouse themselves for yo[ur] judgment ([ם]משפטכ‎ יעורו אמת דורשי עולם נהיה כול‎)." This text occurs in
a section oriented towards the "foolish of heart" (lines 4-9) rather than
the regular addressee of 4QInstruction. In line 7 the ones being judged
are distinguished from "those who seek truth." It also says that this latter
group "exist[s] forever" (עולם נהיה‎).[39] 4Q418 69 ii 13 asserts that the
angels have eternal life and asks rhetorically if they ever tire of the
"works of truth." The phrase "those who seek truth" in 4Q418 69 ii 7
can easily be understood as referring to angels.[40] They do not "wake up"

---

[36] Puech, "Apports des textes apocalyptiques et sapientiels." The promise of eternal
life is thought to imply resurrection: "la resurrection-réveil est l'entrée dans la vie
éternelle du juste."

[37] Tigchelaar, *To Increase Learning*, 211.

[38] John J. Collins, "The Eschatologizing of Wisdom in the Dead Sea Scrolls," in *Sapiential Perspectives: Wisdom Literature in Light of the Dead Sea Scrolls. Proceedings of
the Sixth International Symposium of the Orion Center, 20-22 May 2001* (ed. G. Sterling
and J.J. Collins; Leiden: Brill, forthcoming).

[39] Elgvin, "An Analysis of 4QInstruction," 79, understands the Niphal participle of היה‎
in this line as referring to the past. Tigchelaar, *To Increase Learning*, 210, translates the
relevant phrase as "all who exist for ever." See *DJD 34*, 283. See also section 4.1 of
Chapter 2.

[40] *DJD 34*, 286-87. C.H.T. Fletcher-Louis has proposed that "those who exist forever"
refers not to angels but the angelomorphic priesthood that is a topic of his scholarship.
See his *All the Glory of Adam: Liturgical Anthropology in the Dead Sea Scrolls* (STDJ
42; Leiden: Brill, 2002), 118-21. His discussion focuses on 4Q418 69 ii 10-15. He
argues that the "glory" and "splendor" mentioned in reference to the "s[ons of] heaven"
"is entirely in accord with the tradition of cultic anthropology we have been tracing."
Fletcher-Louis, however, acknowledges that "This may seem like reading too much between the lines." See ibid., 120. There is no compelling reason to avoid interpreting the
"sons of heaven" of 4Q418 69 ii 12-13 in the conventional sense as a term signifying
angels.

but "rouse themselves" against the "foolish of heart." They have a role during judgment that complements that of the "dark regions" that roar.[41] 4Q418 69 ii 7 supports the general perspective of the fragment that judgment is a cosmological ordeal. The entire cosmos, including the heavenly host and Sheol, struggles against the wicked.

That the angels have an ordained role during judgment is also implied by texts from other eschatological sections of 4QInstruction. The word "host" (צבא) occurs three times in the beginning portion of 4Q416 1. None of the attestations are in contexts that survive in full. What remains of 4Q416 1 4 seems to declare that God's universal dominion is carried out in part by angels: "according to their host to r[ule by dominion] ..." Before the fragment's judgment scene in lines 10-13, line 7 proclaims that God created the heavenly host: "the host of heaven he established up[on] (צבא השמים הכ֯י֯ן ע֯[ל]ל) ..."[42] "Host" also appears in line 6.[43] Line 12 mentions the "sons of heave[n]" in another fragmentary context.[44] 4Q418 69 ii 15 mentions a "council of the divine ones," suggesting that God is given some sort of assistance by angelic beings when carrying out judgment.[45] The angels assist in the implementation of judgment in other late Second Temple texts.[46] There is no surviving text

---

[41] Nickelsburg, *1 Enoch*, 209-11.

[42] Elgvin, "An Analysis of 4QInstruction," 238-39, transcribes the last visible letter in this phrase as *mêm*, and reconstructs [קדם]מ֯. He thus translates "The host of heavens he established from [the beginning] ..." Both the *'ayin* and *mêm* are materially possible but the context is too fragmentary to interpret the line properly. See idem, "Early Essene Eschatology," 150; *DJD 34*, 82.

[43] The phrase "according to the needs of their host" (לפי מחסור צבאם) of 4Q416 1 6 is obscure. Strugnell and Harrington, *DJD 34*, 83, translate "the poverty of their host." The term מחסור has a financial usage in terms of needs that are to be met, as discussed in section 3.3 of Chapter 4. But in 4Q416 1 6 it is not clear it should be understood in this way. 4QInstruction does not elsewhere emphasize the "poverty" of the angels. It is perhaps better to understand מחסור in 4Q416 1 6 in the sense of what is needed or necessary—that is, the angels will play their ordained role in the implementation of judgment. Elgvin, "An Analysis of 4QInstruction," 239, translates "needs of their host." See also Tigchelaar, *To Increase Learning*, 179.

[44] The version of this line in *DJD 34*, 81-83, depicts the "sons of heaven" as rejoicing on the day of judgment. Tigchelaar, *To Increase Learning*, 175-76, does not include the supplement "will rejoice" in 4Q416 1 12.

[45] Elgvin, "An Analysis of 4QInstruction," 248-49, transcribes אולים סו[ר[י], which he translates as "[the foun]dation of beginnings." Strugnell and Harrington, *DJD 34*, 281, reconstruct the phrase as אילים ב֯סור. The claim in ibid., 283, that traces of a *bêt* before the *sāmek* are visible cannot be corroborated through examination of its photograph. Tigchelaar, *To Increase Learning*, 211, favors the understanding of the line in *DJD 34*.

[46] *1 Enoch* proclaims that God "will appear with his host" and that he will come "with ten thousand holy ones to execute judgment" (1:4, 9). In the judgment scene of *1 Enoch* 102, the angels carry out commands as well as show fear at God's power (vv. 2-3). The accompaniment of the angels is also clear in the theophany of 1QH 11, in which the foundations shake as "the host of the heavens adds to their noise" (v. 35). The Treatise on the

of 4QInstruction that describes angels as having an aggressive eschatological role. The composition emphasizes God, not the angels, in terms of judgment. But they are nevertheless involved in God's mighty act.

2.2 Judgment in 4QInstruction and the Theophanic Tradition

4Q416 1 and 4Q418 69 ii describe divine judgment as a powerful act that affects the entire cosmos. It places the natural world in a state of fear and tumult. 4Q416 1 emphasizes that divine judgment will disturb the primal waters and produce fear. 4Q418 69 ii depicts the foundations of the firmament shouting. These judgment scenes have drawn comparison with the theophanies of the Hebrew Bible.[47] Some background discussion of the theophanic tradition is warranted to better understand the presentation of judgment in 4QInstruction.

Biblical theophanies are characterized by an advent of God that is accompanied by an upheaval of the natural world.[48] Among the most well-known is Judges 5:4-5:

> Lord, when you went out from Seir, when you marched from the region of Edom, the earth trembled (רעשה), and the heavens poured, the clouds indeed poured water. The mountains quaked before the Lord, the One of Sinai, before the Lord, the God of Israel.

As in 4Q416 1 11-12, in theophanies fear and terror are often reactions to God's appearance: "The mountains saw you, and writhed; a torrent of water swept by; the deep (תהום) gave forth its voice" (Hab 3:10).[49]

Two Spirits promises visitation "at the hands of all the angels of destruction (מלאכי חבל)" (1QS 4:12). These same angels appear in the Damascus Document: "all the angels of destruction (מלאכי חבל) against those turning aside from the path" (CD 2:6). Angels have a central role in the eschatological war described in the War Scroll (e.g., 1QM 1:10), which also mentions the "angels of destruction" (13:12). The martial aspect of the angels is evident in the function of the archangel Michael in Daniel and Revelation. For example, see Dan 12:1, "At that time Michael, the great prince, the protector of your people, shall arise. There shall be a time of anguish, such as has never occurred since nations first came into existence" (cf. 10:13, 21); Rev 12:7, "And war broke out in heaven; Michael and his angels fought against the dragon." Cf. Mark 8:38; Jude 9. See further Maxwell J. Davidson, *Angels at Qumran: A Comparative Study of 1 Enoch 1-36, 72-108 and Sectarian Writings from Qumran* (JSPSup 11; Sheffield: Sheffield Academic Press, 1992), 300-03.

[47] Collins, "The Eschatologizing of Wisdom"; Elgvin, "Early Essene Eschatology," 150; idem, "An Analysis of 4QInstruction," 100. Also note that 4Q418 212 1-2 may have originally been part of a theophanic judgment scene. Only a small portion of this text remains: "the king[dom] will be shaken … on the day of its judgment."

[48] This definition is from Jörg Jeremias, *Theophanie: Die Geschichte einer alttestamentlichen Gattung* (Neukirchen-Vluyn: Neukirchener Verlag, 1965), 1.

Scholarship on biblical theophanies has often been form-critical. Jeremias, for example, delineated the theophany Gattung and argued that its Sitz-im-Leben was military Siegesfeiern ("victory celebrations"), of which the Song of Deborah in Judges 5 is the oldest example.[50] Cross and Miller associate theophanies with the motif of the Divine Warrior and "the march of Yahweh from the southern mountains (or from Egypt) with heavenly armies" that is preserved in archaic Hebrew poetry.[51] They situate the theophanic tradition in the holy war ideology of early Israel. Cross further argues that the Divine Warrior became associated with a ritual "march of conquest" that was rooted in the Gilgal cult.[52]

Even if one does not agree with Cross's argument in its entirety, the concept of the divine overwhelming the natural world is certainly archaic. There is a theophany, for example, in the Baal Epic:

> Baal opened a rift in the clouds; his holy voice Baal gave forth ... At his h[oly] voice the earth quaked; at the issue of his [lips] the mountains were afr[aid]. The ancient [mountains] were afraid; the hills of the ear[th] tottered (KTU 1.4 vii 28-35).[53]

As the pre-Israelite theophanic tradition is appropriated by biblical texts, it is also utilized by post-biblical literature. Cross, for example, ends his discussion of the theophany of the Divine Warrior with a citation from the War Scroll: "Arise, O Warrior, take your captives, O Glorious One, and gather your spoil, Doer of Valor. Put forth your hand on the neck of your enemies, and your foot on the heaps of the slain" (1QM 12:10-11).[54] This text, which does not describe the upheaval of the natural world, underscores the role of divine martial imagery in Cross's understanding

---

[49] A thorough discussion of this verse is available in Francis I. Andersen, *Habakkuk* (AB 25; New York: Doubleday, 2001), 326-32. For more theophanic texts in the Hebrew Bible, see Exod 15:14-16; Deut 32:22; Pss 68:8-9; 97:5; Nah 1:5; Isa 24:17-23; 64:1-3; and Mic 1:3-4. A review of this material is available in Jeffrey J. Niehaus, *God at Sinai: Covenant and Theophany in the Bible and the Ancient Near East* (Grand Rapids: Zondervan, 1995).

[50] *Theophanie*, 136-50. Jeremias was arguing against scholars such as S. Mowinckel and W. Beyerlin, who placed the theophany in the cultus. For a review of scholarship, see Niehaus, *God at Sinai*, 55-77. See also J.K. Kuntz, *The Self-Revelation of God* (Philadelphia: Westminster, 1967).

[51] Frank Moore Cross, *Canaanite Myth and Hebrew Epic* (Cambridge: Harvard University Press, 1997 [orig. pub., 1973]), 100. See also Patrick D. Miller, *The Divine Warrior in Early Israel* (Cambridge: Harvard University Press, 1973); idem, *The Religion of Ancient Israel* (Louisville: Westminster, 2000), 8-12.

[52] Cross, *Canaanite Myth*, 103.

[53] This translation is from Nick Wyatt, *Religious Texts from Ugarit: The Words of Ilimilku and His Colleagues* (Sheffield: Sheffield Academic Press, 1998), 109. For other ancient Near East parallels, see Niehaus, *God at Sinai*, 81-141.

[54] This translation is from Cross, *Canaanite Myth*, 111. See also Miller, *Divine Warrior*, 143.

of the theophany genre. Other late texts colored with apocalyptic imagery describe the advent of God shaking the natural world. Hanson, for example, sees the theophany of the Divine Warrior in Zechariah 14:3-4:

> Then the Lord will go forth and fight against those nations as when he fights on a day of battle. On that day his feet shall stand on the Mount of Olives ... the Mount of Olives shall be split in two from east to west by a very wide valley; so that one half of the Mount shall withdraw northward, and the other half southward (cf. 9:10).[55]

This scene includes both martial imagery and upheaval of the natural order. Elgvin provides additional late Second Temple parallels.[56]

Ben Sira is also familiar with the theophanic tradition:

> Do not say, "I am hidden from the Lord, and who from on high has me in mind? Among so many people I am unknown, for what am I in a boundless creation? Lo, heaven and the highest heaven, the abyss (תהום) and the earth, tremble at his visitation! The very mountains and the foundations of the earth quiver and quake (רעש ירעשו) when he looks upon them ... Who is to announce his acts of justice? Or who can await them? For his decree is far off." Such are the thoughts of one devoid of understanding; a senseless and misguided person thinks foolishly (16:17-23).[57]

In this passage Ben Sira is not dismissive of theophanic descriptions of God. Rather he is critical of the opinion that one can hide from the Lord

---

[55] Paul D. Hanson, *The Dawn of Apocalyptic* (Philadelphia: Fortress, 1979 [orig. pub., 1975]), 321, 374-75. See also Miller, *Divine Warrior*, 140-41.

[56] *Sib. Or.* 3:675-81, "The all-bearing earth will be shaken in those days by the hand of the Immortal, and the fish in the sea and all the wild beasts of the earth ... will shudder before the face of the Immortal and there will be a terror. He will break the lofty summits of the mountains and the mounds of giants and the dark abyss will appear to all." The *Testament of Moses*, like Zechariah 14, includes a late attestation of the theophany of the Divine Warrior: "For the Heavenly One will arise from his kingly throne. Yea, he will go forth from his holy habitation with indignation and wrath on behalf of his sons. And the earth will tremble, even to its ends shall it be shaken. And the high mountains will be made low. Yea, they will be shaken, as enclosed valleys will they fall" (10:3-4). Note also Jdt 16:15: "For the mountains shall be shaken to their foundations with the waters; before your glance the rocks shall melt like wax." The fragmentary text 4Q579 (4QOuvrage hymnique[?]) 1 4 has been reconstructed to read "... abyss that causes trembling ..." 4Q530 (4QEnGiants[b] ar) 2 16-17 proclaims that "The Ruler of the heavens came down to earth, and thrones were erected and the Great Holy One sa[t down" (cf. Dan 7:9-10; *1 En.* 14:18-22; 4Q405 20 ii-21-22 6-14). This vision frightens the giants (l. 20). See Loren T. Stuckenbruck, "The Throne-Theophany of the Book of Giants: Some New Light on the Background of Daniel 7," in *The Scrolls and The Scriptures: Fifty Years After* (ed. S.E. Porter and C. Evans; Sheffield: Sheffield Academic Press, 1997), 211-20; Émile Puech, *Qumrân Grotte 4.XVIII: Textes Hébreux (4Q521-4Q528, 4Q576-4Q579)* (DJD 25; Oxford: Clarendon, 1998), 210; Elgvin, "Early Essene Eschatology," 150.

[57] Argall, *1 Enoch and Sirach*, 226-32; Alexander Di Lella and Patrick W. Skehan, *The Wisdom of Ben Sira* (AB 39; New York: Doubleday, 1987), 275.

since retribution is "far off" (cf. 23:16-21).[58] Elsewhere Ben Sira affirms the inevitability of judgment from God as the Divine Warrior:

> Indeed, the Lord will not delay, and like a warrior will not be patient until he crushes the loins of the unmerciful and repays vengeance on the nations; until he destroys the multitude of the insolent, and breaks the scepters of the unrighteous (35:22-23; cf. 5:7-8).[59]

The theophanic tradition is attested in the undisputed writings of the Dead Sea sect. The appearance of the Divine Warrior tradition in 1QM 12 has already been mentioned. One of the most extensive theophanic judgment scenes in the sectarian corpus is in 1QH 11. Destruction is first associated with Belial overwhelming the natural order:

> When the measuring line falls upon judgment ... and the period of anger with all destruction (לכל בליעל), and the ropes of death enclose with no escape, then the torrents of Belial (בליעל) will overflow all the high banks like a devouring fire in all their watering channels (?) ... It consumes the foundations of clay and the tract of dry land; the bases of the mountain he burns and converts the roots of flint rock into streams of lava. It consumes right to the great deep (תהום) (ll. 27-31; cf. Ps 18:5-6).[60]

This chaos triggers the advent of God and his host:

> The earth cries out at the calamity which overtakes the world, and all its schemers scream, and all who are upon it go crazy, and melt away in the great calamity. For God will thunder (ירעם) with the roar of his strength ... and the host of the heavens adds to their noise, [and] the eternal foundations melt and shake, and the battle of heavenly heroes roams unceas[ingly] over the earth, [un]til the determined eternal unparalleled destruction (ll. 32-36).[61]

This text has some striking similarities with 4QInstruction. The theophany in 1QH 11 includes an auditory dimension, as does 4Q418 69

---

[58] Argall, *1 Enoch and Sirach*, 233-34; Shannon Burkes, *God, Self, and Death: The Shape of Religious Transformation in the Second Temple Period* (JSJSup 79; Leiden: Brill, 2003), 89-91.

[59] There is similar material in Ben Sira 36. This chapter may be a later addition to the composition because of its striking hostility towards foreign nations. This is a theme not found elsewhere in Ben Sira and is easily dated to the Maccabean crisis. See Collins, *Jewish Wisdom*, 109-11; Randal A. Argall, "Competing Wisdoms: *1 Enoch* and *Sirach*," *Henoch* 24 (2002), 175-78 (*The Origins of Enochic Judaism: Proceedings of the First Enoch Seminar. University of Michigan, Sesto Fiorentino, Italy, June 19-23, 2001* [ed. G. Boccaccini]).

[60] John J. Collins, "The Expectation of the End in the Dead Sea Scrolls," in *Eschatology, Messianism, and the Dead Sea Scrolls* (ed. C.A. Evans and P.W. Flint; Grand Rapids: Eerdmans, 1997), 87-88; Elgvin, "Early Essene Eschatology," 143.

[61] Note the parallel in 2 Peter 3:10: "But the day of the Lord will come like a thief, and then the heavens will pass away with a loud noise, and the elements will be dissolved with fire, and the earth and everything that is done on it will be disclosed."

ii 7-9. 1QH 11 mentions the "depths," like 4Q416 1 12 (cf. Exod 15:8; Hab 3:10; Sir 16:18). In the Hodayot the shaking destroys the "eternal foundations"; the foundations of the firmament shout out in 4Q418 69 ii 9.[62] This judgment scene from the Hodayot includes the disruption of mountains, a motif common in biblical theophanies that is not in 4QInstruction.[63] 1QH 11 also accords an important role to Belial, a mythological figure of evil who never appears in 4QInstruction. Despite these differences, their similarities suggest that the Hodayot and 4QInstruction have theophanic traditions in common.[64]

Another important late attestation of the theophanic tradition occurs in the opening chapter of *1 Enoch*:

> The Holy and Great One will come out from his dwelling, and the Eternal God will tread from there upon Mount Sinai, and he will appear with his host ... And all will be afraid, and the Watchers will shake, and fear and great trembling (רבה רעדה ורחלה; cf. Exod 15:15) will seize them unto the ends of the earth. And the high mountains will be shaken (יזועון), and the high hills will be made low, and will melt like wax before the flame. And the earth will sink and everything that is on the earth will be destroyed, and there will be judgment upon all, and upon all the righteous (1:3-7).[65]

1 Enoch and 4QInstruction each begin with a theophanic judgment scene that establishes the eschatological horizon for what follows.[66] The theophany of *1 Enoch* 1 is closer to the biblical theophanies than any 4QInstruction text. *1 Enoch* 1, not 4QInstruction, includes the image of the Divine Warrior marching with his heavenly armies. In *1 Enoch*, they march from heaven to Sinai, whereas in the traditional theophanies they march from Egypt or the southern mountains, indicating *1 Enoch*'s appeal to a revelation beyond that of Sinai.[67] Its effort to move beyond

---

[62] The foundations are also shaken in Ps 18:7, 15 = 2 Sam 22:8, 16; Deut 32:22; Isa 24:18; and Ps 82:5.

[63] Note, however, that Tigchelaar's version of 4Q416 1 11 depicts the earth as shaking. See *To Increase Learning*, 176.

[64] The Hodayot and 4QInstruction are compared more extensively in section 3 of this chapter.

[65] A version of this scene is preserved in the New Testament in Jude 14-15. See also 4QEn[a] 1 i 1-7 (*1 En.* 1:1-6) in J.T. Milik, *The Books of Enoch: Aramaic Fragments of Qumran Cave 4* (Oxford: Clarendon, 1976), 141-45. See further Nickelsburg, *1 Enoch*, 135-49; James C. VanderKam, "The Theophany of Enoch 1 3B-7, 9," in *From Revelation to Canon* (JSJSup 62; Leiden: Brill, 2000), 332-53.

[66] Collins, *Jewish Wisdom*, 126; Elgvin, "Early Essene Eschatology," 150; Harrington, *Wisdom Texts*, 41.

[67] John J. Collins, *The Apocalyptic Imagination* (2nd ed.; Grand Rapids: Eerdmans, 1998 [orig. pub., 1984]), 48. See also Miller, *Divine Warrior*, 142; Andreas Bedenbender, *Der Gott der Welt Tritt auf den Sinai: Entstehung, Entwicklung und Funktionsweise der Fruhjudischen Apokalyptik* (ANTZ 8; Berlin: Institut Kirche und Judentum, 2000), 228-29; George W.E. Nickelsburg, "Enochic Wisdom: An Alternative to the Mo-

Sinai could be a natural development from the biblical theophanies, many of which describe God as the "one of Sinai" (e.g., Deut 33:2; Judg 5:5; Ps 68:8).⁶⁸ Sinai is never mentioned in 4QInstruction. It includes no prominent martial imagery, unlike *1 Enoch*. The beginning of the *Book of the Watchers* emphasizes the trembling of the mountains, whereas 4QInstruction never mentions mountains in this context.⁶⁹ Also, while the Watchers are prominent in *1 Enoch* 1, they play no role whatsoever in 4QInstruction.⁷⁰ The *Epistle of Enoch* incorporates theophanic judgment into an eschatological scenario that includes a period of wickedness in which chaos reigns and the innocent suffer (e.g., *1 En.* 100:1-6; 101:6-7). There is no equivalent period of wickedness in 4QInstruction.⁷¹

The theophanies of these two texts do, however, have features in common. Like 4QInstruction, *1 Enoch*, in both its opening scene and in the *Epistle of Enoch* (cf. 102:2-3), describes the natural order in a state of fear and panic, a common feature of the biblical theophanies.⁷² *1 Enoch* 1:7 stresses, like 4QInstruction, that in this cataclysmic moment all of humanity will be judged.⁷³ Both compositions use "day of judgment" terminology, showing affinity with the prophetic tradition, as Nickelsburg has stressed.⁷⁴ A fragmentary text of 4QInstruction reads: "on the day of its judgment" (בְיֹום משפטה[) (4Q418 212 2).⁷⁵ Elgvin has reconstructed the phrase "day of judgment" (יום משפטה) in 4Q416 1 on the

---

saic Torah?" in *Hesed Ve-Emet: Studies in Honor of Ernest S. Frerichs* (ed. J. Magness and S. Gitin; BJS 320; Atlanta: Scholars Press, 1998), 123-32.

⁶⁸ VanderKam, "The Theophany of Enoch," in *From Revelation to Canon*, 339-40.

⁶⁹ Note however the fragmentary phrase of 4Q418c 10: "[the sum]mit of Carmel will …" The surviving portion of line 5 of this fragment, "[des]troy a[l]l iniquity," suggests that this text may have contained a judgment scene that included the quaking of mountains. But not enough of the text survives to state this conclusively. See *DJD 34*, 502. See also the version of 4Q416 1 11 in Tigchelaar, *To Increase Learning,* 175.

⁷⁰ Argall, *1 Enoch and Sirach*, 170; VanderKam, "The Theophany of Enoch," in *From Revelation to Canon*, 344-46. Compare *1 Enoch* 1:5, in which the Watchers tremble before the judgment occurs, with 91:15 (the *Apocalypse of Weeks*), where the Watchers are judged in the tenth week, after the destruction of sinners and the rewarding of the righteous has taken place. Cf. 10:15; 16:3.

⁷¹ This topic is discussed in section 2.4 of this chapter.

⁷² See, for example, Hab 3:6; Exod 15:14-16; Isa 24:18. Cf. Isa 29:23; Zech 14:13. Also note *T. Levi* 3:9: "So when the Lord looks upon us we all tremble. Even the heavens and earth and the abysses tremble before the presence of his majesty." See also VanderKam, "The Theophany of Enoch," in *From Revelation to Canon*, 343.

⁷³ See section 2.6 of this chapter.

⁷⁴ Nickelsburg, *1 Enoch,* 60-61.

⁷⁵ Also note that 4Q418 184 2 stresses, in an unfortunately fragmentary context, revealed knowledge in relation to a specific "day": "which he revealed to you (lit. "your ear") through the mystery that is to be on the day (בֹיֹם) …" This text may refer to a coming day of judgment.

basis of the extant פטה[of line 13.[76] This reading is plausible and has been endorsed by Tigchelaar.[77] "Day of judgment" language also occurs in *1 Enoch*. For example, the visitation upon Semyaza and other corrupt angels in the *Book of the Watchers* takes place on the "great day" (יומא רבא) of their judgment (4QEn[b] 1 iv 11; cf. *1 En.* 10:12).[78]

The similarities between 4QInstruction and *1 Enoch* regarding judgment do not by themselves warrant the claim that the former used the latter as a source. Even the fact that both texts begin with theophanies does not necessarily imply direct dependence. The biblical books of Nahum and Micah, for example, both begin on a strong theophanic note (see 1:5 and 1:4, respectively). It is possible that 4QInstruction and *1 Enoch* independently continue an established technique by beginning with theophanic language. The theophanic judgment scenes of these two texts have similar depictions of God's judgment and its impact upon the cosmos. The differences between their theophanies, however, problematize the claim of direct dependence.

4Q416 1 and 4Q418 69 ii should be considered examples, along with texts such as *1 Enoch* 1 and Zechariah 14, of the re-emergence of theophanic imagery in the Second Temple period. 4QInstruction uses the theophanic tradition to give additional force to descriptions of the final judgment. They help the composition affirm that judgment is inevitable and that it will be an overwhelming display of divine power.

2.3 *4QInstruction and* 1 Enoch

The previous section examined similarities between 4QInstruction and *1 Enoch* in terms of theophanic judgment. There are others. They both have an eschatological horizon. The two texts are deterministic and claim to disclose higher wisdom to the elect. The vision of Hagu contains angelic wisdom, as do the heavenly tablets of the *Apocalypse of Weeks* and the *Epistle of Enoch* (e.g., *1 En.* 93:1-2; 103:1). Both the *Apocalypse of Weeks* and 4QInstruction periodize history. The *Epistle of Enoch* and 4QInstruction portray the righteous as poor. *1 Enoch* and 4QInstruction also have terminology in common. Both use רז to describe revealed knowledge (*1 En.* 106:19; 4QEn[c] 5 ii 26). The two texts employ קץ to convey the belief that judgment will occur at a specific point

---

[76] "Early Essene Eschatology," 146.

[77] Tigchelaar, *To Increase Learning*, 175. This reconstruction is not found in *DJD 34*, 81.

[78] Milik, *The Books of Enoch*, 175; Michael Knibb, *The Ethiopic Book of Enoch* (2 vols.; Oxford: Clarendon, 1978), 2.91. See also *1 En.* 22:13; 94:9; 98:10; *Jub.* 23:11.

in the future (4QEnᵍ 1 iv 23; 4Q416 1 13).[79] I argued in section 2.4.4 of Chapter 3 that the word תבנית was probably used for the angelic "form" of Noah in *1 Enoch* 106, a description similar to the "spiritual people" of 4QInstruction who are in the likeness of the holy ones (תבנית קדושים) (4Q417 1 i 17).

The main proposal for understanding the affinities between 4QInstruction and *1 Enoch* has been put forward by Torleif Elgvin. He claims that the wisdom text uses Enochic literature as a source. For example, he understands the description of judgment to the "foolish of heart" in 4Q418 69 ii 4-10 as "inspired by" *1 Enoch* 91 and 103:1-104:6.[80] *1 Enoch* 103-104 uses the second person plural, like 4Q418 69 ii, in contrast to most of 4QInstruction. Phrases common to both compositions, such as "inherit the earth" (*1 En.* 5:7; 4Q418 81 14) and "eternal planting" (*1 En.* 10:16; 93:5, 10; 4Q418 81 13), are taken as evidence of direct literary dependence.[81] Elgvin claims that the mystery that is to be should be equated with the "sevenfold wisdom" given to the elect in *1 Enoch* 93:10 and that the vision of Hagu may be a reference to an Enochic text, such as the *Apocalypse of Weeks* or the *Animal Apocalypse*.[82] *1 Enoch* is presented as the central inspiration for the writing of 4QInstruction. Elgvin has claimed that the circles that produced 4QInstruction should be understood as the "bridge" that connects Enochic literature to the Qumran community.[83]

The presence of Enochic manuscripts among the Qumran corpus suggests there is no need to posit a "bridge" to link this material to the Dead Sea sect. The claim that 4QInstruction exhibits direct literary reliance upon *1 Enoch* has been challenged. Loren T. Stuckenbruck has examined some of the phrases that the two texts have in common.[84] He argues that they are used in different ways. For example, 4Q418 69 ii 14 mentions walking in eternal light in relation to angels, whereas this is not the case in *1 Enoch* 92:2-5, which also uses this image.[85] He concludes that while 4QInstruction may have utilized Enochic traditions, a direct literary relationship "is difficult to substantiate."[86] Tigchelaar has put for-

---

[79] This is discussed in the following section.
[80] Elgvin, "An Analysis of 4QInstruction," 169.
[81] Elgvin, "Early Essene Eschatology," 132.
[82] Elgvin, "An Analysis of 4QInstruction," 170.
[83] He writes "*Sap. Work A* represents a bridge between the apocalyptic Enoch literature and the clearly defined sectarian community." See his "Early Essene Eschatology," 164.
[84] Loren T. Stuckenbruck, "4QInstruction and the Possible Influence of Early Enochic Traditions: An Evaluation," in *The Wisdom Texts from Qumran*, 245-61.
[85] Ibid., 257-59.
[86] Ibid., 261.

ward a similar position.[87] He focuses on Elgvin's assertion that 4Q418 69 ii was "inspired by" *1 Enoch* 91 and 103-104. There are clear similarities. 4Q418 69 ii 4-6 reads "And now, foolish of heart ... your return will be to the eternal pit."[88] *1 Enoch* 103:5, 7 includes the phrases "woe to you, you sinners" and "their souls will be made to go down into Sheol."[89] 4Q418 69 ii 7 discusses darkness ("dark regions") and judgment. *1 Enoch* 103:8 likewise mentions darkness and judgment. Tigchelaar also acknowledges differences between 4QInstruction and the *Epistle of Enoch*. For example, key terms of 4Q418 69 ii, such as "foolish of heart" or "truly chosen ones," do not occur in the *Epistle of Enoch*. More importantly, the *Epistle* is preoccupied with the oppression of the righteous at the hands of sinners. This idea is not found in 4QInstruction. Tigchelaar concludes that the "dependence" of 4Q418 69 ii upon *1 Enoch* 103-104 "is improbable, though not impossible."[90]

Stuckenbruck and Tigchelaar successfully revise Elgvin's position regarding the relationship between *1 Enoch* and 4QInstruction. Despite their similarities the two texts have significantly different thoughtworlds. While both the *Epistle of Enoch* and 4QInstruction understand their intended audiences as poor, 4QInstruction frequently uses the refrain "you are poor," whereas the *Epistle* never explicitly calls its audience poor.[91] Rather, it proclaims judgment against oppressors who are clearly rich (e.g., *1 En.* 94:8). 4QInstruction never displays anger towards the wealthy. These texts also have different modes of revelation. The mystery that is to be never occurs in *1 Enoch* and there are no otherworldly journeys or visions mediated by an angel in 4QInstruction. During his celestial journeys Enoch is given information about the heavenly realm and the names and characteristics of numerous angels. 4QInstruction has no encyclopedic interest in the attributes or names of individual angels, or in a geographical description of the heavenly landscape. In the previous section I mentioned differences between the two texts' presentations of theophanic judgment. 4QInstruction's periodization of history displays no interest in an elaborate description of end-time events, unlike the *Apocalypse of Weeks*. 4QInstruction has no period of

---

[87] Tigchelaar, *To Increase Learning*, 212-17. For a related opinion, see M. Knibb, "The Book of Enoch in the Light of the Qumran Wisdom Literature," in *Wisdom and Apocalypticism in the Dead Sea Scrolls and in the Biblical Tradition*. G. Nickelsburg understands the eschatology of 4QInstruction as similar to *1 Enoch* without appealing to the use of one by the other as a source. See his *1 Enoch*, 58-60.

[88] The phrase "eternal pit" is discussed in section 2.5 of this chapter.

[89] Tigchelaar, *To Increase Learning*, 213. See also Caquot, "Les textes de sagesse de Qoumrân," 22.

[90] Tigchelaar, *To Increase Learning*, 216.

[91] See section 3.3 of Chapter 4.

wickedness preceding the final obliteration of the wicked, unlike the seventh week of *1 Enoch* 93:9. In 4QInstruction the wicked are sent to Sheol without emphasis on punishment after death, whereas Enochic texts underscore the anguish the wicked endure in the abyss of fire (e.g., *1 En.* 108:5).[92] While *1 Enoch* is organized around the figure of Enoch, no corresponding figure serves this function in 4QInstruction.

Another important difference between *1 Enoch* and 4QInstruction involves their explanations of human evil. The *Book of the Watchers* attributes evil in the human realm to supernatural forces, in the form of the Watchers. 4QInstruction shows no familiarity with this fallen angel tradition. The main context for 4QInstruction's reflection on the problem of sinful behavior is Genesis 1-3. As examined in Chapter 3, 4QInstruction explains human conduct by positing two contrasting types of humankind, the "spiritual people" and the "fleshly spirit." The existence of these two types is traced back to the two contrasting portrayals of Adam in Genesis 1-3. *1 Enoch* 24-32 shows familiarity with the concept of a tree of knowledge in a garden.[93] But no Enochic text turns to the Eden tradition to explain the problem of human evil.

The claim of direct literary dependence between *1 Enoch* and 4QInstruction is difficult to maintain. Nevertheless, both Tigchelaar and Stuckenbruck grant that it is possible that 4QInstruction was inspired by Enochic literature. While it cannot be proven conclusively, it is reasonable to argue that the author of 4QInstruction was familiar with Enochic texts. Enochic material was popular in the latter half of the Second Temple period. This is suggested by the abundance of Enoch manuscripts found at Qumran and the description of Enoch in *Jubilees* as one who "saw and knew everything and wrote his testimony" (4:19).[94] Familiarity with Enochic literature would help explain the development of 4QInstruction's apocalyptic worldview, as Elgvin has suggested. The author of 4QInstruction would thus attest the popularity of apocalypti-

---

[92] This topic is discussed in section 2.5 of this chapter.

[93] Eibert J.C. Tigchelaar, "Eden and Paradise: The Garden Motif in Some Early Jewish Texts," in *Paradise Interpreted: Representations of Biblical Paradise in Judaism and Christianity* (ed. G.P. Luttikhuizen; Leiden: Brill, 1999), 37-57; James C. VanderKam, "The Interpretation of Genesis in *1 Enoch*," in *The Bible at Qumran: Text, Shape, and Interpretation* (ed. P.W. Flint; Grand Rapids: Eerdmans, 2001), 129-48; Pierre Grelot, "La géographie mythique d'Hénoch et ses sources orientales," *Revue Biblique* 65 (1958): 33-69.

[94] James C. VanderKam, "Enoch Traditions in Jubilees and Other Second-Century Sources," in *From Revelation to Canon*, 305-31.

cism in scribal circles.⁹⁵ But if the author of the wisdom text did read some form of *1 Enoch*, he took from it general ideas, without alluding to Enochic literature directly. In that sense *1 Enoch* has an analogous relationship with the Dead Sea sect. Members of this group possessed copies of Enochic texts. It is reasonable to surmise that the apocalyptic worldview evident in their writings is to some extent shaped by their reading of Enochic literature. But nothing they wrote contains a direct reference to an Enochic text.

2.4 The Periodization of History and Its Culmination in Judgment

4QInstruction proclaims that the act of judgment is to occur at a specific moment in the future. It puts forward this view in part through use of the word קץ ("period"). According to 4Q416 1 13, the elimination of the wicked will happen when "the period of tru[th] (קץ הא[מ]ת]) will be completed." 4QInstruction attests the related expression "period of completion" (קץ שלום) in a fragmentary context (4Q418c 9; cf. 11QMelch 2 15).⁹⁶ The idea of a final destructive period is found in 4Q418 211 4, which is also incomplete: "... [will pe]rish iniquity, for the end will come (כיא יבוֹא סוף)."⁹⁷ The moment of judgment is probably the topic of 4Q418 123 ii 4: "His period (קצו) which God revealed to the ear of the understanding ones through the mystery that is to be" (cf. 4Q416 1 11). A similar understanding of the word "period" is found in the Treatise on the Two Spirits, which declares that the two spirits are under the dominion of God "in compliance with the mysteries of God, until his period (עד קצו)" (1QS 3:23).

4QInstruction's eschatology is also evident in its use of the phrase קץ החרון. 4Q416 4 1 attests the expression "the pe[riod of] wrath," which is based on the extant phrase קֹ[ ]חרון. Materially, this could be transcribed as either קץ אחרון or קץ החרון.⁹⁸ The transcription קץ החרון in 4Q416 4 1 is suggested by 4Q416 3 3: "... until wickedness is completed, for there will be wrath in every per[iod] (חרון בכל קֹ[ץ])." The

---

⁹⁵ J.Z. Smith has emphasized that apocalyptic literature is a "scribal phenomenon." See his "Wisdom and Apocalyptic," in *Map Is Not Territory* (Chicago: University of Chicago Press, 1978), 67-87. See also Collins, *The Apocalyptic Imagination*, 39.

⁹⁶ This phrase is translated in *DJD 34*, 502, as "period of peace."

⁹⁷ Tigchelaar, *To Increase Learning*, 116, disputes the reconstruction of the word translated above, following *DJD 34*, as "[will pe]rish." His rationale has a sound material basis. If Tigchelaar is correct, the text would still describe the destruction of iniquity. The verb in question, if not "perish" (אבד), would be a semantically equivalent term.

⁹⁸ *DJD 34*, 133. Tigchelaar, *To Increase Learning*, 49, transcribes the phrase as קֹ[צ]חרון[.

topic of 4Q416 4 is clearly judgment. Line 2 reads: "... anger, for against them the furnace is fanned" (cf. Ezek 20:20, 22). Since 4QInstruction proclaims a final period of judgment, 4Q416 4 1 probably intends a word-play between קץ החרון and קץ אחרון.

Judgment in 4QInstruction has an eternal aspect. The composition uses the phrase "all the periods" (כול קצים) to refer to the entire chronological order. 4Q418 81 13 uses the phrase to describe the eternal nature of God's glory: "during all periods (עם כול קצים) (is) his splendor" (cf. 4Q415 2 i + 1 ii 8).[99] The phrase כול קצים occurs in 4Q418 69 ii 14 in an incomplete context in reference to walking in "eternal light." In this text כול קצים apparently refers to angels and their possession of eternal life. In 4Q418 123 ii 2 the "periods" are synonymous with years: "for the entering-in of years (שנים) and the going-out of periods (קצים) ..." 4Q416 1 14, just after the "period of tru[th]" in line 13, uses the phrase "in all the eternal periods" (בכל קצי עד). In this material the expression "all the periods" seems to signify the entire sequence of the epochs of history. The chronological order, taken as a whole, is considered "eternal."

Like the epochs of history, judgment is considered "eternal." 4Q417 1 i 7-8, for example, discusses "their reckoning for all the periods of eternity (פקודתם לכול קצי עולם) and the eternal reckoning (// פקודת עד)." That the judgment is "eternal" assumes that its effects are permanent and that it culminates history. 4QInstruction, however, does not give prominence to the view that judgment concludes the sequence of historical periods. By describing judgment as eternal, it is considered to be in a sense effective throughout history, even though it is only implemented at its end. This understanding of the "eternal judgment" explains why 4Q416 3 3 declares that there will be wrath "in every period," although 4Q416 4 1 discusses judgment as coming in one "period of wrath."[100] The semantic contribution of this phrase in 4QInstruction can be elucidated further against the backdrop of its use elsewhere in late Second Temple literature.

The phrase קץ חרון occurs in several late Second Temple texts. In CD 1:5 it refers to a moment of judgment 390 years after Nebuchadnezzar destroyed Jerusalem (cf. 5:20; 19:10). The expression does not refer to a final act of visitation that occurs in the eschatological future. It may

---

[99] Tigchelaar, *To Increase Learning*, 94, considers only the first letter of the word קצים to be visible.

[100] Also note 4Q418 228 3, which is reconstructed in *DJD 34*, 442, as "take the judgment on the time[s] (משפט קץ[ים]) ..." This phrase may reflect the conviction that judgment is evident in all periods, but it is too fragmentary to state this conclusively. Tigchelaar, *To Increase Learning*, 118, disputes the reconstruction of the word קץ in this line.

have been intended as a wordplay with קֵץ אַחֲרוֹן, "the last age," providing an end-time analogy that conveyed the magnitude of this past act of judgment.[101] The theophanic judgment scene of 1QH associates the phrase קֵץ חָרוֹן with the outpouring of wrath upon the world before the advent of God: "the period of anger (קֵץ חָרוֹן) with all destruction ..." (11:28).

Daniel 8:19 uses the term קֵץ to refer to an appointed time of judgment that is to occur in the future: "Behold, I will explain to you what will be in the latter time of wrath (אַחֲרִית הַזַּעַם), for it is the appointed time of the end (מוֹעֵד קֵץ)." This verse includes a play on Habakkuk 2:3, which understands קֵץ as referring to a specific point in time: "For there is still a vision for the appointed time (לַמּוֹעֵד); it speaks of the end (לַקֵּץ), and does not lie" (cf. Sir 36:10).[102] Habakkuk is a contemporary of Jeremiah and Ezekiel, writing after the death of Josiah during the period of neo-Babylonian encroachment into Palestine (cf. 1:6).[103] He proclaims that at a certain point in the future there will be an "end" to this foreign aggression and that God will deliver his people (e.g., 1:12-13; 3:13-15). Daniel 8:19, when alluding to Habakkuk's prophecy, also understands קֵץ as a distinct historical period in which God's wrath will appear to requite unjust aggression—the defilement of the Temple due to the policies of Antiochus Epiphanes (cf. 8:13-14).[104]

In the final chapters of Daniel the word קֵץ refers to a moment in the future in which eschatological events are to unfold. Referring to the struggles of the Maccabean revolt, the book proclaims that "Some of the wise shall fall, so that they may be refined, purified, and cleansed, until the time of the end, for there is still an interval until the time appointed (עַד־עֵת קֵץ כִּי־עוֹד לַמּוֹעֵד)" (11:35). This political conflict shall culminate with the advent of Michael, beginning "a time of anguish (עֵת צָרָה), such as has never occurred since nations first came into existence" (12:1). Daniel is told by an angel that the righteous will be rewarded after this period of upheaval with resurrection and eternal life at the end of the regular flow of history, a moment that was expected in the near

---

[101] John J. Collins, *Daniel* (Hermeneia; Minneapolis: Fortress, 1993), 338.

[102] Collins, *Apocalypticism in the Dead Sea Scrolls*, 65; idem, *Daniel*, 339. See also Andersen, *Habakkuk*, 205-08.

[103] Joseph Blenkinsopp, *A History of Prophecy in Israel* (2nd ed.; Louisville; Westminster John Knox, 1996 [orig. pub., 1983]), 124-29; Andersen, *Habakkuk*, 25-31.

[104] John J. Collins, "The Meaning of 'the End' in the Book of Daniel," in *Of Scribes and Scrolls: Studies on the Hebrew Bible, Intertestamental Judaism, and Christian Origins* (ed. H.W. Attridge et al.; Lanham: University Press of America, 1990), 93. See also Alfred Mertens, *Das Buch Daniel im Lichte der Texte vom Toten Meer* (SBM 12; Stuttgart: Echter KBW Verlag, 1971), 146-48.

future: "you shall rise for your reward at the end of the days (לקץ הימין)"
(12:13; cf. v. 7).[105]

The Pesher on Habakkuk's understanding of Habakkuk 2:3, in a fashion similar to Daniel 11-12, equates the word קץ with "the final age": "Its
interpretation: the final age (הקץ האחרון) will be extended and go beyond all that the prophets say" (7:7-8). The passage continues by interpreting the rest of the verse from Habakkuk:

> "Though it might tarry, wait for it; it definitely has to come and will not de-
> lay." Its interpretation concerns the men of truth … whose hands will not
> desert the service of truth when the final age (הקץ האחרון) is extended be-
> yond them, because all the ages of God (כול קיצי אל) will come at the right
> time, as he established for them in the mysteries of his prudence (ll. 9-14;
> cf. 1QS 4:18).[106]

The Pesher on Habakkuk in its expectation of the end probably intended
a word play between קץ חרון and קץ אחרון, as is apparently the case with
CD 1:5, since 1QpHab proclaims not only that the last age is coming but
that God will display his scorn for the wicked in a coming "day of judgment" (12:14; 13:2-3). Affirmation that the final period of history will
arrive occurs in the context of frustration that it has not yet happened.
The pesher encourages people to maintain confidence in its arrival.[107]

The *Apocalypse of Weeks* also employs the word קץ to refer to a moment of judgment that takes place in the last stage of history. This text
demarcates all of history into ten weeks. Like Daniel and the Pesher on
Habakkuk, it uses קץ to describe the period of judgment. The final judgment, occurring in the tenth week, is described as "the (fixed) time of the
Great Judgment (קץ דינא רבא)" (4QEn^g 1 iv 23; cf. *1 En.* 91:15).[108]

---

[105] Collins, "The Meaning of 'the End,'" 95-98.

[106] Maurya P. Horgan, *Pesharim: Qumran Interpretations of Biblical Books* (CBQMS
8; Washington, D.C.: Catholic Biblical Association, 1979), 38-39.

[107] Habakkuk 2:3 is also used as a prooftext in rabbinic literature that deals with eschatological delays. See, for example, *b. Sanh.* 97b: "What is meant by 'but at the end it
shall speak and not lie?' R. Samuel b. Nahmani said in the name of R. Jonathan: Blasted
be the bones of those who calculate the end. For they would say, since the predetermined
time has arrived, and yet he has not come, he will never come. But [even so], wait for
him, as it is written, 'Though he tarry, wait for him.' … But since we look forward to it,
and He does likewise, what delays [his coming]?—The Attribute of Justice delays it. But
since the Attribute of Justice delays it, why do we await it?—To be rewarded [for hoping]
as it is written, 'blessed are all they that wait for him' (Isa 30:18)." The Attribute of
Justice, a hypostasis of the divine quality of justice, apparently delayed redemption because Israel was not considered ready for it. See also William H. Brownlee, *The Midrash
Pesher of Habakkuk* (SBLMS 24; Missoula: Scholars Press, 1979), 120. For more on the
Attribute of Justice, see Ephraim Urbach, *The Sages* (Cambridge/London: Harvard University Press, 1975), 448-61.

[108] The translation is from Milik, *The Books of Enoch*, 267. There are significant variants among the manuscripts attesting this pericope. See Knibb, *The Ethiopic Book of*

4QInstruction's "period of wrath" should be understood as referring to judgment that takes place in the final stage of history, as in Daniel, the Pesher on Habakkuk, and the *Apocalypse of Weeks*. There is some ambiguity regarding this point, however, since eschatological rewards and punishments are also meted out after death in 4QInstruction.[109] Its use of the word קץ, however, establishes that judgment culminates the chronological order.

4QInstruction's conceptualization of history, as argued in section 4.1 of Chapter 2, is based on a tripartite division of time into the past, present, and future (4Q418 123 ii 3-4; 4Q417 1 i 3-4). This three-fold format covers the full scope of the chronological order, from creation to judgment. Apocalyptic texts such as Daniel 9 and the *Apocalypse of Weeks* also present a schematization of history that culminates in judgment. A key aim of understanding history in this fashion is to discern the stamp of divine control upon the flow of time. Judgment as a core feature of the divine plan guiding reality is emphasized, for example, in the vision of Hagu pericope: "Engraved is the statute, and ordained is all the punishment, because engraved is that which has been ordained by God against all the in[iquities of] the sons of Sheth" (4Q417 1 i 14-15).

4QInstruction's understanding of history, however, is substantially different from that of Daniel or *1 Enoch*. The wisdom text shows no interest in enumerating the periods of history. The central motif of the *Apocalypse of Weeks* is an elaborate description of the events that occur in each of its ten weeks of history. There is no equivalent timetable in 4QInstruction. Unlike Daniel, it never calculates a specific date on which its eschatological scenario is to begin (Dan 8:14; 12:11-12). While Daniel and the Pesher on Habakkuk express a sense of anxiety or frustration that expected end-time events have not yet begun, there is no such sentiment in 4QInstruction.[110]

Enoch, 2.220. Elgvin, "Early Essene Eschatology," 152-53, has argued that the *Apocalypse of Weeks* attests the phrase שביע קשוט (*1 En.* 91:12) and that this is the "Aramaic equivalent" of the phrase קץ האמ[ת] of 4Q416 1 13. *1 Enoch* 91:12 may be a good philological parallel. But making this claim is complicated by the presence of multiple hands in the Aramaic. Milik's edition of 4QEnoch^g 1 iv 15 does not read שביע קשוט but שבוע תמיני קשוט <ר>. See his *The Books of Enoch*, 266. The word תמיני may have been used to replace the phrase שבוע. Even though the proper transcription of this phrase is disputed, it refers to a specific period in which the destruction of the wicked is to take place, as observed by Elgvin. See also Nickelsburg, *1 Enoch*, 436-37.

[109] This issue is examined in section 3 of this chapter.

[110] See, for example, Dan 12:6: "One of them said to the man clothed in linen, who was upstream, 'How long shall it be until the end of these wonders?'" See also Elgvin, "Early Essene Eschatology," 142. Also note that the phrase קץ אחרון that is important in 1QpHab 7 is used in the Treatise on the Two Spirits, as in 4QInstruction, without a sense of immi-

Other motifs associated with eschatological urgency are absent in 4QInstruction. Some late Second Temple texts proclaim that an end-time scenario will begin to unfold soon, or already has begun, by using the phrase the "end of days."[111] For example, the Halakhic Letter character-izes the present in this way: "this is the end of days" (4Q398 11-13 4). The phrase "end of days" never occurs in 4QInstruction.[112] Some Second Temple writings proclaim that eschatological events are unfolding by characterizing the present as a period of wickedness that will be immedi-ately followed by judgment. Daniel 7:25 proclaims that evil will hold sway for "a time, two times, and half a time" before judgment, a figure that corresponds to the second half of the last week in the seventy weeks schema of chapter 9. In the *Apocalypse of Weeks* the judgment transpir-ing in the eighth week follows the seventh in which "an apostate genera-tion will arise" (*1 En.* 93:9; cf. *Jub.* 23:16-21). Elgvin has argued that there is a "period of wickedness" in 4QInstruction that corresponds to the seventh week of the *Apocalypse of Weeks*, but this proposal is not likely.[113] The text affirms that in the present there are wicked people who deserve eschatological punishment. But the composition never chastises the present age as one of wickedness that requires universal punishment. Late Second Temple texts with this viewpoint often depict the present as under the sway of Belial.[114] 4QInstruction exhibits no knowledge of this figure. The composition has no sense of eschatological urgency.

It has been claimed that eschatological woes are evident in 4Q417 2 i 10-12: "[Gaze upon the mystery] that is to be, and grasp the birth-times of salvation (מולדי ישע) and know who is inheriting glory and who ini[qu]ity" (cf. 4Q416 2 iii 20; 4Q418 202 1). Elgvin argues that the phrase מולדי ישע refers to "the pangs of salvation."[115] The nature of end-

---

nent eschatology: "For God has sorted them into equal parts until the last time (קץ אחרון)" (1QS 4:16-17).

[111] A. Steudel, "אחרית הימים in the Texts from Qumran," *Revue de Qumran* 16 (1993): 225-46; Collins, *Apocalypticism in the Dead Sea Scrolls*, 56-58.

[112] Elgvin, "An Analysis of 4QInstruction," 112.

[113] In "Early Essene Eschatology," 151, Elgvin argues that the suffix of the word קצה of 4Q416 1 11 "refers to רשעה ("wickedness") in the preceding line." There is a complete half line, which originally contained perhaps seven or eight words, between the word רשעה of line 10 and the "period" of line 11. It is much more likely that the antecedent of "its period" is a word that is no longer extant.

[114] 1QS 1:18 describes the present as "the dominion of Belial." The War Scroll asso-ciates the "lot of Belial" with the "rule of the Kittim" (Gentiles) (1QM 1:5-6). 4QFlorilegium promises that the advent of the Davidic messiah will provide rest from the "sons of Belial" (4Q174 1 i 8). See further Elgvin, "Early Essene Eschatology," 151.

[115] Torleif Elgvin, "Wisdom and Apocalypticism in the Early Second Century BCE—The Evidence of 4QInstruction," in *The Dead Sea Scrolls Fifty Years After Their Discov-ery: Proceedings of the Jerusalem Congress, July 20-25, 1997* (ed. L.H. Schiffman, E.

time tribulations would thus be disclosed through the mystery that is to be. This reading cannot be supported. 4QInstruction gives no indication that judgment is preceded by eschatological travails. The moment of judgment is theophanic. The composition teaches that the world is overwhelmed during the implementation of judgment, not at any time leading up to this point.

The phrase מולדי ישע should be interpreted as a deterministic understanding of time rather than the 'birth-pangs' of salvation. A similar phrase from the Book of Mysteries, "the time of birth" (בית מולדים), can shed light on the expression from 4QInstruction.[116] Unfortunately, the attestations of this phrase in Mysteries occur in fragmentary contexts. In 4Q299 3a ii-b 13 the phrase is associated with revelation: "... [p]lan of the time of birth (חשבת בית מולדים[מ])) he opened be[fore them ..." (cf. 4Q299 1 4; 4Q299 5 5). This reflects a deterministic mindset, as noted by Schiffman.[117] He understands בית מולדים as referring to human birth on the basis of parallels in rabbinic literature (e.g., *Tg. Onq.* Gen 40:20). For him the phrase means "the time of birth that is seen to affect the future and nature of the individual."[118] The word בית would then correspond to "house" in modern astrological parlance (i.e., born in the house of Neptune). Schiffman's interpretation is supported by astrological texts from Qumran.[119] 4Q186 (4QHoroscope) uses the term בית in this very sense: "His spirit has six (parts) in the house (בית) of light and three in the house (בית) of darkness" (1 ii 7-8; cf. 4Q186 1 iii 5-6).[120] In this text מולד signifies one's astrological sign: "this is the sign (המולד) in which he was born (ילוד)" (1 ii 8; cf. 4Q186 2 i 8).[121] 1QH 20:8 also

---

Tov, and J.C. VanderKam; Jerusalem: Israel Exploration Society/Shrine of the Book, Israel Museum, 2000), 233; idem, "An Analysis of 4QInstruction," 79.

[116] The phrase בית מולדים has been plausibly reconstructed in 4Q415 2 ii 9. There the phrase probably refers to the birth of the woman to whom this fragment is addressed. Its main topic is the conduct of a woman in marriage. Line 9 seems to make a distinction between the woman's life in the house of her birth and in the house of her husband (cf. l. 7). The fragmentary nature of the text makes interpretation difficult. See *DJD 34*, 47-49; Tigchelaar, *To Increase Learning*, 32.

[117] *DJD 20*, 42.

[118] Ibid., 37.

[119] Matthew Morgenstern, "The Meaning of בית מולדים in the Qumran Wisdom Texts," *Journal of Jewish Studies* 51 (2000), 141. See also Caquot, "Les textes de sagesse de Qoumrân," 9.

[120] See Francis Schmidt, "Ancient Jewish Astrology: An Attempt to Interpret 4QCryptic (4Q186)," in *Biblical Perspectives: Early Use and Interpretation of the Bible in Light of the Dead Sea Scrolls* (ed. M.E. Stone and E. Chazon; STDJ 28; Leiden: Brill, 1998), 191-92. See also Strugnell, "Notes en marge," 274-76; *DJDJ 5*, 88-92; *DJD 34*, 117.

[121] According to Schiffman, *DJD 20*, 37, מולד is a rabbinic term for the new moon. See also Schmidt, "Ancient Jewish Astrology," 195-97.

uses the word מולד. In this text the phrase מולדי עת refers not to human
birth but history: "the births of time (מולדי עת), the foundations of the
period, and the course of seasons in their order, by their signs for all their
dominion, in the order established through God's mouth."[122] The expression מולדי עת denotes the beginning of time and God's establishment of
the chronological order.

Both 4QHoroscope and the Hodayot use the word מולד in reference to
time as arranged and determined by God. This provides the key for interpreting the phrase מולדי ישׁע in 4QInstruction. It reflects the composition's deterministic mindset. It should be understood in relation to human birth rather than the beginning of time.[123] 4Q417 2 i 10-12 discusses
the eschatological fate of people. 4QInstruction does not reflect familiarity with the systematic astrological understanding of human birth found
in 4Q186. But the wisdom text exhibits the compatible view that from
the beginning of one's life his fate has been established by God. The
phrase "birth-times of salvation" underscores the perspective that those
who will receive salvation have an inherent predisposition for this fate.[124]

4QInstruction's understanding of history is deterministic and in that
sense is compatible with apocalyptic literature. But in terms of history
the wisdom text is significantly different from many apocalyptic texts
from the late Second Temple period. 4QInstruction is much less ornate
and elaborate, without many of the tropes commonly found in the eschatological scenarios of apocalyptic literature. These differences provide insights into the political and cultural climate in which
4QInstruction was composed. Several of the apocalyptic texts examined
above reflect the social and political uncertainties of the time of their
composition. Daniel 7-12 reflects the upheavals of the Maccabean crisis,
which in chapter 9 is placed in the final week of its seventy-week
schema. It is common to contend that the *Apocalypse of Weeks* was
written during the "seventh week," in which wickedness holds sway.[125]
Many Dead Sea Scrolls texts display an awareness of various political
problems and religious disputes from the second and first centuries BCE,
such as the oppression of Roman rule and tension with the Pharisees and
the Temple establishment. Many of the writings from Qumran reflect

---

[122] *DJD 34*, 182. The word מולד is used in the sense of birth in 1QH 11:11. In this text
the speaker compares his grief to the pain of a woman giving birth.

[123] Morgenstern, "The Meaning of בית מולדים," 142, provides additional support for this
interpretation. He identifies a parallel Syriac expression, *bet yalda*, which refers to human
birth in an astrological sense.

[124] This view is also expressed in 4Q416 2 iii 9-10: "If he restores you to glory, walk in
it, and with the mystery [that] is to be examine one's origins. Then you will know his
inheritance and in righteousness you will walk" (cf. l. 20).

[125] Collins, *The Apocalyptic Imagination*, 64; Nickelsburg, *1 Enoch*, 440.

this climate of tension and uncertainty by declaring that the present is under the dominion of Belial and that divine visitation will arrive soon. The political context influenced the presentation of the final judgment and encouraged the elaboration of forms of eschatological expression. That 4QInstruction's understanding of history is not accompanied by eschatological urgency or a sense of pervasive wickedness in the world suggests that the composition was not written during a time of civil turmoil. The political crises of the author's day, however, may be implied by the economic distress of the addressee. In any case, 4QInstruction does not characterize the present age as an epoch of oppression that warrants divine retribution. This suggests that 4QInstruction was not written in the period in which the undisputed literature of the Qumran community was composed. If the wisdom text is from the same time as the main sectarian texts, it characterizes the contemporary situation in a way that is very different from the writings of the Dead Sea sect.

4QInstruction may have been written before the Maccabean conflict. The composition shows no familiarity with this crisis. A lack of references to historical events is standard, however, in biblical wisdom, and 4QInstruction could be continuing this tradition. A pre-Maccabean origin is possible but a late second century date for the text cannot be excluded. Wisdom texts are often notoriously hard to pin down to a specific date of composition. In this regard 4QInstruction is no exception.[126]

2.5 The Elimination of the Wicked in 4QInstruction and its Depiction of Death

In 4QInstruction judgment against the wicked is a basic element of the natural order. It is ordained that wickedness will be punished. 4Q417 2 i 8, for example, declares that one's retribution will be in measure with his deeds: "the wickedness of his deeds together with his punishment (פקדתו)" (cf. 4Q417 1 i 24). Divine judgment against the wicked is also emphasized in the vision of Hagu pericope, which declares that visitation is decreed "against all the in[iquities of] the sons of Sheth" (4Q417 1 i 14-15). I argued in section 2.2 of Chapter 3 that the phrase "sons of Sheth" is a reference to the wicked, who are also described as the "fleshly spirit." 4Q416 1 12 affirms that this group will be destroyed in the final judgment (cf. 4Q416 2 ii 2-3).

According to 4QInstruction, the wicked will be eliminated completely. 4Q416 1 13 declares that "all iniquity will come to an end (כל עולה תתם)." 4Q418 69 ii 8 asserts that "all the foolish of heart will be

---

destroyed and the sons of iniquity will be found no more." 4Q418 113 1
is a fragmentary text that, like 4Q416 1 13, uses the verb תמם to describe
the destruction of iniquity: "... until ini[quity] is completed (עד תום
[עו]לה)" (cf. 4Q418 211 4).[127]

The judgment scene of the Book of Mysteries employs the verb תמם
twice to describe the end of wickedness:

> And this shall be the sign to you that it is taking place: when the begotten
> of unrighteousness are locked up (בהסגור מולדי עולה), and wickedness is
> removed from before righteousness, as darkness is removed before light.
> (Then,) just as smoke wholly ceases (כתום) and is no more, so shall wick-
> edness cease (יתם) forever (1Q27 1 i 5-6; cf. Ps 104:35).[128]

After judgment, justice and knowledge are to prevail in the world (1Q27
1 i 7). The image of smoke dissipating suggests that the wicked will
completely disappear. This is seemingly in tension with the view that
they are "locked up," as conveyed by the expression בהסגור.

The meaning of the word סגר in other late Second Temple texts relates
to the fate of the wicked in 4QInstruction. It employs סגר to describe
their recompense. 4Q418 126 ii 6-7 reads: "... to repay vengeance to the
workers of iniquity (פעלי און) ... and to shut (the door) upon the wicked
(לסגור בעד רשעים)" (cf. 4Q418 201 2).[129] Milik interprets סגר in 1Q27 1
i 5 as referring to "l'emprisonnement dans l'Enfer" on the basis on 1QH
11:18.[130] In this verse from the Hodayot, the "pit" has doors that are
closed upon the wicked: "And the doors of the pit close upon (יסגרו דלתי
שחת) the one expectant with injustice, and everlasting bolts upon all the
spirits of the serpent."[131] Before this it declares that "Sh[eo]l [and
A]bad[don] open" to receive the wicked (11:16; cf. 4Q418 177 2).[132]

In both Mysteries and the Hodayot, the 'locking up' (סגר) of the
wicked refers to the act of going to Sheol. But this is never explicitly
presented as imprisonment. The focus is this world. Once the wicked
leave it, they are gone forever. The dead may be punished or imprisoned,

---

[127] Compare the beginning of 4Q180 1: "An interpretation concerning the ages: God
made a time to bring to perfect accomplishment (קץ להתם) [all that is] and is to come."
This translation is based on Strugnell, "Notes en marge," 252. See also Elgvin, "Early
Essene Eschatology," 152; *DJD 34*, 340; *DJDJ 5*, 77-78.

[128] *DJD 20*, 38, 106. Schiffman translates the word הסגור as "are delivered up."

[129] Regarding the phrase פעלי און, which is well attested in the Hebrew Bible (e.g., Pss
6:9; 36:12; 101:8), I follow the transcription of Tigchelaar, *To Increase Learning*, 103.
Strugnell and Harrington, *DJD 34*, 350-54, argue that it should be read as בעלי און.

[130] *DJD 1*, 104.

[131] Compare the expression "gates of death" in texts such as Job 38:17; Pss 9:13;
107:18; Wis 16:13; 3 Macc 5:51; and 6:31.

[132] Note the parallel in Prov 15:11: "Sheol and Abaddon lie open before the Lord, how
much more human hearts!" Cf. 27:20; Job 26:6.

but the texts show little interest in their fate after death. Death is depicted as the gates of Sheol closing. By mentioning the "doors of the pit" closing, 1QH 11 provides a fuller portrait of this image than Mysteries. 4Q418 126 ii 6-7 should be interpreted in light of this background. The word סגר in this text signifies the doors of Sheol closing upon the wicked. This understanding of Sheol as a neutral term signifying death is in keeping with biblical tradition.[133] 4Q418 126 ii is consistent with the presentation of the fate of the wicked elsewhere in 4QInstruction. 4Q418 69 ii 8 teaches that after judgment the wicked will be "found no more," and 4Q416 1 13 declares that iniquity will be brought to an end.

That 4Q418 126 ii 6-7 should be viewed as an allusion to Sheol receiving the wicked is supported by the fragmentary reference in 4Q423 5 1 to the "judgment of Korah" (קורח משפט).[134] This is a reference to the well-known story from Numbers 16 about an Israelite who led a rebellion against the leadership of Moses and Aaron in the wilderness period.[135] His group is punished with death for its disobedience:

> The earth opened its mouth and swallowed them up, along with their households—everyone who belonged to Korah and all their goods. So they with all that belonged to them went down alive into Sheol; the earth closed over them, and they perished from the midst of the assembly (16:32-33).

Like 1QH 11, Numbers 16 visualizes the death of the wicked as Sheol swallowing them up (cf. Jude 11). The text from Numbers does not describe Sheol as having gates. But it does emphasize that the earth swallows up the wicked.

That Sheol is the topic of 4Q418 126 ii is also suggested by several references to the "pit" in 4QInstruction (cf. *1 En.* 51:1).[136] Unfortunately, they all occur in fragmentary contexts. "Pit" is found in 4Q418 177 2 in conjunction with "Abaddon."[137] The word "pit" is also employed in

---

[133] For M. Fox, for example, Sheol signifies death "viewed as a location." He thus translates it as "Death-Land." See his *Proverbs 1-9* (AB 18a; New York: Doubleday, 2000), 192.

[134] James M. Scott, "Korah and Qumran," in *The Bible at Qumran: Text, Shape, and Interpretation* (ed. P.W. Flint; Grand Rapids: Eerdmans, 2001), 182-202. Scott does not focus on the description of Korah's death in Numbers 16.

[135] For an overview, see Baruch Levine, *Numbers 1-20* (AB 4A; New York: Doubleday, 1993), 405-32.

[136] For Sheol described as a pit, see, for example, Ps 16:10, "For you do not give me up to Sheol, or let your faithful one see the Pit," and Job 33:22, "Their souls draw near the Pit, and their lives to those who bring death." Cf. Ps 30:10; Isa 38:18; Ezek 28:8; and 31:14.

[137] For occurrences of "Abaddon," see Job 26:6; 28:22; 31:12; Ps 88:12; Prov 15:11; 1QH 11:16, 19, and 32. See also M. Hutter, "Abaddon," in *Dictionary of Deities and Demons in the Bible* (2nd ed.; ed. K. van der Toorn et al.; Leiden: Brill, 1999), 1.

4Q418 102 1 (cf. 4Q418 127 2). Like Proverbs, 4QInstruction relies on Sheol terminology to describe death.[138]

4QInstruction also uses the expression "eternal pit." 4Q418 69 ii 6 proclaims that the "foolish of heart" will go there: "your return will be to the eternal pit (לשחת עולם תשובתכם)."[139] The "eternal pit" refers to death. The image in 4Q418 126 ii 6-7 of the gates of death closing upon the wicked likely presumes the "eternal pit" as the destination of the dead. This is also evident from the composition's references to Sheol and the Korah story. Pit and Sheol function as synonymous terms in 4QInstruction. The pit is described as "eternal" because those who enter it will never return.

4QInstruction's use of the phrase "eternal pit" raises the possibility that its author had a conception of punishment after death. The term שחת can be translated as "destruction" or "damnation."[140] The text contains no explicit description of the "eternal pit" as a place of eternal anguish. The *Book of the Watchers*, by contrast, affirms that the wicked will endure punishment in an "abyss of fire." It proclaims that the fallen angels will be taken to "the abyss of fire; in torment and in prison they will be shut up for all eternity. And then he (Semyaza) will be burnt and from then on destroyed with them" (*1 En.* 10:13-14).[141] In section 2.3 of this chapter I argued that the author of 4QInstruction knew some form of Enochic literature. This suggests that he was familiar with the concept of punishment after death.[142] But the text he wrote shows little interest in this idea. In this regard 4QInstruction is closer to the Book of Mysteries and the Wisdom of Solomon (e.g., 5:14) than *1 Enoch*. Unlike Enochic literature, these texts are more interested in proclaiming the elimination of the wicked from the earth than describing what happens to them afterwards.

---

[138] Proverbs often asserts that the wicked will go to Sheol (e.g., 5:5; 7:27; 9:18; 15:24; 23:14; 27:20).

[139] *DJD 34*, 283. Also note that 4Q418 162 4, if reconstructed correctly, declares that the addressee has been saved from this pit: "[You will be saved from] the eternal pit, and you will have gl[ory] ([וד]כב לכה והיה עולם שׂחת[)." The contrast between "eternal pit" and "glory" makes this a sensible reconstruction of the text. But its fragmentary condition makes interpretation tentative. See ibid., 385-86.

[140] Elgvin, "An Analysis of 4QInstruction," 249.

[141] Cf. *1 En.* 21:7-10; 103:7-8; 108:5; 4Q548 1 ii-2 13. Note the parallel in Revelation 20:3, which depicts the eschatological punishment of the dragon: "(he) threw him into the pit, and locked and sealed it over him, so that he would deceive the nations no more, until the thousand years were ended" (cf. 9:2, 11). For an overview of the topic of punishment after death, see Collins, "The Afterlife," 121-31; Nickelsburg, *1 Enoch*, 224-25.

[142] Puech understands "Shéol et Fosse" in 4QInstruction as "le lieu des châtiments et de perdition éternels où les impies seront anéantis pour toujours." See his "Apports des textes apocalyptiques et sapientiels."

The Treatise on the Two Spirits explicitly describes the "eternal pit" as a place of agony to which the wicked are sent:

> And the visitation of all those who walk in it (wickedness) will be for an abundance of afflictions at the hands of all the angels of destruction, for the eternal pit (לשחת עולמים) by the scorching wrath of the God of revenge, for permanent terror and shame without end with the humiliation of destruction by the fire of the dark regions (מחשכים). And all the ages of their generations (they shall spend) in bitter weeping and harsh evils in the abysses of darkness until their destruction (1QS 4:11-14).[143]

Elsewhere the Community Rule warns sectarians to avoid the "men of the pit," which may, like the "foolish of heart" of 4Q418 69 ii, refer to those who are destined for the eternal pit (1QS 9:16). The Treatise also declares that God "has determined an end to the existence of injustice and on the appointed time of the visitation he will obliterate it for ever" (4:18-19). Their removal from the human realm leads to a utopian existence on earth: "Then truth shall rise up forever (in) the world" (4:19). The Treatise depicts the wicked as burning in the fire of the "dark regions" (מחשכים) (4:13).[144] In 4Q418 69 ii 7 the "dark regions" roar against the "foolish of heart," without any imagery of fire. In the Treatise the "eternal pit" and the "dark regions" help create a vivid portrait of the anguish of the wicked after death. These images occur in 4QInstruction without explicit description of punishment after death. It may have been obvious to its author that the "eternal pit" was a place of eternal torment. The belief may be implied in the image of the angels "rousing themselves" for the judgment of the "foolish of heart" (4Q418 69 ii 7). 1QS 4:12 associates "angels of destruction" with the transport of the wicked to the "eternal pit" (cf. CD 2:6; 1QM 13:12).

In the Treatise the fate awaiting the wicked in the "eternal pit" contrasts the blessed afterlife of the righteous: "And the reward of all those who walk in it will be healing, plentiful peace in a long life ... eternal joy (שמחת עולמים) with endless life, and a crown of glory" (1QS 4:6-7). As examined below, 4QInstruction promises "eternal joy," using the phrase שמחת עולם, to the addressee in 4Q417 2 i 10-12. The Treatise explicitly contrasts "eternal joy" (שמחת עולמים) with the "eternal pit" (שחת עולמים)

---

[143] Compare *4 Ezra* 7:36: "The pit of torment shall appear, and opposite it shall be the place of rest; and the furnace of hell shall be disclosed, and opposite it the paradise of delight." See also the curse of Belial in 4Q286 (4QBlessings^a) 7 ii 4-5, in which Belial and the "spirits of his lot" are "denounced for the plots of the defilement of their [im]purity, fo[r they are a lo]t of darkness and their visitation is to an eternal pit" (cf. 4Q215a 1 ii 3). This translation is from James R. Davila, *Liturgical Works* (ECDSS 6; Grand Rapids: Eerdmans, 2000), 59.

[144] The fires of the "dark regions" of Sheol and Abaddon also consume the wicked in 4Q491 (4QM^a) 8-10 i 15. See Tigchelaar, *To Increase Learning*, 198.

in 1QS 4:6-14. 4QInstruction has a similar contrast. But it never directly distinguishes "eternal joy" from the "eternal pit" in the same text (they occur in 4Q417 2 i 12 and 4Q418 69 ii 7, respectively). The Treatise also describes in more detail than 4QInstruction what is meant by these terms. It is possible that the Treatise's use of the expressions "eternal pit" and "eternal joy" is inspired by the wisdom text. If so, the Treatise made the contrast between the two, and thus the opposing fates of the righteous and wicked, more explicit and elaborate than 4QInstruction. This relationship between the two texts is also suggested by their dualisms, which are quite similar to one another except for the glaring absence of imagery of light and darkness in 4QInstruction.

It is reasonable to conclude that the author of 4QInstruction believed that the wicked would be sent to a place of punishment after death. But this is not an issue that the composition emphasizes. The "eternal pit" represents the fate of the "foolish of heart." Knowing their destiny should encourage the addressee to emulate the angels, as the "truly chosen ones" are encouraged to in 4Q418 69 ii 10-15. 4QInstruction is interested in the "eternal pit" as something to be avoided. In that sense it is not surprising that the text includes no elaborate description of it.

The undisputed writings of the Dead Sea sect depict the elimination of the wicked from the earth. Like *1 Enoch*, they describe their punishment after death. The most explicit evidence for this viewpoint in the Qumran community is the Treatise. This belief is evident elsewhere in the rule-books. The opening section of the Community Rule attests the torment of the wicked after death: "Accursed are you, without mercy, according to the darkness of your deeds, and sentenced to the gloom of everlasting fire (אפלת אש עולמים)" (1QS 2:7-8; cf. 1QpHab 10:5).[145] The Damascus Document attests a similar fate for the wicked. CD 2:5 describes "a great anger with flames of fire" that consumes the wicked. It also affirms that they will be left without "remnant or survivor" (ll. 7-8). When judgment is proclaimed in chapter 8, it emphasizes the deeds of the wicked without describing the nature of their punishment. Punishment after death is not a prominent concept in this text.

The Pesher on Psalm 37 emphasizes the eradication of the wicked from the earth more than their punishment afterwards. Like the Book of Mysteries and the Wisdom of Solomon, this pesher describes the wicked

---

[145] Shortly after this proclamation, it is asserted that the wicked will be wiped out: "his spirit will be obliterated … May God's anger and the wrath of his verdicts consume him for everlasting destruction (כלת עולמים)" (2:14-15). Since the wicked will suffer in the "gloom of everlasting fire," the "eternal destruction" they will endure probably does not imply that they will be destroyed and gone forever but rather that the process of destruction lasts forever.

as disappearing like smoke. It interprets a passage from Psalm 37:20, "Like smoke they all vanish," as referring to "the wi[cke]d princes who oppress his holy people, who will perish like smoke that is los[t in the w]ind" (4Q171 3 7-8; cf. 4Q171 2 8).[146] The Hodayot likewise stresses the destruction of the wicked: "All injustice [and wick]edness you obliterate for ever" (6:15-16; cf. 12:20; 14:30). These texts are more interested in describing the removal of the wicked from earth than what happens to them afterwards. This is also the case with 4QInstruction.

Late Second Temple instructional texts have various conceptions of the fate of the wicked. The Treatise asserts that they will suffer after death. The Book of Mysteries affirms that the wicked will die because of their deeds, without explicit mention of punishment after death. This is similar to traditional wisdom. As Lange has observed, Mysteries places the older sapiential view of the fate of the wicked in an eschatological horizon, proclaiming that they will disappear at a specific moment in the future.[147] 4QInstruction attests a more extensive transformation of wisdom. It is similar to Mysteries in its emphasis on the elimination of the wicked from earth rather than their punishment after death. The two texts also both have an eschatological perspective. 4QInstruction differs from both Mysteries and traditional wisdom in its affirmation of divine agency in judgment. 4QInstruction stresses the role of God in judgment. The depiction of judgment in Mysteries highlights the mystery that is to be rather than God. The Tat-Ergehen-Zusammenhang of the Book of Proverbs does not accentuate an active divine role in punishment. Judgment in 4QInstruction is closer to depictions of retribution in contemporary apocalyptic texts than biblical wisdom.

The Treatise of the Two Spirits, 4QInstruction, and the Book of Mysteries illustrate different ways that Palestinian instructional texts presented the fate of the wicked in the late Second Temple period. As there

---

[146] This translation is from Horgan, *Pesharim*, 197. See also *DJDJ 5*, 46; Strugnell, "Notes en marge," 215. The view that the wicked will evaporate like smoke is also found in later texts. See, for example, *2 Bar.* 82:2-7, "you ought to know that our Creator will surely avenge us on all our brothers according to everything which they have done against us ... they do not keep the statutes of the Most High; but as smoke they will pass away. And we think about the beauty of their gracefulness while they go down in impurities; but like grass which is withering, they will fade away" (cf. 4Q185 1-2 i 9-12; Ps 90:5-6; Is 40:6-8); Wis 5:9-14, "All those things (the wealth and arrogance of the wicked) have vanished like a shadow, and like a rumor that passes by; like a ship that sails through the billowy water, and when it has passed no trace can be found, no track of its keel in the waves ... Because the hope of the ungodly is like thistledown carried by the wind ... it is dispersed like smoke before the wind." Elgvin, "Early Essene Eschatology," 152, observes a similar image from the Rosh Hashanah liturgy: "and all evil will disappear like smoke."

[147] Lange, *Weisheit und Prädestination*, 120.

was debate in sapiential circles in this era regarding the origin of evil, there was variety of opinion regarding the nature of its punishment.[148]

2.6 Judgment of All Humankind

Although 4QInstruction concentrates on the visitation against the wicked, it stresses that all of humanity will be judged.[149] The universality of judgment is emphasized at the beginning of the composition: "[For kingdom] and kingdom, for pr[ovince and province, for each and every man ... And the judgment of all of them belongs to him]" (4Q416 1 4-6).[150] After describing how God fashioned every ruler, 4Q423 5 4 asserts that they, and everyone else, will be judged: "[He will judg]e all of them in truth and visit upon fathers and sons, [upon proselyte]s together with every native born."[151] 4Q418 77 3 presents judgment as a universal aspect of the human condition: "Then you will discern the judgment of humankind (משפט אנוש)." Universal judgment may be emphasized in the phrase "judgment of the flock" (משפט צאן).[152] That all will be judged is clear in 4Q417 2 i 15-16: "F[or] before [his anger] none will stand. Who is righteous in his judgment?" This fragment also reminds the addressee of judgment to foster ethical behavior:

> Do not overlook your [transgress]ions. Be like a humble man when you strive for his judgment ... Then God will appear, his anger will turn aside, and he will take away your sins (ll. 14-15; cf. Sir 18:20).[153]

4QInstruction teaches that everyone will be judged. This is used as an incentive for the addressee to be ethical.

---

[148] See section 2.5 of Chapter 3.

[149] Other Second Temple texts emphasize that all will be judged. *1 Enoch* 1:9 and CD 1:2 describe God as judging "all flesh." This is also stressed in the Community Rule: "I realize that in his hand lies the judgment of every living thing" (1QS 10:16-17).

[150] *DJD 34*, 81. For a slightly different reconstruction of this passage, see Tigchelaar, *To Increase Learning*, 175-76. Also note that the fragmentary text 4Q418 68 has the phrase "generation and generation" in line 1 and repeats the word "visitation" in lines 2-3 (פקודת and פקורות, respectively).

[151] *DJD 34*, 519; Tigchelaar, *To Increase Learning*, 142.

[152] This phrase occurs in 4Q417 3 2; 4Q418 172 13; and 4Q418 239 2. These are small fragments and the exact meaning of the expression cannot be recovered fully. It is possible to understand the flock as the intended audience of 4QInstruction. It could also refer to all humanity. In prophetic literature similar language is used in relation to the judgment of Israel. See, for example, Ezek 34:22; 37:24; Zech 11:7, 11; 13:7.

[153] Contrast Rom 9:16: "So it depends not on human will or exertion, but on God who shows mercy."

2.7 The Awareness of Judgment

The addressee is taught to be aware of judgment. 4QInstruction grants that he might go astray and commit sin. This is explicit, for example, in 4Q417 1 i 23: "do not be contaminated by iniquity" (cf. 4Q418 147 4). This text affirms that the wicked will be recompensed for their deeds: "[the wicked person] will not be treated as guiltless. According to his inheritance in it he will be tr[eated as wicked]" (l. 24). 4QInstruction warns the addressee to avoid the "evil inclination" (יֵצֶר רַע) in 4Q417 1 ii 12. Before this line 11 declares "He will punish all your ways." The addressee is not sinless with his rewards guaranteed. This problematizes Elgvin's claim that salvation is a "present reality" for the addressee.[154] Even though God established him to be among the elect (4Q418 81 1-4), he must earn his ultimate rewards. This attitude is prevalent in the presentation of judgment in 4Q418 69 ii. The "truly chosen ones" who are spared are urged to maintain a high degree of vigilance in their pursuit of righteousness and knowledge by imitating the angels (ll. 13-14). The intended audience is told to act like the angels in part to be spared from the eschatological judgment.

The importance of the addressee's awareness of judgment is also evident from the mystery that is to be. Judgment is one of the topics that he can learn about through contemplation of this mystery. For example, 4Q417 1 i 6-8 reads: "[Day and night meditate upon the mystery that is] to be ... in all their ways with their reckoning for all the periods of eternity, and the eternal reckoning." The final judgment may also be the topic of 4Q418 123 ii 4, which mentions "his period" that has been revealed through the mystery that is to be. 4Q417 2 i 10-12 promises that contemplation of the mystery that is to be will allow the addressee to know "who is inheriting glory and who ini[qu]ity." Some fragmentary texts also associate judgment with the mystery that is to be. 4Q418 77 2 mentions the mystery that is to be and continues in line 3 to provide the addressee with knowledge about the "judgment of humankind." The "judgment of Korah" in 4Q423 5 1 is presumably understood by means of the mystery that is be, which is safely reconstructed in line 2. Although it does not refer to the mystery that is to be, the vision of Hagu pericope stresses that the addressee know that judgment is to take place: "And you, understanding one, inherit your reward by remembering the mi[ght because] it is coming" (4Q417 1 i 13-14).

The role of the final judgment is also indicated by its relationship to the knowledge of good and evil. As examined in Chapter 2, the ad-

---

[154] Elgvin, "Early Essene Eschatology," 144; Collins, "The Eschatologizing of Biblical Wisdom."

dressee can attain the knowledge of good and evil through the mystery
that is to be (4Q417 1 i 6-8). This knowledge is connected to the final
judgment. After declaring God to be a "god of truth" in 4Q416 1 14 (cf.
1QH 7:28), line 15 includes a fragmentary phrase: "to establish a just
standard between good and evil (להכֹּון צדק בין טוב לֹרֹע)" (cf. 4Q418
127 6). Not enough of the latter section of 4Q416 1 remains to make
conclusive assessments. I argued earlier that in 4QInstruction obtaining
the knowledge of good and evil requires an awareness of the divine plan
guiding events. Therefore it is reasonable to think of God's judgment as
helping make knowledge of good and evil possible, or at least valid.
Conduct is to be shaped by the realization that the righteous will be
spared and the wicked punished because that is how God made the
world. In that sense it is not surprising that 4Q418 2 7, a variant of
4Q416 1 15, reads not להכֹּון but להבין, stressing that good and evil is not
established but taught.[155] That 4Q416 1 establishes a theological basis
for ethical conduct is also suggested by the fragmentary reference in line
16 to a "fleshly [incl]ination" (יֹ]צר בשר), a disposition akin to the
"wicked inclination" (4Q417 1 ii 12) that is reminiscent of the "fleshly
spirit." The reality of judgment helps legitimate the proposition that the
knowledge of good and evil is applicable to this world and crucial for
perceiving the nature of God's cosmos. This view is compatible with the
Book of Proverbs, which also relates the outcome of one's actions to the
nature of the created order. But 4QInstruction differs from Proverbs by
situating retribution in an eschatological context, as do contemporary
apocalyptic texts.

3. THE FATE OF THE RIGHTEOUS

According to 4QInstruction, at the moment of judgment some will be
punished and others rewarded. This dualistic perspective is evident in
the distinction between the "foolish of heart" and the "truly chosen ones"
in 4Q418 69 ii 4-15. 4Q416 1 10 proclaims salvation for the righteous
and the judgment of the wicked: "From heaven he will judge over the
work of wickedness. But all the sons of his truth will be accepted with
favor (כל בני אמתו ירצו)." The Treatise on the Two Spirits similarly
describes those who will be rewarded eschatologically as the "sons of
truth" in 1QS 4:6.[156] Like 4QInstruction, the Treatise also contrasts the

---

[155] Tigchelaar, *To Increase Learning*, 190.
[156] For the phrase "sons of your truth," see 1QH 5:29; 17:35; 18:27; 19:11. Cf. 1QH
10:14; 1QM 17:8.

righteous with the wicked who will be destroyed (1QS 4:11-14).[157] The association of the "sons of his truth" with divine favor (ירצו) in 4Q416 1 invites comparison with the "men of favor" of 4Q418 81 10. The addressee can help ensure that they will avoid the fate of the wicked: "You have the ability to turn anger from the men of favor (אנשי רצון)."[158] This group is understood as "those who keep his word" (שומרי דברו) in line 8 of 4Q418 81. Given the association with divine approval, the "men of favor" is likely a reference to the intended audience of 4QInstruction.

While 4QInstruction affirms that the righteous will be rewarded, it contains surprisingly few descriptions of what their reward will be. Although it is never asserted explicitly, 4QInstruction promises its addressee eternal life. This is evident from the composition's theme of joy. Joy is an important eschatological motif in late Second Temple literature, as examined in section 3.5.2 of Chapter 4. 4Q417 2 i 10-12 tells the addressee not to "rejoice (תשמח) in your mourning lest you toil in your life" because "eternal joy" (שמחת עולם) is promised for those in mourning. Eternal joy characterizes his eschatological future. 4Q417 2 i 10-12 distinguishes the state of eternal joy that it promises to the addressee from mourning, which it associates with his present life.

The eschatological significance of joy is evident elsewhere in 4QInstruction. 4Q416 4 1-2 describes the "period of wrath" and the wicked for whom "the furnace is fanned." Line 3 of this text depicts an opposite fate for the addressee: "But you, understanding one, rejoice in the inheritance of truth (שמחה בנחלת אמת)." A similar contrast is made in the fragmentary text 4Q418 102 5: "[from the] iniquity of abomination you will be innocent, and in the joy of truth (בשמחת אמת) you will ..."[159]

When 4Q418 126 ii 7 proclaims that the gates of death will shut upon the wicked, it affirms that God will "raise up the head of the poor (דלים)." That poverty is emphasized suggests that this refers to the addressee. Since the lifting up of the poor is in contrast to the death of the wicked, it probably denotes some sort of exaltation of the poor. This is suggested by a fragmentary phrase in line 8 that reads "in eternal glory

---

[157] Cf. 4Q548 (The Visions of Amram[f]? ar) 1 ii-2 12-14; *T. Ash.* 6:5.

[158] The phrase אנשי רצון has been compared to the expression ἀνθρώποις εὐδοκίας, a term for those favored by God in Luke 2:14. See A. Wolters, "Anthropoi Eudokias (Luke 2:14) and 'ansy rswn (4Q416)," *Journal of Biblical Literature* 113 (1994): 291-97. Note also that 1QH uses the similar expression בני רצונכה, "sons of your favor," in reference to the elect (12:32-33; 19:9). See Joseph A. Fitzmyer, *The Semitic Background of the New Testament* (Grand Rapids/Livonia: Eerdmans/Dove, 1997), 101-04; *DJD 34*, 307; Tigchelaar, *To Increase Learning*, 234.

[159] Part of the word שמחה may appear in 4Q418 69 ii 1. See *DJD 34*, 284. Unfortunately none of the word's context has survived. This possibility is not endorsed in Tigchelaar, *To Increase Learning*, 209-11.

and peace eternal (בכבוד עולם ושלום עד)." This is presumably a description of the fate that awaits the righteous (cf. 4Q418 162 4). 4Q416
2 iii 11-12 similarly promises the addressee an "inheritance of glory."
The addressee of 4QInstruction is offered eschatological salvation in the
form of eternal life, a unique claim in Hebrew wisdom literature.[160]
   Elgvin has suggested that 4QInstruction promises an angelic afterlife
in the form of astral immortality, in which the righteous shine like the
stars as in Daniel 12:3 and *1 Enoch* 104:2-6 (cf. Wis 3:7).[161] However
there is no astral imagery in the composition in relation to the righteous
dead.[162] Nevertheless it is reasonable to associate the eternal life promised to the addressee with the angels. The composition stresses the eternal life of the angels (4Q418 69 ii 13). It emphasizes that the addressee
is like the angels. He is in the lot of the angels (4Q418 81 4-5), and
urged to be like the "spiritual people" who are in the "likeness of the
holy ones" (4Q417 1 i 17). 4Q416 1 10-12 associates the deliverance of
the "sons of his truth" with the "sons of heave[n]," a common term for
angels. Angels are also models for conduct (4Q418 55 8-11; 4Q418 69 ii
13-14). As the addressee is expected to imitate the angels in this world,
his eschatological future is likewise modeled after them.
   Despite the addressee's similarities to the angels, he will experience
death.[163] His physical body will expire: "[More]over your wealth is together with your flesh (הונכה עם בשרכה). [When the days of] your life
[come to an end], they (also) will come to an end together (יתמו יחד)"
(4Q418 103 ii 9).[164] This text uses the same verb, תמם, employed in
4Q416 1 13 and 4Q418 113 1 in reference to the destruction of iniquity.
The addressee is warned to protect his "holy spirit" during his lifetime
through upright living and sound decisions (e.g., 4Q416 2 ii 6; 4Q416 iii

---

[160] Collins, *Jewish Wisdom*, 183.

[161] Elgvin, "Priestly Sages?"; idem, "Early Essene Eschatology," 143. See also
Caquot, "Les textes de sagesse de Qoumrân," 22; Collins, *Daniel*, 393-98; idem, "The
Afterlife," 122-27; Nickelsburg, *1 Enoch*, 529-30. Cf. Luke 20:36; *2 Bar.* 51:10; *2 En.*
22:9-10; *T. Levi* 14:3.

[162] Collins, "The Eschatologizing of Wisdom"; Tigchelaar, *To Increase Learning*, 215.
See further Puech, "Apports des textes apocalyptiques et sapientiels." The Pesher on the
Periods also promises life with the angels for the righteous without using star imagery: "In
accordance with God's compassion ... he approaches some from among the sons of the
world so that they can be considered with him in the com[munity of] [the g]ods to be a
holy congregation in the position of eternal life and in the lot with his holy ones" (4Q181
1 ii 3-4). See *DJDJ* 5, 79-80; Strugnell, "Notes en marge," 254-55.

[163] 4Q418 55 11 distinguishes angels from humans by pointing out that humans die:
"Are they (angels) like man because he is sluggish, or like a human because he dies?"

[164] The rationale for this translation is given in section 3.3 of Chapter 4.

5-7).[165] But his body will die. Having preserved his spirit in life, upon death it simply continues living. His spirit enjoys eternal life with the angels as a reward for ethical conduct in life. That the life of the spirit endures after the death of the body explains why 4QInstruction never appeals to resurrection.[166] This also suggests that it is not necessary for the spirits of the righteous to wait for the theophanic "period of wrath" at the end of history to receive their eschatological rewards. They are also available after death. 4QInstruction displays a degree of ambiguity regarding the fate of the righteous.[167]

The promise of eternal life with the angels is boldly formulated in 4Q416 2 iii 11-12: "Praise his name constantly because he has raised your head out of poverty. With the nobles (נדיבים) he has placed you, and he has given you authority over an inheritance of glory."[168] The נדיבים have been understood as actual elites of Palestinian society.[169] This is unlikely, however, because the addressee is so often considered materially poor. I propose that the word נדיבים refers to the angels, although admittedly the term is not used in this way elsewhere. It is a symbolic depiction of the addressee's numerous affinities with the angels. This is similar to the usage of the term in CD 6:2-11, which interprets the phrase "nobles of the people" (נדיבי העם) of Numbers 21:18 to refer to the elect. The image of being placed with the nobles is apparently an adaptation of 1 Samuel 2:8: "He (God) raises up the poor (דל) from the dust; he lifts the needy from the ash heap, to make them sit with princes (נדיבים) and inherit a throne of glory (כסא כבוד נחלם)" (cf. Ps 113:7-8).[170] In this verse from Hannah's prayer, the elevation of the poor demonstrates the might of God and his control over the human realm.

---

[165] See section 3.5.1 of Chapter 4. Also note that in 4Q418 127 the addressee has oppressed people (line 4) and is depicted as craving death: "Your soul will desire that you will enter in its (Sheol's) gates and that [the earth] bury and co[ver you] ..." (line 2). See *DJD 34*, 357; Tigchelaar, *To Increase Learning*, 104.

[166] See section 2.1 of this chapter.

[167] A similar ambiguity is in Ben Sira. He uses eschatological language to describe death. See, for example, 5:7-8, "Do not delay to turn back to the Lord ... for suddenly the wrath of the Lord will come upon you, and at the time of punishment you will perish"; 18:24, "Think of his wrath on the day of death, and of the moment of vengeance when he turns away his face."

[168] Note the parallel in Eph 2:6: "(God has) raised us up with him and seated us with him in the heavenly places in Christ Jesus."

[169] John Strugnell, personal communication. The issue is left unresolved in *DJD 34*, 118. In Ben Sira 13:9 the word refers to a person of high social standing.

[170] *DJD 34*, 118.

He brings life and death and is the cause of one's wealth or poverty (1 Sam 2:6-7).[171]

Theologically the situation is similar in 4Q416 2 iii 11-12. The salvation of the addressee is construed as a form of wealth (cf. 4Q418 126 ii 7).[172] In this sense it is fitting to describe the angels as "nobles." The eschatological rewards of the addressee are in contrast to the poverty he endures in this world. His possession of an "inheritance of glory" in life anticipates the eternal life he will enjoy with the angels after death. By affirming that he is already seated with the nobles, 4QInstruction blurs the distinction between the addressee's regular life and the one he will enjoy after death with the angels. Elsewhere the composition stresses this distinction. 4Q417 2 i 10-12 contrasts mourning with "eternal joy." This suggests that 4Q416 2 iii 11-12 should not be interpreted literally. It does not put forward a claim as extreme as the Self-Glorification Hymn, whose speaker declares "I am counted among the gods" (4Q491c 1 7).[173] 4Q416 2 iii 11-12 reflects the deterministic idea that the addressee's elect status and his eschatological rewards are a feature of God's plan. But the composition also emphasizes that attaining life with the angels after death is predicated on righteous conduct. In a sense, as Elgvin has suggested, 4QInstruction can be said to have a form of "realized eschatology," in that the addressee realizes his destiny through proper behavior.[174] But the addressee has the potential not to act in this way (4Q417 1 ii 12). The full attainment of "eternal joy" is reached after he has led a righteous life.

The afterlife of the righteous according to 4QInstruction invites comparison with the eschatological rewards promised to the Dead Sea sect.[175]

---

[171] Compare 4Q427 (4QHª) 7 ii 8-9: "(God) brings down the arrogant spirit without even a remnant; and he raises the poor from the dust to ... up to the clouds he extols him in stature and together with the gods in the congregation of the community" (cf. 1QH 26:1-2).

[172] See section 3.3 of Chapter 4.

[173] This text was formerly known as 4Q491 11. For an overview of this fragment, see Collins, *Apocalypticism in the Dead Sea Scrolls*, 143-47. See also Maurice Baillet, *Qumrân Grotte 4.III (4Q482-4Q520)* (DJD 7; Oxford: Clarendon, 1982), 27; Martin G. Abegg, Jr., "Who Ascended to Heaven? 4Q491, 4Q427, and the Teacher of Righteousness," in *Eschatology, Messianism, and the Dead Sea Scrolls* (ed. C.A. Evans and P.W. Flint; Grand Rapids: Eerdmans, 1997), 62-70; Esther Eshel, "4Q471b: A Self-Glorification Hymn," *Revue de Qumran* 17 (1996): 175-202; Michael O. Wise, "מי כמוני באלים: A Study of 4Q491c, 4Q471b, 4Q427 7 and 1QHª 25:35-26:10," *Dead Sea Discoveries* 7 (2000): 173-219.

[174] Elgvin, "Early Essene Eschatology," 144.

[175] The promise of an angelic afterlife is common in late Second Temple literature. Daniel 12:3 and *1 Enoch* 104:2-6 have been mentioned above. Note also *T. Ash.* 6:5, "if anyone is peaceful with joy he comes to know the angel of peace and enters eternal life"; *T. Mos.* 10:9, "And God will raise you to the heights. Yea, he will fix you firmly in the

Members of the Qumran community expected to attain eternal life. The hymns of the Hodayot describe the sectarians' eternal life with the angels. The theophanic judgment scene in 1QH 11 is prefaced by the speaker giving thanks for his salvation:

> I thank you, Lord, because you saved my life from the pit (שחת) (cf. 1QS 11:13), and from the Sheol of Abaddon have lifted me up to an everlasting height, so that I can walk on a boundless plain ... The depraved spirit you have purified from great offence so that he can take a place with the host of the holy ones, and can enter in communion with the congregation of the sons of heaven (ll. 19-22).

1QH 19:10-13 declares that the "sons of your favor" (בני רצונכה; l. 9) has in a sense already joined the angels:

> For the sake of your glory, you have purified man from offence, so that he can make himself holy for you ... to become united wi[th] the sons of your truth and in the lot with your holy ones (בגורל עם קדושיכה), to raise the

---

heaven of the stars"; *4 Ezra* 7:97, "it is shown them how their face is to shine like the sun, and how they are to be made like the light of the stars, being incorruptible from then on." Cf. Phil 2:15; Matt 13:43; Mark 12:25; *T. Levi* 4:3. See James H. Charlesworth, "The Portrayal of the Righteous as an Angel," in *Ideal Figures in Ancient Judaism: Profiles and Paradigms* (ed. J.J. Collins and G.W.E. Nickelsburg; SBLSCS 12; Chico: Scholars Press, 1980), 135-51; Nickelsburg, *Resurrection, Immortality, and Eternal Life*, 161, 171-76; Collins, *Daniel*, 393; Davidson, *Angels at Qumran*, 316-17; Elgvin, "An Analysis of 4QInstruction," 113-17.

In terms of the afterlife of the righteous, there are several similarities between the Wisdom of Solomon and 4QInstruction. In the Wisdom of Solomon the righteous will have eternal life with the angels. This suggests some reliance on Palestinian traditions. In a manner similar to 4Q418 81 4-5, the wicked ask about the righteous: "Why have they been numbered among the children of God? And why is their lot among the saints?" (Wis 5:5). It also associates the afterlife with the stars: "In the time of their visitation they will shine forth, and will run like sparks through the stubble" (3:7). Compare Col 1:12: "the Father, who has enabled you to share in the inheritance of the saints in the light" (cf. Eph 1:18). Like 4QInstruction, the Wisdom of Solomon never predicates this afterlife on any form of resurrection, utilizing instead the Hellenistic idea of the immortality of the soul. Both the Wisdom of Solomon and 4QInstruction associate the eschatological rewards of the righteous with a restoration of God's original relationship with humankind. 4QInstruction depicts the addressee as similar to Adam, as examined in section 2.4.1 of Chapter 3. The Wisdom of Solomon, by claiming that God did not make death (1:13), underscores the view that God originally created humankind to have eternal life, which it promises to the righteous. Death was not an original feature of the created order. It is attributed to the devil's pollution of this system (2:23-24). It should also be noted that a minority position holds that the Wisdom of Solomon was written originally in Hebrew. See John J. Collins, "The Mysteries of God: The Category 'Mystery' in Apocalyptic and Sapiential Writings," in *Wisdom and Apocalypticism in the Dead Sea Scrolls and in the Biblical Tradition*; idem, *Jewish Wisdom*, 185-87; Shannon Burkes, "Wisdom and Apocalypticism in the Wisdom of Solomon," *Harvard Theological Review* 95 (2002): 21-44; Chrysostome Larcher, *Le Livre de la Sagesse ou la Sagesse de Salomon* (3 vols.; Paris: Gabalda, 1983), 1.285; David Winston, *The Wisdom of Solomon* (AB 43; New York: Doubleday, 1979), 17.

worms of the dead from the dust, to an ever[lasting] community (cf. 4Q427 7 ii 9).[176]

The relationship of the righteous to the angelic world asserted in the Hodayot represents a bolder claim than that of 4QInstruction. The Hodayot can be said to have a 'realized angelology', since the elect are depicted as enjoying fellowship with the angels in the present.[177] In 4QInstruction, by contrast, full participation with the angelic world is realized after death.

The Qumran rulebooks do not associate the eternal life of the righteous with the angels as forcefully as the Hodayot. Nevertheless it is an important theme in this material. 1QS 11:7-9 declares that the elect have "an inheritance in the lot of the holy ones" and that the sectarians will be an "eternal planting throughout all future ages" (cf. 1QSb 3:25-26; 4:24-26; 1QM 12:1-5). The rulebooks also present eternal life as "the glory of Adam."[178] The Damascus Document declares that those who remain steadfast "will acquire eternal life (חיי נצח), and all the glory of Adam is for them" (CD 3:20). The Treatise on the Two Spirits promises that the righteous will be rewarded with "eternal life" (חיי נצח; cf. 4Q418 238 4) and declares that the righteous have been "chosen for an everlasting covenant and to them shall belong all the glory of Adam" (1QS 4:7, 22-23). The Hodayot associates the "glory of Adam" with long life, declaring that God has given those who serve him "all the glory of Adam [and] abundance of days" (1QH 4:15). The association of Adam with eternal life evident in the phrase the "glory of Adam" may indicate that all of humanity, as "sons of Adam," has the potential to achieve eternal life, but that only the righteous attain it. The phrase may reflect the belief that eternal life is a consequence of having knowledge of good and evil (cf. Gen 3:22).

The Qumran sectarians understood the eternal life that was promised to them in light of the angelic fellowship they purportedly possessed during their lifetimes. The writings of this group claim that its members participated in angelic life and worship. The hymns of the Hodayot are the most explicit witness to this belief among the undisputed writings of

---

[176] The phrase "to raise the worms of the dead from the dust" has been interpreted as a reference to resurrection, but it could also be a metaphorical assessment of the human condition, reflecting the Niedrigskeitsdoxologie of the composition. See Collins, *Apocalypticism in the Dead Sea Scrolls*, 121.

[177] Collins, *Apocalypticism in the Dead Sea Scrolls*, 120; Nickelsburg, *Resurrection, Immortality, and Eternal Life*, 152-54; Björn Frennesson, *"In a Common Rejoicing": Liturgical Communion with Angels in Qumran* (SSU 14; Uppsala: University of Uppsala Press, 1999). See also Fletcher-Louis, *All the Glory of Adam*, 104-12.

[178] Fletcher-Louis, *All the Glory of Adam*, 95-97; Puech, *La Croyance des Esséniens*, 2.438-39.

the Dead Sea sect. Although not all would agree that it is a product of this group, communion with the angelic world in the present is a pivotal concept of the Songs of Sabbath Sacrifice (e.g., 4Q400 2 1-8).[179] The eternal life members of the sect could attain was an extension of the holy existence they enjoyed in this world.[180] This is compatible with the continuation of the life of the addressee's spirit after death in 4QInstruction.

There are important differences between 4QInstruction and the main texts of the Dead Sea sect regarding the eschatological rewards of the righteous. The Hodayot and other writings of the Qumran community offer a fully "realized eschatology" that includes fellowship with the angels both in this world and after death. 4QInstruction does not celebrate the addressee's communion with the angels in this life. The composition does not stress that eschatological rewards are wholly attained in the present. Rather the addressee must heed instruction in order to join the angels after death. This fate is presented as a feature of God's divine plan, and in that sense the addressee already possesses an "inheritance of glory" (4Q416 2 iii 11-12). 4QInstruction has a type of "realized eschatology," but it is not as "realized" as that of the Hodayot. This suggests that the two texts did not come from the same milieu but that they are not completely unrelated. Tigchelaar has argued that 4QInstruction was used as a source by the Hodayot, particularly columns 5 and 6.[181] This is a reasonable assessment of the relationship between the two texts.[182] If 4QInstruction is considered a source of inspiration for the Hodayot, it took ideas from the wisdom text and developed them. This is compatible with the argument in section 4.5 of Chapter 2 that the Treatise on the Two Spirits used 4QInstruction as a source but developed a type of dualism that is more extreme than that of the wisdom text.

Many Second Temple texts promise the righteous eternal life with the angels. Among these texts 4QInstruction is distinguished by its use of the angels as a model for conduct in daily life (4Q418 55 8-11; 4Q418 69 ii 13-14). Acting like an angel in life results in joining them after death. This prospect was clearly an incentive for righteous conduct in the apocalyptic tradition, although texts such as Daniel 12 or *1 Enoch* 104 do not highlight this as explicitly as 4QInstruction.

---

[179] Collins, *Apocalypticism in the Dead Sea Scrolls*, 140-43.

[180] Ibid., 123.

[181] Tigchelaar, *To Increase Learning*, 206-07.

[182] This is suggested by the large number of manuscripts of 4QInstruction found at Qumran, that the wisdom text is generally dated earlier than the Hodayot, and that 4Q418 55 10 and 1QH 18:27-28 have material in common. These issues are discussed in section 3 of Chapter 6.

4QInstruction uses the motif of an angelic afterlife to fill out the eschatological consequences of its understanding of humankind. In Chapter 3 I argued that 4QInstruction discusses the "spiritual people" and the "fleshly spirit" to describe two different ways of being human. The flesh of the "fleshly spirit" will fade away, and its spirit will go down to Sheol after death. The spirit of the "spiritual people," by contrast, will rise to be with the angels after the demise of the physical body. The addressee must be like the "spiritual people" if he is to achieve the eschatological rewards that have been promised to him.

4. CONCLUSION

Eschatology is a crucial feature of 4QInstruction. It begins with a judgment scene and teaches that judgment is ordained to occur as a feature of natural order. It calls this visitation the "period of wrath" (4Q416 4 1). It represents the ordained end of the historical order, although eschatological rewards and punishments are also meted out after death. 4QInstruction teaches that history is composed of a sequence of chronological periods, as in apocalyptic texts such as Daniel 9 and the *Apocalypse of Weeks*. The periodization of history in the wisdom text, however, is less elaborate than that of the apocalypses. There are also several eschatological motifs found in apocalyptic literature that are absent in 4QInstruction, such as a final period of wickedness or messianism. Additionally, the wisdom text has no sense of eschatological urgency. These factors suggest that it was not written in a period of turmoil and upheaval.

4QInstruction's description of the final judgment is theophanic. Drawing upon archaic Israelite traditions, the composition construes judgment as a moment filled with divine power that overwhelms the natural order. Theophanic judgment is a point of similarity between 4QInstruction and *1 Enoch*. When judgment occurs the wicked will be eliminated from this world. They will die, with death depicted as Sheol with its gates wide open. 4QInstruction does not emphasize that Sheol is a place of torment. The righteous will die but this only affects their flesh. With their transient aspects removed, only that which is eternal remains. After death they enjoy eternal life with the angels. The righteous will be spared from the punishment of the final judgment and receive eschatological salvation.

The eternal life that is promised to the righteous is not guaranteed. It is obtained by upholding the standards of ethical conduct and piety that 4QInstruction imparts to them. Rather than proclaim the creation of a new earth that is much better than the present one (e.g., Rev 21:1; Isa 65:17; *1 En.* 91:16), 4QInstruction's eschatology encourages people to improve their conduct in this world. The text's apocalyptic worldview cannot be separated from its practical advice. 4QInstruction's ethical teachings are rooted in an eschatological perspective.

CHAPTER SIX

4QINSTRUCTION'S TRANSFORMATION OF WISDOM

1. INTRODUCTION

4QInstruction is a sapiential text that attests a transformation of wisdom.[1] Its author was steeped in the traditional wisdom of Israel. This is evident from the text's similarities to the Book of Proverbs. Biblical wisdom influences 4QInstruction's advice on practical topics such as debts, marriage, and social relations. The impact of the sapiential tradition on the composition is also evident in its eudemonistic ethos (e.g., 4Q418 221 3; 4Q418 81 17). Its teachings provided a better life in this world for its addressee.

Some features of 4QInstruction are alien to the biblical wisdom tradition. It frequently grounds instruction in an appeal to higher revelation through the mystery that is to be. It proclaims that God will destroy the wicked in the final judgment. 4QInstruction displays considerable interest in the angels and claims that the addressee is in their lot (4Q418 81 4-5). As I argued in the previous chapter, the text also provides him with the prospect of eternal life after death.

The worldview of 4QInstruction is well illustrated by a comparison with Ben Sira.[2] Both texts draw on traditional wisdom and incorporate it into their teaching. Ben Sira identifies the Torah as a fully sufficient source of wisdom. This allows him to disparage esoteric appeals to a higher source of revelation. 4QInstruction fits Ben Sira's description of the kind of speculation that he dismisses: "Do not meddle in matters that are beyond you, for more than you can understand has been shown you" (3:23).[3] 4QInstruction, by contrast, claims to disclose higher wisdom to the addressee. This includes the knowledge, for example, that he has

---

[1] Torleif Elgvin, "An Analysis of 4QInstruction" (diss.; Hebrew University of Jerusalem, 1997), 59-62.

[2] Daniel J. Harrington, "Two Early Jewish Approaches to Wisdom: Sirach and Qumran Sapiential Work A," *Journal for the Study of the Pseudepigrapha* 16 (1997): 25-38.

[3] R.A. Argall has observed that *1 Enoch* also accords with Ben Sira's description of the speculation of mysteries. See his *1 Enoch and Sirach* (SBLEJL 8; Atlanta: Scholars Press, 1995).

been separated from the "fleshly spirit" (4Q418 81 1-2). He can acquire eschatological wisdom through the contemplation of revealed mysteries: "[Gaze upon the mystery] that is to be, and grasp the birth-times of salvation and know who is inheriting glory and who ini[qu]ity" (4Q417 2 i 10-12). If Ben Sira can be said to merge the sapiential and covenantal traditions, 4QInstruction combines the sapiential and apocalyptic traditions.

4QInstruction has an apocalyptic worldview. Its epistemology is closer to Daniel and *1 Enoch* than Proverbs. The Qumran wisdom text invokes the mystery that is to be. This mystery reveals knowledge that would be otherwise unavailable, such as the nature of history and the beginning of creation.[4] This reflects the deterministic mindset of the composition. It portrays the flow of events and the fate of the individual as arranged by God. The text has a periodization of history, albeit one that is not as elaborate as that of the *Apocalypse of Weeks* or Daniel 9. 4QInstruction also has an eschatological horizon. It asserts that there will be a final judgment. While 4QInstruction is a wisdom text in terms of genre, many aspects of its belief system are apocalyptic.

4QInstruction's apocalyptic elements should not be separated from its practical wisdom into separate strata.[5] Material from both traditions is utilized to help the addressee acquire wisdom. Possessing wisdom denotes both the ability to have a successful and ethical life and knowledge of the divine plan guiding events. The revelation that is given to the addressee bears on his ordinary life. For example, 4Q416 2 iii 17-18 connects the mystery that is to be with a call to revere one's parents: "as he revealed to you through the mystery that is to be, honor them for the sake of your glory." 4QInstruction teaches that the revelation of God's dominion demands an ethical response.

The combination of sapiential and apocalyptic material in 4QInstruction demonstrates that the wisdom tradition, as it was passed on, could be combined with ideas and traditions that had no place in the ancient Israel in which it originally developed. 4QInstruction is an example of Jewish wisdom in the late Second Temple period. Before the discovery of the Dead Sea Scrolls, the only extant example of a Palestin-

---

[4] See sections 4.1-2 of Chapter 2.

[5] Elgvin has argued that the two should be separated from one another. See section 3.2 of Chapter 1. For more on the compatibility of wisdom and apocalypticism, see John J. Collins, "Wisdom, Apocalypticism and Generic Compatibility," in *Seers, Sibyls and Sages in Hellenistic Roman Judaism* (JSJSup 54; Leiden: Brill, 1997), 385-404; Shannon Burkes, *God, Self, and Death: The Shape of Religious Transformation in the Second Temple Period* (JSJSup 79; Leiden: Brill, 2003), 253-62. See further Florentino García Martínez, "Wisdom at Qumran: Worldly or Heavenly?" in *Wisdom and Apocalypticism in the Dead Sea Scrolls and in the Biblical Tradition* (ed. F. García Martínez; BETL 168; Leuven: Peeters-Leuven University Press, forthcoming).

ian wisdom text from this period was Ben Sira. His instruction provides practical wisdom while dismissing speculation of mysteries and visions, which are both characteristic features of apocalyptic literature. *1 Enoch* and other apocalyptic texts frequently characterize the knowledge they reveal as wisdom (e.g., *1 En.* 93:10), but they generally show minimal interest in giving advice regarding specific areas of ordinary life. The testaments combine apocalyptic and parenetic material but in terms of genre are not wisdom texts.[6] Before the Dead Sea Scrolls came to light there was scant evidence of apocalyptic elements preserved in wisdom literature.[7]

4QInstruction attests a Second Temple trajectory of the wisdom tradition that was poorly attested before the publication of the Dead Sea Scrolls. This stream of the sapiential tradition is characterized by the combination of traditional wisdom with an apocalyptic worldview. The Treatise on the Two Spirits and the Book of Mysteries are also examples of this type of wisdom.[8] The Treatise, though not modeled directly after biblical wisdom, is an instruction (cf. 1QS 3:13) that presents a dualistic and deterministic presentation of reality. It has an eschatological horizon and proclaims a time of visitation. Rewards and punishments will be meted out at that moment (1QS 4:6-14). As 4QInstruction connects the knowledge of good and evil to the mystery that is to be (4Q417 1 i 6-8), the Treatise declares that its deterministic teachings have been set before its readers "so that they know good [and evil]" (1QS 4:26). I speculated in section 4.5 of Chapter 2 that 4QInstruction might be a source for the Treatise. It seems to elaborate 4QInstruction's dualism with imagery of light and darkness and its dichotomy between "eternal joy" and the "eternal pit." The Book of Mysteries is another wisdom text with an eschatological horizon. It claims to disclose higher wisdom (e.g., 4Q299 8 6) and emphasizes eschatological judgment. Like 4QInstruction, it invokes the mystery that is to be (1Q27 1 i 2, 4). Mysteries also includes practical advice, albeit fragmentary, regarding money (1Q27 1 ii 2-6). All three texts are examples of a type of Second Temple wisdom that is characterized by influence from the apocalyptic tradition.

---

[6] John J. Collins, "Testaments," in *Jewish Writings of the Second Temple Period* (ed. M.E. Stone; CRINT 2.2; Assen/Philadelphia: Van Gorcum/Fortress, 1984), 325-55; Robert A. Kugler, *The Testaments of The Twelve Patriarchs* (Sheffield: Sheffield Academic Press, 2001).

[7] The judgment scene in Wisdom of Solomon 5 is a rare example of an apocalyptic motif in sapiential literature that was known before the emergence of the Dead Sea Scrolls. See John J. Collins, *Jewish Wisdom in the Hellenistic Age* (OTL; Louisville: Westminster John Knox, 1997), 184.

[8] A. Lange also emphasizes the similarities of these works. He argues that they have a common provenance. See section 3.1 of Chapter 1.

The main proposal regarding 4QInstruction's relationship to the apocalyptic tradition is Elgvin's claim that 4QInstruction used Enochic literature as a source.[9] There is no explicit evidence, however, of direct literary dependence. Nevertheless it is entirely possible that the author of the wisdom text developed its apocalyptic worldview in part by reading Enochic material.

2. 4QINSTRUCTION AND THE SECTARIAN QUESTION

4QInstruction is devoted to an addressee with elect status. He has access to higher wisdom through revelation and is proclaimed to be among the lot of the angels. He has been granted authority over the garden of Eden (4Q423 1 2), an assertion that presents his elect status as a restoration of the relationship God originally enjoyed with Adam.[10] The addressee's "inheritance" is superior to that which is allotted to most people (4Q416 2 iii 11-12). These claims suggest that the composition was designed for some sort of sectarian milieu.

4QInstruction generally uses the second person singular. Yet it is clear that the composition is addressed to more than one person. This is above all evident from the diversity of addressees. Some texts are addressed to a farmer, such as 4Q418 103 ii. Others give instruction to one with "manual skill" (חכמת ידים), who is some sort of artisan (4Q418 81 15).[11] The composition posits at least two separate professions, although some of its addressees could have been farmers with artisan skills. Other texts assume the addressee is a servant who works for a harsh superior (4Q416 2 ii 9-15). Some texts understand the addressee to be engaged in trade. 4Q415 2 ii 1-9 is intended for a woman. This text encourages her to honor her father-in-law as her own father.[12] There are also 4QInstruction texts that use the plural. 4Q418 55 4 employs the first person plural: "But vigilance will be in our heart [at all times] and assurance in all our ways." This group is distinguished from the foolish, also in the plural, who have "not sought after under[standing]" (l. 5). 4Q418 69 ii is addressed to two contrasting groups, the "foolish of heart" in lines 4-9 who will be destroyed at God's judgment, and the "truly chosen

---

[9] This issue is discussed in section 2.3 of Chapter 5.
[10] See section 2.4.1 of Chapter 3.
[11] See section 3.2 of Chapter 4.
[12] Daniel J. Harrington, "Ten Reasons Why the Qumran Wisdom Texts are Important," *Dead Sea Discoveries* 4 (1997), 252. Also note that 4Q415 11 gives advice to a male addressee concerning his wife.

ones" who in lines 10-15 are urged to follow the example of the angels.
4Q416 1 10 proclaims "all the sons of his truth will be accepted with
favor (ירצו)." 4Q418 81 10 also mentions a group with special status,
"the men of favor (אנשי רצון)." Line 8 of this fragment enjoins the addressee to treat with compassion "all those who keep his word." While
4QInstruction normally refers to the addressee as מבין in the singular, it
also uses the term in the plural: "God revealed to the ear of the understanding ones (מבינים) through the mystery that is to be" (4Q418 123 ii 4;
cf. 4Q415 11 5; 4Q418 221 3). Terms such as "the sons of his truth" and
"men of favor" describe a group that has elect status. The addressee
should be considered a member of this group.[13] The preference for the
singular is a rhetorical maneuver designed to engage the addressees in a
more personal and direct manner.[14]

4QInstruction's dedication to a group with elect status is analogous to
the social setting of the *Apocalypse of Weeks*. This text has a sense of
group identity in that it proclaims higher wisdom to an elect community:
"the chosen righteous from the eternal plant of righteousness will be
chosen, to whom will be given sevenfold teaching concerning his whole
creation" (*1 En.* 93:10). The *Animal Apocalypse* may have also been
intended for a specific audience (cf. 90:6-7).[15] The social setting of these
groups cannot be recovered with precision.[16] There is not enough evidence to reconstruct an Enochic movement in the manner of Boccaccini[17]
or, following Hengel, attribute Enochic texts to the Hasidim.[18]

---

[13] Also note the phrase "children of Eve" in 4Q418 126 ii 9. The context of this phrase
is too fragmentary to interpret properly. Given the association of the addressee with
Adam, the expression may be another term signifying the intended audience of the composition. Line 8 of the fragment mentions "eternal glory" and separating the "spirit of life."
Strugnell and Harrington, *DJD 34*, 352, suggest this spirit is separated from the "spirit of
darkness."

[14] Stephen Fraade has made a similar point with regard to a switch from the second
person plural to the second person singular in 4QMMT. See his "To Whom It May Concern: 4QMMT and Its Addressee(s)," *Revue de Qumran* 19 (2000), 513. The frequent use
of the first person singular in the Hodayot has also been understood in this way. See
Bonnie Kittel, *The Hymns of Qumran* (SBLDS 50; Atlanta: Scholars Press, 1981), 10-11.

[15] George W.E. Nickelsburg, *1 Enoch: A Commentary on the Book of 1 Enoch, Chapters 1-36, 81-108* (Hermeneia; Minneapolis: Fortress, 2001), 361-63.

[16] John J. Collins, *The Apocalyptic Imagination* (2nd ed.; Grand Rapids: Eerdmans,
1998 [orig. pub., 1984]), 70-79.

[17] Gabriele Boccaccini, in his *Beyond the Essene Hypothesis: The Parting of the Ways
Between Qumran and Enochic Judaism* (Grand Rapids: Eerdmans, 1998), has offered a
possible but hypothetical reconstruction of sectarian dynamics in the Second Temple
period.

[18] Martin Hengel has argued that the Hasidim mentioned in 1 Maccabees 2 should be
linked to a large number of texts, such as Daniel, the Damascus Document, the *Apocalypse of Weeks*, and the *Animal Apocalypse*. These texts are far too different to posit that

One of the more important group terms in 4QInstruction is the "spiritual people." They are opposed to the "fleshly spirit." The contrast between the two groups is compatible with the distinction between the "truly chosen ones" and the "foolish of heart." The "spiritual people" and the "fleshly spirit" are not specific segments of society. Rather they represent two contrasting ways of being human. The "spiritual people" are in the likeness of the angels (4Q417 1 i 16-17). This predisposes them to righteousness. The "fleshly spirit" does not have knowledge of good and evil (4Q417 1 i 18-19), a lack that would lead them to commit iniquities. I argued in Chapter 3 that by providing the addressee with an enigmatic account of two different kinds of people, 4QInstruction teaches him that there are two different paths he could take—a right one and a wrong one. The addressee, upon reflection of the brief account of these types of people, is to realize that he has affinity with the "spiritual people." He is distinguished from the "fleshly spirit," as are the "spiritual people." He is in the lot of the angels, a status similar to the "spiritual people" who are in the likeness of the holy ones. As the "spiritual people" have revealed knowledge through the vision of Hagu, the addressee has the mystery that is to be. The "spiritual people" represent an ideal to which the addressee is to aspire, while the "fleshly spirit" signify a way of being human that is to be avoided.

Although the addressee is predisposed to righteous behavior, being in the lot of the angels, he must nevertheless choose to live in this way. He is warned about the evil *yēṣer* (4Q417 1 ii 12). He can turn to wickedness despite his elect status. One's "inheritance" is not automatically granted. It is something allotted by God that must be earned. It requires a full knowledge of the elect status accorded to him. He should understand that it is an ordained feature of the divine framework guiding events. This knowledge is acquired through contemplation of the mystery that is to be and the provision of ways to understand his special status, such as having authority over the garden of Eden. It also requires ethical and practical instruction.

Since 4QInstruction has a sectarian mentality, the question arises if it is a product of the Qumran community. Scholarship is divided on the question. Several commentators contend that no member of the Dead Sea sect wrote 4QInstruction. Strugnell and Harrington claim that the text was used to train administrative scribes and functionaries of the royal court in the third and second centuries BCE.[19] They also suggest

---

they stem from the same group. See his *Judaism and Hellenism* (2 vols.; Philadelphia: Fortress, 1973), 1.97-99, 189.

[19] *DJD 34*, 20-21.

that its audience was comprised of priests on the basis of texts such as 4Q418 81 3. This text uses Numbers 18, a text that justifies the Aaronids' entitlements as priests, to explain the elect status of the addressee.[20] Tigchelaar argues that 4QInstruction is not a product of a school or narrow group setting but rather was addressed to society at large, giving instruction to people of all levels of society.[21] Lange has claimed, on the basis of the text's cultic elements and use of Torah, that 4QInstruction was produced by circles close to the Jerusalem Temple around the time of Jason and Menelaus (175-164 BCE).[22]

Others have argued that 4QInstruction should be considered a product of the Qumran sectarians or their direct predecessors. James Scott has claimed that 4QInstruction's use of the Korah story from Numbers 16 (4Q423 5 1) is a veiled reference to schisms within the Qumran community.[23] Geza Vermes has argued that 4QInstruction was written by the Dead Sea sect because of its similarities to texts such as the Community Rule and the Hodayot.[24] Émile Puech, while he does not explicitly affirm that 4QInstruction is a product of the Dead Sea sect, contends that the composition stems from the "même milieu culturel que les compositions esséniennes."[25] John Collins has also argued that the wisdom text comes from a setting that is similar to that of the Dead Sea sect, without affirm-

---

[20] C. Fletcher-Louis has argued that 4Q418 81 1-14 is addressed to Aaronic priests. See his *All the Glory of Adam: Liturgical Anthropology in the Dead Sea Scrolls* (STDJ 42; Leiden: Brill, 2002), 178-83.

[21] Eibert J.C. Tigchelaar, "The Addressees of 4QInstruction," in *Sapiential, Liturgical and Poetical Texts from Qumran: Proceedings of the Third Meeting of the International Organization for Qumran Studies, Oslo 1998* (ed. D. Falk et al.; STDJ 35; Leiden: Brill, 2000), 62-75; idem, *To Increase Learning for the Understanding Ones: Reading and Reconstructing the Fragmentary Early Jewish Sapiential Text 4QInstruction* (STDJ 44; Leiden: Brill, 2001), 248. Patrick Tiller has also argued that 4QInstruction is not necessarily a product of the Dead Sea sect. See his "The 'Eternal Planting' in the Dead Sea Scrolls," *Dead Sea Discoveries* 4 (1997): 312-35.

[22] Armin Lange, "In Diskussion mit dem Tempel: zur Auseinandersetzung zwischen Kohelet und weisheitlichen Kreisen am Jerusalemer Tempel," in *Qohelet in the Context of Wisdom* (ed. A. Schoors; BETL 136; Leuven: Leuven University Press/Peeters, 1998), 157. See also Jörg Frey, "Flesh and Spirit in the Palestinian Jewish Sapiential Tradition and in the Qumran Texts: An Inquiry into the Background of Pauline Usage," in *The Wisdom Texts from Qumran and the Development of Sapiential Thought* (ed. C. Hempel, A. Lange, and H. Lichtenberger; BETL 159; Leuven: Leuven University Press/Peeters, 2002), 399-400.

[23] James M. Scott, "Korah and Qumran," in *The Bible at Qumran: Text, Shape, and Interpretation* (ed. P.W. Flint; Grand Rapids: Eerdmans, 2001), 182-202.

[24] Geza Vermes, *The Complete Dead Sea Scrolls in English* (New York: Penguin, 1997), 402.

[25] See his "Apports des textes apocalyptiques et sapientiels de Qumrân à l'eschatologie du judaïsme ancien," in *Wisdom and Apocalypticism in the Dead Sea Scrolls and in the Biblical Tradition.*

ing that the composition was written by that group.[26] Torleif Elgvin considers 4QInstruction to be "pre-Essene."[27] He argues that its apocalyptic material is the product of a community that dates to the early second century BCE. 4QInstruction, he claims, circulated among the "camps" of the Essene movement throughout Palestine that are described in the Damascus Document.

4QInstruction has no red-flag markers of provenance from the Dead Sea sect. It shows no awareness of a Teacher of Righteousness or the communal structures and rituals described in the Qumran rulebooks. It uses the term יחד but never in an explicitly sectarian manner.[28] Such differences do not by themselves eliminate the possibility that 4QInstruction was written by the Qumran group. Many of these elements are also not found in the Hodayot, which many regard as a sectarian composition. Several important features of 4QInstruction are compatible with the writings of the Dead Sea sect. Like this corpus, the wisdom text claims to provide higher wisdom to the elect. It also shares with this material an eschatological horizon and the expectation of final judgment. 4QInstruction and the undisputed literature of the Qumran community have a deterministic understanding of the natural order. They both affirm that the elect enjoy a form of angelic fellowship. Priestly terms are used to describe both the intended audience of 4QInstruction, as in 4Q418 81 3, and the Qumran sectarians, who are called the "sons of Zadok" (e.g., CD 4:3).

There are indications that there is a relationship between 4QInstruction and the Qumran community. At least six manuscripts of 4QInstruction were found at the Qumran site. 1QS 11 invokes the mystery that is to be. While only 4QInstruction appeals to the vision of Hagu, the Rule of the Congregation (1QSa) and the Damascus Document

---

[26] John J. Collins, "Sectarian Consciousness in the Dead Sea Scrolls," Grand Rapids Conference on the Dead Sea Scrolls, April 2003; idem, "Wisdom, Apocalypticism and the Dead Sea Scrolls," in *Seers, Sibyls and Sages*, 376.

[27] Torleif Elgvin, "Wisdom and Apocalypticism in the Early Second Century BCE— The Evidence of 4QInstruction," in *The Dead Sea Scrolls Fifty Years After Their Discovery: Proceedings of the Jerusalem Congress, July 20-25, 1997* (ed. L.H. Schiffman, E. Tov, and J.C. VanderKam; Jerusalem: Israel Exploration Society/Shrine of the Book, Israel Museum, 2000), 246. Daryl Jefferies has argued that 4QInstruction is "extra-Qumranic" and should be situated in the "camps" mentioned in the Damascus Document. He contends that it is a product of the Qumran community on the basis of terminology common to 4QInstruction and the undisputed literature of this sect. See his *Wisdom at Qumran: A Form-Critical Analysis of the Admonitions in 4QInstruction* (Gorgias Dissertations, Near Eastern Studies 3; Piscataway: Gorgias Press, 2002), 323.

[28] Eibert J.C.Tigchelaar, "הבא ביחד in *4QInstruction (4Q418* 64 + 199 + 66 par *4Q417* 1 i 17-19) and the Height of the Columns of *4Q418*," *Revue de Qumran* 18 (1998): 589-93. This topic is discussed in section 3.4 of Chapter 4.

mention a "Book of Hagu." Even more striking, 4Q418 55 10 shares
material with 1QH 18:27-28: "... [ac]cording to their knowledge they are
glorified, each more than his neighbor."

There are important differences between 4QInstruction and the undisputed writings of the Dead Sea sect. They differ fundamentally in terms
of halakhah. 4QMMT, which provides sectarian interpretations of legal
issues, indicates the importance of halakhic concerns for the Qumran
group. This is also indicated by the Damascus Document's copious legal
material.[29] Occasionally 4QInstruction shows an interest in halakhah.
4Q418 103 ii applies the prohibition from Leviticus 19 and Deuteronomy
22 against mixing diverse things together to farming methods. 4Q416 2
iv 8-9 declares that the husband has authority over his wife's vows: "And
every oath binding on her, that she would vow a v[ow,] you will annul it
by an utterance of your mouth" (cf. CD 16:10-12).[30] This is similar to
Numbers 30:6-15. But legal concerns on the whole are not prominent in
the wisdom text. A comparison of the Damascus Document's instruction
on marriage with that of 4QInstruction aptly illustrates their different
approaches.[31] 4QInstruction associates the proper ethical attitude one
should have in marriage with poverty: "you have married a woman in
your poverty" (4Q416 2 iii 20). CD never connects marriage to poverty.
Its discussion of marriage is more halakhic. CD 5:9-11 argues that the
ban against marrying your mother's sister (cf. Lev 18:13) applies not
only to males, but also to females in relation to the brother of the father.
This stringent interpretation of biblical law has no analogue in
4QInstruction. CD 13:16-18 specifies that any group member who mar-
ries or divorces will inform the Inspector and heed his advice. No group
leader is mentioned when 4QInstruction gives advice on marriage.

4QInstruction also differs from the writings of the Dead Sea sect with
regard to cultic issues. 4Q423 3 4-5 stipulates a liturgical consecration
of the first-born: "[you shall come before your God wit]h the firstborn of
your womb and the firstborn of all [your cattle. You shall come before
you]r [God] and say: 'I consecrate [to God] everyone [who opens the
womb'] ..."[32] This seems to present participation in the Temple cult as a

---

[29] Charlotte Hempel, *The Laws of the Damascus Document: Sources, Tradition and
Redaction* (STDJ 29; Leiden: Brill, 1998). See also Lawrence H. Schiffman, *Reclaiming
the Dead Sea Scrolls* (ABRL; New York: Doubleday, 1995), 273-87.

[30] *DJD 34*, 125.

[31] See also Lawrence H. Schiffman, "Halakhic Elements in the Sapiential Texts," in
*Sapiential Perspectives: Wisdom Literature in Light of the Dead Sea Scrolls. Proceed-
ings of the Sixth International Symposium of the Orion Center, 20-22 May 2001* (ed. G.
Sterling and J.J. Collins; Leiden: Brill, forthcoming).

[32] Tigchelaar, *To Increase Learning*, 141-42, does not include several of the supplements found in the reconstruction of this text in *DJD 34*, 514.

normal activity.[33] This issue, by contrast, is contentious for the Qumran group. An interest in cultic affairs in 4QInstruction is more the exception than the rule. It offers general ethical advice without legal reflection on how exactly it is to be heeded. It frequently calls on the addressee to praise God and the angels (e.g., 4Q416 2 iii 11; 4Q418 81 11), but never in connection with observance of festal days or prescribed methods of prayer. It never adjusts its instruction to accommodate the Sabbath, unlike the Damascus Document (e.g., CD 12:4). 4QInstruction shapes conduct in a way that is closer to Proverbs than Leviticus.

In complete contrast to the main texts of the Qumran community, 4QInstruction displays minimal interest in national affairs. The group it addresses is not presented as the remnant of Israel through which restoration shall occur. The Community Rule is addressed to a group that is depicted as an interim temple "to atone for the land" while the rest of Israel is under the sway of wickedness (1QS 8:10). The Damascus Document recounts the history of the sect against the wider backdrop of biblical history.[34] This text also describes Israel as a "stray heifer" (CD 1:13) and criticizes the Pharisees, with a pun on "halakhah," as seekers of "easy interpretations" (חלקות) (1:18). 4QInstruction has no clear attestation of the word "Israel," and its intended audience is never charged with the responsibility of atoning for the land. In contrast to the Damascus Document, the wisdom text never recites the history of the group to which it is addressed, or understands this community in relation to the history of Israel. Moreover, 4QInstruction is never critical of the Pharisees. It shows no familiarity with this type of Judaism whatsoever.

Another key difference between 4QInstruction and the main texts of the Qumran community regards the status of Torah. The wisdom text bases its instruction upon the Torah but does not make it a prominent theme in its own right. It uses the Torah without invoking it as a source of authority. The Torah has a more important status for the movement associated with the Teacher of Righteousness. The Damascus Document often prooftexts scripture when describing the history of the sect. The Community Rule is directed to a group that is devoted to the recitation and interpretation of the Torah: "And in the place in which the Ten (men

---

[33] Elgvin, the official editor of 4Q423, suggests this text is an expansion of the biblical command to consecrate your firstborn (e.g., Exod 13:12-15). The Torah never mentions a liturgical ceremony that accompanies this act. See *DJD 34*, 514-15. See also his "Priestly Sages? The Milieus of Origin of 4QMysteries and 4QInstruction," in *Sapiential Perspectives: Wisdom Literature in Light of the Dead Sea Scrolls. Proceedings of the Sixth International Symposium of the Orion Center, 20-22 May 2001* (ed. G. Sterling and J.J. Collins; Leiden: Brill, forthcoming).

[34] Maxine L. Grossman, *Reading for History in the Damascus Document* (STDJ 45; Leiden: Brill, 2002).

of the Community council) assemble there should not be missing a man
to interpret the law day and night, always, one relieving another" (1QS
6:6-7). The addressee of 4QInstruction is never commanded to read the
Torah and his elect status is never explained through citation of scripture.
The Damascus Document, not 4QInstruction, cites Proverbs (CD 14:2).
The wisdom text uses Genesis 1-3 but never cites it verbatim. It turns to
these chapters to provide support for its view of humankind but draws
from it quite loosely. Aspects of the text that do not accord with its perspective, such as the ban against eating the fruit of the tree, are simply
left out. The composition does not interpret scripture in the manner of a
pesher. The status of the Torah in 4QInstruction is fundamentally different from its centrality for the Teacher movement.

4QInstruction and the main texts of the Qumran sect differ in terms of
poverty. 4QInstruction frequently uses the refrain "you are poor." I
argued in Chapter 4 that the text often considers its addressee to be materially poor. The composition uses his elect status as a basis for advice
that bears on his financial affairs. It explains, for example, that the addressee should pay off debts quickly because he should exchange his
"holy spirit for no price" (4Q416 2 ii 6). 4QInstruction thematizes poverty.

The poverty of group members is a less important theme for the Qumran sectarians. Several of their texts, most notably the Pesher on Psalm
37, occasionally portray the elect as poor. The Damascus Document
consistently shows sympathy for the poor but only once portrays the elect
as poor (19:9).[35] While the Community Rule has an interest in the financial affairs of group members (e.g., 1QS 1:11-12), it never describes
them as poor. Group members probably led a frugal lifestyle and many
could have been poor.[36] But self-identification as "poor" is less prominent than in 4QInstruction. There is no equivalent to the "you are poor"
refrain in the undisputed literature of the Dead Sea sect.

These differences suggest that 4QInstruction was not written by the
Qumran community. The text does not seem, however, completely unrelated to this group. 4QInstruction was clearly popular among the members of the Dead Sea sect, as indicated by the number of manuscripts of
the document at Qumran. It is reasonable to presume with Elgvin that
the text circulated among the "camps," since they were comprised of
people with elect status who were engaged in ordinary life. That the
mystery that is to be is found in the Community Rule (1QS 11:3-4) and

---

[35] Catherine M. Murphy, "The Disposition of Wealth in the *Damascus Document* Tradition," *Revue de Qumran* 19 (1999): 83-129; eadem, *Wealth in the Dead Sea Scrolls and
the Qumran Community* (STDJ 40; Leiden: Brill, 2002), 25-102.
[36] Ibid., 454-55.

that 1QH 18:27-28 matches 4Q418 55 10 are clear signals that 4QInstruction was used by the Qumran community.[37] In chapters 2 and 5 I argued that the wisdom text can be considered a source for both the Treatise on the Two Spirits and the Hodayot. Like *1 Enoch* and *Jubilees*, 4QInstruction is a document that influenced the Dead Sea sect.

Elgvin has argued that 4QInstruction is an "early Essene" text, written by non-priestly teachers with an Enochic, apocalyptic orientation who later merged with a Zadokite priestly group, producing the Dead Sea sect.[38] It is possible that some members of the intended audience of 4QInstruction, or their heirs, joined the Dead Sea community, bringing the wisdom text with them. The Qumran community drew upon multiple strands of Second Temple culture in the formation of their belief system. The community utilized not only the Torah, but also priestly, sapiential, and apocalyptic traditions. It is not a simple merger of 4QInstruction's group with Zadokites. There is no evidence of a direct genealogical link between the Qumran community and the intended audience of 4QInstruction. The wisdom text can be considered "pre-Essene" (or "early Essene") but this designation must be qualified. The main writings of the Qumran sect suggest that its members read 4QInstruction and borrowed ideas and specific phrases from it. Many key elements of the Dead Sea group, however, were not inspired by 4QInstruction. These include the institutional structure of the Qumran community, its legal code, posture towards the cult, management of financial affairs, and the status of the Torah. There is a relationship between 4QInstruction and the Qumran community. But it is one that is rather loose.[39]

Contra Tigchelaar, 4QInstruction is addressed to a specific group and not humankind writ large. It is unlikely the author of 4QInstruction would give advice to anyone considered to be like the "fleshly spirit." The elect status of the addressee suggests a sectarian milieu. But the nature of the group to which 4QInstruction is devoted is substantially different from the Dead Sea sect. There is no founding ideology that Israel has gone astray or disagreements over the calendar. The composition contains no reverence for a leader that is analogous to the Teacher of Righteousness. There is no indication that daily life was regulated to the

---

[37] Also note that it is claimed in *DJD 34*, 59, that 4Q271 (4QD^f) 3 7-9 quotes from 4Q415 11, which requires a man betrothing his daughter to tell her husband about her "blemishes." See further Joseph M. Baumgarten, *Qumran Cave 4.XIII: The Damascus Document (4Q266-273)* (DJD 18; Oxford: Clarendon, 1996), 175-77; Murphy, *Wealth in the Dead Sea Scrolls*, 195.

[38] Elgvin, "Early Essene Eschatology," 164.

[39] Collins, "Sectarian Consciousness."

extent stipulated in the Qumran rulebooks. The Dead Sea sect is not a
good model for understanding the group behind 4QInstruction.

3. THE DATE AND SOCIAL SETTING OF 4QINSTRUCTION

Unlike Ben Sira, the author of 4QInstruction gives no biographical information about himself. But he is a clearly a scribe educated in the
traditional wisdom of Israel. Also in contrast to Ben Sira, the author of
the Qumran wisdom text probably did not come from an upper-class
background. His instruction never reflects an aristocratic setting. Along
with elect status, poverty is a key indicator for assessing the group to
which 4QInstruction is addressed. Many members earned a living
through common professions of the day. The addressee is often considered a farmer and/or artisan. His means of sustenance were tenuous and
he was often forced to borrow. 4QInstruction encourages its addressee to
treat creditors with honesty and to maintain good standing with them
(4Q417 2 i 21-24). This advice demonstrates his need for credit. Some
instruction is designed for one who is destitute (4Q417 2 i 20). The addressee could easily be at the mercy of his work supervisor.
4QInstruction recommends that the addressee become "like an eldest
son" to his superior, although he may hate his boss (4Q416 2 ii 13-14).
His precarious financial situation accords with the nature of the economy
of the latter half of the Second Temple period. There was no middle
class in the modern sense and most people were subsistence farmers.
The typical addressee of 4QInstruction is a commoner who struggles to
make ends meet.

The poverty of the addressee helps determine the nature of the intended audience of 4QInstruction. The claim that 4QInstruction provided training for royal scribes that was put forward in *DJD 34* should be
rejected. Such diplomatic training would presume that it was designed
for young aristocratic men. Ben Sira trains his students how to conduct
themselves at formal banquets and in the presence of the powerful (e.g.,
13:9; 32:9). This is also the case with some of the sayings in the Book of
Proverbs (e.g., 23:1-3). 4QInstruction provides no etiquette for high
society. Some of its addressees were women (4Q415 2 ii 1-9). This by
itself suggests that the group was not composed of aristocratic scribes.[40]

---

[40] If Ben Sira is any indication, aristocratic scribal circles at the time exhibited animos-
ity towards women (e.g., 25:16-26; 42:14). By contrast, there is no misogyny in
4QInstruction. See Daniel J. Harrington, "Wisdom at Qumran," in *The Community of the*

4QInstruction's women also call into question the claim made in *DJD 34* that the text is addressed to priests. That festal days, halakhic observance, or ritual purity are not major themes also casts doubt on this view.[41] It is safer to conclude that 4QInstruction uses priestly traditions to describe the addressee's elect status.

The financial difficulties that the addressees of 4QInstruction endured in their day-to-day lives provide insight into the rationale for the group's formation.[42] There is no evidence that its members were brought together by theological disputes or by oppression from foreign rulers. Many of the problems facing the addressees relate to their economic circumstances. Unlike the *Epistle of Enoch,* 4QInstruction does not seethe with disdain for the wealthy (e.g., *1 En.* 94:6-11; cf. 4Q417 2 i 2). There was no need for such anger because the wisdom text provides the larger setting in which the addressee's ordinary life, with all of its difficulties, should be understood. Material wealth, like one's physical body, will pass away (4Q418 103 ii 9). The addressee was given the prospect of eternal life after death. 4QInstruction describes this reward as joining the "nobles," a term that likely refers to the angels, and being lifted out of poverty (4Q416 2 iii 11-12; cf. 4Q418 126 ii 7).[43] The addressee is not angry at the wealthy because he is promised eschatological rewards that are more valuable than anything possessed by the rich. Reassured that he has an "inheritance of glory," he can maintain a state of reverence and proper ethical comportment while enduring financial hardship—even when dealing with creditors and harsh superiors. 4QInstruction offers its intended audience a way to find dignity and respect amidst degrading circumstances.

4QInstruction is older than the Community Rule and the Hodayot since it can reasonably be posited as a source for these texts. This excludes dating 4QInstruction to the first century BCE. A third century dating is not impossible, but unlikely. The influence of the apocalyptic tradition on 4QInstruction, and its apparent familiarity with a version of *1 Enoch,* suggest the wisdom text was written at a time when the apocalyptic tradition enjoyed a degree of popularity and was no longer in its early stages of development. This suggests a second century date for 4QInstruction. While the earliest Jewish apocalypses are Enochic compositions that date to the third century (the *Book of the Watchers* and the

---

Renewed Covenant: The Notre Dame Symposium on the Dead Sea Scrolls (ed. E. Ulrich and J. VanderKam; Notre Dame: University of Notre Dame Press, 1994), 148.

[41] Tigchelaar, *To Increase Learning,* 235.

[42] Matthew J. Goff, "The Mystery of Creation in 4QInstruction," *Dead Sea Discoveries* 10 (2003), 23-24.

[43] See section 3 of Chapter 5.

Astronomical Book), most Jewish texts that have an apocalyptic world-view were written in the second and first centuries BCE.

If 4QInstruction can be situated in the second century, the question arises as to when in this century it was written. Elgvin has suggested that 4QInstruction should be dated to the first quarter of the second century BCE.[44] The document shows no knowledge of the Maccabean crisis that took place during the reign of Antiochus IV Epiphanes (175-164 BCE). The text displays no familiarity with Seleucids, and shows little interest in Gentiles in general. 4QInstruction lacks eschatological urgency and many of the tropes that typically accompany end-time scenarios, such as Belial, the "end of days," or messianism. This suggests that it was not written in a period of political upheaval. These factors support a pre-Maccabean dating. An early second century dating is a valid possibility.

However determining a specific date within the second century is difficult. 4QInstruction's lack of eschatological tropes that are common in other second century texts does not necessitate an early second century dating. It could simply attest the diversity of eschatological views in the century. Relatively early second century texts such as Daniel or the *Animal Apocalypse* are extremely eschatological. A text from the early part of the century can have many of the eschatological tropes not found in 4QInstruction. The wisdom text never describes political persecution at the hands of Gentile rulers in the manner of the Book of Daniel. But 4QInstruction often assumes that the addressee is suffering from economic distress. His difficult situation may simply be a matter of the inherent inequity of an agrarian economy. But the economic problems of the addressee's day could have been exacerbated by political instability. That 4QInstruction does not mention the Maccabean conflict does not necessarily mean it is pre-Maccabean. It could have been written late in the century when the Maccabean persecution was no longer a pressing issue. The omission may be an issue of genre. Most wisdom texts do not discuss contemporary historical events.

Since 4QInstruction can be understood as a source for the Treatise and the Hodayot, the history of the Dead Sea sect bears on the question of dating the wisdom text. It is beyond the scope of the present work to discuss fully the provenance of the Qumran community. The standard consensus holds that the Teacher of Righteousness was active in the mid-second century and that the community at Qumran flourished in the first century.[45] Such a view favors placing 4QInstruction, as a source docu-

---

[44] Elgvin, "Priestly Sages?"

[45] For standard treatments of the subject, see Frank Moore Cross, *The Ancient Library of Qumran* (3rd ed.; Minneapolis: Fortress Press, 1995 [orig. pub., 1958]); Schiffman, *Reclaiming the Dead Sea Scrolls*, 65-95.

ment for the Qumran sect, earlier in the second century rather than later but does not necessarily exclude a later date. Recent scholarship has re-evaluated the traditional consensus regarding the date of the Teacher of Righteousness and his community at Qumran. Jodi Magness, on the basis of the pottery and coins found at the site, concludes "it is reasonable to date the initial establishment of the sectarian settlement to the first half of the first century B.C.E. (that is, some time between 100-50 B.C.E.)."[46] According to the method of dating the paleography of the scrolls established by Frank Moore Cross, many of the texts of the Dead Sea sect date to the first century.[47] Michael Wise has argued that both the Teacher and the *floruit* of his movement should be dated to the first century BCE.[48] A later date for the Teacher and the origin of his movement allows for a later dating of 4QInstruction. The time of the Teacher and the movement associated with him are major debates that are far from settled. For the present it will suffice to say that the use of 4QInstruction as a source for the Community Rule and the Hodayot suggests a second century date for the wisdom text. While several factors suggest an early second century dating, the evidence for this position is not rock solid. A safer conclusion is that 4QInstruction was written in the second century BCE.

A second century dating places 4QInstruction in the same era as Ben Sira. His instruction can be safely dated to around 180 BCE as established by its prologue, which was written by his grandson in 132 BCE. These two texts draw on traditional wisdom and give instruction on topics such as filial piety and finances. Both emphasize the importance of praising God and claim to provide wisdom. They ask similar questions but often approach them with different perspectives and frequently provide different answers. Ben Sira's wisdom is more Torah centered, whereas 4QInstruction claims to disclose higher wisdom. The two texts come from different segments of society. As examined in section 3.1 of Chapter 4, Ben Sira advises his students to lend even though the borrowers might not repay the loan, while 4QInstruction warns the addressee to be kind to creditors or else they will be wary to lend (4Q417 2 i 22-24; Sir 29:5-7). The former generally assumes that his addressee is rich, the latter that he is poor. In terms of worldview and social location, Ben Sira

---

[46] Jodi Magness, *The Archaeology of Qumran and the Dead Sea Scrolls* (Grand Rapids: Eerdmans, 2002), 65.

[47] Frank Moore Cross, "The Development of the Jewish Scripts," in *The Bible and the Ancient Near East* (ed. G.E. Wright; New York: Doubleday, 1961), 133-202.

[48] Michael O. Wise, "Dating the Teacher of Righteousness and the *Floruit* of His Movement," *Journal of Biblical Literature* 122 (2003): 53-87.

and 4QInstruction provide an impression of the diversity of Jewish wisdom in the second century BCE.

The editors of *DJD 34* have claimed that 4QInstruction is a "missing link" in the transmission of the sapiential tradition in the Second Temple period.[49] Since 4QInstruction's wisdom is not combined with national traditions, Strugnell and Harrington consider the text representative of a stage of Jewish wisdom that predates Ben Sira. This assessment provides no explanation of 4QInstruction's apocalyptic worldview. There are many crucial aspects of the composition, such as its eschatological horizon and appeals to revelation, that are similar to beliefs commonly found in the apocalyptic literature of the late Second Temple period. This is not the case with Proverbs and Ben Sira. But, in a sense, 4QInstruction can be understood as a "missing link." The composition sheds light on a poorly attested trajectory of Second Temple wisdom. 4QInstruction is the best example available of a Second Temple wisdom text that has an apocalyptic worldview. The Book of Mysteries and the Treatise on the Two Spirits indicate that this is a sapiential development broader than 4QInstruction itself.

---

[49] *DJD 34*, 31.

BIBLIOGRAPHY

Abegg, Martin G., Jr., "Who Ascended to Heaven? 4Q491, 4Q427, and the Teacher of Right-eousness," in *Eschatology, Messianism, and the Dead Sea Scrolls* (ed. C.A. Evans and P.W. Flint; Grand Rapids: Eerdmans, 1997), 61-73.

Aitken, James K., "Apocalyptic, Revelation and Early Jewish Wisdom Literature," in *New Heaven and New Earth: Prophecy and the Millennium. Essays in honour of Anthony Gelston* (ed. P.J. Harland and C.T.R. Hayward; VTSup 77; Leiden: Brill, 1999), 181-93.

Albertz, Rainer, *A History of Israelite Religion in the Old Testament Period* (OTL; 2 vols.; Louisville: Westminster/John Knox, 1994).

Allegro, John M., *Qumrân Cave 4.I (4Q158-4Q186)* (DJDJ 5; Oxford: Clarendon, 1968).

Alster, B., *The Instructions of Suruppak: A Sumerian Proverb Collection* (Copenhagen: Akademisk Forlag, 1974).

——, *Proverbs of Ancient Sumer: The World's Earliest Proverb Collections* (2 vols.; Be-thesda: CDL Press, 1997).

Andersen, Francis I., *Habakkuk* (AB 25; New York: Doubleday, 2001).

Anderson, Bernhard W., *Contours of Old Testament Theology* (Minneapolis: Fortress, 1999).

Applebaum, S., "Judaea as a Roman Province: The Countryside as a Political and Economic Factor," in *Aufstieg und Niedergang der romischen Welt* II.8 (Berlin/New York: de Gruyter, 1977), 355-96.

Argall, Randal A., *1 Enoch and Sirach* (SBLEJL 8; Atlanta: Scholars Press, 1995).

——, "Competing Wisdoms: *1 Enoch* and *Sirach*," *Henoch* 24 (2002): 169-78 (*The Origins of Enochic Judaism: Proceedings of the First Enoch Seminar. University of Michigan, Sesto Fiorentino, Italy, June 19-23, 2001* [ed. G. Boccaccini]).

Asher, Jeffrey R., *Polarity and Change in 1 Corinthians 15: A Study of Metaphysics, Rhetoric, and Resurrection* (HUT 42; Tübingen: Mohr-Siebeck, 2000).

——, "Σπείρεται: Paul's Anthropogenic Metaphor in 1 Corinthians 15:42-44," *Journal of Biblical Literature* 120 (2001): 101-22.

Attridge, Harold, et al., *Qumran Cave 4.VIII: Parabiblical Texts, Part 1* (DJD 13; Oxford: Clarendon, 1994).

Aune, David, *Revelation 1-5* (WBC 52a; Dallas: Word Books, 1997).

Baillet, Maurice, *Qumrân Grotte 4.III (4Q482-4Q520)* (DJD 7; Oxford: Clarendon, 1982).

Barthélemy, D., and J.T. Milik, *Qumran Cave 1* (DJD 1; Oxford: Clarendon, 1955).

Barthélemy, D., and O. Rickenbacher, *Konkordanz zum hebräischen Sirach* (Göttingen: Van-denhoeck & Ruprecht, 1973).

Bartholomae, Christian, *Altiranisches Wörterbuch* (Strassburg: Verlag von Karl J. Trübner, 1904).

Basser, H.W., "The Rabbinic Attempt to Democratize Salvation and Revelation," *Sciences Religieuses/Studies in Religion* 12 (1983): 27-33.

Baumann, Gerlinde, *Die Weisheitsgestalt in Proverbien 1-9* (FAT 16; Tübingen: J.C.B. Mohr [Paul Siebeck], 1996).

Baumgarten, Joseph M., *Qumran Cave 4.XIII: The Damascus Document (4Q266-273)* (DJD 18; Oxford: Clarendon, 1996).

Bedenbender, Andreas, *Der Gott der Welt Tritt auf den Sinai: Entstehung, Entwicklung und Funktionsweise der Frühjüdischen Apokalyptik* (ANTZ 8; Berlin: Institut Kirche und Judentum, 2000).

——, "Jewish Apocalypticism: A Child of Mantic Wisdom?" *Henoch* 24 (2002): 189-96 (*The Origins of Enochic Judaism: Proceedings of the First Enoch Seminar. University of Michigan, Sesto Fiorentino, Italy, June 19-23, 2001* [ed. G. Boccaccini]).

Beentjes, P.C., *The Book of Ben Sira in Hebrew* (VTSup 68; Leiden: Brill, 1997).

Benoit, P., J.T. Milik, and R. de Vaux, *Les Grottes de Murabba'at* (DJD 2; Oxford: Clarendon, 1961).

Bernstein, Moshe, "Contours of Genesis Interpretation at Qumran: Contents, Context, and Nomenclature," in *Studies in Ancient Midrash* (ed. J.L. Kugel; Cambridge: Harvard University Center for Jewish Studies, 2001), 57-85.

Beyerle, Stefan, "Und dann werden die Zeichen der Wahrheit erscheinen ..." (Habilitationsschrift; Rheinischen Friedrich-Wilhelms-Universität, 2001).

Bickerman, Elias J., *The Jews in the Greek Age* (Cambridge: Harvard University Press, 1988).

Black, Matthew, ed., *Apocalypsis Henochi Graeci in Pseudepigrapha Veteris Testamenti* (PVTG 3; Leiden: Brill, 1970).

Blenkinsopp, Joseph, *A History of Prophecy in Israel* (2nd ed.; Louisville: Westminster John Knox, 1996 [orig. pub., 1983]).

——, *Isaiah 1-39* (AB 19; New York: Doubleday, 2000).

——, *Wisdom and Law in the Old Testament: The Ordering of Life in Israel and Early Judaism* (Oxford: Oxford University Press, 1995).

Boccaccini, Gabriele, *Beyond the Essene Hypothesis: The Parting of the Ways Between Qumran and Enochic Judaism* (Grand Rapids: Eerdmans, 1998).

Bockmuehl, Markus, *Revelation and Mystery in Ancient Judaism and Pauline Christianity* (Grand Rapids: Eerdmans, 1990).

Bonner, Campbell, ed., *The Last Chapters of Enoch in Greek* (Darmstadt: Wissenschaftliche Buchgesellschaft, 1968).

Boström, Lennart, *The God of the Sages: The Portrayal of God in the Book of Proverbs* (Stockholm: Almqvist & Wiksell, 1990).

Böttrich, Christfried, "Früjüdische Weisheitstraditionen im slavischen Henochbuch und in Qumran," in *The Wisdom Texts from Qumran and the Development of Sapiential Thought* (ed. C. Hempel, A. Lange, and H. Lichtenberger; BETL 159; Leuven: Leuven University Press/Peeters, 2002), 297-321.

Boyarin, Daniel, *A Radical Jew: Paul and the Politics of Identity* (Berkeley: University of California Press, 1994).

Bremmer, Jan N., *The Rise and Fall of the Afterlife: The 1995 Read-Tuckwell Lectures at the University of Bristol* (London/New York: Routledge, 2002).

Brin, Gershon, "Studies in 4Q424, fragment 3," *Vetus Testamentum* 46 (1996): 271-95.

——, "Studies in 4Q424, fragments 1-2," *Revue de Qumran* 18 (1997): 21-42.

Brooke, George J., "Biblical Interpretation in the Wisdom Texts from Qumran," in *The Wisdom Texts from Qumran and the Development of Sapiential Thought* (ed. C. Hempel, A. Lange, and H. Lichtenberger; BETL 159; Leuven: Leuven University Press/Peeters, 2002), 201-20.

Brooke, George J., et al., *Qumran Cave 4.XVII: Parabiblical Texts, Part 3* (DJD 22; Oxford: Clarendon, 1996).

Brown, Raymond E., *The Semitic Background of the Term "Mystery" in the New Testament* (Biblical Series 21; Philadelphia: Fortress Press, 1968).

Brownlee, William H., *The Midrash Pesher of Habakkuk* (SBLMS 24; Missoula: Scholars Press, 1979).

Buchanan, George Wesley, "The Old Testament Meaning of the Knowledge of Good and Evil," *Journal of Biblical Literature* 75 (1956): 114-20.

Buckley, Michael J., *At the Origins of Modern Atheism* (New Haven/London: Yale University Press, 1987).

Burkes, Shannon, *God, Self, and Death: The Shape of Religious Transformation in the Second Temple Period* (JSJSup 79; Leiden: Brill, 2003).

——, "Wisdom and Apocalypticism in the Wisdom of Solomon," *Harvard Theological Review* 95 (2002): 21-44.

Calduch-Benages, Núria, "God, Creator of All (Sir 43:27-33)," in *Ben Sira's God: Proceedings of the International Ben Sira Conference, Durham, Ushaw College 2001* (ed. R. Egger-Wenzel; BZAW 321; Berlin/New York: de Gruyter, 2002), 79-100.

Callaway, Phillip, "Remarks on Some Sapiential Texts from Qumran," *The Qumran Chronicle* 8 (1998): 121-27.

Callender, Dexter E., Jr., *Adam in Myth and History: Ancient Israelite Perspectives on the Primal Human* (HSS 48; Winona Lake: Eisenbrauns, 2000).

Caquot, André, "Les textes de sagesse de Qoumrân (Aperçu préliminaire)," *Revue d'histoire et de philosophie religieuses* 76 (1996): 1-34.

Cathcart, Kevin J., "Numbers 24:17 in Ancient Translations and Interpretations," in *The Interpretation of the Bible: The International Symposium in Slovenia* (ed. J. Krasovec; JSOTSup 289; Sheffield: Sheffield Academic Press, 1998), 511-20.

Charles, R.H., *The Book of Enoch* (Oxford: Clarendon, 1912).

Charlesworth, James H., ed., *The Old Testament Pseudepigrapha* (2 vols.; New York: Doubleday, 1983).

———, "The Portrayal of the Righteous as an Angel," in *Ideal Figures in Ancient Judaism: Profiles and Paradigms* (ed. J.J. Collins and G.W.E. Nickelsburg; SBLSCS 12; Chico: Scholars Press, 1980), 135-51.

Chazon, Esther, "The Creation and Fall of Adam in the Dead Sea Scrolls," in *The Book of Genesis in Jewish and Oriental Christian Interpretation: A Collection of Essays* (ed. J. Frishman and L. van Rompay; Leuven: Peeters, 1997), 13-24.

Clifford, Richard, *Proverbs* (OTL; Louisville: Westminster John Knox, 1999).

Cohen, Jeremy, *"Be Fertile and Increase, Fill the Earth and Master It": The Ancient and Medieval Career of a Biblical Text* (Ithaca: Cornell University Press, 1989).

Cohn, Norman, *Cosmos, Chaos, and the World to Come: The Ancient Roots of Apocalyptic Faith* (New Haven/London: Yale University Press, 1993).

Collins, John J., "The Afterlife in Apocalyptic Literature," in *Judaism in Late Antiquity. Part 4: Death, Life-After-Death, Resurrection and the World-to-Come in the Judaisms of Late Antiquity* (ed. J. Neusner and A.J. Avery-Peck; Leiden: Brill, 2000), 119-38.

———, *The Apocalyptic Imagination* (2nd ed.; Grand Rapids: Eerdmans, 1998 [orig. pub., 1984]).

———, *Apocalypticism in the Dead Sea Scrolls* (London/New York: Routledge, 1997).

———, *Between Athens and Jerusalem* (2nd ed.; Grand Rapids/Livonia: Eerdmans/Dove, 2000 [orig. pub., 1983]).

———, *Daniel* (Hermeneia; Minneapolis: Fortress, 1993).

———, "The Eschatologizing of Wisdom in the Dead Sea Scrolls," in *Sapiential Perspectives: Wisdom Literature in Light of the Dead Sea Scrolls. Proceedings of the Sixth International Symposium of the Orion Center, 20-22 May 2001* (ed. G. Sterling and J.J. Collins; Leiden: Brill, forthcoming).

———, "The Expectation of the End in the Dead Sea Scrolls," in *Eschatology, Messianism, and the Dead Sea Scrolls* (ed. C.A. Evans and P.W. Flint; Grand Rapids: Eerdmans, 1997), 74-90.

———, *Jewish Wisdom in the Hellenistic Age* (OTL; Louisville: Westminster John Knox, 1997).

———, "In the Likeness of the Holy Ones: The Creation of Humankind in a Wisdom Text from Qumran," in *The Provo International Conference on the Dead Sea Scrolls* (ed. D.W. Parry and E. Ulrich; STDJ 30; Leiden: Brill, 1999), 609-19.

———, "The Meaning of 'the End' in the Book of Daniel," in *Of Scribes and Scrolls: Studies on the Hebrew Bible, Intertestamental Judaism, and Christian Origins* (ed. H.W. Attridge et al.; Lanham: University Press of America, 1990), 91-98.

———, "The Mysteries of God: The Category 'Mystery' in Apocalyptic and Sapiential Writings," in *Wisdom and Apocalypticism in the Dead Sea Scrolls and in the Biblical Tradition* (ed. F. García Martínez; BETL 168; Leuven: Peeters-Leuven University Press, forthcoming).

———, "The Sage in Apocalyptic and Pseudepigraphic Literature," in *The Sage in Israel and the Ancient Near East* (ed. J.G. Gammie and L.G. Perdue; Winona Lake: Eisenbrauns, 1990), 343-54.

———, *The Scepter and the Star: The Messiahs of the Dead Sea Scrolls and Other Ancient Literature* (ABRL; New York: Doubleday, 1995).

———, "Sectarian Consciousness in the Dead Sea Scrolls," Grand Rapids Conference on the Dead Sea Scrolls, April 2003.

———, *Seers, Sibyls and Sages in Hellenistic Roman Judaism* (JSJSup 54; Leiden: Brill, 1997).

———, "Testaments," in *Jewish Writings of the Second Temple Period* (ed. M.E. Stone; CRINT 2.2; Assen/Philadelphia: Van Gorcum/Fortress, 1984), 325-55.

———, "Wisdom Reconsidered, in Light of the Scrolls," *Dead Sea Discoveries* 4 (1997): 265-81.

Cook, Stephen L., *Prophecy and Apocalypticism* (Minneapolis: Fortress, 1995).

Cotton, H.M., and A. Yardeni, *Aramaic, Hebrew, and Greek Documentary Texts from Nahal Hever and Other Sites* (DJD 27; Oxford: Clarendon, 1997).

Coughenour, Robert, "The Wisdom Stance of Enoch's Redactor," *Journal for the Study of Judaism* 13 (1982): 47-55.

Crawford, S.W., "Lady Wisdom and Dame Folly at Qumran," *Dead Sea Discoveries* 5 (1998): 355-66.

Crenshaw, James, *Education in Ancient Israel* (ABRL; New York: Doubleday, 1998).

———, *Old Testament Wisdom: An Introduction* (Atlanta: John Knox Press, 1981).

———, ed., *Theodicy in the Old Testament* (Philadelphia: Fortress, 1983).

———, "Wisdom and Authority: Sapiential Rhetoric and its Warrants," in *Congress Volume: Vienna, 1980* (VTSup 32; Leiden: Brill, 1981), 10-29.

Cross, Frank Moore, *The Ancient Library of Qumran* (3rd ed.; Minneapolis: Fortress Press, 1995 [orig. pub., 1958]).

———, *Canaanite Myth and Hebrew Epic* (Cambridge: Harvard University Press, 1997 [orig. pub., 1973]).

———, "The Development of the Jewish Scripts," in *The Bible and the Ancient Near East* (ed. G.E. Wright; New York: Doubleday, 1961), 133-202.

Dalley, Stephanie, *Myths from Mesopotamia* (Oxford: Oxford University Press, 1989).

Davidson, Maxwell J., *Angels at Qumran: A Comparative Study of 1 Enoch 1-36, 72-108 and Sectarian Writings from Qumran* (JSPSup 11; Sheffield: Sheffield Academic Press, 1992).

Davies, W.D., "'Knowledge' in the Dead Sea Scrolls and Matthew 11:25-30," *Harvard Theological Review* 46 (1953): 113-39.

Davila, James R., *Liturgical Works* (ECDSS 6; Grand Rapids: Eerdmans, 2000).

Davis, Ellen F., *Proverbs, Ecclesiastes, and the Song of Songs* (Louisville: Westminster John Knox, 2000).

Delcor, M., *Les Hymnes de Qumran (Hodayot)* (Paris: Letouzey et Ané, 1962).

Denis, Albert-Marie, *Les Thèmes de connaissance dans le document de Damas* (Studia Hellenistica 15; Louvain: Publications universitaires de Louvain, 1967).

Di Lella, Alexander, and Patrick W. Skehan, *The Wisdom of Ben Sira* (AB 39; New York: Doubleday, 1987).

Dimant, Devorah, "Men as Angels: The Self-Image of the Qumran Community," in *Religion and Politics in the Ancient Near East* (ed. A. Berlin; Bethesda: University Press of Maryland, 1996), 93-103.

———, "Noah in Early Jewish Literature," in *Biblical Figures Outside the Bible* (ed. M.E. Stone and T.A. Bergen; Harrisburg: Trinity Press International, 1998), 123-50.

———, "The Qumran Manuscripts: Contents and Significance," in *Time to Prepare a Way in the Wilderness* (ed. D. Dimant and L.H. Schiffman; STDJ 16; Leiden: Brill, 1995), 23-58.

———, "Qumran Sectarian Literature," in *Jewish Writings of the Second Temple Period* (ed. M.E. Stone; CRINT 2.2; Assen/Philadelphia: Van Gorcum/Fortress, 1984), 483-548.

Dochhorn, J., "'Sie wird dir nicht ihre Kraft geben'—Adam, Kain und der Ackerbau in 4Q423 2₃ und Apc Mos 24," in *The Wisdom Texts from Qumran and the Development of Sapiential Thought* (ed. C. Hempel, A. Lange, and H. Lichtenberger; BETL 159; Leuven: Leuven University Press/Peeters, 2002), 351-64.

Dunn, James D.G., "Biblical Concepts of Revelation," in *Divine Revelation* (ed. P. Avis; Grand Rapids/Cambridge: Eerdmans, 1997), 1-22.

———, *The Theology of Paul the Apostle* (Grand Rapids: Eerdmans, 1998).

Dupont-Sommer, A., *The Essene Writings from Qumran* (trans. G. Vermes; Cleveland: Meridian, 1962).

Eisenman, Robert, and Michael Wise, *The Dead Sea Scrolls Uncovered* (New York: Barnes and Noble, 1992).

Elgvin, Torleif, "Admonition Texts from Cave 4," in *Methods of Investigation of the Dead Sea Scrolls and the Khirbet Qumran Site: Present Realities and Future Prospects* (ed. M.O. Wise et al.; Annals of the New York Academy of Sciences 722; New York: New York Academy of Sciences, 1994), 179-96.

——, "An Analysis of 4QInstruction" (diss.; Hebrew University of Jerusalem, 1997).

——, "Early Essene Eschatology: Judgment and Salvation according to Sapiential Work A," in *Current Research and Technological Development on the Dead Sea Scrolls: Conference on the Texts from the Judean Desert, Jerusalem, 30 April 1995* (ed. D.W. Parry and S.D. Ricks; STDJ 20; Leiden: Brill, 1996), 126-65.

——, "The Mystery to Come: Early Essene Theology of Revelation," in *Qumran between the Old and New Testaments* (ed. F.H. Cryer and T.L. Thompson; JSOTSup 290; Sheffield: Sheffield Academic Press, 1998), 113-50.

——, "Priestly Sages? The Milieus of Origin of 4QMysteries and 4QInstruction," in *Sapiential Perspectives: Wisdom Literature in Light of the Dead Sea Scrolls. Proceedings of the Sixth International Symposium of the Orion Center, 20-22 May 2001* (ed. G. Sterling and J.J. Collins; Leiden: Brill, forthcoming).

——, "The Reconstruction of Sapiential Work A," *Revue de Qumran* 16 (1995): 559-80.

——, "'To Master His Own Vessel': 1 Thess 4:4 in Light of New Qumran Evidence," *New Testament Studies* 43 (1997): 604-19.

——, "Wisdom and Apocalypticism in the Early Second Century BCE—The Evidence of 4QInstruction," in *The Dead Sea Scrolls Fifty Years After Their Discovery: Proceedings of the Jerusalem Congress, July 20-25, 1997* (ed. L.H. Schiffman, E. Tov, and J.C. VanderKam; Jerusalem: Israel Exploration Society/Shrine of the Book, Israel Museum, 2000), 226-47.

——, "Wisdom, Revelation, and Eschatology in an Early Essene Writing," in *Society of Biblical Literature Seminar Papers 1995* (SBLSP 34; Atlanta: Scholars Press, 1995), 440-63.

——, "Wisdom With and Without Apocalyptic," in *Sapiential, Liturgical and Poetical Texts from Qumran: Proceedings of the Third Meeting of the International Organization for Qumran Studies, Oslo 1998* (ed. D. Falk et al.; STDJ 35; Leiden: Brill, 2000), 15-38.

Elgvin, Torleif, et al., *Qumran Cave 4.XV: Sapiential Texts, Part 1* (DJD 20; Oxford: Clarendon, 1997).

Emetan, Aturpati-i, *The Wisdom of the Sasanian Sages (Denkard VI)* (trans. S. Shaked; Boulder: Westview Press, 1979).

Engberg-Pedersen, Troels, ed., *Paul Beyond the Judaism/Hellenism Divide* (Louisville: Westminster John Knox, 2001).

Eshel, Esther, "4Q471b: A Self-Glorification Hymn," *Revue de Qumran* 17 (1996): 175-202.

Eshel, Esther, et al., *Qumran Cave 4.VI: Poetical and Liturgical Texts, Part 1* (DJD 11; Oxford: Clarendon, 1998).

Evans, Craig A., ed., *The Interpretation of Scripture in Early Judaism and Christianity: Studies in Language and Tradition* (JSPSup 33; Sheffield: Sheffield Academic Press, 2000).

Farmer, William R., "The Economic Basis of the Qumran Community," *Theologische Zeitschrift* 11 (1955): 295-308.

Feldman, Louis H., *Flavius Josephus: Translation and Commentary. Volume 3: Judean Antiquities 1-4* (Leiden: Brill, 2000).

Fensham, F. Charles, "Widow, Orphan, and the Poor in Ancient Near Eastern Legal and Wisdom Literature," *Journal of Near Eastern Studies* 21 (1962): 129-39.

Fiensy, David A., *The Social History of Palestine in the Herodian Period: The Land is Mine* (Lewiston/Queenston/Lampeter: The Edwin Mellen Press, 1991).

Fishbane, Michael, *Biblical Interpretation in Ancient Israel* (Oxford: Clarendon, 1985).

——, "From Scribalism to Rabbinism: Perspectives on the Emergence of Classical Judaism," in *The Sage in Israel and the Ancient Near East* (ed. J.G. Gammie and L.G. Perdue; Winona Lake: Eisenbrauns, 1990), 439-56.

——, "The Well of Living Water: A Biblical Motif and its Ancient Transformations," in *Sha'arei Talmon: Studies in the Bible, Qumran, and the Ancient Near East presented to Shemaryahu Talmon* (ed. M. Fishbane and E. Tov; Winona Lake: Eisenbrauns, 1992), 3-16.

Fitzmyer, Joseph A., *The Genesis Apocryphon of Qumran Cave 1: A Commentary* (2nd ed.; BibOr 18a; Rome: Biblical Institute Press, 1971).

——, *The Semitic Background of the New Testament* (Grand Rapids/Livonia: Eerdmans/Dove, 1997).

Fletcher-Louis, Crispin H.T., *All the Glory of Adam: Liturgical Anthropology in the Dead Sea Scrolls* (STDJ 42; Leiden: Brill, 2002).
——, "Some Reflections on Angelomorphic Humanity Texts among the Dead Sea Scrolls," *Dead Sea Discoveries* 7 (2000): 292-312.
Flusser, D., "The Four Empires in the Fourth Sibyl and in the Book of Daniel," *Israel Oriental Studies* 2 (1972): 148-75.
Fontaine, Carol R., "Wisdom in Proverbs," in *In Search of Wisdom: Essays in Memory of John G. Gammie* (ed. L.G. Perdue et al.; Louisville: Westminster/John Knox, 1993), 99-114.
Fox, Michael V., *Proverbs 1-9* (AB 18a; New York: Doubleday, 2000).
Fraade, Steven D., *Enosh and His Generation: Pre-Israelite Hero and History in Postbiblical Interpretation* (SBLMS 30; Chico: Scholars Press, 1984).
——, "To Whom It May Concern: 4QMMT and Its Addressee(s)," *Revue de Qumran* 19 (2000): 507-26.
Frankfort, H., ed., *The Intellectual Adventure of Ancient Man* (Chicago: University of Chicago Press, 1977 [orig. pub., 1946]).
Frennesson, Björn, *"In a Common Rejoicing": Liturgical Communion with Angels in Qumran* (SSU 14; Uppsala: University of Uppsala Press, 1999).
Frey, Jörg, "Flesh and Spirit in the Palestinian Jewish Sapiential Tradition and in the Qumran Texts: An Inquiry into the Background of Pauline Usage," in *The Wisdom Texts from Qumran and the Development of Sapiential Thought* (ed. C. Hempel, A. Lange, and H. Lichtenberger; BETL 159; Leuven: Leuven University Press/Peeters, 2002), 367-404.
——, "The Notion of 'Flesh' in 4QInstruction and the Background of Pauline Usage," in *Sapiential, Liturgical and Poetical Texts from Qumran: Proceedings of the Third Meeting of the International Organization for Qumran Studies, Oslo 1998* (ed. D. Falk et al.; STDJ 35; Leiden: Brill, 2000), 197-226.
——, "Die paulinische Antithese von 'Fleisch' und 'Geist' und die palästinisch-jüdische Weisheitstradition," *Zeitschrift für die neutestamentliche Wissenschaft* 90 (1999): 45-77.
Fujita, S., "The Metaphor of Plant in Jewish Literature in the Intertestamental Period," *Journal for the Study of Judaism* 7 (1976): 30-45.
Galling, K., *Die Krise der Aufklärung in Israel* (Mainzer Universitätsreden 19; Mainz: Verlag der Johannes Gutenberg-Buchhandlung, 1952).
Gammie, John G., "From Prudentialism to Apocalypticism: The Houses of the Sages amid the Varying Forms of Wisdom," in *The Sage in Israel and the Ancient Near East* (ed. J.G. Gammie and L.G. Perdue; Winona Lake: Eisenbrauns, 1990), 479-97.
——, "Spatial and Ethical Dualism in Jewish Wisdom and Apocalyptic Literature," *Journal of Biblical Literature* 93 (1974): 356-85.
García Martínez, Florentino, *The Dead Sea Scrolls Translated* (trans. W.G.E. Watson; 2nd ed.; Leiden/Grand Rapids: Brill/Eerdmans, 1996).
——, *Qumran and Apocalyptic* (STDJ 9; Leiden: Brill, 1992).
——, "Wisdom at Qumran: Worldly or Heavenly?" in *Wisdom and Apocalypticism in the Dead Sea Scrolls and in the Biblical Tradition* (ed. F. García Martínez; BETL 168; Leuven: Peeters-Leuven University Press, forthcoming).
García Martínez, Florentino, and Eibert J.C. Tigchelaar, *The Dead Sea Scrolls Study Edition* (2 vols.; Leiden: Brill, 1997-98).
García Martínez, Florentino, et al., *Qumran Cave 11.II (11Q2-18, 11Q20-31)* (DJD 23; Oxford: Clarendon, 1998).
Giese, Ronald L., Jr., "Compassion for the Lowly in Septuagint Proverbs," *Journal for the Study of the Pseudepigrapha* 11 (1993): 109-17.
Gilbert, Maurice, "Wisdom of the Poor: Ben Sira 10,19-11,6," in *The Book of Ben Sira in Modern Research: Proceedings of the First International Ben Sira Conference, 28-31 July 1996, Soesterberg, Netherlands* (ed. P.C. Beentjes; BZAW 255; Berlin/New York: Walter de Gruyter, 1997), 153-69.
Ginzberg, Louis, *The Legends of the Jews* (7 vols.; Philadelphia: Jewish Publication Society of America, 1961 [orig. pub., 1909]).
——, *An Unknown Jewish Sect* (New York: Ktav, 1976 [orig. pub., 1922]).
Goff, Matthew J., "The Mystery of Creation in 4QInstruction," *Dead Sea Discoveries* 10 (2003): 1-24.

——, "The Worldly and Heavenly Wisdom of 4QInstruction" (diss.; University of Chicago, 2002).

Golb, Norman, *Who Wrote the Dead Sea Scrolls?* (New York: Scribner, 1995).

Goldin, Judah, *The Fathers According to Rabbi Nathan* (YJS 10; New York/London: Yale University Press, 1983 [orig. pub., 1955]).

Goldstein, Jonathan A., *1 Maccabees* (AB 41; Garden City: Doubleday, 1976).

Goodman, Martin, "The First Jewish Revolt: Social Conflict and the Problem of Debt," *Journal of Jewish Studies* 33 (1982): 419-28.

——, *The Ruling Class of Judaea: The Origins of the Jewish Revolt, A.D. 66-70* (Cambridge: Cambridge University Press, 1987).

Gordis, Robert, "The Knowledge of Good and Evil in the Old Testament and the Qumran Scrolls," *Journal of Biblical Literature* 76 (1957): 122-38.

Grelot, Pierre, "L'eschatologie des Esséniens et le livre d'Hénoch," *Revue de Qumran* 1 (1958): 113-31.

——, "La géographie mythique d'Hénoch et ses sources orientales," *Revue Biblique* 65 (1958): 33-69.

Grindheim, Sigurd, "Wisdom for the Perfect: Paul's Challenge to the Corinthian Church (1 Corinthians 2:6-16)," *Journal of Biblical Literature* 121 (2002): 689-709.

Grossman, Maxine L., *Reading for History in the Damascus Document* (STDJ 45; Leiden: Brill, 2002).

Hahn, I., "Die Eigentumsverhältnisse der Qumransekte," *Wissenschaftliche Zeitschrift* 12 (1963): 263-72.

Hanson, Paul D., *The Dawn of Apocalyptic* (Philadelphia: Fortress, 1979 [orig. pub., 1975]).

——, "Rebellion in Heaven: Azazel and Euhemeristic Heroes in 1 Enoch 6-11," *Journal of Biblical Literature* 96 (1977): 195-233.

Harrington, Daniel J., "The Qumran Sapiential Texts in the Context of Biblical and Second Temple Literature," in *The Dead Sea Scrolls Fifty Years After Their Discovery: Proceedings of the Jerusalem Congress, July 20-25, 1997* (ed. L.H. Schiffman, E. Tov, and J.C. VanderKam; Jerusalem: Israel Exploration Society/Shrine of the Book, Israel Museum, 2000), 256-62.

——, "The Raz Nihyeh in a Qumran Wisdom Text (1Q26, 4Q415-418, 423)," *Revue de Qumran* 17 (1996): 549-53.

——, "Ten Reasons Why the Qumran Wisdom Texts are Important," *Dead Sea Discoveries* 4 (1997): 245-55.

——, "Two Early Jewish Approaches to Wisdom: Sirach and Qumran Sapiential Work A," *Journal for the Study of the Pseudepigrapha* 16 (1997): 25-38.

——, "Wisdom and Apocalyptic in 4QInstruction and 4 Ezra," in *Wisdom and Apocalypticism in the Dead Sea Scrolls and in the Biblical Tradition* (ed. F. García Martínez; BETL 168; Leuven: Peeters-Leuven University Press, forthcoming).

——, "Wisdom at Qumran," in *The Community of the Renewed Covenant: The Notre Dame Symposium on the Dead Sea Scrolls* (ed. E. Ulrich and J. VanderKam; Notre Dame: University of Notre Dame Press, 1994), 137-53.

——, *Wisdom Texts from Qumran* (London: Routledge, 1996).

Harrington, Daniel J., and John Strugnell, "Qumran Cave 4 Texts: A New Publication," *Journal of Biblical Literature* 112 (1993): 491-99.

Hartman, L., *Asking for a Meaning: A Study of 1 Enoch 1-5* (Lund: Gleerup, 1979).

Hayes, Christine, "Intermarriage and Impurity in Ancient Jewish Sources," *Harvard Theological Review* 92 (1999): 3-36.

Hempel, Charlotte, *The Laws of the Damascus Document: Sources, Tradition and Redaction* (STDJ 29; Leiden: Brill, 1998).

——, "The Qumran Sapiential Texts and the Rule Books," in *The Wisdom Texts from Qumran and the Development of Sapiential Thought* (ed. C. Hempel, A. Lange, and H. Lichtenberger; BETL 159; Leuven: Leuven University Press/Peeters, 2002), 277-95.

Hengel, Martin, *Judaism and Hellenism* (2 vols.; Philadelphia: Fortress, 1973).

——, *The Zealots* (Edinburgh: T. & T. Clark, 1989 [orig. pub., 1961]).

Hill, Andrew, *Malachi* (AB 25D; New York: Doubleday, 1998).

Himmelfarb, Martha, *Ascent to Heaven in Jewish and Christian Apocalypses* (New York/Oxford: Oxford University Press, 1993).
Holm-Nielsen, Svend, *Hodayot: Psalms from Qumran* (Aarhus: Universitetsforlaget, 1960).
Hölscher, Gustav, "Die Entstehung des Buches Daniel," *Theologische Studien und Kritiken* 92 (1919): 113-38.
Horgan, Maurya P., *Pesharim: Qumran Interpretations of Biblical Books* (CBQMS 8; Washington, D.C.: Catholic Biblical Association, 1979).
Horsely, Richard, *Bandits, Prophets, and Messiahs: Popular Movements in the Time of Jesus* (2nd ed.; Harrisburg: Trinity Press International, 1999 [orig. pub., 1985]).
Horst, Pieter van der, *The Sentences of Pseudo-Phocylides* (Leiden: Brill, 1978).
Hultgård, Anders, "Persian Apocalypticism," in *The Encyclopedia of Apocalypticism* (ed. J.J. Collins, B. McGinn, and S. Stein; 3 vols.; New York/London: Continuum, 1998), 1.39-84.
Hurtado, Larry W., *One God, One Lord: Early Christian Devotion and Ancient Jewish Monotheism* (2nd ed.; Edinburgh: T. & T. Clark, 1998 [orig. pub., 1988]).
Hutter, M., "Abaddon," in *Dictionary of Deities and Demons in the Bible* (2nd ed.; ed. K. van der Toorn et al.; Leiden: Brill, 1999)
Ibba, Giovanni, "Il 'Libro dei Misteri' (1Q27, f.1): testo escatologico," *Henoch* 21 (1999): 73-84.
Jefferies, Daryl, "Wisdom at Qumran: A Form-Critical Analysis of the Admonitions in 4QInstruction" (diss.; University of Wisconsin-Madison, 2001).
——, *Wisdom at Qumran: A Form-Critical Analysis of the Admonitions in 4QInstruction* (Gorgias Dissertations, Near Eastern Studies 3; Piscataway: Gorgias Press, 2002).
Jeremias, Jörg, *Theophanie: Die Geschichte einer alttestamentlichen Gattung* (Neukirchen-Vluyn: Neukirchener Verlag, 1965).
Jewett, Robert, *Paul's Anthropological Terms: A Study of their Use in Conflict Settings* (AGJU 10; Leiden: Brill, 1971).
Johnson, Elizabeth E., *The Function of Apocalyptic and Wisdom Traditions in Romans 9-11* (SBLDS 109; Atlanta: Scholars Press, 1989).
Kampen, John, "The Diverse Aspects of Wisdom at Qumran," in *The Dead Sea Scrolls after Fifty Years: A Comprehensive Assessment* (2 vols.; ed. P.W. Flint and J.C. VanderKam; Leiden: Brill, 1998), 1.211-43.
Kandler, Hans-Joachim, "Die Bedeutung der Armut im Schriftum von Chirbet Qumran," *Judaica* 13 (1957): 193-209.
Keck, L.E., "The Poor among the Saints in Jewish Christianity and Qumran," *Zeitschrift für die Neutestamentliche Wissenschaft* 57 (1966): 54-78.
Kittel, Bonnie, *The Hymns of Qumran* (SBLDS 50; Atlanta: Scholars Press, 1981).
Klausner, J., "The Economy of Judea in the Period of the Second Temple," in *The Herodian Period* (ed. M. Avi-Yonah; New Brunswick: Rutgers University Press, 1975), 179-205.
Klijn, A.F.J., *Seth in Jewish, Christian and Gnostic Literature* (NovTSup 46; Leiden: Brill, 1977).
Kloppenborg, John S., *The Formation of Q* (Harrisburg: Trinity Press International, 1999 [orig. pub., 1987]).
Knibb, Michael, "The Book of Enoch in the Light of the Qumran Wisdom Literature," in *Wisdom and Apocalypticism in the Dead Sea Scrolls and in the Biblical Tradition* (ed. F. García Martínez; BETL 168; Leuven: Peeters-Leuven University Press, forthcoming).
——, "Enoch Literature and Wisdom Literature," *Henoch* 24 (2002): 197-203 (*The Origins of Enochic Judaism: Proceedings of the First Enoch Seminar. University of Michigan, Sesto Fiorentino, Italy, June 19-23, 2001* [ed. G. Boccaccini]).
——, *The Ethiopic Book of Enoch* (2 vols.; Oxford: Clarendon, 1978).
Kobelski, Paul J., *Melchizedek and Melchiresa'* (CBQMS 10; Washington, D.C.: Catholic Biblical Association, 1981).
Koch, Klaus, "Gibt es ein Vergeltungsdogma im Alten Testament?" *Zeitschrift für Theologie und Kirche* 52 (1955): 1-42.
——, *The Rediscovery of Apocalyptic* (Naperville: Allenson, 1972).
Koester, Helmut, *Ancient Christian Gospels* (Harrisburg: Trinity Press International, 1990).

Kreissig, H., "Die landwirtschaftliche Situation in Palästina vor dem judäischen Krieg," *Acta Antiqua* 17 (1969): 223-54.

Küchler, Max, *Frühjüdische Weisheitstraditionen* (OBO 26; Freiburg: Universitätsverlag, 1979).

Kugel, James L., *The Bible As It Was* (Cambridge: Harvard University Press, 1997).

———, "Some Instances of Biblical Interpretation in the Hymns and Wisdom Writings of Qumran," in *Studies in Ancient Midrash* (ed. J.L. Kugel; Cambridge: Harvard University Center for Jewish Studies, 2001), 155-69.

Kugler, Robert A., *The Testaments of The Twelve Patriarchs* (Sheffield: Sheffield Academic Press, 2001).

Kuhn, Heinz-Wolfgang, "The Wisdom Passage in 1 Corinthians 2:6-16 between Qumran and Proto-Gnosticism," in *Sapiential, Liturgical and Poetical Texts from Qumran: Proceedings of the Third Meeting of the International Organization for Qumran Studies, Oslo 1998* (ed. D. Falk et al.; STDJ 35; Leiden: Brill, 2000), 240-53.

Kuhn, Karl Georg, ed., *Konkordanz zu den Qumrantexten* (Göttingen: Vandenhoeck & Ruprecht, 1960).

Kuntz, J.K., *The Self-Revelation of God* (Philadelphia: Westminster, 1967).

Lambert, W.G., *Babylonian Wisdom Literature* (Winona Lake: Eisenbrauns, 1996 [orig. pub., 1963]).

Lange, Armin, "The Determination of Fate by the Oracle of the Lot in the Dead Sea Scrolls, the Hebrew Bible and Ancient Mesopotamian Literature," in *Sapiential, Liturgical and Poetical Texts from Qumran: Proceedings of the Third Meeting of the International Organization for Qumran Studies, Oslo 1998* (ed. D. Falk et al.; STDJ 35; Leiden: Brill, 2000), 39-48.

———, "In Diskussion mit dem Tempel: zur Auseinandersetzung zwischen Kohelet und weisheitlichen Kreisen am Jerusalemer Tempel," in *Qohelet in the Context of Wisdom* (ed. A. Schoors; BETL 136; Leuven: Leuven University Press/Peeters, 1998), 113-60.

———, "Die Endgestalt des protomasoretischen Psalters und die Toraweisheit," in *Der Psalter in Judentum und Christentum* (ed. E. Zenger; Herders Biblische Studien 18; Freiburg: Herder, 1998), 101-36.

———, "Eschatological Wisdom in the Book of Qohelet and the Dead Sea Scrolls," in *The Dead Sea Scrolls Fifty Years After Their Discovery: Proceedings of the Jerusalem Congress, July 20-25, 1997* (ed. L.H. Schiffman, E. Tov, and J.C. VanderKam; Jerusalem: Israel Exploration Society/Shrine of the Book, Israel Museum, 2000), 817-24.

———, "Kognitives *lqh* in Sap A, im Tenak und Sir," *Zeitschrift für Althebraistik* 9 (1996): 190-95.

———, *Weisheit und Prädestination: Weisheitliche Urordnung und Prädestination in den Textfunden von Qumran* (STDJ 18; Leiden: Brill, 1995).

———, "Die Weisheitstexte aus Qumran: Eine Einleitung," in *The Wisdom Texts from Qumran and the Development of Sapiential Thought* (ed. C. Hempel, A. Lange, and H. Lichtenberger; BETL 159; Leuven: Leuven University Press/Peeters, 2002), 3-30.

———, "Wisdom and Predestination in the Dead Sea Scrolls," *Dead Sea Discoveries* 2 (1995): 340-54.

Larcher, Chrysostome, *Le Livre de la Sagesse ou la Sagesse de Salomon* (3 vols.; Paris: Gabalda, 1983).

Larsen, Kasper Bro, "Visdom og apokalyptik i Musar leMevin (1Q/4QInstruction) [Wisdom and Apocalyptic in Musar leMevin (1Q/4QInstruction)]," *Dansk Teologisk Tidsskrift* 65 (2002): 1-14.

Lebram, Jürgen Christian, "Die Theologie der späten Chokma und häretisches Judentum," *Zeitschrift für die alttestamentliche Wissenschaft* 77 (1965): 202-11.

Leeuwen, Raymond C. van, "Scribal Wisdom and a Biblical Proverb at Qumran," *Dead Sea Discoveries* 4 (1997): 255-65.

———, "Wealth and Poverty: System and Contradiction in Proverbs," *Hebrew Studies* 33 (1992): 25-36.

Lehmann, Manfred R., "Ben Sira and the Qumran Literature," *Revue de Qumran* 3 (1961): 103-16.

——, "Jewish Wisdom Formulae: Ben Sira, the Dead Sea Scrolls, and Pirke Avot," in *Proceedings of the Eleventh World Congress of Jewish Studies, Jerusalem, June 22-29, 1993, Division A: The Bible and the World* (Jerusalem: The World Union of Jewish Studies, 1994), 159-62.

Levenson, Jon D., *Creation and the Persistence of Evil: The Jewish Drama of Divine Omnipotence* (Princeton: Princeton University Press, 1988).

——, *The Death and Resurrection of the Beloved Son* (New Haven: Yale University Press, 1993).

——, "The Sources of Torah: Psalm 119 and the Modes of Revelation in Second Temple Judaism," in *Ancient Israelite Religion: Essays in Honor of Frank Moore Cross* (ed. P.D. Miller et al.; Philadelphia: Fortress, 1987), 559-74.

Levine, Baruch, *Numbers 1-20* (AB 4A; New York: Doubleday, 1993).

Levison, J.R., *Portraits of Adam in Early Judaism from Sirach to 2 Baruch* (Sheffield: JSOT, 1988).

Lichtenberger, H., "Eine weisheitliche Mahnrede in den Qumranfunden (4Q185)," in *Qumrân: sa piété, sa théologie et son milieu* (ed. M. Delcor; BETL 46; Paris: Duculot, 1978), 151-62.

——, "Der Weisheitstext 4Q185—Eine neue Edition," in *The Wisdom Texts from Qumran and the Development of Sapiential Thought* (ed. C. Hempel, A. Lange, and H. Lichtenberger; BETL 159; Leuven: Leuven University Press/Peeters, 2002), 127-50.

Lichtheim, Miriam, *Ancient Egyptian Literature* (3 vols.; Berkeley: University of California Press, 1973-80).

——, *Late Egyptian Wisdom Literature in the International Context: A Study of Demotic Instructions* (OBO 52; Göttingen: Vandenhoeck & Ruprecht, 1983).

Lim, Timothy H., *Pesharim* (Sheffield: Sheffield Academic Press, 2002).

Lindenberger, James M., *The Aramaic Proverbs of Ahiqar* (Baltimore/London: Johns Hopkins University Press, 1983).

Lipscomb, W. Lowndes, and James A. Sanders, "Wisdom at Qumran," in *Israelite Wisdom: Theological and Literary Essays in Honor of Samuel Terrien* (ed. J.G. Gammie et al.; Missoula: Scholars Press, 1978), 277-85.

Lohfink, Norbert, *Lobgesänge der Armen* (Stuttgart: Verlag Katholisches Bibelwerk, 1990).

Lohse, Eduard, *Colossians and Philemon* (Hermeneia; Philadelphia: Fortress, 1971).

Löning, Karl, "Die Konfrontation des Menschen mit der Weisheit Gottes: Elemente einer sapientialen Soteriologie," in *Rettendes Wissen: Studien zum Fortgang weisheitlichen Denkens im Frühjudentum und im frühen Christentum* (ed. K. Löning; AOAT 300; Münster: Ugarit-Verlag, 2002), 1-41.

Mach, Michael, *Entwicklungsstadien des jüdischen Engelglaubens in vorrabbinischer Zeit* (TSAJ 34; Tübingen: J.C.B. Mohr [Paul Siebeck], 1992).

Magness, Jodi, *The Archaeology of Qumran and the Dead Sea Scrolls* (Grand Rapids: Eerdmans, 2002).

Marböck, J., *Weisheit im Wandel* (Bonn: Hanstein, 1971).

Margalioth, Mordecai, *Sepher Ha-Razim* (Jerusalem: Yediot Achronot, 1966).

Martin, Dale, *The Corinthian Body* (New Haven: Yale University Press, 1995).

Martin Hogan, Karina, "The Exegetical Background of the 'Ambiguity of Death' in the Wisdom of Solomon," *Journal for the Study of Judaism* 30 (1999): 1-24.

Mastin, B.A., "Wisdom and Daniel," in *Wisdom in ancient Israel: Essays in honour of J.A. Emerton* (ed. J. Day et al.; Cambridge: University of Cambridge Press, 1995), 161-69.

McKane, William, *Proverbs: A New Approach* (OTL; Philadelphia: Westminster, 1970).

Mertens, Alfred, *Das Buch Daniel im Lichte der Texte vom Toten Meer* (SBM 12; Stuttgart: Echter KBW Verlag, 1971).

Milik, J.T., *The Books of Enoch: Aramaic Fragments of Qumran Cave 4* (Oxford: Clarendon, 1976).

——, *Ten Years of Discovery in the Wilderness of Judaea* (trans. J. Strugnell; Naperville: Allenson, 1959).

Miller, J. Maxwell, "In the 'Image' and 'Likeness' of God," *Journal of Biblical Literature* 91 (1972): 289-304.

Miller, Patrick D., *The Divine Warrior in Early Israel* (Cambridge: Harvard University Press, 1973).
——, *The Religion of Ancient Israel* (Louisville: Westminster, 2000).
Morgan, Michael A., *Sepher Ha-Razim: The Book of Mysteries* (Chico: Scholars Press, 1983).
Morgenstern, Matthew, "The Meaning of בית מולדים in the Qumran Wisdom Texts," *Journal of Jewish Studies* 51 (2000): 141-44.
Mulder, Martin J., ed., *Mikra* (CRINT 2.1; Assen/Maastricht and Philadelphia: Van Gorcum/Fortress Press, 1988).
Müller, H.-P., "Mantische Weisheit und Apokalyptik," *Congress Volume: Uppsala 1971* (VTSup 22; Leiden: Brill, 1972), 268-93.
Murphy, Catherine M., "The Disposition of Wealth in the *Damascus Document* Tradition," *Revue de Qumran* 19 (1999): 83-129.
——, *Wealth in the Dead Sea Scrolls and the Qumran Community* (STDJ 40; Leiden: Brill, 2002).
Murphy, Frederick J., *Early Judaism: The Exile to the Time of Jesus* (Peabody: Hendrickson, 2002).
Murphy, Roland E., "Death and Afterlife in the Wisdom Literature," in *Judaism in Late Antiquity. Part 4: Death, Life-After-Death, Resurrection and the World-to-Come in the Judaisms of Late Antiquity* (ed. J. Neusner and A.J. Avery-Peck; Leiden: Brill, 2000), 101-16.
——, *The Tree of Life: An Exploration of Biblical Wisdom Literature* (3rd ed.; Grand Rapids: Eerdmans, 2002 [orig. pub., 1990]).
——, "Wisdom and Creation," *Journal of Biblical Literature* 104 (1985): 3-11.
——, "Wisdom and Yahwism Revisited," in *Shall Not the Judge of All the Earth Do What is Right?: Studies on the Nature of God in Tribute to James L. Crenshaw* (ed. D. Penchansky and P.L. Redditt; Winona Lake: Eisenbrauns, 2000), 191-200.
——, "*Yeṣer* in the Qumran Literature," *Biblica* 39 (1958): 334-44.
Nel, Philip, "Authority in the Wisdom Admonitions," *Zeitschrift für die alttestamentliche Wissenschaft* 93 (1981): 418-26.
——, *The Structure and Ethos of the Wisdom Admonitions in Proverbs* (BZAW 158; Berlin/New York: Walter de Gruyter, 1982).
Newman, Carey C., et al., ed., *The Jewish Roots of Christology* (JSJSup 63; Leiden: Brill, 1999).
Newsom, Carol, "The Sage in the Literature of Qumran: The Functions of the Maskil," in *The Sage in Israel and the Ancient Near East* (ed. J.G. Gammie and L.G. Perdue; Winona Lake: Eisenbrauns, 1990), 373-83.
Nickelsburg, George W.E., *1 Enoch: A Commentary on the Book of 1 Enoch, Chapters 1-36, 81-108* (Hermeneia; Minneapolis: Fortress, 2001).
——, "Apocalyptic and Myth in 1 Enoch 6-11," *Journal of Biblical Literature* 96 (1977): 383-405.
——, "Enochic Wisdom: An Alternative to the Mosaic Torah?" in *Hesed Ve-Emet: Studies in Honor of Ernest S. Frerichs* (ed. J. Magness and S. Gitin; BJS 320; Atlanta: Scholars Press, 1998), 123-32.
——, "The Epistle of Enoch and the Qumran Literature," *Journal of Jewish Studies* 33 (1982): 333-48.
——, *Jewish Literature Between the Bible and the Mishnah* (Philadelphia: Fortress, 1981).
——, *Resurrection, Immortality, and Eternal Life in Intertestamental Judaism* (HTS 26; Cambridge: Harvard University Press, 1972).
——, "Revealed Wisdom as a Criterion for Inclusion and Exclusion: From Jewish Sectarianism to Early Christianity," in *To See Ourselves as Others See Us: Christians, Jews, and 'Others' in Late Antiquity* (ed. J. Neusner and E.S. Frerichs; Chico: Scholars Press, 1985), 73-91.
——, "Revisiting the Rich and Poor in 1 Enoch 92-105 and the Gospel according to Luke," in *Society of Biblical Literature Seminar Papers 1998* (SBLSP 37; Atlanta: Scholars Press, 1998), 579-605.
——, "Riches, the Rich, and God's Judgment in 1 Enoch 92-105 and the Gospel according to Luke," *New Testament Studies* 25 (1979): 324-44.

——, "Wisdom and Apocalypticism in Early Judaism: Some Points for Discussion," in *Society of Biblical Literature Seminar Papers 1994* (SBLSP 33; Atlanta: Scholars Press, 1994), 715-32.

Niehaus, Jeffrey J., *God at Sinai: Covenant and Theophany in the Bible and the Ancient Near East* (Grand Rapids: Zondervan, 1995).

Niehr, H., "Die Weisheit des Achikar und der *musar lammebin* im Vergleich," in *The Wisdom Texts from Qumran and the Development of Sapiential Thought* (ed. C. Hempel, A. Lange, and H. Lichtenberger; BETL 159; Leuven: Leuven University Press/Peeters 2002), 173-86.

Niggemeyer, Jens-Heinrich, *Beschwörungsformeln aus dem "Buch der Geheimnisse" (Sefär ha-razim): Zur Topologie der magischen Rede* (Hildesheim/New York: Georg Olms Verlag, 1975).

Nitzan, Bilha, "The Idea of Creation and Its Implications in Qumran Literature," in *Creation in Jewish and Christian Tradition* (ed. H.G. Reventlow and Y. Hoffman; Sheffield: Sheffield Academic Press, 2002), 240-64.

Nötscher, Friedrich, *Zur theologischen Terminologie der Qumran-Texte* (BBB 10; Bonn: Peter Hanstein Verlag, 1956).

Oppenheim, A.L., *Ancient Mesopotamia* (2nd ed.; Chicago: University of Chicago Press, 1977 [orig. pub., 1964]).

Orlov, Andrei A., "The Flooded Arboretums: The Garden Traditions in the Slavonic Version of *3 Baruch* and the *Book of Giants*," *Catholic Biblical Quarterly* 65 (2003): 184-201.

Osten-Sacken, Peter von der, *Die Apokalyptik in ihrem Verhältnis zu Prophetie und Weisheit* (München: C. Kaiser, 1969).

——, *Gott und Belial* (SUNT 6; Göttingen: Vandenhoeck & Ruprecht, 1969).

Otzen, Benedikt, "Old Testament Wisdom Literature and Dualistic Thinking in Late Judaism," in *Congress Volume: Edinburgh 1974* (VTSup 28; Leiden: Brill, 1975), 146-57.

——, *Tobit and Judith* (Sheffield: Sheffield Academic Press, 2002).

Pastor, Jack, *Land and Economy in Ancient Palestine* (London/New York: Routledge, 1997).

Patrick, Dale, *The Rhetoric of Revelation in the Hebrew Bible* (Minneapolis: Fortress, 1999).

Paul, Shalom, *Amos* (Hermeneia; Minneapolis: Fortress, 1991).

——, "Heavenly Tablets and the Book of Life," *Journal of the Ancient Near Eastern Society of Columbia University* 5 (1973): 345-53.

Pearson, Birger Albert, *The Pneumatikos-Psychikos Terminology in 1 Corinthians: A Study in the Theology of the Corinthian Opponents of Paul and its Relation to Gnosticism* (SBLDS 12; Missoula: Society of Biblical Literature, 1973).

Perdue, Leo G., "Cosmology and the Social Order in the Wisdom Tradition," in *The Sage in Israel and the Ancient Near East* (ed. J.G. Gammie and L.G. Perdue; Winona Lake: Eisenbrauns, 1990), 457-78.

——, "Revelation and the Problem of the Hidden God in Second Temple Wisdom Literature," in *Shall Not the Judge of All the Earth Do What is Right?: Studies on the Nature of God in Tribute to James L. Crenshaw* (ed. D. Penchansky and P.L. Redditt; Winona Lake: Eisenbrauns, 2000), 201-22.

——, "The Vitality of Wisdom in Second Temple Judaism during the Persian Period," in *Passion, Vitality, and Foment: The Dynamics of Second Temple Judaism* (ed. L.M. Luker; Harrisburg: Trinity Press International, 2001), 119-54.

——, *Wisdom and Creation: The Theology of Wisdom Literature* (Nashville: Abingdon, 1994).

——, *Wisdom and Cult: A Critical Analysis of the Views of Cult in the Wisdom Literatures of Israel and the Ancient Near East* (SBLDS 30; Missoula: Scholars Press, 1977).

Pfann, Stephen J., et al., *Qumran Cave 4.XXVI: Cryptic Texts and Miscellanea, Part 1* (DJD 36; Oxford: Clarendon, 2000).

Pinnick, Avital, *The Orion Center Bibliography of the Dead Sea Scrolls (1995-2000)* (STDJ 41; Leiden: Brill, 2001).

Piper, Otto A., "The 'Book of Mysteries' (Qumran I 27): A Study in Eschatology," *Journal of Religion* 38 (1958): 95-106.

Pleins, J. David, "Poverty in the Social World of the Wise," *Journal for the Study of the Old Testament* 37 (1987): 61-78.

——, *The Social Visions of the Hebrew Bible: A Theological Introduction* (Louisville: Westminster John Knox, 2001).
Pritchard, J.B., *The Ancient Near East* (2 vols.; Princeton: Princeton University Press, 1958).
Puech, Émile, "Apports des textes apocalyptiques et sapientiels de Qumrân à l'eschatologie du judaïsme ancien," in *Wisdom and Apocalypticism in the Dead Sea Scrolls and in the Biblical Tradition* (ed. F. García Martínez; BETL 168; Leuven: Peeters-Leuven University Press, forthcoming).
——, *La Croyance des Esséniens en la Vie Future: Immortalité, Résurrection, Vie Éternelle?* (2 vols.; Paris: Gabalda, 1993).
——, *Qumrân Grotte 4.XVIII: Textes Hébreux (4Q521-4Q528, 4Q576-4Q579)* (DJD 25; Oxford: Clarendon, 1998).
——, *Qumrân Grotte 4.XXII: Textes Araméens, Première Partie (4Q529-549)* (DJD 31; Oxford: Clarendon, 2001).
Puech, Émile, and Annette Steudel, "Un nouveau fragment du manuscrit 4QInstruction (XQ7 = 4Q417 ou 4Q418)," *Revue de Qumran* 19 (2000): 623-27.
Qimron, Elisha, *The Hebrew of the Dead Sea Scrolls* (HSS 29; Atlanta: Scholars Press, 1986).
Qimron, Elisha, and John Strugnell, *Qumran Cave 4.V (Miqṣat Ma'aśe Ha-Torah)* (DJD 10; Oxford: Clarendon, 1994).
Rabinowitz, Isaac, "The Authorship, Audience and Date of the De Vaux Fragment of an Unknown Work," *Journal of Biblical Literature* 71 (1952): 19-32.
——, "The Qumran Author's *spr hhgw/y*," *Journal of Near Eastern Studies* 20 (1961): 109-14.
Rad, Gerhard von, *Old Testament Theology* (2 vols.; New York: Harper & Row, 1965).
——, *Wisdom in Israel* (London/Valley Forge: SCM Press Ltd./Trinity Press International, 1972).
Reicke, Bo, "The Knowledge Hidden in the Tree of Paradise," *Journal of Semitic Studies* 1 (1956): 193-201.
Reiterer, Friedrich Vinzenz, "Die Immateriellen Ebenen der Schöpfung bei Ben Sira," in *Treasures of Wisdom: Studies in Ben Sira and the Book of Wisdom. Festschrift M. Gilbert* (ed. N. Calduch-Benages and J. Vermeylen; BETL 143; Leuven: Leuven University Press, 1999), 91-127.
Richter, Hans-Peter, *A Preliminary Concordance to the Hebrew and Aramaic Fragments from Qumran Caves II-X* (Göttingen: privately published, 1988).
Rigaux, B., "Révélation des Mystères et Perfection à Qumran et dans le Nouveau Testament," *New Testament Studies* 4 (1958): 237-62.
Ringgren, Helmer, *The Faith of Qumran: Theology of the Dead Sea Scrolls* (Philadelphia: Fortress, 1963).
Robinson, James M., ed., *The Nag Hammadi Library* (San Francisco: Harper & Row, 1981).
Rofé, Alexander, "Revealed Wisdom: From the Bible to Qumran," in *Sapiential Perspectives: Wisdom Literature in Light of the Dead Sea Scrolls. Proceedings of the Sixth International Symposium of the Orion Center, 20-22 May 2001* (ed. G. Sterling and J.J. Collins; Leiden: Brill, forthcoming).
Romaniuk, Casimir, "Le Thème de la Sagesse dans les Documents de Qumran," *Revue de Qumran* 9 (1978): 429-35.
Rowley, H.H., *Jewish Apocalyptic and the Dead Sea Scrolls* (London: The Athlone Press, 1957).
Russell, D.S., *The Method and Message of Jewish Apocalyptic* (OTL; Philadelphia: Westminster Press, 1964).
Rylaarsdam, J. Coert, *Revelation in Jewish Wisdom Literature* (Chicago: University of Chicago Press, 1946).
Sacchi, Paolo, *Jewish Apocalyptic and Its History* (JSPSup 20; Sheffield: Sheffield Academic Press, 1990).
Safrai, Ze'ev, *The Economy of Roman Palestine* (London/New York: Routledge, 1994).
Sanders, Jack T., "When Sacred Canopies Collide: The Reception of the Torah of Moses in the Wisdom Literature of the Second-Temple Period," *Journal for the Study of Judaism* 32 (2001): 121-36.
Sauer, G., "Weisheit und Tora in qumranischer Zeit," in *Weisheit ausserhalb der kanonischen Weisheitsschriften* (ed. B. Janowski; Gütersloh: Kaiser, 1996), 107-27.

Savedow, Steve, *Sepher Rezial Hemelach: The Book of the Angel Rezial* (York Beach: Samuel Weiser, 2000).

Sawyer, John F.A., "The Meaning of אלהים בצלם ('In the Image of God') in Genesis I-XI," *Journal of Theological Studies* 25 (1974): 418-26.

Schellenberg, Annette, *Erkenntnis als Problem: Qohelet und die alttestamentliche Diskussion um das menschliche Erkennen* (OBO 188; Fribourg: Fribourg University Press, 2002).

Schiffman, Lawrence H., "4QMysteries^a: A Preliminary Edition and Translation," in *Solving Riddles and Untying Knots: Biblical, Epigraphic, and Semitic Studies in Honor of Jonas C. Greenfield* (ed. Z. Zevit et al.; Winona Lake: Eisenbrauns, 1995), 207-60.

——, "4QMysteries^b: A Preliminary Edition," *Revue de Qumran* 16 (1993): 203-25.

——, *The Eschatological Community of the Dead Sea Scrolls: A Study of the Rule of the Congregation* (SBLMS 38; Atlanta: Scholars Press, 1989).

——, "Halakhic Elements in the Sapiential Texts," in *Sapiential Perspectives: Wisdom Literature in Light of the Dead Sea Scrolls. Proceedings of the Sixth International Symposium of the Orion Center, 20-22 May 2001* (ed. G. Sterling and J.J. Collins; Leiden: Brill, forthcoming).

——, *Reclaiming the Dead Sea Scrolls* (ABRL; New York: Doubleday, 1995).

Schmidt, Francis, "Ancient Jewish Astrology: An Attempt to Interpret 4QCryptic (4Q186)," in *Biblical Perspectives: Early Use and Interpretation of the Bible in Light of the Dead Sea Scrolls* (ed. M.E. Stone and E. Chazon; STDJ 28; Leiden: Brill, 1998), 189-205.

Schnabel, Eckhard J., *Law and Wisdom from Ben Sira to Paul* (WUNT 2/16; Tübingen: J.C.B. Mohr [Paul Siebeck], 1985).

Schneemelcher, Wilhelm, ed., *New Testament Apocrypha* (rev. ed.; 2 vols.; Louisville/Cambridge: Westminster/James Clarke & Co Ltd, 1991).

Scholem, Gershom, *Origins of the Kabbalah* (Princeton: Princeton University Press/Jewish Publication Society, 1987 [orig. pub., 1962]).

Schoors, A., "The Language of the Qumran Sapiential Works," in *The Wisdom Texts from Qumran and the Development of Sapiential Thought* (ed. C. Hempel, A. Lange, and H. Lichtenberger; BETL 159; Leuven: Leuven University Press/Peeters, 2002), 61-95.

Schürer, Emil, *The History of the Jewish People in the Age of Jesus Christ* (rev. ed.; ed. G. Vermes, F. Millar, and M. Black; 3 vols.; Edinburgh: T. & T. Clark, 1973-87).

Scott, James M., "Korah and Qumran," in *The Bible at Qumran: Text, Shape, and Interpretation* (ed. P.W. Flint; Grand Rapids: Eerdmans, 2001), 182-202.

Scroggs, R., *The Last Adam: A Study in Pauline Anthropology* (Philadelphia: Fortress Press, 1966).

Segal, M.H., השלם סירא בן ספר (Jerusalem: Bialik, 1958).

Shanks, Hershel, "Chief Scroll Editor Opens Up: An Interview with Emanuel Tov," *Biblical Archaeology Review* 28 (May/June 2002), 32-35, 62.

Shupak, Nili, *Where can Wisdom be found?* (OBO 130; Fribourg/Göttingen: University Press/Vandenhoeck & Ruprecht, 1993).

Smith, Jay E., "Another Look at 4Q416 2 ii.21, a Critical Parallel to First Thessalonians 4:4," *Catholic Biblical Quarterly* 63 (2001): 499-504.

Smith, Jonathan Z., "Wisdom and Apocalyptic," in *Map Is Not Territory* (Chicago: University of Chicago Press, 1978), 67-87.

Stadelmann, H., *Ben Sira als Schriftgelehrter* (WUNT 2/6; Tübingen: Mohr, 1981).

Stegemann, Hartmut, *The Library of Qumran: On the Essenes, Qumran, John the Baptist, and Jesus* (Leiden/Grand Rapids: Brill/Eerdmans, 1998).

——, "Methods for the Reconstruction of Scrolls from Scattered Fragments," in *Archaeology and History in the Dead Sea Scrolls* (ed. L.H. Schiffman; Sheffield: Sheffield Academic Press, 1990), 189-220.

Steiner, R.C., "The Heading of the 'Book of the Words of Noah' on a Fragment of the Genesis Apocryphon: New Light on a 'Lost' Work," *Dead Sea Discoveries* 2 (1995): 66-71.

Steinmetz, Devora, "Sefer HeHago: The Community and the Book," *Journal of Jewish Studies* 52 (2001): 40-58.

Steudel, Annette, "הימים אחרית in the Texts from Qumran," *Revue de Qumran* 16 (1993): 225-46.

——, "Probleme und Methoden der Rekonstruktion von Schriftrollen," in *Qumran—die Schriftrollen vom Toten Meer: Vorträge des St. Galler Qumran-Symposiums vom 2./3. Juli 1999* (ed. M. Fieger et al.; Freiburg/Göttingen: Universitätsverlag/Vandenhoeck & Ruprecht, 2001), 97-109.

Stone, Michael E., *4 Ezra* (Hermeneia; Minneapolis: Fortress, 1990).

——, "Apocalyptic Literature," in *Jewish Writings of the Second Temple Period* (ed. M.E. Stone; CRINT 2.2; Assen/Philadelphia: Van Gorcum/Fortress, 1984), 383-437.

——, "Lists of Revealed Things in the Apocalyptic Literature," in *Magnalia Dei: The Mighty Acts of God* (ed. F.M. Cross et al.; Garden City: Doubleday, 1976), 414-51.

——, *Selected Studies in Pseudepigrapha & Apocrypha* (SVTP 9; Leiden: Brill, 1991).

Stordalen, Terje, *Echoes of Eden: Genesis 2-3 and Symbolism of the Eden Garden in Biblical Hebrew Literature* (Leuven: Peeters, 2000).

Strugnell, John, "More on Wives and Marriage in the Dead Sea Scrolls (4Q416 2 ii 21 [Cf. 1 Thess 4:4] and 4QMMT, B)," *Revue de Qumran* 17 (1996): 537-47.

——, "Notes en marge du volume V des 'Discoveries in the Judaean Desert of Jordan,'" *Revue de Qumran* 7 (1970): 163-276.

——, "The Sapiential Work 4Q415ff. and the Pre-Qumranic Works from Qumran: Lexical Considerations," in *The Provo International Conference on the Dead Sea Scrolls* (ed. D.W. Parry and E. Ulrich; STDJ 30; Leiden: Brill, 1999), 595-608.

——, "The Smaller Hebrew Wisdom Texts Found at Qumran: Variations, Resemblances, and Lines of Development," in *The Wisdom Texts from Qumran and the Development of Sapiential Thought* (ed. C. Hempel, A. Lange, and H. Lichtenberger; BETL 159; Leuven: Leuven University Press/Peeters, 2002), 31-60.

——, "Le travail d'édition des fragments de Qumrân: Communication de J. Strugnell," *Revue Biblique* 63 (1956): 64-66.

Strugnell, John, and Daniel J. Harrington, *Qumran Cave 4.XXIV: Sapiential Texts, Part 2. 4QInstruction (Mûsār Lĕ Mēvîn): 4Q415ff. With a re-edition of 1Q26* (DJD 34; Oxford: Clarendon, 1999).

Stuckenbruck, Loren T., "4QInstruction and the Possible Influence of Early Enochic Traditions: An Evaluation," in *The Wisdom Texts from Qumran and the Development of Sapiential Thought* (ed. C. Hempel, A. Lange, and H. Lichtenberger; BETL 159; Leuven: Leuven University Press/Peeters, 2002), 245-61.

——, *Angel Veneration and Christology: A Study in Early Judaism and in the Christology of the Apocalypse of John* (WUNT 2/70; Tübingen: J.C.B. Mohr [Paul Siebeck], 1995).

——, "'Angels' and 'God': Exploring the Limits of Early Jewish Monotheism," in *Exploring Early Jewish and Christian Monotheism* (ed. L.T. Stuckenbruck and W. Sproston North; New York/London: Continuum, forthcoming).

——, *The Book of Giants from Qumran* (TSAJ 63; Tübingen: Mohr-Siebeck, 1997).

——, "The Throne-Theophany of the Book of Giants: Some New Light on the Background of Daniel 7," in *The Scrolls and The Scriptures: Fifty Years After* (ed. S.E. Porter and C. Evans; Sheffield: Sheffield Academic Press, 1997), 211-20.

Tanzer, Sarah, "The Sages at Qumran: Wisdom in the *Hodayot*" (diss.; Harvard University, 1987).

Taylor, Joan E., *The Immerser: John the Baptist within Second Temple Judaism* (Grand Rapids: Eerdmans, 1997).

Tcherikover, Victor, *Hellenistic Civilization and the Jews* (trans. S. Applebaum; Philadelphia/Jerusalem: Jewish Publication Society of America/The Magnes Press, 1961).

Tigchelaar, Eibert J.C., "הבא ביחד" in *4QInstruction (4Q418 64 + 199 + 66 par 4Q417 1 i 17-19) and the Height of the Columns of 4Q418*," *Revue de Qumran* 18 (1998): 589-93.

——, "The Addressees of 4QInstruction," in *Sapiential, Liturgical and Poetical Texts from Qumran: Proceedings of the Third Meeting of the International Organization for Qumran Studies, Oslo 1998* (ed. D. Falk et al.; STDJ 35; Leiden: Brill, 2000), 62-75.

——, "Eden and Paradise: The Garden Motif in Some Early Jewish Texts," in *Paradise Interpreted: Representations of Biblical Paradise in Judaism and Christianity* (ed. G.P. Luttikhuizen; Leiden: Brill, 1999), 37-57.

——, *To Increase Learning for the Understanding Ones: Reading and Reconstructing the Fragmentary Early Jewish Sapiential Text 4QInstruction* (STDJ 44; Leiden: Brill, 2001).

——, "Towards a Reconstruction of the Beginning of 4QInstruction (4Q416 Fragment 1 and Parallels)," in *The Wisdom Texts from Qumran and the Development of Sapiential Thought* (ed. C. Hempel, A. Lange, and H. Lichtenberger; BETL 159; Leuven: Leuven University Press/Peeters, 2002), 99-126.

Tiller, P.A., *A Commentary on the Animal Apocalypse of 1 Enoch* (SBLEJL 4; Atlanta: Scholars Press, 1993).

——, "The 'Eternal Planting' in the Dead Sea Scrolls," *Dead Sea Discoveries* 4 (1997): 312-35.

Tobin, Thomas H., "4Q185 and Jewish Wisdom Literature," in *Of Scribes and Scrolls: Studies on the Hebrew Bible, Intertestamental Judaism and Christian Origins* (ed. H.W. Attridge et al.; Lanham: University Press of America, 1990), 145-52.

Un-Sok Ro, Johannes, *Die sogennante "Armenfrömmingkeit" im nachexilischen Israel* (BZAW 322; Berlin: de Gruyter, 2002).

Urbach, Ephraim, *The Sages* (Cambridge/London: Harvard University Press, 1975).

VanderKam, James C., "The Birth of Noah," in *Intertestamental Essays in Honour of Jósef Tadeusz Milik* (ed. Z.J. Kapera; Krakow: Enigma, 1992), 213-31.

——, *The Book of Jubilees* (Sheffield: Sheffield Academic Press, 2001).

——, *Calendars in the Dead Sea Scrolls: Measuring Time* (London/New York: Routledge, 1998).

——, *Enoch and the Growth of an Apocalyptic Tradition* (CBQMS 16; Washington, D.C.: Catholic Biblical Association, 1984).

——, *From Revelation to Canon: Studies in the Hebrew Bible and Second Temple Literature* (JSJSup 62; Leiden: Brill, 2000).

——, "The Interpretation of Genesis in *1 Enoch*," in *The Bible at Qumran: Text, Shape, and Interpretation* (ed. P.W. Flint; Grand Rapids: Eerdmans, 2001), 129-48.

——, "Mantic Wisdom in the Dead Sea Scrolls," *Dead Sea Discoveries* 4 (1997): 336-53.

Vattioni, F., *Ecclesiastico: Testo ebraico con apparato critico e versioni greca, latina e siriaca* (Naples: Istituto Orientale di Napoli, 1968).

Vaux, Roland de, "La Grotte des manuscrits hébreux," *Revue Biblique* 66 (1949): 589-610.

Vermes, Geza, *The Complete Dead Sea Scrolls in English* (New York: Penguin, 1997).

——, "Genesis 1-3 in Post-Biblical Hebrew and Aramaic Literature before the Mishnah," *Journal of Jewish Studies* 43 (1992): 221-25.

Verseput, Donald J., "Wisdom, 4Q185, and the Epistle of James," *Journal of Biblical Literature* 117 (1998): 691-707.

Wacholder, Ben Zion, and Martin G. Abegg, *A Preliminary Edition of the Unpublished Dead Sea Scrolls: The Hebrew and Aramaic Texts from Cave Four* (2 vols.; Washington, D.C.: Biblical Archaeology Society, 1992).

Wacker, Marie-Theres, "'Rettendes Wissen' im äthiopischen Henochbuch," in *Rettendes Wissen: Studien zum Fortgang weisheitlichen Denkens im Frühjudentum und im frühen Christentum* (ed. K. Löning; AOAT 300; Münster: Ugarit-Verlag, 2002), 115-54.

Washington, H.C., *Wealth and Poverty in the Instructions of Amenemope and the Hebrew Proverbs* (SBLDS 142; Atlanta: Scholars Press, 1994).

Watson, Duane F., "The Oral-Scribal and Cultural Intertexture of Apocalyptic Discourse in Jude and 2 Peter," in *The Intertexture of Apocalyptic Discourse in the New Testament* (ed. D.F. Watson; SBLSymS 14; Atlanta: Society of Biblical Literature, 2002), 187-213.

Weeks, Stuart, *Early Israelite Wisdom* (Oxford: Clarendon, 1994).

Weinfeld, Moses, *Deuteronomy and the Deuteronomic School* (Oxford: Oxford University Press, 1972).

——, *The Organizational Pattern and the Penal Code of the Qumran Sect* (NTOA 2; Fribourg/Göttingen: Éditions Universitaires/Vandenhoeck & Ruprecht, 1986).

Werman, Cana, "'The תורה and the תעודה' Engraved on the Tablets," *Dead Sea Discoveries* 9 (2002): 75-103.

——, "What is the Book of Hagu?" in *Sapiential Perspectives: Wisdom Literature in Light of the Dead Sea Scrolls. Proceedings of the Sixth International Symposium of the Orion Center, 20-22 May 2001* (ed. G. Sterling and J.J. Collins; Leiden: Brill, forthcoming).

Wernberg-Møller, P., "A Reconsideration of the Two Spirits in the *Rule of the Community* (1QSerek III, 13 – IV, 26)," *Revue de Qumran* 3 (1961-62): 413-41.

Westermann, Claus, *The Roots of Wisdom* (Louisville: John Knox Press, 1995).

Whybray, R.N., *The Book of Proverbs: A Survey of Modern Study* (Leiden: Brill, 1995).

——, *Wealth and Poverty in the Book of Proverbs* (JSOTSup 99; Sheffield: Sheffield Academic Press, 1990).

Widengren, G., "Les quatre Âges du monde," in *Apocalyptique iranienne et dualisme qoumrânien* (ed. G. Widengren, M. Philonenko, and A. Hultgård; Paris: Maisonneuve, 1995), 23-62.

Winston, David, *The Wisdom of Solomon* (AB 43; New York: Doubleday, 1979).

Winter, P., "Ben Sira (33 [36], 7-15) and the Teaching of 'Two Ways,'" *Vetus Testamentum* 5 (1955): 315-18.

Wischmeyer, Oda, *Die Kultur des Buches Jesus Sirach* (BZNW 77; Berlin: Walter de Gruyter, 1995).

Wise, Michael O., "מי כמוני באלים: A Study of 4Q491c, 4Q471b, 4Q427 7 and 1QHᵃ 25:35-26:10," *Dead Sea Discoveries* 7 (2000): 173-219.

——, "Dating the Teacher of Righteousness and the *Floruit* of His Movement," *Journal of Biblical Literature* 122 (2003): 53-87.

Wise, Michael O., Martin Abegg, Jr., and Edward Cook, *The Dead Sea Scrolls: A New Translation* (San Francisco: HarperSan Francisco, 1996).

Wolters, A., "Anthropoi Eudokias (Luke 2:14) and 'ansy rswn (4Q416)," *Journal of Biblical Literature* 113 (1994): 291-97.

Worrell, John, "Concepts of Wisdom in the Dead Sea Scrolls" (diss.; Claremont Graduate School, 1968).

——, "עצה: 'Counsel' or 'Council' at Qumran?" *Vetus Testamentum* 20 (1970): 65-72.

Woude, A.S. van der, "Wisdom at Qumran," in *Wisdom in ancient Israel: Essays in honour of J.A. Emerton* (ed. J. Day et al.; Cambridge: University of Cambridge Press, 1995), 244-56.

Wright III, Benjamin G., "The Categories of Rich and Poor in the Qumran Sapiential Literature," in *Sapiential Perspectives: Wisdom Literature in Light of the Dead Sea Scrolls. Proceedings of the Sixth International Symposium of the Orion Center, 20-22 May 2001* (ed. G. Sterling and J.J. Collins; Leiden: Brill, forthcoming).

——, "Putting the Puzzle Together: Some Suggestions Concerning the Social Location of the Wisdom of Ben Sira," in *Society of Biblical Literature Seminar Papers 1996* (SBLSP 35; Atlanta: Scholars Press, 1996), 133-49.

Wyatt, Nick, *Religious Texts from Ugarit: The Words of Ilimilku and His Colleagues* (Sheffield: Sheffield Academic Press, 1998).

Yadin, Yigael, *The Temple Scroll* (New York: Random House, 1985).

Yarbro Collins, Adela, "The Seven Heavens in Jewish and Christian Apocalypses," in *Death, Ecstasy, and Other Worldly Journeys* (ed. J.J. Collins and M. Fishbane; Albany: State University of New York Press, 1995), 57-93.

Zangenberg, Jürgen, "Wildnis unter Palmen? Khirbet Qumran im regionalen Kontext des toten Meeres," in *Jericho und Qumran: Neues zum Umfeld der Bibel* (ed. B. Mayer; Regensberg: Verlag Friedrich Pustet, 2000), 129-64.

INDEX OF AUTHORS

INDEX OF TEXTS

HEBREW BIBLE

APOCRYPHA

DEAD SEA SCROLLS AND RELATED LITERATURE

JOSEPHUS AND PHILO

RABBINIC SOURCES

EARLY CHRISTIAN SOURCES

CLASSICAL SOURCES